CESARE PAVESE

Cesare Pavese

*A study of
the major novels and poems*

DOUG THOMPSON

CAMBRIDGE UNIVERSITY PRESS

Cambridge

London   New York   New Rochelle

Melbourne   Sydney

Published by the Press Syndicate of the University of Cambridge
The Pitt Building, Trumpington Street, Cambridge CB2 1RP
32 East 57th Street, New York, NY 10022, USA
296 Beaconsfield Parade, Middle Park, Melbourne 3206, Australia

© Cambridge University Press 1982

First published 1982

Printed in Malta by Interprint Ltd

Library of Congress catalogue card number: 81–15467

British Library Cataloguing in Publication Data
Thompson, Doug
Cesare Pavese
1. Pavese, Cesare—Criticism and interpretation
I. Title
858'.91209   PQ4835.A846
ISBN 0 521 23602 9

For June

being here is much, and ... all this that's here, so fleeting, seems to require us and strangely concerns us.

Rainer Maria Rilke: *Duino elegies*

Contents

Frontispiece: Cesare Pavese
(reproduced by permission of Giulio Einaudi Editore, Torino)

	page
Preface	ix
1 The world of Cesare Pavese (1908–1950)	1
2 'Lavorare stanca' and the evolution of Pavese's verse in the nineteen-thirties	13
3 Imprisonment, solitude and salvation in 'Il carcere'	40
4 'Paesi tuoi' and the myth of America	55
5 The search for maturity and the 'search for a style' in 'La bella estate' and 'La spiaggia'	71
6 The 'once and for all event': symbolic reality in 'Feria d'agosto'	96
7 The language of myth in 'Dialoghi con Leucò'	115
8 'Not fear, not the usual sort of cowardice'	149
9 Structure and style as myth in 'Il diavolo sulle colline'	178
10 Being and seeming in 'Tra donne sole'	204
11 History, symbol and myth in 'La luna e i falò'	223
12 The celebration of a rite: last poems, 1945–1950	249
13 'To bring order and design where there is chaos'	261
Notes	271
Bibliography of Pavese's works	280
Selected criticism of Pavese's works	283
Index	285

Preface

Many years ago, as a young research student eager for unpublished anecdotes about Pavese, I was suddenly, if only temporarily, deflected from my purpose by a not-too-approving Massimo Mila. I had sensed a certain reticence, for though he was willing enough to answer specific questions about Pavese, he flatly refused to 'reminisce', eventually explaining that in his view what was needed most of all was a balanced critical assessment of Pavese's works, for they and not the author's private life were what mattered ultimately. At the time I was unconvinced, for couldn't I have undertaken *that* unexciting task without ever leaving my desk, in England?

As the years passed and a steady stream of studies and articles on Pavese continued to use his writings to underscore particular theses about the failed life and the complex psychology of the man, I long ago came to share Mila's view. The trouble is that with Pavese it is very difficult to avoid that sort of personalised approach, given the centrality of the contemplative 'I' in his work and the apparently desired posthumous publication of his diary. Yet all too often that approach has assumed the character of an inquisition. Therefore, mindful of his own plea of 'Non fate troppi pettegolezzi' ('Don't indulge in too much gossip'), this book is an attempt to chart Pavese's 'search for a style' in his literary works and to assess the effects of his 'theory of myth' on the results of that quest. I have tried to avoid going over ground which has already been well trodden and have thus referred to other writers on Pavese only where my own argument seemed to demand it. The bibliography of selected criticism, I hasten to add, reflects a much wider range of views and approaches than my own.

My comments are, of course, based on analysis of the Italian texts, and wherever it has seemed necessary – particularly when some stylistic or linguistic point is at issue – I have quoted Pavese's Italian.

I here wish to record my thanks to all those who have assisted and advised in the production of this book, particularly to my sometime colleague, Joan Hall, for her help with some of the translations; to Professor Brian Moloney, for his extremely useful and constructive criticisms; and to my wife, June, for her unceasing encouragement, her practical assistance in a thousand different ways and, most especially, for her thoughtful reading and discussion of the manuscript at all stages of its production.

Finally, my grateful thanks are due to Peter Owen Ltd, for kind permission to translate extensively from Pavese's works; to Manchester University Press, for permission to reproduce a page from the introduction to my edition of Pavese's *La luna e i falò* (1979), in chapter 11; and to the editors of *Italian Studies*, for allowing me to quote at great length from my article, '"Slow rotation suggesting permanence": history, symbol and myth in Pavese's last novel,' also in chapter 11.

Doug Thompson

Cambridge, November 1980

1
The world of Cesare Pavese
(*1908–1950*)

Between Turin and the sea, in the direction of Savona, is an area of high, steep-sided hills and narrow valleys, known as the Langhe. Its terrain, though frequently beautiful, is rugged and inhospitable, and seems, in its very wildness, to deny the presence of men, despite the fact that for centuries they have struggled to scratch a meagre living from its soil. The struggle with this land has left its mark upon the people. They are men of few words, more at their ease in action than in words; they are closed, wary of outsiders, stubborn and courageous. Poverty has hardened them, and even after the years of economic boom which followed the Second World War, their lives underwent no very significant changes, despite the relative proximity of the great industrial conurbation between Turin, Genoa and Milan. They remain what they have been for centuries, a peasant community in a depressed area, left, economically speaking, further behind than ever by the great technological advancement of recent years.

It was here, on 9 September 1908, that Cesare Pavese was born, in the village of Santo Stefano Belbo. His parents, though both of peasant origin, had already lived for some years in the regional metropolis of Turin, where his father held a modest though secure post as a bailiff in the Law Courts. However, each year the family went off to the countryside to escape the dry, stifling heat of the city during the long summer months. It was towards the end of one such period that Pavese was born, the second (and last) surviving child of his parents' marriage; his sister, Maria, was then six years old.

The minutiae of his life in those early years, even if known, would probably make very dull reading; yet certain factors and events, which are important if one is to understand the man and his writing, must not go unrecorded. Reference has already been made to the regional 'type' produced by the Langhe, and Pavese, partly because of his yearly visits and partly because of his home circumstances, inherited much of the closedness and stubbornness associated with the people of the region. In 1914, when the boy was only six years old, his father died of a brain tumour, and he was then left solely under the care and influence of his mother and sister, and this too seems to have left its mark upon him. His mother appears to have been an austere, almost unapproachable woman, and warmth and affection seem to have been withheld from him at a time when he was most in need of them, for his mother was incapable of sharing her sadness and her sense of loss with anyone. The boy became resentful and sullen, often remaining silent for long periods or going off on his own to play or read in the woods (if they happened to be in the Langhe) or in his room. It was in those years that the habit of solitude developed in him with its attendant shyness and uneasiness in the presence of strangers. His relationship with his mother seems always to have been difficult – not because of any lack of affection on either side, but because of the undemonstrative nature, in the first place of the woman, but later, as he grew, of Cesare himself. In that particular society, the absence of a man's influence in his early life must have been a strong contributory factor to the growing complexity of his personality, and perhaps in part explains the reverence and awe in which he held his schoolmaster, Augusto Monti, in his middle and later teens. At the centre of his life there appears to have been an emotional vacuum which he was to try repeatedly to fill, always without success. Had his mother been more open, more obviously loving, the course of his life might have been very different.

Though the Langhe figured prominently in the development of Pavese's *forma mentis*, the amount of time that he actually spent there could not have been very great, for even after the death of her husband, his mother continued to live in the city. Moreover, because of the financial strain she was eventually compelled to sell the house in Santo Stefano where Cesare had been born, so that for a longish period visits to the region were made only at the invitation of relatives. From his earliest years, Pavese's home was the city of Turin, and it too played its part in shaping his personality.

Of all Italian cities, Turin has a character which is truly unique, a strange mingling of Italian and North European, symmetrical and austere, subjected to heavy mists coming from the river Po and icy winds from the Alps, which tower away behind it. This city was to be at the centre of Pavese's work as it was of his life. There was another sense, quite apart from the physical one, in which its atmosphere was different from that of other Italian cities, and that was in its political life, particularly after the First World War. Even before the advent of Fascism in 1922 it had become a stronghold of working-class politics, for it was the home of Antonio Gramsci, the founder of the Italian Communist Party. It was from here that he directed his political journal, *L'ordine nuovo* (The new order), and, from 1923, the Communist daily, *L'Unità*, until his arrest and imprisonment in 1926. Despite the disappearance of Gramsci from the political arena, Turin was to remain an important centre of anti-Fascism. Quite apart from the activity of the Communists it was also a centre of progressive Liberalism, and Piero Gobetti, friend of Gramsci, organised a political movement around his own reviews, *La rivoluzione liberale* (Liberal revolution) and *Il Baretti*, in the early nineteen-twenties. Although Pavese was at this time still a boy at school, he came indirectly in contact with these movements, particularly the latter, through Augusto Monti, who was a close associate of Gobetti. It is doubtful whether Pavese ever achieved political consciousness in any orthodox sense, despite his post-war commitment to the Communist Party, but certainly in his early years politics had little or no conscious importance in his life. From a very early date, he had decided he wanted to be a writer, but living at a time when culture and society were seriously adrift from each other, he never really considered that a writer might have a socially or a politically creative role to play through his writing. We see from his youthful letters that aesthetics and art stand apart from the concerns of daily life,[1] being rather the realm of the ineffable, of the sublime. Yet, by the time he published his first poems he had moved away from this rarefied view to something bordering on social – at times, even political – awareness. The circumstances and location of his education were instrumental in leading him along paths which, temperamentally, he was perhaps unsuited to follow.

Pavese's elementary schooling was completed in Turin – all but for one year when he attended the local school in Santo Stefano. His early secondary education he received at a Jesuit school in the city, but it was not until he transferred to the Ginnasio Moderno that he began to show any interest or make any noticeable progress in his education. It was at this particular school that he met Mario Sturani who, for many years, was to be his closest friend. It was here too that his vocation for poetry emerged, and many of his first attempts at writing were shared with Sturani, who was himself then showing great promise as a painter.

One of the most significant events in Pavese's young life was his transfer, at the age of sixteen, to the Liceo Massimo d'Azeglio where he was to complete his schooling before going on to the University of Turin, in 1927. Here, under the guidance of Monti, his enthusiasm for literature blossomed and developed. Pavese was extremely impressionable and Monti's purposeful teaching served to channel his thoughts and emotions towards self-discovery and self-expression through the written word. Many tributes have been paid to the work of Monti since the nineteen-thirties, and almost all of them have spoken of his passionate devotion to human rights, which he regarded as fundamental to his role as an educator, as well as of the tremendous respect which he inspired in his pupils. It was, in all probability, the moral strength of the man and his clear sense of direction which drew Pavese to him, for both factors had hitherto been largely absent from his own life.

At the end of his first year at the Massimo d'Azeglio Sturani left in order to continue his studies at an art college in Monza, with the result that their friendship was carried on by letter, except of course, during vacations. In his letters we see Pavese the precocious literary pundit, giving voice to a mixture of Crocean idealism and the aestheticism of d'Annunzio and Papini. Poetry – 'the queen of the world, indeed, a goddess' – appears to demand a suffering servitude which Pavese accepts humbly, even willingly. Throughout his life as a writer there was always present a sense of the virtue which supposedly derives from the hard work of literary creation, an attitude which was perhaps little more than a compensation or even a justification for his own relative ineptitude in the practicalities of day-to-day living. He seems to have sensed, at a relatively early date, that the 'word' could provide a refuge for the self from the world of not-self, whilst ostensibly attempting to communicate through it with that world. This kind of equivocation was very occasionally to be reflected even in his later writing in which he claimed to be trying to clarify those personal myths which have a determining role for the individual. Like Dante the pilgrim, he learns that reason can take him only so far in the realisation of self-knowledge and that reality is ultimately an unfathomable mystery. Alienation, for Pavese, was a long-standing habit which eventually came to be recognised, particularly in his post-war novels, as a deep-seated, human problem, characteristic of the twentieth century. As a conscious attitude it derives, in part, from the *fin de siècle* writers whose literary opinions he reiterates in his early letters to Sturani. For one already pointed, by the circumstances of his own life, towards withdrawal, theories involving idealism or literary elites, kneeling at the shrine of 'Art', seemed a safe haven in a stormy sea. This influence, assimilated by an impressionable, lonely youth at the outset of his writing life, was never wholly purged from Pavese's work, and Monti himself was to be a vociferous critic of what he saw as a decadent, even destructive strain in his writing.

In 1927, Pavese registered as a student in the Faculty of Letters at the University of Turin. During the years in which he was a student he seems, for a time, to have become more accessible and was often to be found in the company of both old and newly made friends. Many of the ex-pupils of the Massimo d'Azeglio continued to associate with each other in those years, and under the direction of Monti and Leone Ginzburg their discussions became ever more politically oriented and eventually their group was to become a part of the Giustizia e Libertà (Justice and Freedom) movement, organised against Fascism. Although Pavese found himself closely associated with this kind of activity he continued to remain essentially aloof from it and completely unaligned. His apparent vocation for solitude continued to manifest itself in his pastimes. He swam a good deal in the river Po and its tributary, the Sangone, and also developed a passion for rowing. He became physically much stronger than he had ever been previously in his life, and the asthma which had earlier troubled him, and was to do so again later, virtually left him. Yet another interest which came to the fore in his years at university was the cinema, and he would go, usually alone, to see English and American films at the small picture houses in the suburbs of the city. It was through these films that he made his first contact with American culture, and thus began, whilst still a student, to read and translate the works of contemporary American writers. For the subject of his degree thesis he chose the poetry of Walt Whitman and although the finished work was at first rejected – a political significance was imputed to it – it was eventually accepted (apparently through the influence of his friend Ginzburg) and he was awarded his degree.

In November 1930, his mother died. This event seems to have left him in a state of shock, and he cut himself off from his friends, at least for a time. He was probably temporarily saved from himself at that time by the first love of his adult life, the woman to whom his biographer, Davide Lajolo, refers as 'the woman with the hoarse voice'. From Lajolo's description of her,[2] it seems that in some ways she resembled his mother and was thus perhaps able to help him through a difficult period. However, it is likely that his ever-increasing dependence upon her was a chief cause of her decision to break with him when the opportunity arose, as it did so tragically in 1935.

In order to supplement his earnings from his translations Pavese found work as a teacher. As he was not a member of the Fascist Party it was difficult to obtain a secure post,[3] particularly in the city, and he was therefore generally compelled to go further afield, to the outlying country districts of Piedmont or, alternatively, to teach evening classes in the city. Besides his work as a translator of English and American novels, Pavese wrote a good number of articles on American literature for the review *La cultura*, which was edited by Arrigo Cajumi. In 1933, this review amalgamated with Luigi Einaudi's *La riforma sociale* and was thereafter directed by the newly formed Einaudi Publishing House. Not long after its formation the Publishing House fell foul of the Fascist authorities. Many of those associated with it were suspected or known anti-Fascists and were under constant surveillance by the police, and early in 1934 Leone Ginzburg, who had become director of the new *La cultura*, was arrested. Pavese applied for the vacant post and was appointed, not least because his non-partisan views might possibly serve to remove some of the pressure, coming from the Fascist authorities, under which the Publishing House was constrained to work. For a year Pavese held this post but then resigned, mainly because he found it impossible to do the job without commitment to the political values which the review represented.

These were the years of triumphant Fascism and in the cultural sphere Italy was being slowly strangled from within. It took a great deal of courage for a writer to write as he pleased, especially if opposed to the Regime, and the risk which he ran was shared equally by anyone who dared to publish his controversial work. The official censorship was at its most vigilant (even if not always efficient), particularly with publishers who were already suspect, such as Einaudi, and so Pavese, with the help of his friend Mila, attempted to have his first poems published by the Solaria Press in Florence. Solaria was directed by Alberto Carocci, and it too, like Einaudi, published its own review, whose express aim was to maintain a link between European and Italian culture, an aim which, in the twenties and thirties, ran counter to the isolationist policy of Fascism. Independently, Pavese had made his own researches beyond the confines of what was called, by Fascist critics, the 'pure Latin spirit', in his discovery of the literature of the United States, and it therefore seemed logical and perhaps even inevitable that he should eventually gravitate towards a review such as *Solaria*. Elio Vittorini, himself greatly interested in American literature, had been connected with *Solaria* for some years, and it was to him that Carocci gave Pavese's poems. He read them with considerable interest and recommended that in principle they ought to be published by the Solaria Press, but it was also clear that certain modifications would have to be made before they could be presented to the censor without fear of incriminating either the author or the publisher. In fact, it was to be almost two years before the poems of *Lavorare stanca* (Working is tiresome)[4] appeared, in January 1936, and by that time, Pavese himself had become a political prisoner of the Regime.

In May 1935, the Fascist police made over two hundred arrests in Turin, mainly of people suspected of involvement in the Giustizia e Libertà movement. Pavese's woman-friend ('the woman with the hoarse voice'), an ardent anti-Fascist, had asked him to receive letters for her at his own home, for she knew herself to be closely watched. One of her correspondents was Altiero Spinelli, at that time a Communist, who was serving a prison sentence at the Regina Coeli prison in Rome. One morning the police called on Pavese, searched the house and found an incriminating letter which had come from Spinelli. Pavese refused to divulge the name of its intended recipient and as a result was imprisoned in Turin. He was eventually transferred to Regina Coeli himself and was there finally brought to trial and committed to three years' political *confino* at Brancaleone,[5] a remote town on the coast of Calabria.

Although he served only eight months of his three-year sentence before it was suspended, Pavese suffered greatly as a result of the experience and the terrible anti-climax of his return to Turin in mid-March 1936. The period of his *confino* is well documented for not only do many of his letters remain but there is also his diary, which was begun at Brancaleone, and which was published after his death. From the very outset his writing, whether letters, diary or poems, betrays a sense of futility and utter helplessness in the face of his destiny – a feature which was to pervade almost all of his subsequent work. The following much-quoted letter, written to Adolfo Ruata in November 1935, about a month after his arrival at Brancaleone, is typical:

Study is impossible; you can do nothing worth doing in this state of uncertainty, nothing other than to savour utter boredom, misery, spleen and gut-ache.
I indulge in the most squalid pastimes. I catch flies, translate from

Greek, I make myself not look at the sea, I wander round the fields, smoke, keep a diary, reread my letters from home and observe a meaningless chastity. (*Lett. I*, p. 462)

It is typical in that it is dominated by the 'I' which, in his life, was the apparently insurmountable obstacle that prevented him from reaching out and becoming a part of the world of others and their collective concerns. There was no sense of the historicity of what had happened to him. It remained only a personal fact, an unshared experience, an unkind twist of fate. His perspective was to be consistently that of the contemplative observer of himself who seeks, through that contemplation, to break out of his solitude and yet who continually fails to do so.

In the eight months that Pavese spent at Brancaleone, his woman-friend seems to have written to him only once. This in itself might have had no other significance than the desire to avoid drawing attention to herself, on the assumption that she was of more use to the anti-Fascist cause outside prison. Pavese appears to have accepted and understood her silence. He in all probability consoled himself with the knowledge of the sacrifice that he had made for her and the promise of their eventual reconciliation. It therefore must have come as a terrible shock to him to find that she was to be married to someone else shortly after his release. For him, any positive meaning that that imprisonment and solitude might have depended solely on their reunion, and when that was denied him the futility and hopelessness of the many days spent at Brancaleone were confirmed. The *Esame di coscienza* (Soul-searching), dated 10 April 1936, which appears in his diary,[6] reveals something of the depression which followed:

I have no reason to reject my obsessive idea that whatever happens to a man is determined by the whole of his past life, and is, in fact, merited. Obviously, I must have offended greatly to have come to this pass.

It is interesting that the determinism which he observes here becomes almost a superstition with him, in the suggestion that his suffering is deserved. This degeneration of the rational/historical viewpoint into the subjective/irrational is continued in the second sentence, where some cosmic force appears to be responsible for exacting retribution on him. This kind of lapse is typical of the early diary and recurs from time to time in his letters at various periods of his subsequent life. Later, in this same passage, he continues:

The terrible thing is that all I have left now is not sufficient to put me back on my feet because, the betrayals apart, I've already been in a similar position in the past and I didn't manage to find any moral salvation then. It's obvious that I shan't find any this time either.

Pavese had begun to see a pattern emerging from his own life. The pattern, he reasoned, is inescapable because it is the logical outcome of all that one is – is a destiny, in fact. Speaking of his broken love affair, he says:

I've had an adventure in which I have been judged and declared unfit to go on. In comparison with this kind of collapse the wretchedness of the lover, terrible though it is, or loss of position, which is serious enough, are as nothing.

His life had collapsed because he interpreted what had taken place in an absolute sense. One woman had 'declared' him 'unfit to go on', therefore he must remake himself in a different mould. For many weeks after his return from Brancaleone, he avoided all contact with his friends, and his 'reconstruction' was begun in virtual isolation, in the conviction that by sheer strength of will and self-discipline he could create a new self and another destiny. He found that there was a close resemblance between the way in which he had hitherto lived his life and his attitude towards the writing of verse, and came to see them as merely different facets of the same underlying malady, a dilettantish approach, a life-technique which was casual, disorderly and largely dictated by emotion.

The parallel between an intensely subjective life and the composition of short, separate poems, one every now and again, without regard for any sense of unity between them, is no mere coincidence. It is that sort of attitude that makes one live by fits and starts, without any sense of progress or purpose.

The moral, therefore, is this: construct in art as in life; expel gratuitous emotion from art as from life; exist tragically. (*MV* 20 April 1936)

The most significant lesson that he had learned from his experience with the woman he had lost he expressed in his diary on 25 November 1937, and it confirms the path of solitude and alienation which had in part been thrust upon him by circumstances, but which, in part, his temperament had chosen:

You must never again take anything seriously which does not depend on you entirely; such as love, friendship and acclaim.

Those things which do depend only on you, does it matter very much whether you take them seriously or not? Who will know if you don't? If you are alone then there isn't any 'who'. Even the 'I' disappears. Better and better.

Pavese did recover from the setbacks of 1935–6; however, it is impossible to know what lasting effect they had upon him, for the wound clearly never fully healed. Once more, he began to write, more and more in prose, much less in verse, for this was the period in which he worked in the short story form, as well as composing his first novel, *Il carcere* (The political prisoner), which was not published until 1947, and his first published novel, *Paesi tuoi* (Your part of the country), which appeared in 1941.

In the years immediately preceding the outbreak of the Second World War, Pavese found himself once again closely associated with anti-Fascism in Turin. In 1942, he was taken on to the full-time staff of the Einaudi Publishing House, but by this time Italy had entered the war, and Turin began to suffer heavy bombardment from the Allies. The following year found Pavese in Rome, and it was there that he was drafted into the army. However, owing to the asthma which had troubled him since early childhood, he was judged unfit for military service. He returned to Turin to find it devastated and empty.

After September 1943 the various anti-Fascist movements re-formed in armed resistance to Mussolini's newly created Nazi-Fascist Republic of Salò. Italy was divided and in the throes of a civil war, as well as being the battleground for the retreating Germans and the Allies. In order to escape the bombing, Pavese left Turin with his sister and her family and lived for a time in the village of Serralunga, near Crea, in the province of Monferrato. Eventually, however, he went to live in a convent school where he gave private lessons. It was in these circumstances, in almost total isolation, in the midst of war, that Pavese pursued the connection between literature and myth that he had continually glimpsed in his earlier studies and writings. His writing, both during and immediately after the war, was heavily influenced by his reflections on myth, and a seam was opened up which, many critics have maintained, was both pretentious and counter-productive, for it appears to create or to perpetuate a sense of mystery surrounding human experience rather than to reduce it, through reason, to history. Pavese himself sincerely believed that he had stumbled across something momentous, and all his subsequent writing was to be an exploration of contemporary experience in the light of his developing theory of myth.

Pavese took no active part in the Resistance. Many of his friends, among them Ginzburg, Pintor and Pajetta, had died in the struggle and Pavese suffered both grief at the loss and remorse at his own inability to take sides. But going beyond the personal level, he was also profoundly shocked by the visible signs of suffering amongst the thousands of people whom he did not know, when he emerged once again from the relative security of the hills and returned to Turin and to Rome. It was in these circumstances that he decided to become a member of the Italian Communist Party. He wrote a series of articles for the Communist daily *L'Unità* in 1945–6, but it is clear from what he wrote that he was very unsure of his ground, and that it required a good deal more than he was able or perhaps prepared to give, to become politicised in the current Communist mould. His association with the Party was not a happy one, and it is not difficult to understand why. He was too much the individual and too much the professional writer, a man full of contradictions inclining strongly towards intellectualism in what he wrote, and as a result, he came in for much criticism from the intelligentsia of the Party.

In 1946 he embarked on the most productive, though sadly short period of his writing career, and very quickly reached a maturity and confidence in his work as a novelist that were always lacking in his everyday life. Each year, he wrote at least one novel, sometimes more, and in 1950, shortly before his death, was awarded the Strega Prize for his trilogy *La bella estate* (The beautiful summer). By this time he was regarded, in Italy, as a major novelist, and had become something of a public figure. However, all this was on the surface. Inside, the situation was very different, for Pavese was already caught up in what proved to be the final crisis of his life.

Towards the end of 1949 he came to know an American actress, Constance Dowling, who had come to Italy in search of success in the newly emerged film industry. Once again Pavese, by this time over forty years of age, fell in love, catching sight, albeit for a fleeting moment, of the possible fulfilment of his lifelong ambition of attaining the normality of a wife, a home and perhaps even a family. But the dream remained a dream. The young actress, perhaps dazzled initially by Pavese's success, flattered by his attentions, soon tired of him and returned to America. It is clear from his diary that this blow had a staggering effect upon him and was undoubtedly a main contributory factor in his decision to take his own life. Decision it most certainly was, for, with characteristic thoroughness, he constructed it like the plot of one of his novels, working towards it for several weeks beforehand, sorting out his personal papers, arranging his diary for publication and writing letters to various friends, even checking that the newspapers had suitable photographs of him. He wanted his death to appear as a positive gesture, as a choice which had been made clearly and rationally, and the methodical way in which it was prepared and executed gave it just such an appearance. On the afternoon of 26 August 1950, he took a room at the Hotel Roma in Turin, and on the following evening, a Sunday, his body was discovered there. He had taken a huge quantity of sleeping tablets.

The manner of his death, the documented torment of his day-to-day existence, the obvious alienation, all have undoubtedly played their part in adding a romantic dimension to the figure of Cesare Pavese, which has, in many cases, served to cloud the judgement of his critics. These same factors have also contributed to his popularity, particularly amongst succeeding generations of the younger reading public in Italy, for at a certain age identification with Pavese comes easily. But perhaps this fact alone should indicate to us the kind of problems we are likely to find in seeking to appreciate his work. He created no main character in any of his novels who was not a fairly obvious manifestation of his own problematical self. Indeed, characterisation has generally been regarded as a weak factor in his writing. He even attempted to construct a theory of the novel which was based not on character but upon what he called 'the rhythm of events' (usually filtered through the consciousness of the main character or a narrator–character), and this, in its way, is perhaps yet another pointer towards his failure in the business of living. Yet, for all his apparent self-deceptions, contradictions and faults, his writing is of much more than average significance in the Italian, and indeed the European, literary traditions of the twentieth century. He was a writer who tried to resolve the practical problems of his own life by contemplating them, reorganising them and writing about them at a time when any kind of meaningful action, at either an individual or a collective level, was extremely difficult. In his sense of futility and alienation and his restless search for salvation, he sharply reflected the needs of the majority of Italians during the two decades of Fascist domination. That there was rarely, if ever, a conscious political motive in his writing gives his work an authenticity which is perhaps lacking, because suspect, in other more politically committed writers of the same period.

2

'Lavorare stanca' and the evolution of Pavese's verse in the nineteen-thirties

Only in 1962, with the publication by Einaudi of *Poesie edite e inedite* (Published and unpublished poems),[1] did it become possible to trace the development of Pavese's poetry during the nineteen-thirties. Up to then there had been two editions of the verse he had written in the thirties – the Solaria edition of *Lavorare stanca* (Working is tiresome)[2] of 1936 and the Einaudi edition of 1943. Even these had revealed substantial differences in tone, point of view and technique, although about half the poems in the second edition had made up the bulk of those in the first. Of the one hundred and four poems in *Poesie edite e inedite* written before 1940, twenty-seven of them were published for the first time. In addition, there were six poems which had appeared in the Solaria *Lavorare stanca* (a limited edition, soon exhausted) but which had been excluded from the Einaudi edition. Thus about a third of the poems belonging to that all-important decade were to all intents and purposes unknown until well after Pavese's death. Had *Poesie edite e inedite* gone no further than bringing these poems to light its contribution to Pavese scholarship would have been considerable. However, it also provided first drafts of individual poems, often reconstructed, with some difficulty, from Pavese's own papers. Thus in a good number of cases it is possible to see how the poem gradually took shape in the poet's mind. The edition drew attention to the connection between certain poems, or groups of poems, and the events of Pavese's life, by establishing in many cases their date and place of composition. This was particularly important with regard to the troubled period in Pavese's life between August 1935 and the end of 1937. Of the twenty-eight poems belonging to that period eleven, including almost all of the group which Pavese called the *Poesie del disamore* (Poems of disaffection), were published for the first time in 1962.

How then did Pavese's verse develop and what did he hope to achieve in it? One of the most valuable sources when seeking to answer these questions is *Il mestiere di poeta* (The poet's craft). This short commentary on his own work was written by Pavese at the end of November 1934, when all but eight of the forty-five poems which were to make up the Solaria edition of *Lavorare stanca* had already been composed. In those poems, we are told, the guiding principle had been 'every poem a story' (*poesia–racconto*), whilst technically Pavese had sought to make his verse 'clear and distinct, muscular, objective, essential'. He explains that what he had tried to achieve, almost instinctively, had been 'an essential expression of essential facts' without falling into what he called 'the usual introspective abstraction, expressed in a language which, because it is bookish is allusive, and masquerades all too easily as essential'. The word 'usual' needs explanation, for what Pavese is referring to is the type of poetry which was being written contemporaneously in Italian, that which Francesco Flora dubbed 'poesia ermetica' (Hermetic poetry).[3]

As Fascism gradually tightened its grip on every aspect of Italian life, writers whose views conflicted with the 'official' views of the Regime found it increasingly difficult to write with reference to their own society lest they become victims of persecution. Some went into exile, either for the duration of the Regime, like Silone, or temporarily, like Moravia. However, others, although unwilling to compromise themselves with the Regime, did continue to write. Their poetry tended to be introspective, often abstruse, as they sought refuge from the forbidden territory of contemporary society as they saw it in delicate creations of musical words, rhythms and personal symbols. Since the fall of Fascism, debate has continued about the ethical and the poetical significance of Hermetic poetry. Whether or not it represented moral and political cowardice is irrelevant to the present discussion, but there can be no doubt at all that it played a part in refining the language, technique and sensibility of many poets, amongst them Ungaretti, Sereni, Montale and Quasimodo, so that when at last comparative freedom had been restored they were fully equipped to produce their most mature work.

Pavese, to judge from what he says about his poems in *Il mestiere di poeta* and, more importantly, from the poems themselves, refused to be restricted by current circumstances. For him the 'basic condition of every attempt at poetry, however sophisticated, is always a close reference to the ethical, and of course, practical demands of the environment in which one is living'. Thus when Italian poetry was undergoing a period of withdrawal, Pavese was taking a 'committed' stand which, although not overtly political, nonetheless raised embarrassing questions so far as the Regime was concerned. In accordance with this commitment he endeavoured to avoid certain traditional features of Italian poetry in his own verse, notably with regard to the use of imagery and metre. His poems he saw, with some justification, as 'a linguistic creation which is fundamentally dialectal or at least based on the language of speech'. With its insistence upon objects, rather than images, upon the language of speech rather than that of any literary tradition, the verse Pavese wrote between 1930 and the time of his arrest in May 1935 was fundamentally Naturalistic. In this, the two most recognisable influences upon his work are those of Walt Whitman, whose poetry he had carefully studied to write his degree thesis, and, to a somewhat lesser degree, his own earlier fellow-Piedmontese, Guido Gozzano. His debt to Whitman is manifold, even though the influence is wholly absorbed and transformed into a style which is uniquely Pavese's own. The opening sequence of Whitman's 'There was a child went forth' highlights this influence, and not only with regard to the long line which both poets favoured; indeed, in his degree thesis, Pavese had referred to 'the gaze which was serene yet full of surprise of "There was a child went forth"', and this seemingly paradoxical combination was to become an ideal at the centre of Pavese's own verse:[4]

There was a child went forth every day,
And the first object he look'd upon, that object he became,
And that object became part of him for the day or a certain part of the day,
Or for many years or stretching cycles of years.

The early lilacs became part of this child,
And grass and white and red morning-glories, and white and red clover, and the song of the phoebe-bird,
And the Third-month lambs and the sow's pink-faint litter, and the mare's foal and the cow's calf,
And the noisy brood of the barnyard or by the mire of the pond-side,
And the fish suspending themselves so curiously below there, and the beautiful curious liquid,
And the water-plants with their graceful flat heads, all became part of him.

Structural features such as the copious use of parataxis, the repetition of words, phrases and specific rhythms are obvious enough, but Whitman's influence in general, though particularly on this poem, extends well beyond these. Though temperamentally very different – Pavese certainly did not share the American's cosmic optimism in his own 'myth of discovery'[5] – themes and motifs found here are often echoed or developed in Pavese's verse which, like Whitman's, is consciously 'primitive', attempting to see with the 'occhio vergine' (virgin eye) of the child.[6] Pavese transforms the central image of the child, who goes out each day and discovers the world and in discovering it both creates and discovers himself, into 'lo scappato di casa' (the runaway child), the *fons et origo* of the theory of myth which he developed later. Other motifs were perhaps first suggested by Whitman's 'the father, strong, self-sufficient, manly', 'men and women crowding fast in the streets', 'the light falling on roofs', 'the village on the highland seen from afar at sunset', 'all the changes of city and country', 'the old drunkard staggering home' and 'the horizon's edge' – all from this one poem. In his thesis on Whitman, Pavese continually draws attention to 'the discovery of mysterious influences in ordinary things – even the sea and the daily monotony experienced by the sailors – and the consequent serenity and joy of life and song' ('Thesis' fols 63–4) and 'the tone of amazed simplicity with which objects, the appearances of the world, are noted and made to follow endlessly, one after the other' ('Thesis' fol. 66), so that it becomes impossible not to connect this tendency with Pavese's *stupore*. There is too a strong sense of continuity and tradition, such as is found in 'I mari del Sud' (The South Seas, *Poesie* p. 11) and 'Antenati' (Forbears, *Poesie* p. 23).

In 'Song of Myself' and many other of Whitman's poems, there is a conscious didacticism which Lorenzo Mondo rightly connected with 'Antenati' and with 'Paesaggio i' (Landscape i),[7] and which is often expressed aphoristically:

> Apart from the pulling and the hauling stands what I am

or authoritatively:

> Do you guess I have some intricate purpose?
> Well I have, for the Fourth-month showers have, and the mica on the side of a rock has

where, incidentally, the first suggests that separation of *essere* and *fare* which Pavese was to insist on later ('A person counts for what he *is*, not for what he *does*' – *MV* 22 October 1940) and which is reflected even in his earliest poems in the contemplative observer, Pavese's narrator,[8] a not too distant cousin of Whitman's 'loafer' or 'magnificent idler'.[9] It would have been strange indeed had Pavese not absorbed some of the lessons he observed and analysed in Whitman's poetry and prose. The tone of his thesis is one of admiration, and the degree of identification with the American's purposes is striking.

A tendency 'to name objects and events stripped to the banality of the everyday and commonplace',[10] common in Whitman's verse, suggested to Lorenzo Mondo a certain influence of Gozzano on Pavese, and this possibility is further strengthened when we recall the habit of the earlier poet of incorporating place names and direct speech into his poems, both devices which Pavese used in his own, earlier verse, notably in 'I mari del Sud', though even before that. However, in spite of other obvious similarities such as the simplicity of Gozzano's language and style in his homely, discursive poetry, which frequently focuses on aspects of the provincial life of Piedmont, it is all too easy to overstate his impact on Pavese's work. Technically, his poetry is for the most part very different, adhering as it does to more traditional verse forms and length of line than does Pavese's, and relying much on rhyme for its effects. In tone, it is usually far removed from Pavese, whose verse does not have that lugubrious sentimentalism, that penchant for melodrama, which Gozzano indulges in poems such as 'Invernale' (Wintertime), 'La signorina Felicità ovvero la Felicità!' (Miss Felicity, or Happiness), 'Il gioco del silenzio' (The play of silence) and many others. Montale has rightly characterised Gozzano's verse as 'that poetry of the *faux exprès*, of semitones and harmonies in grey, that poetry which is clearly not heroic but rather *en pantoufles*',[11] and in so doing has incidentally emphasised its difference from Pavese's. The motif which is perhaps most typical of Gozzano is the relationship between a man and a woman, either realised or potential, remembered now, years after, as though it had been the unrecognised threshold of paradise. The poems are full of naturalistic detail, and Pavese's earliest attempts at poetry are frequently reminiscent of them in this respect. However, he had already managed to control any inclination towards sentimentalism by the time he came to write 'I mari del Sud', where a much greater sense of emotional detachment is in evidence than in most of Gozzano's verse. It is only in fleeting moments that we glimpse any point of contact between them, and even then, despite the major differences already observed in that field, it is in the realm of *tecnica* rather than *Weltanschauung*. Mondo's suggestion that Gozzano provides 'the missing link which joins [Pavese's] youthful, emotional outpourings to "I mari del Sud"'[12] seems greatly exaggerated. Indeed,

Gioanola's claim that Gozzano's influence furnished 'a negative model revealing to Pavese how he couldn't write, rather than a positive model to imitate'[13] seems nearer the mark. Pavese's most typical poetry between 1930 and 1935 is very different from what is most typical of Gozzano. Admittedly, the two poets move in the same provincial world, but Gozzano's attention is continually riveted on its middle-class inhabitants and their day-to-day concerns, whereas Pavese focuses on the outdoor world of the peasant or of those who live on the margins of urban society. With Pavese the whole poem grows out of memory, usually without any special emphasis on the 'act' of remembering, whereas with Gozzano the subject of the poem is a *specific* memory, and even though a lost innocence or new innocence are sometimes implicit in Pavese's material, it is never weighed down with remorse, regret or irony which colour Gozzano's harking back. There is considerable difference in tone and purpose in their approach to past experience, as a direct comparison between an early poem of Pavese's, 'Le maestrine' (The schoolmistresses) – chosen because its subject could well have appealed to Gozzano – and the closing section of 'Paolo e Virginia' will illustrate.

'Le maestrine' (*Poesie* p. 15), like many of Pavese's earlier poems, reconstructs the process whereby a personal myth is created – that of the relatively well-to-do young women schoolteachers so much a part of, and yet so out of place in, the rural setting of the narrator's childhood:

> Le mie terre di vigne, di prugnoli e di castagneti
> dove sono cresciute le frutta che ho sempre mangiato,
> le mie belle colline – hanno un frutto migliore
> che fantastico sempre e non ho morso mai.

(these lands of vines, sloes and chestnut trees, where grow the fruits that I have always eaten, these beautiful hills of mine – they have a better fruit which I dream about continually and have never tasted.)

Here, 'frutto' is synonymous with 'myth', that which recurs 'seasonally', continually renewing that sense of joy in vitality, associated with the 'maestrine', the subject of the poem. The contradiction is highlighted between these young schoolteachers and their environment, whether human or natural; they are fixed forever in their youthfulness – indeed the narrator refuses to think of them as ever growing old – and they are left in our mind's eye 'with their fine parasols and dressed in bright colours', and we are fully aware of that sense of delight in them, which is eternally renewable for the narrator, 'my own fruit, the best, which every year returns'. Wretchedness and beauty coexist in the poem but, significantly, it is the latter which is exalted.

Such optimism – or indeed, such an organic style – are not found in the closing lines of 'Paolo e Virginia'; life goes on, certainly, but diminished, for the richness of the love experience is not carried forward into the future, only the oppressive awareness that 'there hath passed away a glory from the earth':

> Il mio sogno è distrutto
> per sempre e il cuore non fiorisce più.

(My dream is destroyed for ever and my heart no longer blooms.)

It is in this final stanza, with its insistent, dead ring – 'morii', 'distrutto', 'per sempre', 'non ... più', 'invano', 'lutto', etc. – that the preceding narrative finds its *raison d'être*, being entirely at the service of Paolo's personal 'unburdening' – not for the *loss* of Virginia, but for the *effect* her death has had upon him – 'il cuore non fiorisce più' – the real subject and purpose of the poem. With few exceptions, Pavese did not publish this kind of 'poetry of unburdening'[14] during his *poesia–racconto* period (roughly speaking, that of the pre-Brancaleone poems) and when he did write *and* publish poems which expressed a personal sense of desolation (1935–8) they were rarely in the narrative vein. On the contrary, they achieved a much greater compression through the *immagine–racconto*, in which objects and the relationships between them became symbols of the instinctive, essential self; landscapes of the soul.[15] For Pavese, poetry was ever an instrument of self-discovery; for Gozzano, a catharsis and a consolation.

Although Pavese was to modify his views in the intervening years, particularly with regard to the image, he eventually came to realise that the poems of the Solaria edition of *Lavorare stanca* had represented an extraordinary moment in the history of modern Italian poetry:

At a time when Italian prose was a 'weary discussion with itself' and poetry was 'a painful silence', I was talking in prose and in verse with peasants, labourers, sand-diggers, prostitutes, prisoners, factory girls and young people. I wouldn't dream of boasting about it. I liked them and still like them. They were my sort of people.[16]

Lavorare stanca was an attempt, whatever its shortcomings, at a direct confrontation with reality; more specifically, with the life and problems of the people of Piedmont and Turin. Indeed, its significance would seem to lie more in its moral and historical perspective than in any intrinsically poetic merit it might have, for technically it raised as many problems for Pavese as it solved and eventually he abandoned it in favour of prose. It was more the idea than the practice of great poetry. Nonetheless it clearly defined, once and for all, the content of Pavese's poetical world. He himself recognised its relevance in his work when he referred to it as the 'grosso monolito' (great monolith) from which all his most important works had been 'chipped'. The Soliara *Lavorare stanca* has therefore a twofold importance in contemporary Italian literature, the one historical, as the first sustained attempt at *neo-realismo* in verse, the other personal.

If the whole work is indeed the 'great monolith', then – to continue the metaphor – the poem which opens the collection, 'I mari del Sud', is the 'plinth' on which it stands. It contains almost everything which was to be typical of Pavese's writing, and yet, in itself, it is not a consistently good poem:

> Camminiamo una sera sul fianco di un colle,
> in silenzio. Nell'ombra del tardo crepuscolo
> mio cugino è un gigante vestito di bianco,
> che si muove pacato, abbronzato nel volto,
> taciturno.

(We walk one evening up the side of a hill, in silence. In the late twilight shadows my cousin is a giant dressed in white, who moves silently; his face is sunburnt and he does not speak.)

Two features of the poem become apparent in its opening section: the conversational tone and the unusually long line which is employed. In his attempt to sever all links with traditional verse forms, Pavese sought space in which to develop the *racconto* (story) aspect of each poem, and quite by chance (so he would have us believe)[17] he stumbled across the thirteen-syllable line. Occasionally, as in the sixth line, it becomes stretched to as many as sixteen syllables, and proves extremely unwieldy, loosening the bonds of poetic form until the verse becomes indistinguishable from prose. The majority of the poems in the Solaria edition of *Lavorare stanca* are based on the thirteen-syllable line, and there are very few where the poet is entirely in control. The main problem is the caesura, which often reveals that the line is in reality two lines of shorter duration, both of which are common traditional types; for example,

> Camminiamo una sera   sul fianco di un colle

Here, the first part of the 'line' is a perfectly regular seven-syllable line (*settenario*), stressed on the third and sixth syllables, whilst the second part is of six syllables (*senario*), having its stress on the second and the fifth.

> Mio cugino ha parlato stasera. Mi ha chiesto
> se salivo con lui: dalla vetta si scorge
> nelle notti serene il riflesso del faro
> lontano, di Torino. 'Tu che abiti a Torino ...'
> Mi ha detta '... ma hai ragione. La vita va vissuta
> lontano dal paese: si profitta e si gode
> e poi, quando si torna, come me a quarant'anni,
> si trova tutto nuovo. Le Langhe non si perdono.'
> Tutto questo mi ha detto e non parla italiano,
> ma adopera lento il dialetto, che, come le pietre
> de questo stesso colle, è scabro tanto
> che vent'anni di idiomi e di oceani diversi
> non gliel'hanno scalfito. E cammina per l'erta
> con lo sguardo raccolto che ho visto, bambino,
> usare ai contadini un poco stanchi.

(My cousin has spoken this evening. He asked me if I would go up the hill with him. From the top, on clear nights, you can see the reflection of the far-off beacon of Turin. 'You who live in Turin ...,' he said to me, '... but you're right. Life goes on far away from home, you profit from it and enjoy it and then, when you come back, like I did at the age of forty, you find everything is new. You don't lose the Langhe.' He said all this to me, but he doesn't speak Italian; speaking slowly, he uses the dialect which, like the stones of this very hill, is so rugged that twenty years of different languages and different parts of the world have left no mark on it. And he walks up the slope with that look of concentration on his face that I saw him turn on the peasants who were a bit tired, when I was a child.)

The verbal theme of the first section, that of silence ('silenzio', 'taciturno', 'tacere'), is taken up again here only to be broken. But the fact that the cousin 'has spoken' is, to the mind of the narrator, worthy of comment. There is about it that mild sense of *stupore* (amazement) which often accompanies the observation (often by children in Pavese's poems) of an event or state of affairs which would normally pass without comment. One of the most notable features of this poem is the sense of awe in which the narrator holds his cousin, and what the poem relates, almost as an undercurrent, is the myth-making process which had been going on for him for as long as he could remember. The cousin is, for the narrator, a living myth.

In this part of the poem, the two poles of Pavese's world, the Piedmontese countryside (*campagna*) and the city of Turin (*città*), are present, but at a great distance from each other. Later, they develop as two totally different worlds in Pavese's writing, and it is interesting that even here the city, which came to represent history, progress and civilisation in his mind (as opposed to the prehistory represented by *campagna*), should be described in terms of light – the 'far-off beacon' whose reflection may be seen only 'on clear nights'.

For the cousin, what is important is the sense of belonging which has accompanied him wherever he has travelled in the world and which has ultimately determined his return to the Langhe. His return involves both memory and discovery, and an awareness of something immutable. In the Langhe, the alienation of man from the world of nature has never taken place.

In the third section ('Vent'anni è stato in giro per il mondo'), the narrative swings away from the present to the past and memory, from the cousin to his continuous absence and its myth-making significance in the childhood of the narrator.

The personal memories of the narrator in the third section become a definite introspection in the fourth ('Oh da quando ho giocato ai pirati malesi'), and the objective-present with which the poem began has by this time developed into the subjective-past, a movement which, after 1935, had taken place in the whole of Pavese's poetry. The desired objectivity and immediacy of the Solaria poems were achieved only through a tremendous effort of self-discipline, and proved impossible to maintain in his isolation at Brancaleone. The lament in this part of 'I mari del Sud' is for the lost world of childish illusion and innocence, a world which has been supplanted by the intangible, almost inexpressible horrors of modern city life:

> La città mi ha insegnato infinite paure:
> una folla, una strada mi han fatto tremare,
> un pensiero talvolta, spiato su un viso.
> Sento ancora negli occhi la luce beffarda
> dei lampioni a migliaia sul gran scalpiccio.

(The city has taught me countless fears: a crowd or a street have made me tremble; sometimes even a thought glimpsed on someone's face. In my eyes I still feel the mocking light of thousands of street-lamps way above the great shuffling of people in the streets.)

This stanza proves to be parenthetic, though developing naturally enough out of the circumstances dealt with in the first three. Pavese himself rightly spoke of 'I mari del Sud' as being 'a poem which is somewhere between the psychological and reportage'. In the fifth section ('Mio cugino è tornato, finita la guerra'), the events of the cousin's life return, whilst the pessimism of his relatives continues, providing a thematic link with the third section.

> Mio cugino ha una faccia recisa. Comprò un pianterreno
> nel paese e ci fece riuscire un garage di cemento
> con dinanzi fiammante la pila per dar la benzina
> e sul ponte ben grossa alla curva una targa reclame.
> Poi ci mise un meccanico dentro a ricevere i soldi
> e lui girò tutte le Langhe fumando.

(My cousin has a determined face. He bought a piece of land in the village and had a garage built there out of concrete, and he put a shiny petrol pump in front of it, and on the bend at the bridge a great big placard. Then he put a mechanic in the garage to collect the money whilst he wandered all over the Langhe smoking.)

The garage, which was to return in the poem 'Atlantic Oil' (*Poesie* p. 54),[18] becomes a symbol of modern, urban society and of change being imposed upon the almost timeless atmosphere which characterises the Langhe in Pavese's poetry. But in 'I mari del Sud' the resistance to change is evidently too great, and the failure of the project emphasises the cousin's ever-increasing awareness of himself and the tradition to which he belongs:

> al mattino batteva le fiere e con aria sorniona
> contrattava i cavalli. Spiegò poi a me,
> quando fallì il disegno, che il suo piano
> era stato di togliere tutte le bestie alla valle
> e obbligare la gente a comprargli i motori.
> 'Ma la bestia' diceva 'più grossa di tutte,
> sono stato io a pensarlo. Dovevo sapere
> che qui buoi e persone son tutta una razza.'

(he would scour the markets in the mornings, and, with an air of cunning about him, would bargain for horses. He explained to me later, after the plan had failed, that his intention had been to buy up all the animals in the valley, and in that way force people to buy cars from him. 'But the biggest animal of the lot', he said, 'was me, for having thought of it. I should have known that here people and animals are all the same race.')

From his experience he has also learnt that there are more important values in life than financial gain. He has to accept the region as it is, for he cannot change it, and this realisation makes him more human. Here, as earlier in the poem, there are hints that the cousin is still regarded as a rolling stone. The details which the narrator tells about him are suggestive of the air of myth and mystery which surrounds him in the narrator's own consciousness. There is almost a reluctance to admit that the cousin has returned for good, that he is human after all, and therefore the narrator, though perhaps not consciously, tries to persuade us and himself that his cousin is continuing his exotic life, albeit on a smaller scale. He wanders all over the Langhe, he marries a woman who is not typical of the region, he tries to introduce modern 'city' ideas and, perhaps most important of all, he maintains that solitude and taciturnity which have been the fertile ground upon which the myth has flourished. But the sense of the exotic, if ever it existed at all for the cousin, no longer plays any significant part in his life. It is only for those who, like the narrator, have not travelled and have not seen for themselves, and who have lived the far away places only in their imagination, that a sense of the exotic exists.

The next stanza ('Camminiamo da più di mezz'ora') moves, once again, to the present, for the cousin's life, a denial of the narrator's myth of it, is always lived for the present, without nostalgia or regret. For Pavese, the cousin of 'I mari del Sud' (an actual relation of Pavese's) remained always the model of strength and self-sufficiency to which he aspired. Almost at the end of his life, in a letter to his cousin's daughter, he still referred to him as 'the only one of the Paveses who has counted for something up to now and who was a real man'.[19]

> Mio cugino si ferma d'un tratto e si volge: 'Quest'anno
> scrivo sul manifesto: *Santo Stefano*
> *è sempre stato il primo nelle feste*
> *della valle del Belbo* – e che la dicano
> quei di Canelli.'
>   e io penso alla forza
> che mi ha reso quest'uomo, strappandolo al mare,
> alle terre lontane, al silenzio che dura.
> Mio cugino non parla dei viaggi compiuti.
> Dice asciutto che è stato in quel luogo e in quell'altro e pensa ai suoi
> motori.

(Suddenly my cousin stops and turns to me: 'This year I'll write on the placard: *The Festival of Santo Stefano has always been the best in the Belbo valley* – and that they admit it even in Canelli' ... and I think about the strength that this man has given me, tearing himself away from the sea, from distant lands, from the endless silence. My cousin doesn't talk about the voyages he has made. He says drily that he's been in this place or that, and he thinks about his motors.)

From the proud words to be inscribed on the placard, we realise that the cousin has in truth arrived home. The narrator derives an inner strength from the knowledge that his cousin, who has been everywhere and seen everything, has finally rejected a life of adventure in returning to what was always his deepest reality – the only reality the narrator has ever known. Yet the cousin, though a realist, is by no means insensitive for he does have one special memory, though like everything else in his life it too is controlled. It is a memory devoid of nostalgia, and it lives on in him because of its suggestiveness – of beauty, of struggle and of strength:

> e ha veduto volare i ramponi pesanti nel sole,
> ha veduto fuggire balene tra schiume di sangue
> e inseguirle e innalzarsi le code e lottare alla lancia.
> Me ne accenna talvolta.

(he saw heavy harpoons flying in the sun, he saw whales fleeing in the foam lathered with blood and saw the chase and the lifted tails and the struggle with the lance. He mentions it to me sometimes.)

One is reminded of Hemingway in the motif of the bloody struggle to the death, but the original here, as indeed with Hemingway, is Herman Melville, whose *Moby-Dick* Pavese was soon after to translate into Italian.[20] The fascination which America and its writers had for Pavese in the years when he was composing the first *Lavorare stanca* is often present in one way or another in those poems, and will be discussed in chapter 4 below.

Certain features of 'I mari del Sud' make it quite unlike any other Italian poetry being written at the time. Firstly, its language. There is nothing abstruse, nor even allusive. What few images there are do not serve as nuclei around which the poem is constructed. Pavese later explained in *Il mestiere di poeta* that he did not want them in his poetry because they would jeopardise his 'adored immediacy' and because he wanted to avoid the 'facile, gushing lyricism of the imagists'. Indeed, the sparseness of formal imagery suggests the language of prose rather than that of poetry; little meaning is evoked, rather is it described and explained. Nevertheless, this *is* poetry because, quite apart from the intricate rhythms, other formalising elements are at work, and it is in these that we best see Pavese's 'essential expression of essential facts'. An organic unity is created by the repetition of key words or phrases (*riprese*). Reference has already been made to the verbal theme of 'silence' in the first stanza and this appears yet again in the 'endless silence' of the seventh. There is a whole network of such themes, amongst them the 'dressed in white' and 'sunburnt face' of the first and sixth stanzas, the 'hilltop' of the second and seventh, 'the slope' which appears again in the second and seventh, and so on. Quite apart from these *riprese* there are others which are, like the 'silence' of the first, characteristic of one stanza; amongst these are 'far-off' and 'Turin' in the second; 'women', 'stamp', 'they forgot' and the derivatives of 'morte' (death) in the third; the 'quanto(a) tempo (vita) è trascorso(a)' (what a long time/how much life has passed) and the rhetorical use of 'altri' (others) in the fourth. This was to prove a constant and unifying feature in Pavese's poetry, the *riprese* being carried over from one work to another.

Another interesting aspect of this poem is its use of near-authentic speech within the metric scheme – a moderately successful experiment which is repeated occasionally in later poems, notably 'Estate di San Martino' (Indian summer, *Poesie* p. 36) and 'Il vino triste' (Sad wine, *Poesie* p. 21), while the use of place names has already been noted in the context of Pavese's debt to Gozzano.

The Naturalistic character of the poetry of the first *Lavorare stanca* lies not only in the use of regional Italian (occasionally dialectal) and regional topics but in the great attention paid to descriptive detail. The cousin

> è un gigante vestito di bianco,
> che si muove pacato, abbronzato nel volto,
> taciturno

whilst the arrival of the postcard triggers off the boyish flight of fancy, in which place names and their associations are sufficient to set his heart beating faster:

> veniva da un'isola detta Tasmania
> circondata da un mare più azzurro, feroce di squali,
> nel Pacifico, a sud dell'Australia.

(It had come from an island called Tasmania, which was surrounded by the bluest of seas, teeming with sharks, in the Pacific, to the south of Australia.)

One significant feature of 'I mari del Sud' is sharply at variance with the theories of Naturalism – the involvement of the story-teller in the events he is narrating. Pavese's narrator is not the protagonist, yet the poem is as much about the protagonist's effect on the narrator as it is about the cousin himself. There is some detachment, but nothing like that found in the chief exponents of Naturalism. Shortly after the end of this decade, Pavese realised the value of incorporating his narrator, as a character in his own right, into his novels, and after *La spiaggia* (The beach), written in 1940–1, this became his common practice.

Pavese, as is clear from his diary and the poems of his youth, was extremely introverted, and it is not surprising that in several poems, even in his emotionally most controlled period 1930–5, the narrator and the protagonist are one and the same. However, the resultant poetry is rarely, if at all, morbidly subjective. Poems such as 'Antenati' (Forbears) and 'Mania di solitudine' (Mania for solitude, *Poesie* p. 52) define the links between the narrator–protagonist and his environment; they are not concerned with his alienation – which, generally speaking, becomes the chief preoccupation of Pavese's poetry for a long time after the events of 1935.

The more or less Naturalistic standpoint taken in 'I mari del Sud' was precariously maintained in 'Donne perdute' (Fallen women, *Poesie* p. 18), 'Fumatori di carta' (Smokers of cheap cigarettes, *Poesie* p. 30) and other compositions of the years 1930–3, but even in many of those poems there is an undercurrent of *inquietudine* (anxiety) which stems primarily from the sexual preoccupations of their narrators.

It was in a poem written in 1933, 'Paesaggio ı' (Landscape ı, *Poesie* p. 37), that Pavese first noted any substantial development in his verse. It was here, he tells us in *Il mestiere di poeta*, that he first 'discovered' the image. Nevertheless, he refused to admit to himself that he was using the image in a conventional manner. He claimed, instead, to have created a 'fanciful relationship' between the hermit, the subject of the poem, and the landscape in which he had placed him. This relationship consisted simply in the direct application to the hermit of words used first of all to describe the landscape ('le felci'; 'bruciate':)

> Quando fuma la pipa in disparte nel sole,
> se lo perdo non so rintracciarlo, perchè è del colore
> delle felci bruciate.

(When he's smoking his pipe away from his cave, in the sun, if I lose sight of him he's difficult to find again, because he is the same colour as the *scorched bracken*.)

As a result of this discovery, though he misunderstood it, Pavese came to see poetry as 'a complex of fanciful relationships which constitute one's own perception of a reality', and he began consciously to move away from an objective towards a subjective viewpoint. It was in 'Paesaggio ı' that the first world of Pavese's poetry, the countryside of the Langhe, became established in the 'punti di riferimento' (objective correlatives) already referred to as *riprese*,[21] though without example. It is an elemental–natural world consisting of 'la collina' (the hill), 'la roccia' (rock), 'terra' (earth), 'cespugli' (shrubs and bushes), 'sole' (sun), 'vigne' (vines), 'il cielo' (the sky), 'le valli' (valleys), 'la pianura' (the plain), 'foglie' (leaves), 'acqua' (water), 'pioggia' (rain) and 'pozzi' (pools), a world inhabited by 'la capra' (the goat), 'la biscia' (the snake), 'villani' (peasants) and 'vagabondi' (tramps).

In this early period, Pavese frequently achieves a suggestiveness which is a kind of optimism at the root of the poem: for example, the opening lines of 'Due sigarette' (Two cigarettes, *Poesie* p. 44), composed in 1933:

> Ogni notte è la liberazione. Si guarda i riflessi
> dell'asfalto sui corsi che si aprono lucidi al vento.
> Ogni rado passante ha una faccia e una storia.
> Ma a quest'ora non c'è più stanchezza: i lampioni a migliaia
> sono tutti per chi si sofferma a sfregare un cerino.

(Freedom comes every night. You look at the reflections on the asphalt along the streets which open out, glistening in the wind. Each rare passer-by has a face and a story. But by this time you are no longer tired. The street-lamps in their thousands are for anyone who stops to strike a match.)

In the poem that optimism is justified, for the story-teller meets a woman with whom he smokes a cigarette and talks a while, and in the last line goes off to spend the night with her. The street or the piazza, in the Solaria *Lavorare stanca*, is the place where 'ogni cosa può accadere' (anything might happen), and this is in sharp contrast with the constricted world of the post-1935 poems, for there, only the child can still feel that unlimited possibility is offered by each street. For the grown man the street becomes a place in which his solitude is emphasised, and even in the poem 'Lavorare stanca' (*Poesie* p. 99), which dates from 1934, there is an evident retreat from the mood of 'Due sigarette', and the poem ends on a note of desperate optimism:

> Non è giusto restare sulla piazza deserta.
> Ci sarà certamente quella donna per strada
> che, pregata, vorrebbe dar mano alla casa.

(It isn't right to stay in the empty piazza. Surely, somewhere in these streets there is a woman who, if she were asked, would like to lend a hand in the house.)

The opening line of 'Due sigarette' touches on one of the most prominent themes of the first *Lavorare stanca*, that of freedom. The majority of characters encountered live outside, or on the very edge of, moral or social normality. They are, for the most part, solitary figures whose outstanding characteristic is generally their self-sufficiency. Many reveal a definite antipathy towards organised work, which is regarded as a limitation, whilst others, like the sand-diggers of 'Crepuscolo di sabbiatori' (The sand-diggers' twilight, *Poesie* p. 56) or the cousin of 'I mari del Sud', tend to be isolated by the work they do. There are also those who are morally unacceptable, the prostitutes Dina[22] and Deola,[23] the drunkards of 'Disciplina antica' (Ancient discipline, *Poesie* p. 75) and 'Indisciplina' (Lack of discipline, *Poesie* p. 76), the tramps of 'Casa in costruzione' (House under construction, *Poesie* p. 64) and 'Il tempo passa' (Time goes by, *Poesie* p. 95), and even the hermit of 'Paesaggio i'. The frequency with which they occur, in one form or another, makes it difficult not to see Pavese himself behind these various *personae*. This feeling is reinforced when we realise that another great limiting factor in *Lavorare stanca* is the question of sexual relationships, for there is enough documentary evidence, letters and diary entries, to show that Pavese always found this an insurmountable problem in his life. It is so for the narrators of 'Tradimento' (Betrayal, *Poesie* p. 25) and 'Lavorare stanca' (*Poesie* p. 60), and if these poems are an expression of Pavese's own difficulties, then we can also perhaps understand the compensatory significance of the virile, self-sufficient 'giants' such as the one described in 'Balletto' (Dance, *Poesie* p. 66):

> Il gigante s'avvia e la donna è una parte di tutto il suo corpo,
> solamente più viva. La donna non conta,
> ogni sera è diversa ...

(The giant moves and the woman is a part of his whole body, only more alive. The woman doesn't matter, every evening she is a different one ...)

This virility is often manifested as a scorn for women, which at its most extreme represents a petulant misogyny. A key poem in this context, in that it links the themes of the sexual giant, the insignificance of woman and the opposition to work, is 'Antenati':

> E le donne non contano nella famiglia.
> Voglio dire, le donne da noi stanno in casa
> E ci mettono al mondo e non dicono nulla

> e non contano nulla e non le ricordiamo.
> ...
>
> > il solo lavoro non basta a me e ai miei;
> > noi sappiamo schiantarci, ma il sogno più grande
> > dei miei padri fu sempre un far nulla da bravi.

(And women don't matter in the family. What I mean is that with us women stay inside and bring us into the world and have no say in anything and no meaning and we don't remember them ... work by itself isn't enough for me and my family. We know how to work till we drop, but the grandest dream that my forbears had was to do nothing at all just like the well-to-do.)

The 'sogno' (dream) voiced here is one of many which underlie the attempted objective presentation of real situations in *Lavorare stanca*. The compensatory principle, present in the virile 'giant', can also be extended to the kind of situation outlined in 'Due sigarette' or 'Piaceri notturni' (Night pleasures, *Poesie* p. 71) which, whatever else, certainly have the appearance of dream fulfilments. This attitude towards women may be interpreted in the same way. Women, the object of desire and the denial of its fulfilment for Pavese, are frequently humbled and made the tool or scapegoat of his men. It seems that only in this way can woman be possessed and her mystery be destroyed. However, it is not my intention to imply that Pavese's poems are interesting only as case histories; but it is an aspect which cannot be ignored.

The notion of freedom depending on a rejection of the fundamental condition of the individual's participation in society – that of work – coupled with the strength associated with solitude, leads one to suspect that Pavese himself aspired, as a writer, to just such a position. Assuming its feasibility, does this represent an espousal of something akin to d'Annunzio's poet – superman, or a less than conscious reaction to the pressures on the writer under Fascist rule? In other words, was it a choice Pavese would have made whatever the historical circumstances or *force majeure* – that is, no choice at all? Pavese eventually rejected the negative attitude to work which is characteristic of *Lavorare stanca*, yet he continued to see himself as an outsider. His youthful letters to Sturani suggest that he inherited and unquestioningly accepted the *fin de siècle* notion of the artist, refusing to be possessed by a vulgar, materialistic society, seeing his artistic freedom in his rejection of its values. Between 1930 and 1935, Pavese found himself in a historical situation in which those circumstances actually prevailed. Whether consciously or not, he had schooled himself for a role he was called upon to play. His poetry began to look more and more like that of the *ermetici*, but once the historical pressures were removed then *as a writer* he took up a more or less 'committed' stand, though *as a human being* he continued to see himself as an outsider.

His sense of alienation was real enough, and more and more he came to see his writing as a means of breaking through the barriers which stood between himself and his fellow men. It is obvious from those poems in which sex is seen as the basis of a relationship that doubt and anxiety increase in Pavese's mind, so that within the space of one year he moves from the apparently sure standpoint of 'Due sigarette' (1933) to that of 'Lavorare stanca' (1934). The events of 1935 hit Pavese at a time when he had already begun to sense the inevitability of his own inadequacy as a man, and undermined the confidence and harmony which his earlier poems had sought to create. To make distinctions between man and writer may seem heretical; but Pavese himself does just this in the penultimate entry in his diary, for there he says:

In my work, then, I am king. I've done it all in ten years. Just think of the hesitations I experienced then.

In my life I am more desperate and lost than ever I was then. What have I constructed? Nothing. For several years I have ignored my defects and have lived as though they didn't exist. I have been stoical. Was it heroism? No, it cost me nothing. Then at the first assault of the 'restless anxiety' I have fallen back into quicksand. Since March I've been floundering in it. Names don't matter. Are they anything other than names turned up by chance, accidental names – if not those, wouldn't there have been others? It happens that now I know which is my greatest triumph – and this triumph lacks flesh, lacks blood, is lifeless.

There is nothing more I want on this earth, except that which fifteen years of failure have put beyond my reach. (*MV* 17 August 1950)

A comparison of the poems written before and after Pavese's arrest in 1935 reveals that in the earlier poems solitude is a source of strength and is therefore desired, whilst in the later ones it is seen as an inescapable weakness which is interpreted as personal failure. Having once experienced an imposed solitude, it seems he was unable to see it in the same light as before. Ironically, Pavese's success as a writer is achieved as an observer who stands on the edge of a world and reveals it, and his failure at the personal level comes from the self-same standpoint, for he is unable to enter that world and participate in it.

Freedom, with which this discussion began, became noticeably associated with children,[24] and also with old men,[25] in a small group of poems composed in 1934 and early 1935. Because they do not work, children and old men have time to observe and savour the world about them. However, real freedom exists only for the child, because life, for him, is still anticipation, whilst for the old it is memory and the realisation that active participation is forever past. Both enjoy a measure of peace, the child in that he does not yet know the frustrations and anxieties which stem from work and sexuality, and the old man in that those torments, once experienced, now lie behind him. These poems suggest Pavese had begun to believe that adult life was all restriction and suffering because it was then that one lost the self-sufficiency of the child and depended, for the fulfilment of one's greatest needs, particularly sexual, upon the will of others. Brancaleone and its tragic personal sequel for Pavese confirmed him in this view, and set him searching for 'l'isolamento che basta a se stesso' (solitude which is self-sufficiency) which became his definition of 'maturity'.

The inevitable suffering associated with work and with sex is also present in those poems which bring together *campagna* and *città* in individual lives. In 'Gente che non capisce' (People who don't understand, *Poesie* p. 62) the girl Gella works in the city but travels back and forth each day, for her home is in the country. She experiences a different way of life but at the same time a growing sense of alienation, in that she can no longer identify with the countryside to which her family belongs. Her reaction – 'she sits in silence' whilst they discuss their work in the country – is symptomatic of her withdrawal, illustrated by the fantasies she creates to solve her problem. Environment and tradition represent security for the characters in Pavese's poems, so that change is followed by bewilderment and suffering. It is the same in 'Città in campagna' (City in the country, *Poesie* p. 58), where the child, returning home to the country after a visit with his father to the city, experiences a sense of dissatisfaction; as a result of this visit his life will never again resume the tranquillity and balance it has had before. An apparently absolute reality has been shown to be merely relative.

Change, of whatever sort, assumes the character and mask of injustice in Pavese's poetry. Human life has thus a built-in element of injustice and suffering, quite apart from those injustices like work, which man imposes on himself, or sex, which is imposed on him by nature. Here Pavese draws close to Leopardi, for both poets recognise a tragic human condition which can never be substantially altered but whose suffering could perhaps be alleviated if men were to make a real effort to minimise their injustices to each other. In 'Fumatori di carta', Pavese makes as impassioned a plea as does the Leopardi of 'La ginestra' (The broom-flower) for an improvement of man's lot through human solidarity. Pavese's poem speaks of the poverty and wretchedness of life in the city of Turin:

> Imparò a lavorare
> nelle fabbriche senza un sorriso. Imparò a misurare
> sulla propria fatica la fame degli altri,
> e trovò dappertutto ingiustizie.

(He learned how to work in the factory without a smile. He learned how to measure the hunger of others by his own labour, and everywhere he found injustices.)

Then a statement which is untypically – if ingenuously – bold for the Pavese of 1932:

> Accettava il lavoro
> come un duro destino dell'uomo. Ma tutti gli uomini
> lo accettassero e al mondo ci fosse giustizia.

(He accepted work as the harsh destiny of mankind. But if only all men would accept it there might be justice in the world.)

The worker curses his destiny which compels him and his brother to toil day in and day out to feed their ageing parents. The fatalism seems to have emerged as a sense of powerlessness in the face of Destiny, but this is not final, for at the end of the poem there is a statement which signals nothing less than the awakening of a political consciousness:

> D'un tratto gridò
> che non era il destino se il mondo soffriva,
> se la luce del sole strappava bestemmie:
> era l'uomo colpevole. *Almeno potercene andare,*
> *far la libera fame, rispondere no*
> *a una vita che adopera amore e pietà,*
> *la famiglia, il pezzetto di terra, a legarci le mani.*

(All of a sudden he cried out that it wasn't Destiny that made the world suffer, that caused the sunlight to bring forth nothing but curses, it was man who was to blame. 'If only we could go away, be hungry in freedom, say no to a life which uses love and pity, the family or a bit of land to tie our hands.')

It is not surprising that this poem was omitted from the Solaria *Lavorare stanca*, for whether Pavese's intention had been overtly anti-Fascist (which seems unlikely) or a general statement about the human lot, the case dealt with in the poem was typical of too many in Fascist Italy for it not to have landed Pavese and the Solaria Press in trouble.

The sixteen poems which Pavese wrote whilst he was detained at Brancaleone reveal a more obvious subjectivity than those composed before. There is an insistence on nostalgia and memory, solitude and disillusionment and an all-pervading sense of futility and stagnation. The world of these poems is one of 'pioggia' (rain), 'mare' (sea), 'fumo' (smoke), 'nebbia' (mist), 'freddo' (cold) and 'ombra' (shadow), and a sad reflective music runs through them.

Turin becomes the focus of nostalgia and loses the 'infinite paure' (numberless fears) which had been identified with it in 'I mari del Sud'. In 'Paesaggio vi' (Landscape vi, *Poesie* p. 119) it becomes 'la bella città, in mezzo a prati e colline' (the beautiful city, set among meadows and hills) and 'le donne dai vivi colori/vi camminano' (women in bright colours walk there). That sense of possibility which had been a significant element in 'Due sigarette' returns here, but no longer with reference to the here and now. This Turin is the city of earlier memories, considered from the other end of Italy, and is mythologised into something resembling the earthly paradise. It becomes the place of memory, of reality, of security; the future to which he will one day return:

> Ogni via, ogni spigolo schietto di casa
> nella nebbia, conserva un antico tremore:
> chi lo sente non può abbandonarsi.

(Every street, every angle of a house showing through the mist retains a ripple of memory from days gone by: no-one who feels it can let himself go.)

The theme of childhood and freedom (and its obverse – adulthood and limitation) continues in 'Poetica' (Poetics, *Poesie* p. 125) and 'Mito' (Myth, *Poesie* p. 127); and is most fully developed in the latter, where the connection between childhood and the immortality of the gods, to emerge later in *Dialoghi con Leucò*, is made. The poem turns on the contrast between a child and the man he will become, and the note of disillusionment and resignation predominates.

Reference has already been made to the 'sad, reflective music' of the Brancaleone poems, and this raises the question of Pavese's versification once again. The poem 'Mito' illustrates the many weaknesses in Pavese's poetic technique. He had begun by aiming at a verse which was 'naked and almost prose-like' to avoid the niceties of traditional metres, verse forms and imagery as they were being used by the *ermetici*. However, he had found the balance difficult to achieve because of the many restraints he imposed upon himself. The long line easily became disjointed, not only because of the sense stops (including punctuation), but because of the inevitable caesuras and awkward enjambements. What becomes evident in 'Mito' is that Pavese had opened the door to all kinds of effects that at one time he would never have admitted into his verse. We find him using rhyme, as in the second stanza ('splendori'/'Fragori'/'colore'), or introducing alliteration, as in

> il corpo di un uomo
> pensieroso si piega, dove un dio respirava

where there is interplay between the 's' and 'p' sounds, or in

> trascorre remoto/arrossando la spiaggia

where the relevant sounds are the 'r' and the 's', whilst in the third stanza generally there is a preponderance of 'r' and 'v' sounds. A word repeated more than once in close proximity, noted in connection with the fourth stanza of 'I mari del Sud', makes a double appearance here – once at the beginning of the third stanza ('è ... e ... e') and, perhaps more noticeably, in the second with the word 'più'. This second example has added interest in that on all three occasions it is followed by a caesura, two words of three or four syllables and a substantial marked stop. The effect is to break up the rhythm and to give an emphatic sense of finality which is in keeping with the sense of collapse conveyed semantically.

Attention has already been drawn to the strong tendency of the thirteen-syllable line to divide into what are, in effect, two lines of shorter duration. The third stanza of 'Mito' is a good example, being made up almost entirely of *settenari* (seven-syllable lines). The fourth stanza, like the second, is disjointed. Only two lines (including the last one) are end-stopped, and yet the stanza contains three other full stops and a colon. Pavese's intention, it would seem, was to isolate each unit of meaning in areas of silence so as literally to give pause for thought, but once again the rhythm disintegrates and form almost collapses, so that it is debatable whether this stanza is verse at all.

On the positive side, there is an undeniable organic unity which springs, as ever, from reliance upon the *riprese*. In this poem they are mainly single words which appear both within the individual stanza and outside it; occasionally they recur in the same position in the line, like 'uomo', which is found five times in the end position. Besides the many single words (amongst which 'spiagge', 'estate', 'sole', 'dio', 'terra') there are also phrases or clauses which have a similar function, notably 'senza pena' found in an identical position in the first and fourth stanzas; 'il giovane dio' with its additional divisions into its single components; 'ignorava la morte' which occurs at the end of contiguous sentences; and, with perhaps more significance than Pavese (who in his early verse is rarely allusive) intended to give it, the opening 'Verrà il giorno', which seems to echo all the foreboding and prophecy with which Fra Cristoforo's 'Verrà un giorno' is charged in Manzoni's *I promessi sposi* (*The betrothed*).

The disillusionment which colours 'Mito' is there too in 'Semplicità' (Simplicity, *Poesie* p. 128). In this poem, the sense of futility and the motif of the 'uomo solo' (man who is alone) suggest the idea that it is far better to remain in prison and dream of life outside than to experience release and the inevitable collapse of the dream. This latter theme was to become central to the short stories which Pavese wrote between 1936 and 1938, and to his first novel, *Il carcere* (The political prisoner).

The theme of futility is best seen in 'Paternità' (Paternity, *Poesie* p. 130) and 'Lo steddazzu' (The morning star, *Poesie* p. 134), where 'l'uomo solo' reflects and waits and feels no hope. In the former he is

> dinanzi all'inutile mare,
> attendendo la sera, attendendo il mattino

(before the useless sea, waiting for evening, waiting for morning).

The poem has an ominous, dead ring in its adjectives – 'inutile' (useless), 'torbido' (gloomy), 'madide' (soaked), 'sola' (alone), 'stanco' (tired), 'nera' (black) – and is reminiscent of Leopardi in its insistence on 'il gran vuoto ch'è sotto le stelle' (the great emptiness beneath the stars) and 'le stelle, che non odono nulla' (the stars, which hear nothing).

'Lo steddazzu' reaches the most extreme point of despair expressed in these poems. There is the futility associated with the sea, and the desperate sense of solitude, but also the destruction of the traditional symbols of hope, 'le stelle' (the stars) and 'l'alba' (the dawn):

> Domani tornerà l'alba tiepida con la diafana luce
> e sarà come ieri e mai nulla accadrà.
> L'uomo solo vorrebbe soltanto dormire.
> Quando l'ultima stella si spegne nel cielo,
> l'uomo adagio prepara la pipa e l'accende.

(Tomorrow the tepid dawn will return with its diaphanous light and will be just like yesterday and nothing will ever happen. The man who is alone would like only to sleep. When the last star goes out in the sky, the man slowly fills his pipe and lights it.)

Many of the poems have a delicate beauty which derives from the pathos and suggestiveness of the images which they create. In 'Lo steddazzu' the 'pipa' (pipe) which 'tra i denti/pende spenta' (hangs unlit between his teeth) becomes a symbol of the stagnation which the sense of futility imposes, and this is echoed and extended a little later in

> Pende stanca nel cielo
> una stella verdognola, sorpresa dall'alba.

(a greenish star hangs tired in the sky, surprised by the dawn.)

Of the poems written after Brancaleone little need be said. The *Poesie del disamore* Pavese regarded as a means of coming to terms with a personal tragedy, and never intended them for publication. In them, the motif of the return, the search for a new beginning, is prominent – in one poem, 'Ritorno di Deola' (Deola's return, *Poesie* p. 165), it is, perhaps significantly, the return of another 'outsider', a prostitute – but it is shot through with the realisation that something vital has disappeared forever. No attempt is made to escape from the memories of the past, nor to disguise the longing for its return, but at the same time the futility of this obsessive preoccupation is fully acknowledged. There is the realisation that actions and people and places can no longer have the same significance in his future life as they had in his past. The sense of stagnation persists:

> La notte avrà il volto
> dell'antico dolore che riemerge ogni sera
> impassibile e vivo. Il remoto silenzio
> soffrirà come un'anima, muto, nel buio.
> Parleremo alla notte che fiata sommessa.

(The night will have the face of a former grief which re-emerges every evening, impassive though living. The remote silence will suffer like a soul, unspeaking in the darkness. We shall speak to the night which breathes softly.) ('L'amico che dorme' – The friend who is sleeping – *Poesie* p. 140)

The tone, lexis and imagery of this poem resemble those of the much later *Verrà la morte e avrà i tuoi occhi* (Death will come and its eyes will be yours),[26] though technically the latter are far superior. The last of these poems, 'Risveglio' (Reawakening, *Poesie*

p. 144), announces;

> E' finita la notte
> dei rimpianti e dei sogni. Ma quel giorno non torna.

(The night of dreams and remorse is over. But that day will not come back.)

This recalls the end of summer as the end of childhood, found in 'Mito',

> La breve finestra
> beve il freddo sapore che ha dissolta l'estate.
> Un vigore ci attende, sotto il cielo deserto.

(The window, barely glimpsed, absorbs the cold taste that has dissolved the summer. Strength awaits us beneath the empty sky.)

The poems written between the end of 1937 and 1940 slip gradually away from the old ideals of 'immediatezza' and 'oggetto' into *poesia ermetica*. Poems such as 'La notte' (Night, *Poesie* p. 153), 'Mattino' (Morning, *Poesie* p. 160) and 'Notturno' (Nocturne, *Poesie* p. 163) are full of music and suggestion, but there is little in them that is tangible; they speak of 'voci e risa remote' (far-off laughter and voices – 'Paesaggio VIII,' *Poesie* p. 159), of 'le voci morte' which 'assomigliano al frangersi di quel mare' (the dead voices ... resemble the breaking of the sea), of 'un'ombra fuggevole, come di nube' (a fleeting shadow, like that of a cloud – 'Mattino'). We learn that by this time,

> Non resta,
> di quel tempo di là dai ricordi, che un vago ricordare.

(Nothing remains of that time beyond memory, but a vague remembering – 'La notte')

The woman whom these poems speak of is

> Come una nube
> intravista fra i rami

(like a cloud glimpsed through the branches – 'Notturno')[27]

and in the same poem 'una nube dolcissima' (a very gentle cloud). The accent is always on her insubstantiality. She is seen as an illusion, always far away beyond his reach. She is associated with silence and a 'vano dolore' (useless grief): the time of unconscious happiness, the 'vivere assorto' (living absorbedly) that is connected with childhood in the poems of 1934–5, is merged in Pavese's fantasy 'nel ricordo d'allora' (in the memory of that time) when she was still his and the events of 1935–6 had yet to happen.

Although there is a tenuous beauty in these poems, they seemed to Pavese to lead nowhere. For five years almost, poetry was called upon to clarify or at least to examine the poet's personal difficulties – a far narrower task than he had originally envisaged for it. In the three years between 1938 and 1940 he composed very little in verse: in *Poesie edite e inedite* there are only fourteen poems dating from those years. By that time too he had turned to writing in prose, particularly the short story form, between 1936 and 1938, and had gone on to experiment with the novel. At the time when 'Notturno', chronologically the last poem in this decade of verse, was being written, Pavese had already completed three novels and was probably engaged upon the fourth, *La spiaggia*. When he turned again to writing in verse, in 1945, it was technically far superior to any of that written earlier – for one thing, he had learned how to create real, unselfconscious images – but one thing that verse did have in common with the majority of poems dating from 1937 to 1940 was that it was written about a woman and his inability to comprehend her. Never again was he to attempt to tell a story in verse, for that became, with ever-increasing success, the business of Pavese's novels.

3

Imprisonment, solitude and salvation in 'Il carcere'

In the two years immediately following his political *confino* at Brancaleone, Pavese became obsessed with the questions of imprisonment and alienation. This persistent line of investigation may be traced from its origins in the poems 'Legna verde' (Green wood, 1934), 'Poggio Reale' (the name of the prison in Naples where Pavese was held whilst in transit for Brancaleone; the poem dates from 1935), 'Terre bruciate' (Scorched lands, 1935), and 'Parole del politico' (The political prisoner's words, 1935), through his diary and the short stories 'Terra d'esilio' (Land of exile), 'L'intruso' (The intruder) and 'Carogne' (Carrion), all three dating from 1936–7, and culminates in the short novel *Il carcere* (The political prisoner), written in 1938–9. The theme recurred so frequently because it constituted Pavese's attempt to come to terms with an area of his personal experience which had seen the collapse of his former attitudes and values, and changed the direction of his inner life. The short stories and the novel proved to be the first fruits of his poetical regeneration after the bitter experiences of 1935–6.

The experience of physical confinement, whether in a narrow cell or in some other less rigidly restricted area, brought Pavese to the view that prison was primarily a state of mind and that, for him at any rate, it had probably existed even before his arrest. Brancaleone and his experience of other forms of imprisonment in 1935 had merely enhanced his awareness of it.

In 'L'intruso', Pavese explores his own equivocal attitude to solitude when it is imposed on the individual by circumstances over which he has no control. In the characters of the narrator, a young prisoner, and his cell-mate, Lorenzo, an older man, two sides of Pavese's own personality seem to be locked in a state of tension and conflict. With the narrator there is the problem of how to escape from his sense of alienation, of no longer belonging to the world of normality; whilst with Lorenzo the problem is quite the reverse – how, in fact, to protect that solitude when it is threatened from outside, as it is by the intrusion of the younger man. Lorenzo has learnt how 'to make a home of a prison cell'. It represents security and privacy, as well as liberation from responsibility: 'Qui si vede com'è fatta la gente, che s'infuria se la mettono sola.'[1] (It's in these circumstances you see what people are really made of – if they go to pieces when they're put on their own.) The problem for Stefano, the protagonist in *Il carcere*, is how to make the transition from the unresolved anxiety of the young narrator in 'L'intruso' to the rationalised acceptance of Lorenzo. In the short story we are confronted by two attitudes which are apparently irreconcilable, whereas in the novel Pavese shows us the process by which the one may eventually be transformed into the other.

When Stefano arrives at his place of *confino* in the far South of Italy, after having been shut away in prison for so long, he feels a real freedom in the sense of space all about him and a whole new environment which is all to be discovered. He soon realises, however, that the sense of freedom is precariously balanced, and that when 'the new discoveries have all become a part of his routine' the feeling of being shut in will return. This sense of precariousness is intensified by an anguish which is rooted in the temporary nature of the life he is compelled to live. This anguish begins to colour his whole attitude:

Nobody makes a home of a prison cell, and Stefano was always conscious of the invisible walls all about him. At times, when he was playing cards in the bar, sitting among the friendly or tense faces of those men, Stefano would become aware of how alone he was and how precarious his existence, how cut off he was by his invisible walls – even there in the midst of those temporary people.[2]

This same sense of 'temporariness' had already been encountered by the engineer–narrator of 'Terra d'esilio' which, so far as environment and themes are concerned, may be regarded as a first sketch for *Il carcere*.

The memory of his past and of his future elsewhere makes Stefano feel that whatever he does in his land of exile is without meaning in the terms of his own reality. Despite the sense of futility brought about by the interruption in his personal destiny, he begins to form relationships with people in the village and particularly with Elena and Giannino. These relationships, however, are the expression of his immediate needs and little else. He is determined to give nothing of himself away and in this sense is conscious that he is exploiting the people who are closest to him:

> The existence of Giannino helped him feel that he was not Elena's slave and gave a meaning to his hanging about in the inn and his conversations with the others. (*Carcere* p. 35)

Shortly after his arrival he is made forcibly aware of the absurdity of the life into which he is settling. It is on the day of the feast of Our Lady of September when everyone, Stefano included, goes up the hill to the old village which lies inland, behind Stefano's village, to join in the festivities:

> The hill was a real Mount of Olives, parched the colour of ashes. When he had been up at the top Stefano had looked at the sea and the far-off houses. From the whole trip he had particularly seized on the illusion that his room and Elena's body and the beach he visited every day were so minute and absurd a world that all he need do to hide it all was bring his thumb up in front of his eyes. And yet that curious world, seen from a place that was even more curious, contained him also. (*Carcere* p. 35)

The absurdity does not end there, for although that life is temporary for him, for the villagers it is everything; it is their reality. 'For them the illusion that their whole horizon could disappear behind a hand was real enough' (pp. 37–8). This new awareness intensifies his reluctance and he becomes resentful of any attempt to draw him and possess him:

> Their eyes which were full of intrigue and their over-familiar fingers made him shudder. He felt bits of himself to be at the mercy of others. That Elena who spoke to him with such familiarity and presumed to scold him with her look; his most private self on public display at the inn, the sufferings of night on view in broad daylight. Stefano would close his eyes and his face would become hard. (*Carcere* p. 40)

At the very centre of his life there are, he realises, 'the invisible walls, the habit of the prison cell which cut him off from all human contact' – his own intense desire for the absolute privacy of solitude.

If his aim is indeed to close himself within himself, he has to cease being dependent on anyone for anything and become entirely self-sufficient. However, from his first days there, he has shared a sexual relationship with Elena, his landlady's daughter, who comes each day to tidy his room. Elena is as much a mother figure as a lover, and it is her over-possessive, maternal attitude towards Stefano which he soon comes to resent so much. He realises eventually that this relationship, this dependence, is nothing less than a point of vulnerability, and yet he feels incapable of ending it, not wishing to renounce a pleasure which apparently costs him nothing. He makes up his mind that Elena should agree 'to let him have her without asking anything in return'. If she will accept that he recognises no responsibility towards her and yet continue their relationship then his retreat within himself will succeed – or so he reasons. This attitude is found in several of the short stories which preceded *Il carcere*, notably in 'Viaggio di nozze' (Honeymoon) and 'Suicidî' (Suicide)[3] where the women, Cilia and Carlotta, are sacrificed to the absolute, unbending egotism of the male protagonist–narrators.

There is yet another relationship which Stefano enters into; not a real one, but one which exists in his fantasy and which grows out of his desire for the rough, ignorant, servant girl, Concia, whom he sees from time to time but does not know. More and more, it is she who comes to represent the mystery and the savage spirit of that land. He realises that by using Elena's body he can, in his imagination, possess Concia also – a motif which Pavese had most probably encountered in d'Annunzio's first novel, *Il piacere* (Pleasure, 1889).

The result, then, of his withdrawal is something resembling peace of mind, as he realises on one occasion when waking from an afternoon siesta:

He didn't move, so that he could hold on to that moment for as long as possible, whilst something which was even more pleasant slowly rose up from deep inside him – the certainty that he was no longer asleep and that that sense of peace was therefore real, and that prison by this time was so far away that in his drowsiness he could allow his thoughts to carry him back there and yet still remain calm. (*Carcere* pp. 49–50)

Yet, for all that, his state of mind fluctuates alarmingly, for the sense of imprisonment returns often and for many reasons. Once, for example, he is told that the sergeant of the *carabinieri* (the official directly responsible for him as a *confinato*) is looking all over for him and immediately he feels afraid. In that moment he attributes his fear to the possibility that the 'scrap of paper' – the order of which he lives in constant dread – has arrived, and that he is to be sent back to a real prison. But then, when he has found the officer and the mystery has been resolved, he realises that the emotion which he has at first taken to be fear is, in reality, the hope that what has arrived is notification of his pardon and release. That being the case, he must still regard himself as imprisoned and the life he has created is a game, a fiction. With that awareness he drives himself with renewed vigour and determination really to create that state of mind whose precarious, indeed illusory existence has been revealed by this trivial incident.

The only way to defeat that sense of precariousness is to accept his prison unreservedly for what it is – which means without Elena or Concia. He must have no past and no memories, no future and no hopes. The only time must be the present and the only place that in which he finds himself in any given moment:

> All pleasure, all contact, every abandonment to feeling must remain locked up in his heart as in a prison and be disciplined like a vice, and nothing else must show outwardly or reach his consciousness. Nothing must depend on what was outside him, neither objects nor people must have any claim on him.
>
> Stefano's lips tightened into a grimace, for he felt the bitter, fecund strength growing inside him. He must no longer have any hopes but forestall all unhappiness by accepting it, by devouring it in his solitude. He must ever think of himself as being in prison. (*Carcere* pp. 57–8)

With this paradoxical, absolute capitulation, by and by there comes a miraculous sweetening of his earliest memories of the place. He realises that 'even the hardest lot can become pleasurable provided it is of our own choosing', and, on looking back over the time he has already spent there that it has seemed 'short and unreal'. He seems to understand how the

> illusions and the atmosphere of that whole summer had quietly got into his blood, into his room, just as Concia had got there without her brown feet ever having crossed the threshold. (*Carcere* pp. 68–9)

Occasionally, sexual frustration brings him perilously close to slipping back into his dependence on Elena once again:

> Stefano roused himself in the darkness, disgusted at having fallen back into his old, wavering frame of mind. He even wished that Elena would come back to him. His ironical solitude was crumbling, and if it was giving way on that particular evening which was filled with so many new developments and sudden memories, how would he manage to resist in the morning? Stefano realised that without a struggle it isn't possible to be alone, yet being alone means precisely not wanting to struggle any more. (*Carcere* p. 72)

The situation is absurd: he is seeking an absolute acceptance of his 'new' destiny against which his whole humanity revolts. Yet, for Stefano, his situation is clear enough: if he chooses solitude it becomes bearable, if it is imposed from outside it represents an intolerable prison. The distinction is fine but his peace of mind turns on it. His problem is to convince himself, by a continually renewed act of will and the exercise of an ascetic discipline, that his imposed destiny and his personal choice are effectively the same.

When he learns of Giannino's arrest – and Giannino is the only man with whom he shares more than a casual acquaintance – he strives to keep the memory of him alive, surmising that it is really only memory which gives meaning to one's life. Now Giannino is gone Stefano can begin to regret his loss. There is a seeming hypocrisy here, for Stefano admits to himself that with the disappearance of Giannino there 'vanished the ultimate obstacle to his real solitude'. In truth, Giannino has never been a threat because their relationship has never made any demands upon him:

Giannino was the only one who knew how to fill Stefano's solitude with things left unsaid. It was for this reason that between them there was always that rich expectancy of a first encounter. (*Carcere* p. 70)

He regrets losing the companionship Giannino has given him, even though that loss is convenient to his purpose. Stefano is conscious of trying to construct a life for himself in the same way as one would construct a play or a novel. In doing so he is putting into practice something of what Pavese himself means by 'construct in art as in life; expel gratuitous emotion from art as from life; exist tragically' (*MV* 20 April 1936).

When Elena has left Stefano, she, like Giannino, is regretted, though without any depth of feeling or even sincerity: 'I'm sorry you've gone, little mother', he thinks. He is aware, in both cases, that something resembling indifference is his true frame of mind – 'in fact, he felt neither real grief nor anxiety' – which suggests that his planned withdrawal has been at least in part successful. He had feared that through contact with its people that land, his prison, might already have claimed him, 'possibly the brine, the figs, the moisture from the earth had been getting into his bloodstream in the months that had passed' (*Carcere* p. 80), but now it appears not to be the case. He has kept it at bay.

So fully does he come to accept his solitude that he manages to blunt the impact of those events and objects which might otherwise disturb his tranquillity, such as the arrival of letters from home. Now, however, through the application of his iron discipline, he finds himself marvelling that he has ever lived there at all. He has constructed a rhythm of life, absurd because it excludes all but the most superficial contact, because it has only a limited future, and yet he guards it jealously. Even the plea for solidarity made by another *confinato* (who lives in the old village) is rejected, though admittedly not without some misgivings. Stefano would like to give the man 'the comfort of knowing he was not abandoned' but he calculates it would cost him too much. It is ironical, however, that his future need to avoid the area which he knows to be frequented by the other has added another 'human wall' to his own prison.

Stefano's final 'triumph' comes when he is introduced to Annetta, a prostitute brought to the village from the city. Her precursor had figured in one of the Brancaleone poems, 'Tolleranza' (Tolerance, *Poesie* p. 133). He discovers that although he wants her body, he is afraid to make use of her, for fear of 'feeling himself seized by the spirit of that land'. He goes to the house in which she is staying, so as not to seem ungrateful to those who believe they are doing him a favour by offering to share her with him, but he does no more than talk with her, then goes away.

Stefano began to realise how much strength he had derived from that poor Annetta whom he had respected for no very good reason. The strength didn't come from her so much as from his own body, which was beginning to establish its own equilibrium and in return was giving him real peace of mind. He told himself how foolish he had been in his pride, trying to isolate his thoughts and leaving his body to languish on Elena's breast. To be really alone a mere trifle – abstinence – was sufficient. (*Carcere* p. 103)

Stefano has built a rhythm of life 'on the monotonous emptiness of time', without being drawn into the life around him. Nevertheless, he is never entirely free from the 'constant anxiety and tension [which] arose from uncertainty, from his dependence on a scrap of paper, from the suitcase that stood open on his table'. He asks himself how many years he will remain here, and realises that 'if they had said for life, perhaps he could have faced his future with greater calm' (p. 106).

Other people, the 'human walls', can destroy his artificial world so easily, as becomes apparent when his pardon comes, for everything collapses, leaving him 'dazed and discontented'. The message which he leaves to be passed on to Giannino, whenever he returns, is the lesson of his experience, both as prisoner and as *confinato*:

Tell him you feel a greater sense of satisfaction coming out of a real prison than from leaving this kind of detention. The world on the other side of the bars is beautiful, but the life of the *confinato* is like ordinary life, just a little bit more squalid. (*Carcere* pp. 107–8)

He has come to the discovery that life itself, with the responsibilities it imposes, is the absurd prison. Stefano has only in part been possessed by his prison, for as he is waiting in the company of one or two of the villagers for the train to come and take him back to the life from which he had been abstracted,

Stefano had the illusion, while the train was arriving, that the faces and the names of all those who were not there were being whirled up in a vortex like leaves being swept away. (*Carcere* p. 109)

He has succeeded in coming to terms with his destiny, but his solution had rendered him less human and more alone.

Stefano's attitude fluctuates continuously between *indifferenza* – for those who surround him in the present – and *inquietudine* – a sense of anxiety which is rooted in the knowledge that his fate is not, ultimately, *his* decision but that of some intangible, nebulous authority which is symbolised by that dreaded 'scrap of paper'. However, in so far as he is master of his own fate, Stefano attempts to distance himself from others, not only in a physical sense, but in time also. Meaning is transferred from present to past, for once an individual or an experience has become a part of his past and lives only in memory, Stefano is secure, for he can no longer be touched or threatened by any change within it, he can control and possess it absolutely, manipulating it at will. The disappearance of Giannino is a clear enough example. Abstracted physically from the novel, he simultaneously acquires a significance for Stefano which he has never had in reality. His search is for an absolute, fixed condition, but this – as the novel demonstrates – is never possible, for we are always, to some degree, the possession of the people and objects which constitute our immediate environment. Stefano's real discovery is that there is no freedom, only varying degrees of imprisonment, for prison is 'human walls', it is dependence on someone or something outside oneself and is an obstacle, either real or potential, to the individual will. Recognising this, Stefano tries to empty the present, to make of it a silence, a pure contemplation, a picture, a landscape, a memory, an unassailable peace. There is a link between this point of view and the *fin de siècle* poetry of Pascoli, which is dominated by memories which lie on the other side of his own personal tragedies. There, the fear and rejection of both present and future, which, in the last analysis, is probably fear of death, turns the poet towards a contemplation of a recreated past, which represents security because no longer subject to the wounds inflicted by the passing of time. Yet, fixity is achievable for the human being only in death, so that paradoxically that which is feared becomes that which is desired. A similar kind of attitude is there in Pavese's Stefano, for in order to escape his prison he attempts to accept it absolutely; as Pavese himself argued, 'the only way to escape from the abyss is to look at it, get the measure of it, sound it and descend into it' (*MV* 24 April 1936).

The style of the novel is, in some of its features, close to that which Pavese had used in writing the poems of *Lavorare stanca* and which he had developed in some of the short stories written between 1936 and 1938. It is a style based upon what he called the *immagine–racconto* – the story image. There is a note in Pavese's diary, made whilst he was working on *Il carcere*, which casts some light on what he was there attempting to achieve:

To suggest with a repeated action, or a name, or any other means of recall, that a character or an object or a situation has a fantastic link with another in the story is to take away materiality from each of the two subjects and to create the story of this link, of this image in place of that of the separate materiality of each of them. (*MV* 4 December 1938)

It is this dependence upon the image which makes much of Pavese's prose poetic in character. Pavese himself felt this to be particularly true of *Il carcere*, for years after he had written it he had occasion to speak of its 'entirely evocative, imaginative style', whilst the critic Geno Pampaloni drew attention to its character 'which lies somewhere between the introspective and the lyrical'. Examples are not difficult to find: the villa of Giannino's parents reminds Stefano of 'the villas of his childhood, closed and empty in the land of memory'; the descent from the hill (after the festival of Our Lady of September) and the singing of the faithful bring him 'a sudden memory of his distant childhood, when the drunks were coming down the hill and making a din as they went by the house'. The image is here used to project Stefano's experience into the past and to suggest the hold which that past has even over his present and future experience. In this sense, he is the prisoner of his own past, and this spiritual 'inwardness' parallels and reflects the physical prison motif throughout the novel, so that the latter becomes a metaphor of that spiritual condition. This tendency to look back over his shoulder, as it were, for the key to meaning is already a pointer towards the theory of the personal myth which Pavese was to formulate during the war years. The following passage is typical of his technique in *Il carcere*:

Imprisonment, solitude and salvation in 'Il carcere'   49

That particular morning he had got up before daybreak for a definite reason. He had gone out into the yard well wrapped up and there he had lit a short-stemmed pipe, which was like Giannino's, beneath a black, silent sky. The weather was bitter, but in the shadows it came up from the sea like a breeze, accompanying the twinkling of countless stars. Stefano's thoughts had gone back to that morning of the hunt, before anything had as yet happened, when Giannino had smoked and Concia's house, pale and shuttered, still awaited him. But his real memory was of something else, something more remote, the point about which the whole of his life silently glowed, and the shock of coming upon it again had taken his breath away. Stefano had not been able to sleep on that last night he had spent in prison; then, with his case locked and his papers signed, he had waited for the final moments in a sort of corridor that he didn't know and which had high, flaking walls covered with mildew, and which had enormous windows opening on to an empty sky; and the summer had sweetened the silence and the warm stars, that Stefano had thought were fireflies, had been twinkling. For months on end he had seen nothing but hot walls behind prison bars. All of a sudden it had come to him that that was the night sky, and that he could see such a great distance, and that when day came he would be on a train, crossing the countryside in summer, free to spread himself out for ever towards the invisible human walls. That was the real limit, and the whole of his silent prison had faded away into nothingness, into the night.

Now, in the subdued calm of the little courtyard, Stefano, smoking like Giannino and listening to the monotonous roar of the waves, had watched for the dawn. (*Carcere* p. 86)

In this passage there are three time-levels: the present ('Now, in the subdued calm ...'), the recent past ('that morning of the hunt ...') and the remoter past ('the last night he had spent in prison ...'). They are linked, in Stefano's mind, by objects and elements which are common to each, and it is the combination and recombination of those elements which evokes the memory of the events which surrounded them on different occasions. In this way the separate elements take on the role of symbols which serve to telescope the whole span of time that separates the events one from another, reducing personal experience to something like a quintessence. The effect is, as Pavese was later to suggest, that of taking us out of the flow of time into a new dimension which, because those symbolic experiences recur continually, has much the same kind of existence and function as myths in society. However, when Pavese wrote *Il carcere* he was still a long way from the conscious formulation of that theory which was to dominate his writing and thinking in the last six years of his life. Thus, the linking elements or symbols in this passage – 'a short-stemmed pipe, which was like Giannino's', Giannino smoking, the twinkling stars, the dark sky before the dawn, the silence and so on – are important only for the memories they evoke, not, as was to be the case later, for their own sakes, as the 'once and for all events' or personal myths around which Pavese came to see every individual life revolving and which gave it its unique character.

The 'shock of coming upon it [the particular memory] again had taken his breath away', Pavese tells us, and this element of surprise, which was akin to the *stupore* of the child in *Lavorare stanca*, was to play a significant role in the theory of myth as it was applied in Pavese's last novels. There it was to indicate the recognition, usually of the protagonist, that he was undergoing a pattern of experience already lived through in his remoter past, but a formative experience, one of his own personal myths.

Just as images and symbols are used to direct Stefano's attention towards his own past, they have the added function of interiorising everything which has objective existence and making it a part of Stefano's *paesaggio interiore* – a map, almost, of his own essential self. For example, in the following passage, we see how Stefano gradually 'assimilates' the objective world which he begins by describing and ends by reducing to a symbol of his own condition:

The shadow of the station at that hour made the piazza cool, all except for one single shaft of sunlight which fell from the forbidden glass door across the silent, shimmering lines. The platform was a leap into the void. Like Stefano, the station-master also lived on that void, coming and going at the edge of goodbyes, within the uncertain equilibrium of this invisible wall. (*Carcere* p. 76)

We are led into the station and on to the platform by 'one single shaft of sunlight' which is reflected on a glass door. The first indication of movement towards interiorisation is the word 'forbidden', which establishes a relationship between what has been described and Stefano. Then, following the 'shaft of sunlight' with our eye we 'leap' with it to the lines, the 'silence' of which perhaps suggest the 'void' which, for Stefano, is everywhere and nowhere. But at this point, Stefano's fantasising has taken us over, so that what is described is the progression of his own thoughts in which the experience of the station-master is encapsulated and brought into line with his own. Yet, the relationship between Stefano and the station-master remains only at the level of imagination and is not translated into the day-to-day reality of their lives in the village. In this sense, the station-master and Concia – as well as Elena and Giannino – populate Stefano's fantasy world, but they are not allowed to impinge upon his self-imposed solitude in reality. Here, the identification of Stefano with the station-master is similar to that with Giannino after his imprisonment, for it is based on a sense of mutual deprivation and even suffering. People, for Stefano, thus become symbols, for their significance for him is fixed by his own fantasy which selects and operates on the basis, largely, of emotional need.

By employing a style which has many affinities with the stream of consciousness – despite the third person narrative – Pavese creates and acknowledges in *Il carcere* the inevitability of the gulf which his own experience in the years immediately preceding the writing of the novel had convinced him separates the subject from objective reality. That gulf, it would seem, may only be spanned by the imagination, for at the level of real relationships Pavese's protagonist searches for that alienation as the desired object of choice, believing it to be protection and security in the face of a fear which is derived from temporariness and uncertainty, whether of his situation or of his strange environment. The imposed imprisonment can sting only if it can penetrate and Stefano's whole object is to prevent that happening. He struggles in order not to have to struggle, for the peace which comes with the cessation of struggle is, paradoxically, freedom – even within the walls of a prison. His desire for peace at whatever cost seems to echo the mood of conciliation and appeasement, so much in vogue in the year in which the novel was written – that of Munich, and its ensuing 'peace in our time'.

One further interesting aspect of Pavese's technique in *Il carcere* is his attempt to create a 'rhythm of events' by the continued repetition of, and variations on, certain key images and epithets. It is this repetition, coupled with the 'fantastic relationships' evoked by the *immagine–racconto*, which give the novel its organic unity. The more obvious examples are Giannino's beard and pipe, Concia's red geraniums and the pitcher she carries, Pierino's yellow collar badges, Vincenzo's newspaper, the constant references to the sea which comes to symbolise the utter futility of Stefano's static existence; and the suitcase which remains open but unpacked, constant reminder of his *inquietudine* – the void at the centre of his life.

This repetition of images is further reinforced by a feature which Pavese tells us he had observed in Homer, the reservation and application of certain epithets to an individual whenever he appears – as, for example, 'the bald Vincenzo' and the 'dark, goat-like face of Concia'.

There is continual reference to the bizarre nature of the countryside – its strange plants and its strange characters, such as the beggar, Barbariccia (who had his precursor in the Ciccio of 'Terra d'esilio') – as well as to its strange events, such as the silent procession following behind a priest, bearing a coffin along the track outside the village. An exotic-seeming environment is created, but that is because the normality of the extreme South is being viewed through the eyes of the cultured Northerner. Yet is it the normality of the South? Carlo Levi in *Cristo si è fermato a Eboli* (*Christ stopped at Eboli*) also had occasion to comment frequently upon what he saw in the South which was strange, often with unconcealed amusement, yet, nonetheless, there filters unmistakably through his narrative the sense of poverty and ignorance and of a moral, humanitarian duty vis-à-vis the South, which is the responsibility of everyone. The social dislocation of the South is there in his book, as well as the eye of the Northerner. This dimension is mainly absent from *Il carcere*, for Pavese's perspective and intention were very different from Levi's.

As a novel *Il carcere* succeeds in creating a style, 'a way of possessing one's own experience', by putting a man in a set of circumstances which is very different from what he is familiar with and exploring how he comes to terms with it. Fundamentally, this is the method of the majority of Pavese's earlier novels: in *Paesi tuoi* (Your part of the country) there is the spectacle of the townsman in the country; in *La bella estate* (The beautiful summer) that of the girl entering the adult world; whilst in *La spiaggia* (The beach) we find the problem of adjustment to a marriage relationship in a strange environment observed and explored.

Il carcere came at the end of three of the most painful years in Pavese's life. In the withdrawal of its protagonist it stands comparison with Svevo's *Senilità* (*As a man grows older*, 1898), in which Emilio Brentani rejects all responsibility towards others and, ignoring their reality, creates in its place a world of fantasy which is continually manipulated and modified by him. The parallel is more than coincidental, for both novels are expressive of what seems to be a common feature of societies in a state of stagnation: intense egotism as a form of self-defence against an often indefinable fear.

Il carcere had something of a therapeutic significance for Pavese, for with it he seems to have written himself out of the morbid depression which gripped him after Brancaleone. Yet, had not a superficially similar set of circumstances to Brancaleone (the civil war in the Piedmontese hills between 1943 and 1945) occurred in Pavese's life, it is doubtful whether it would ever have been published in his lifetime. Its publication in 1949, together with *La casa in collina* (The house on the hill) under the highly evocative joint title of *Prima che il gallo canti* (Before the cock crows), seemed to confirm Pavese's by then fully developed theory of human history and individual personality, summed up in his frequently reiterated maxim 'come è stato, così sarà' ('what has been determines what will be'). The most significant difference between the two novels is in their underlying circumstances. In the earlier one there is the absence of struggle with all but self, because the place of *confino* (i.e. enforced isolation) is an imposed withdrawal from all but a small section of society but, equally, an imposed coexistence with that particular section of society – and the one facet is as important in determining Stefano's attitude as is the other. In the later novel, there is the perennial Pavesian struggle for mastery of self, but the war, the all-pervading struggle, gradually breaks down the protagonist's persistent refusal to be involved so that, at the end of the novel, he predicts the imminent breaking of his habit of solitude as a result of the pressure of events.

The two novels span the ten years 1938–48, and in their attitudes towards individual responsibility and individual security give expression to one of the key problems in the development of Italian history in that tormented decade. Stefano's withdrawal is indefensible on moral and political grounds and reflects the acquiescence without conviction of the vast majority of Italians, which helped to sustain the power of the Fascist Regime for so long. In Stefano, Pavese explores, in entirely subjective terms, the most pressing problem of contemporary Italian life, that of how to continue living under the suffocating conditions imposed by Fascism. Stefano's is but one kind of compromise. In his attempts to save himself, whatever the cost in human relationships, he presents the dilemma of the intellectual living under the Regime. In artistic terms the 'Hermetic' poets, for example, took a course which was similar to that taken by Stefano in his day-to-day life. Stefano, like many Italians in the Fascist era, sees the problem both passively and subjectively: how to adjust himself to his situation rather than how to overcome it by acting against it. It is this attitude which underlines the limitations, in human terms, and the historical authenticity, of *Il carcere*. As a novel it succeeds because it represents a scrupulously honest attempt to reconstruct and comprehend a state of mind, rooted in fear and weakness, which its author knew well enough from direct experience. With a sense of haunting beauty and a lasting fascination, this novel refuses the facile heroic myths of Fascists and anti-Fascists alike, transcending both in a wholly realistic revelation of man to himself. If it is indeed true that great writers are 'significant in terms of the human awareness they promote',[4] Pavese's first short novel, though in a minor key, can with some justification be regarded as a classic, one which unfortunately has been greatly underrated.

4

'Paesi tuoi' and the myth of America

In 1918, America had emerged from the holocaust of the First World War as the *deus ex machina* which had not only resolved the problem of the war but which promised a similar resolution of the problems of peacetime. Although the myth of America as 'the land of opportunity' had existed before the war it now grew to immense proportions in the minds of many Europeans. For Italians, in particular, the United States became both the Promised Land and the land of exile, the bitter-sweet experience of the new beginning. This ambivalent attitude towards America was to be further complicated by the restrictive immigration laws passed by the United States in 1921, together with the increasing hostility shown towards that country by the ruling Fascist party after October 1922. For the first generation of Italians living under Fascism, the real America became more remote and alien than it had ever been. Communication between the two countries was minimal and the popular Italian view of America was largely the creation of Fascist propaganda. However, the second generation, which was Pavese's, began to reject the common view of the United States just as it began to reject Fascism which, many of them realised, was very far from being the 'hope of the world'.

Emilio Cecchi is the literary figure who best illustrates the complex view of America held by the earlier generation. His genuine curiosity about America and its culture led him to make a journey through the States to see for himself what was happening there. The result of that journey was his book *America amara* (Bitter America), the very title of which betrays the spirit in which it is written. Though greatly impressed by American organisation, and technical and economic achievement, he saw the country as a cultural wasteland, violent and materialistic. *America amara* is, however, an account not only of what Cecchi observed in the States, but also of what he took with him in the shape of his own essentially nineteenth-century Florentine *forma mentis*.

Cecchi had established himself as a leading figure in the

cosmopolitan–aesthetic tradition of the reviews *La voce* (The voice) and *La ronda* (The patrol), and his views are representative of a decadent Romanticism which lingered on in Italian literature well into the present century. His search was for what was aesthetically satisfying and in America he claimed to have found an 'aesthetic of cruelty'. He looked upon the newly emerging life of America with the sentimental eyes of the old world and saw only a brash inferiority. His move towards America had been cautious and seemed to corroborate many of the views currently expressed by Fascist propaganda. Yet, by the time the book was published, a new generation had already gone a long way to forming its own ideas, and Giaime Pintor, writing in 1943, explained why he and his contemporaries rejected Cecchi's blinkered view:

Tuscany, this over-civilised region, is present in his every judgement, and the by now commonplace images used to describe the Tuscan landscape are, for him, the limits of every other. He is a man who is stubbornly closed in the prejudices of a single country.[1]

Pintor's rejection of Cecchi's views was also a rejection of the values which had created them:

Whilst in the Europe of the post-war years the themes of a decadent culture were taken up once again or formulas such as Surrealism were worked out – both inevitably without any future – America was expressing itself in a new narrative and in a new language, was inventing the cinema.[2]

What Pintor heard from America – and here he spoke for Pavese, Vittorini and others of his generation – was 'a voice which was very very close, that of true friends and of the first contemporaries'. His reference to the American cinema is significant, for it played an important part in Pavese's own move towards America.

In Roosevelt's 'new deal' Elio Vittorini thought he saw a step towards his own ideal in the search for a new innocence and, in literature, for a new purity of language. What he sought, and believed he had found in contemporary American literature, was a language capable of extending human consciousness because it was more accessible than any other literary language that he knew. He was attracted, as was Pavese, by the willingness of American writers to experiment with form and language, particularly in the novel. In Europe, as Pintor observed, tradition was everything, but in that it was misinterpreted as fixity, it was also dead.

In Italy, as in America, there was a new reality to be expressed, but the best responses that Italian literature could produce were

Surrealism, Futurism and Hermeticism, all inadequate to the task because fundamentally evasions of it. Pavese himself attacked 'tradition' in his essay on Herman Melville, written in 1932 as a preface to his translation of *Moby-Dick*. There he rightly maintained that 'to have a tradition is less than nothing, it is only by constantly looking for it that it can be lived'. Pintor, searching for a new humanism, took up the same theme, arguing that

> the figures who count for something among the American writers of today, Hemingway, Faulkner and Saroyan, are, above all else, creators of a style. However, theirs is a style in which materiality still remains fresh, one which owes its fullness to the presence of new objects: of new machines, new houses and new relationships between men.[3]

The names Pintor cites are not those which Pavese would have chosen, but then Pavese's concern with the Americans was almost a decade older than Pintor's, and like Vittorini's was that of the pioneer. Nonetheless, the essential point is made by Pintor in his recognition of the search for a style as a way of first possessing a new reality.

It was as the pioneers of new ways of expressing contemporary reality that Vittorini and Pavese most valued the Americans, seeing in them the models for a future literature which would be European as well as American. Their approach, as Pavese perceived, was classical, mimetic, dynamic, and they were not forever looking back over their shoulders for reassurance.

Almost alone, Vittorini and Pavese were responsible for opening up a channel along which there came, for many young Italian intellectuals like Pintor, the first hints that somewhere else in the world there was a way of life which was very different from that lived under Fascism. However, the activities of Vittorini and Pavese were not limited to the translation and popularisation of contemporary American literature, for both attempted in their own writing to practise many of the lessons they had learnt, and with *Conversazione in Sicilia* (*Conversations in Sicily*)[4] and *Paesi tuoi* (Your part of the country) they infused new blood into a currently anaemic literature.

When *Paesi tuoi* appeared in 1941 it was greeted with a derision which had little to do with literary values. All its reviewers, including the small group who saw in it certain positive features, pointed to the American influences which lurked behind it. Even Cecchi, who praised Pavese's experiments with language, connected it with the neo-Realism of contemporary American writers, and likened it to Steinbeck's *Of mice and men*.[5] The critics felt the novel had confirmed their suspicions about Pavese's translations and essays on American writers, and he was branded 'Americanista' – a term of abuse in the Italy of 1941.

Pavese himself saw no reason to deny the American influence in *Paesi tuoi*, but it needs definition. The novel was the first creative work of Pavese's to appear since *Lavorare stanca* (January 1936), and as the collection of poems was virtually unknown, it is understandable that Pavese should have been seen as a writer infatuated with a foreign literature. What was not known until the end of Pavese's life, or even after, was that in the five years which separated *Lavorare stanca* from *Paesi tuoi* he had dealt with specifically Italian subjects in his short stories and in *Il carcere*,[6] and that an extremely unbalanced impression of his work had therefore been received in 1941. In these circumstances, the opinion of Nemi d'Agostino appears sound, for he suggests that in *Paesi tuoi*,

what we undoubtedly have is a calculated experiment for which there was very little enthusiasm, given that in the same years Pavese tried out, in *Carcere* and in *La spiaggia*, styles which are very different from American neo-Realism, and at the same time was beginning to think about a new form of narrative with a rhythmic base and structure, and to search for its links with the European tradition.[7]

In searching beyond the frontiers of Italy for a style and an inspiration, Pavese had fallen foul of those many critics who took it upon themselves to defend the Fascist policy of cultural isolationism. There was much talk of the 'pure Latin spirit' and 'Latin genius' in Fascist Italy, and it was not until the cultural 'revisionism' of Giuseppe Bottai (Fascist Minister of National Education in the late nineteen-thirties) had been tentatively established that any general move was made towards other cultures by the Fascist intelligentsia. In this sense, *Paesi tuoi* appeared a little too early to receive the full benefit of the 'thaw'.

In a statement made after the war, Pavese explained what he felt had taken place in Italian literature in the thirties:

The decade 1930–40, which will pass into the history of our culture as the period of translations, was not a period of idleness for any of us, Vittorini, Cecchi or the others. It was a decisive moment, and indeed it was only in the apparent exoticism and rebellion that the vital thread in our recent poetical culture was to be located ... We discovered Italy – and this is the point – by looking for men and for words in America, Russia, France and Spain. (*La lett. am.* p. 247)

This, however, was a view in retrospect, expressed only when it had become possible to piece together the many diverse aspects of the historical and cultural circumstances of the thirties. Pavese had not worked to a conscious plan; his approach had been largely intuitive, empirical; what he had sought at the time is indicated in his essay 'Middle West e Piemonte' (1931):

A work of art moves us and gives us insight only in so far as it has historical interest for us, in that it corresponds to some difficulty that we experience – that is, that it resolves some problem in our daily lives. (*La lett. am.* p. 33)

In America, Pavese saw a gigantic country in turmoil, a polyglot society striving to achieve some sense of national consciousness and unity. The concern of its writers was to give a voice and a direction to that process. Their art became the servant of the practical, everyday needs of American life and Pavese saw this as an ideal model for any literature. The best of those writers (in Pavese's opinion), Melville, Whitman, Thoreau, Lee Masters and Sherwood Anderson, were not only writers. They were 'practical' men who had had many years in other jobs and professions, and had travelled widely, inside America and beyond, and the America they wrote about was that of their own experience. Their writing, argued Pavese, contained 'something of that harmony we normally call Greek'. For him, they represented the continuation of what was best in the European tradition.

The theme to which Pavese perhaps instinctively pays most attention in those writers, particularly Lewis and Anderson, is that of the alienation of the individual as a result of the rapidly changing economic and social scene. In the main, the American writers were not merely observers of a changing world. Their work implied a humanistic criticism of what was happening and being allowed to happen, and this feature of their work attracted even Antonio Gramsci to them. In the Europe of the twenties and thirties, especially Italy, the critical function of the writer had all but disappeared. Pavese too approves of that criticism – which finds its way into many of the poems of the first *Lavorare stanca*. Speaking of Sinclair Lewis's characters and their tendency to 'hit the bottle' he argues:

It is, in fact, a protest against a social order which suffocates them and denies them life ... these drinkers are not exotic types, but clerks, factory workers, newspapermen, common people, people you meet every day. They don't have any violent disposition to satisfy, they are not damned.

They are wretched men, slaves of a job, who sometimes have recourse to this ultimate manifestation of individual revolt. (*La lett. am.* p. 6).

Pavese easily identified with one aspect of Sherwood Anderson's writing, indicated in 'Middle West e Piemonte':

For Anderson, the whole modern world is a confrontation between city and countryside, between sincerity and empty pretence, between nature and insignificant men. The extent to which this idea affects us goes without saying. However, our lack of vitality, in comparison with young America, can be seen in the fact that a problem which has given America works like these has given us nothing but a literary caricature – *stracittà* and *strapaese*. (*La lett. am.* p. 36)[8]

For Pavese, the vitality and strength of the Americans lay in their ability to bring about a 'transfiguration of reality' in which 'a new ideal of American life' might be perceived. It was this criterion which endeared Sherwood Anderson to Pavese, and which caused him to note serious limitations in Lewis. Undoubtedly Pavese's critical views about the relative merits of the American novelists are coloured by his own ideal; this was the essence of the myth of America, not an objective assessment but a subjective identification. What Pavese detected was a series of parallels between the United States and Italy, and the Americans' superior way of handling them in their literature.[9]

American literature was created by provincial writers and Pavese realised that 'without provincials a literature lacks vigour'. However, unlike the adherents of the *strapaese* movement, Pavese was not interested in regionalism for its own sake, but rather as the fertile soil from which a national language and culture might grow. He considered this question during his months at Brancaleone, concluding that a writer should only write about what he knows 'in the blood', that is, from long experience of them. This meant that the life of a region or a particular city would form the nucleus of every writer's work, and in practice this is what has happened in Italian literature this century. How clearly Pavese saw this with reference to Italy in the early nineteen-thirties is debatable; but certainly it was a process which was already well under way, starting with Verga and Sicily, Deledda and Sardinia, moving on through Svevo and Trieste, to Pavese's own contemporaries, with Pratolini and Florence, Moravia and Rome, Vittorini and Sicily and, of course, Pavese himself and Piedmont. The region, which for Pavese was synonymous with the familiar, was to be the centre of a literature that did not seek its effects in the exotic or the bizarre.

Real discovery, he argued, exists not in 'a virgin subject' – which is a kind of superficiality – but in what is most familiar and therefore, paradoxically, is most neglected. In theory, he sought what was common or typical, that which his reason told him should be the subject of his art, but in practice it didn't always work out that way. Pavese had an eye for the bizarre – as we noted with reference to *Il carcere* – and it continually appeared in his writing, as an element of his makeup which refused to be purged and whose aesthetic effects he could not resist. Though his discovery was of the commonplace, it had to be accompanied by a sense of wonder (*stupore*), which seemed to call for the transformation of the ordinary into the extraordinary, suggesting the kind of conflict which went on in Pavese between his ideal of a reasoned classicism and an apparently instinctive exoticism – though often, there is no denying, with pleasing effect.

The widespread use of dialect in his work he rejected for two reasons. Firstly because it was a key feature of the Naturalism he was consciously seeking to escape and secondly because it too, to all but its users, was another form of the exotic. Augusto Monti had written novels which were deeply rooted in the life of Piedmont, but he had written in a regional variation of Italian and this, for Pavese, constituted a mistaken perspective. His own aim was to draw the life of the region into the national orbit, and this, he reasoned, could only be done in Italian. He had many models to draw on, in America and in Italy. By refusing a regional language he was following in the footsteps of Alessandro Manzoni, who rewrote his masterpiece, *I promessi sposi* (*The betrothed*), in Florentine Italian (which he considered to be by far the most worthy contender as the national literary language of Italy) fifteen years after it had been first published in what was fundamentally the regional Italian of his native Lombardy.[10] Pavese was very much aware of the problems he was facing, because they were the same as those which had confronted the American writers who had, according to Pavese, dealt with them successfully. In his diary he wrote:

Ranged against the suspicion that I am attempting a *Piedmontese Revival* [in English in the original] is my readiness to believe in a possible extension of Piedmontese values. My justification? Just this. Mine is not a dialect literature – for a long time I struggled instinctively and rationally against dialect. I don't want my writing to appear trivial – and I have learnt from experience. I try to nourish it on the best of the traditional, national juices. I try to keep my eyes open to the world and have been particularly sensitive to the experiments and achievements of the North Americans, for at one time I felt I had discovered amongst them a formative struggle which was similar to my own. (*MV* 11 May 1935)

There was a Piedmontese tradition which had succeeded in transcending the merely regional, and Pavese was clearly aware of this, as he shows in 'Middle West e Piemonte':

One has only to think of the discovery of the regions in Italian literature which took place at the same time as the search for national unity at the end of the eighteenth century and during the whole of the nineteenth. All the Italian writers, from Alfieri onwards, who strive, often unconsciously, to reach a deep national unity by penetrating ever more deeply their regional character, their real nature, arrive at the creation of a human consciousness and language which are enriched with the blood of the province and with all the dignity of a revitalised way of life. (*La lett. am.* p. 34)

Like the cousin of 'I mari del Sud', Pavese had (metaphorically speaking) gone all the way round the world to arrive back and discover what had been there all the time. Yet, without that experience of that 'journey', it is reasonable to suppose that the discoveries would never have been made. However mistaken Pavese's assessment of the American writers, collectively or individually, *what he thought he saw in them* had a profound effect upon his own development. Theirs was the seminal influence in his search for the ordinary man in a recognisable environment, at a time when Italian literature could not, or would not, deal with that reality.

Paesi tuoi[11] tells the story, through the words and reflections of Berto, a Torinese worker, of yet another 'journey' of self-discovery. Coming out of prison and finding himself without a job or plans for the future, Berto decides to accept the offer of Talino, his former cell-mate, to return to the country with him. Talino has been imprisoned for burning down a farmhouse, and is afraid of reprisals against him. He invites Berto to return to his father's farm, ostensibly to work the harvester but, Talino hopes, also as a bodyguard. Berto, who is nobody's fool, is aware of Talino's half truth but goes nevertheless.

At the farm he meets the rough, brutal Vinverra, Talino's father, and his sisters, amongst them Gisella, with whom he begins a convenient relationship. He gradually becomes aware of Talino's incestuous passion for Gisella, but even he is taken completely by surprise when a trifling incident suddenly flares up into the scene which results in her death. Talino stabs her in the neck with a pitchfork, then runs away to hide, whilst Gisella's life slowly ebbs away, watched by the fatalistic women of the household. Talino is caught, Gisella dies and Berto returns to the comparative safety and sanity of the city.

The most immediately recognisable theme of the novel is the confrontation of two different ways of life, those of *città* and *campagna*. Berto, like the child of the earlier poem 'Il dio-caprone' (The goat-god) (and the teacher in the short story 'Notte di festa'),[12] discovers that 'the countryside is a land of green mysteries'. He has lived all his life in the city and is out of his element among people who are closed and very different from any he has known before. Despite a certain bravado he is really afraid and is continuously suspicious of the actions and motives of the people about him. His suspicion amounts almost to superstition at times. He takes refuge in the city-dweller's supposed superiority over those who live in the country, and affects to despise them. However, his sense of difference and therefore isolation arouses in him feelings which are akin to those experienced by other of Pavese's 'prisoners' (of their own experience) in the stories which preceded *Paesi tuoi*. Berto's determination not to be possessed by his new environment is identical to Stefano's in *Il carcere*:

> If the old man [i.e. Talino's father] thought he was going to get me as a full-time labourer, he had another think coming. There wasn't any need to marry his daughters. Washed and dressed up, Gisella could have looked all right even in Turin, but even she was too ignorant. In a place where there wasn't even a billiard-hall they weren't going to get me in their clutches. (*Paesi* p. 88)

Identification with Stefano can be taken a stage further because both characters try to break out of their isolation, manifested most strongly in their sexual needs, by entering into relationships with women whom, fundamentally, they despise. The 'prison' motif, implicit throughout, surfaces in Berto's comment, when, having finished supper one evening, he realises there is nothing at all to do:

> Just as well I was tired and my bones ached; but all the same I wouldn't have minded a trip to the café and a game or two of billiards. Otherwise it was just like in the Nuove [the prison in Turin]: you turn out the light and get into your bunk. (*Paesi* p. 95)

The main theme of the 'green mysteries' culminates in the 'blood on the earth' motif, in the death of Gisella. It was this aspect which suggested to Emilio Cecchi the influence of Steinbeck's *Of mice and men*; but it was a common enough theme in the work of other American writers, and indeed, of recent Italian writers, particularly Verga and d'Annunzio.

The novel's atmosphere is reminiscent of that created in 'Notte di festa'. It is heavy and oppressive, like that which precedes a summer storm – 'hot and stuffy as in a closed room' – and indeed, constant reference is made to the heat. The imagery of the novel plays continuously around the burnt farm-house, for Talino's crime seems to have fixed itself within Berto's sub-conscious mind, for several times he uses the word 'fire' when describing his environment – 'I suddenly thought about Talino's fire ...' (p. 38); 'it was like a fire before my eyes ...' (p. 121); 'you could hear the sound of the sun as if there were a fire ...' (p. 144). Added to this, there is Vinverra's continually expressed fear of fire – for example, when Berto is examining the harvester – 'I'm looking in the tank and I strike a match, and there's Vinverra cursing and telling me to be careful' (p. 51).

The references to heat and fire suggest the metaphorical heat of passion, which is there continuously in the relationships of the characters, whether in the burning of houses, incestuous love or simply in a father unmercifully beating his grown-up daughter. The death of Gisella, at the hands of Talino, is the logical culmination of so much violence and passion. That the passion is predominantly sexual in character is strongly suggested by the introduction of the goat, which escapes and terrifies Berto as he is waiting for Gisella in the darkness, musing on the pleasures he hopes she will give him. In this symbolism we are again reminded of 'Il dio-caprone' (*Poesie* p. 50).

The incest theme grows as a suspicion in Berto's mind until it becomes a reality:

At that moment [whilst Berto was looking for Talino after the stabbing of Gisella] I can just see him going for Gisella, and her yelling, and him on top of her like a wild beast, just about breaking her back to hold her down. (*Paesi* p. 146)

It begins for Berto as a private joke turned up by his wry humour:

Watch it now, we're not in Turin any more, I says to myself in the heat. This guy here, with the excuse that he's stupid, will have me gored by a bull the first chance he gets *if I don't leave his sisters to him.* (*Paesi* pp. 39–40; my italics)

Then it revives, suddenly, when he realises Gisella is not a virgin

'Paesi tuoi' and the myth of America

and that because of the remoteness of the farm the number of men who can possibly have been responsible is restricted. In Monticello he talks in a bar with the owner and with another man about Vinverra and his family, and it comes out that Miliota (Gisella's sister) 'had been telling everybody that her sister had had a haemorrhage one week'. The proprietress is convinced someone 'had done the dirty on her'. Berto becomes convinced of incest and questions Gisella, who denies that Talino had ever touched her. Adele, another of Gisella's sisters, does not deny that Talino was responsible for Gisella's 'wound' (Gisella claims that she has been injured falling on a rake); she merely says: 'You'd better ask Gisella. Is anything wrong?'

Beginning with Gisella's explanation – 'I lost a lot of blood. I thought I was dying' – the references to blood are as frequent as those to heat and fire, and they too seem to culminate logically in Gisella's death, almost as if they had prophesied it:

In that sun, seeing him [Talino] come along, I was thinking that bloodshed makes less of an effect out in the country than it would in the shadow of some building in Turin. Once I saw some blood on the streetcar tracks after an accident, and it scared me; but here, if you think of somebody bent over bleeding in the stubble it seems more natural, like at the slaughter house. (*Paesi* p. 111)

These thoughts are recalled, and refuted, by the shock of Talino's crime and by Gisella's long downhill struggle into death. On two occasions before Talino stabs Gisella, Berto anticipates the event and, without explaining precisely what, hints that something is to come to an abrupt end. The first time:

Back home we found the rabbit and the *peperonata*, and a nice *polenta* Gisella had turned out on the board. I remember it as it was now, because *later on that evening nobody had time to cook anything and I ate two hunks of it cold and it seemed to taste like blood and my teeth were chattering, because right there in front of me on the table I could see a basin full of blood and I could feel my heart in my mouth, colder than the polenta.* (*Paesi* p. 113; my italics)

The second time, after Berto had confronted Gisella with the possibility of incest:

We could still have done a lot of nice things, and because of a silly mistake *we miss our last chance.* (*Paesi* p. 116; my italics.)

Thus, without realising it, we are prepared for Gisella's death. What impresses Berto above all is her blood which stains the earth, for he continually refers to it, and it is even suggested by the 'red and black of the *carabinieri*' who came to take Talino away:

> In the doorway you could still see big spots of blood. What's so special about that, I thought, every day the streets soak some up. But looking at it and thinking that that muddy mess was Gisella's warmth going away, I went cold as well. (*Paesi* p. 131)

The style of *Paesi tuoi* is certainly more ambitious than that of *Il carcere*. *Paesi tuoi* seeks not only to present events and Berto's reactions to them, but to enter into his way of thinking and his whole personality and experience as a man of the working classes.

The pundits of Fascist culture, obsessed with 'purity' and 'tradition', turned their backs on the regions and dialects of Italy as they had on all cultural influences from outside Italy. Pavese realised that dialect and regional Italian had tremendous possibilities for the enrichment of the Italian language if only a formula could be worked out through which the transformation into *lingua* (standard national language) could take place. The close adherence to 'tradition' in poetry had stunted the growth of Italian. The flow of history continually turned up new realities which could not be expressed by the language of the nineteenth-century tradition of *belles-lettres*. The fundamental question to be answered was precisely where the new experiences were taking place. Pavese saw quite clearly that it was in the regions, in the real Italy, not in the abstract concept of the Italy of Fascist propaganda, and that that experience was being possessed in the first instance in the spoken language of the regions, the dialects. The Fascist neglect of the regions in the nineteen-thirties therefore caused the severance of the main artery through which flowed the lifeblood of an all-embracing national language, and hampered the growth even of a true national consciousness. The language of contemporary literature had to be 'anti-literary' if it was to express contemporary history, for the problem which Pavese saw was that of how to synthesise the varied and widely dispersed experience of Italy, how, in fact, to transform dialect into language. In this his view brought him very close to this opinion of Gramsci's (though without the same consciously anti-Fascist implications):

> Whenever the question of the language comes to the fore, in one way or another, it means that a whole series of other problems is making itself felt – the need to establish closer and securer relationships between the governing groups and the popular masses of the nation.

In *Paesi tuoi* what Pavese attempted was not a badly executed neo-

Realism, for if neo-Realism had been his aim then Berto would have been made to speak in dialect. What concerned him was that formula by means of which the essentially flexible spoken language of Piedmont could begin to pass into the mainstream of the Italian language. Pavese understood that that fusion must take place at a deeper level than the merely lexical and therefore used the structures of Piedmontese Italian and even dialect, whilst the words were, in the main, Italian:

> The language [of the novel] ... is anything but a Naturalistic impressionism. I didn't write imitating Berto's way of speaking – he is the only one who speaks – but rather translating his thoughts, his bewilderment, his plans and so on, as he would say them *if he spoke Italian*. I only wrote ungrammatically when doing so indicated a studied carelessness, a complexity, or something obsessive in his mind. I didn't want to show how Berto speaks by forcing himself to speak Italian (which would have been dialectal impressionism) but how he would speak if his words, by some Pentecostal miracle, were to become Italian. How he thinks, in fact. (*MV* 4 December 1939)

However, the experiment was not entirely successful, for although the structure of Berto's thoughts is regional or dialectal, Pavese is unable to free him from ideas and observations which are more in keeping with the intellectual than the worker. In this sense, Pavese fails to create a satisfactory alternative to the language of Stefano in *Il carcere*. The author remains visible at the centre of his novel, still attempting to 'possess his own reality'.

Pavese had been inspired and impressed by similar American experiments, particularly Anderson's:

> Anderson's style! Not the crude dialect which is still too localised in the manner of our dialect specialists who, even in their best works, always retain something which is a bit raw; but rather a remoulding of English, made up of American idioms, of a style which is no longer dialect, but language which is thought over, reworked – which is poetry. (*La lett. am.* p. 42)

The most striking feature is that the main narration is given in the present tense, whilst occasionally lapsing into a past tense, as indeed might happen if a man of Berto's background and education were telling the story of his own experience. The following is typical:

> I go on laughing and laughing, and then I stop because I was going crazy. Somebody over in the stubble was laughing back at me, but it wasn't Gisella: it was an animal noise, sounded like an old woman, a voice to

make your teeth chatter. I come out all in a sweat. Then I see it stop in the middle of the field, a black thing moving along slowly, and it laughs again by itself.

It was a goat. I sit down against the wall and look at it, because it was coming straight to me. Lucky thing Gisella wasn't there and didn't see me. The goat stops about three yards away and looks at me: then she rushes off to one side and throws herself into the canes like a deer. She crashed about a bit; then silence.

Berto, go off and hide, I says, looking all around me. What if Talino had seen you then! (*Paesi* pp. 68–9)

So closely tied up with Berto's character is the method of narration that it is difficult to separate the two. Berto is a product of the industrial society of Turin and doubtless, in the city, is well able to take care of himself. In the country it is a different matter. There his sense of isolation, of difference, is manifested in fear, suspicion, superstition and prejudice. His choice of words often hints at the kind of life he is used to. When he uses a simile or a metaphor to try and clarify something he has seen or heard, the comparison usually turns on a typically city experience, as for example, 'It was like the theatre ...' (when everyone is quarrelling, p. 75); 'It was a good job the sun was going down and catching Talino's legs and the crash barriers and the dust from the side, and making them all gold, like a car's headlights at night' (p. 30); '... and the first thing I see is the hill of La Grangia which filled the whole arcade. It was like Turin when you go out first thing in the morning ...' (p. 48). When he leaves the country after Gisella's death, he gladly returns to Turin, his yard-stick of reality and security throughout the novel.

The world of the main part of the novel is centred, for Berto, around 'a bit of a hill that seemed like a tit' ('We're in between two tits, I say; nobody here has seen it, but we're in between two tits' – p. 42) and this connection of woman with the earth is continued throughout the novel. Sometimes the 'tit' refers to the hill, sometimes to Gisella. Pavese believed this image to be 'a real epithet, which expresses the sexual reality of that countryside' (*MV* 10 December 1939).

Indeed, the whole experience, people included, comes to be regarded by Berto as something less, or more, than human: 'animal eyes', 'muzzle', 'cow', 'feet that seemed like blocks of earth' are all terms which are applied to members of Vinverra's family.

The novel is written entirely from Berto's point of view, but the narration is, if anything, more objective than in *Il carcere*, in that it deals with events far more than the earlier novel, which concentrates on the inner world of conflict and feeling of its protagonist. Cecchi commented, in passing, on the sketchiness of the characters other than Berto. Pavese, however, was fully aware of this apparent deficiency and mentions it in his diary as a deliberate feature soon after the novel was completed:

taking up certain of my ideas once again, the work is a symbol in which the characters as much as the environment are the means to the telling of a little parable, which is the tap root of inspiration and interest: the 'journey of the soul' of my Divine Comedy. (*MV* 4 December 1939)

Later, when writing a review of Italo Calvino's first novel, *Il sentiero dei nidi di ragno* (*The path to the spider's lair*), Pavese had occasion to praise this same 'deficiency' in a younger disciple:

At twenty-three years of age Italo Calvino is already aware that to tell a story it isn't necessary 'to create characters', but rather to translate acts into words. (*La lett. am.* p. 273)

What really mattered, Pavese argued, was the 'rhythm of events' and not the individuals who maintained that rhythm. Some critics have taken exception to this attitude, and it has even been suggested that as Pavese was incapable of creating character, the 'rhythm of events' argument was merely an attempt to make a virtue of necessity. Be that as it may, the question of rhythm is there in *Paesi tuoi*, for recurrent symbols of Berto's experience are numerous, among them 'the well', 'the water that tastes like cherries', 'the crash of a bucket in the well', 'the moon' and of course 'Turin'. These constitute, for Berto, the only recognisable reality he encounters, for all the rest has a bizarre, nightmarish touch which, with the death of Gisella, seems unequivocally confirmed.

The label of 'neo-Realism', quickly appended to *Paesi tuoi* by orthodox Fascist critics, was well wide of the mark. The 'realism' of the novel is limited to the attempt to explore the *forma mentis* of the workman, Berto, whilst the setting and the other characters extend that predilection for the bizarre and the exotic already encountered in *Il carcere*. The reality of the countryside centres on the 'green mysteries' and a 'blood' cult, reminiscent of Hemingway, but that 'reality' is Berto's subjective interpretation of a way of life which is totally alien to him. That interpretation is akin to that of the 'virgin eye' of the child as he encounters experience for the first time – the subject of much of *Feria d'agosto*, which Pavese was to write during the war.

It is very necessary to appreciate the two conflicting trends in *Paesi tuoi*. The novel approaches what we have since come to expect of neo-Realism in that it has a lower-class hero and deals with peasant life. Certainly the actions, environment and relationships are typical of a neo-Realistic novel; yet the interpretation of that life and those actions, which is intended to represent Berto's point of view, seems like a major concession to a mystical neo-Romanticism. In its stylistic ambivalence the novel represents both development and *conformismo*, and in a wider sphere is indicative of the quiet cultural revolt against Fascism which surfaced during the late nineteen-thirties. With *Paesi tuoi*, more than with any other of his first four novels, Pavese helped to pave the way for the much more significant achievements in social realism of Vittorini, Pratolini, Levi and those who came after them in the mid nineteen-forties. The novel is uneven in quality, and is not amongst Pavese's best, yet its importance in his development as a novelist cannot be ignored, for with it he had succeeded in applying many of the lessons he had learnt from the Americans to an imagined episode in contemporary Italian regional life.

5

The search for maturity and the 'search for a style' in 'La bella estate' and 'La spiaggia'

At the time when Pavese had probably only recently completed *La bella estate* (The beautiful summer, written in 1940), and was about to begin *La spiaggia* (The beach),[1] which he completed on 18 February 1941, he noted:

Life is not a search for experience but for oneself. When a person discovers his own basic stratum he realises that it perfectly fits his own destiny and he finds peace. (*MV* 8 August 1940)

Pavese aimed at uncovering that 'basic stratum' so as to arrive at the self-awareness and calm of those solitary figures already encountered in *Lavorare stanca*, those who have become 'padroni di se stessi' (master of themselves). It is worth recalling Pavese's earlier definition of a style:

a way of understanding life (time as it flows by) so that it becomes a new awareness. (*MV* 24 October 1938)

Ginia, the young protagonist of *La bella estate*, and Doro, Clelia and Berti in *La spiaggia*, are all trying desperately to find 'a way of understanding life', to arrive at the 'basic stratum' of themselves. All display that sense of *inquietudine* which lies at the heart of the Pavesian novel, signifying some internal personal drama. With Ginia and Berti that drama is the process of integration into the world of adults. For Doro and Clelia who have recently married, the *inquietudine* characterises the period of adjustment to the 'otherness' of their marriage-partner. Pavese does not question the reality of their love for each other, but suggests that it is nothing unless it becomes a basis from which to construct a mutually inclusive meaning to their lives together. When we meet them they are still very much adrift from each other, and the limbo-like quality of the novel's beach resort setting is suggestive of the 'no man's land' of the time before their 'new awareness' is attained.

These two novels have much in common despite their differences in environment and the social class of their main characters. The most obvious thematic link is that of the psychological differences between adolescent youth and maturity:

One ceases to be young [Pavese argued] when one distinguishes between oneself and others. Youth is not possessing one's own body. Maturity is solitude which is self-sufficiency. (*MV* 8 December 1938)

In these novels we see characters who are at different stages in their passage from adolescence to maturity; none of them, not even the teacher–narrator of *La spiaggia*, is entirely free from *inquietudine*. All are still searching for that 'basic stratum', the psychological equivalent of the twenty years at sea which had brought peace and a 'new awareness' to the cousin of 'I mari del Sud'. Even as early as the end of 1938, Pavese had indicated that he was much more interested in the 'internal world' of his characters than in the external one of environment:

It is no longer necessary to move in the external world, living our anxiety there: we need only brief hints to know that it exists and exists in us, to conjure up a world made entirely of an inner life which by now has assumed the novelty and fecundity of nature. Maturity is this also: to search no longer outside oneself but to let the inner life speak with its own rhythms, which is all that matters. The external world now seems impoverished and materialistic compared with the deep, unexpected ripeness of our memories. (*MV* 6 December 1938)

La bella estate (published 1949) charts the experiences of a sixteen-year-old girl, Ginia, who lives with her brother, Severino, keeping house for him and working in an *atelier*. She and her brother live quite separate lives, for Severino works nights and sleeps during the daytime. The first few pages of the novel show Ginia living the hectic, carefree life of a young teenager; then suddenly everything changes, for her friend, Rosa, is afraid she may be pregnant. Ginia had not the slightest suspicion that her friends had begun to have that kind of experience. She feels left out, wondering why her friends have not confided in her. She takes a self-righteous, condemnatory attitude, which is nothing but the exaltation of her own ignorance to the status of 'astuteness'. She comes to know Amelia, an older girl, who works as a free-lance artist's model. Amelia has much more experience than Ginia, and through her the latter is introduced to many situations which are new and terrifying. However, it is the question of nudity which becomes the apparently unsurmountable barrier between her own world and Amelia's. It is much more than being able to stand unashamedly naked before others. Gradually, Ginia does become more aware of her own body, and that, by Pavese's definition, is crucial in the passage to maturity. Nudity raises the question of sexual experience, already in Ginia's mind because of Rosa, and she struggles to put it in perspective, sensing that it is limiting and destructive. Her own initiation into the mysteries of sex comes when she is introduced by Amelia to Guido, a soldier and aspiring artist, and Rodriguez, his Portuguese friend. Ginia falls in love with Guido but experiences only frustration and disillusionment because he does not take her seriously. Bit by bit, her childhood, the 'beautiful summer' of the title, disintegrates and she is left floundering in a world which is cruel and strangely alien. Pavese had commented on 'youthful enthusiasm' in his diary, about a year before the novel was begun, and Ginia exemplifies much of what he had had in mind:

The inadequacy of youthful enthusiasm consists essentially in the refusal to recognise one's own limitations. The distinction between oneself and others, which comes with mature years, tends to convince the *self* that there is no access to others ...

Since knowing other people (and the only real knowledge comes through identification in love) is an enrichment, anyone who refuses to love them (=to know them) thereby impoverishes himself. From this fact is derived the fullness of youth – in the intemperate nature of those years one feels the thrill of universal knowledge. But this sense of fullness is without foundation; hence the disappointments which are impressed upon us by the experience of maturity. (*MV* 9 February 1939)

Ginia's crisis comes at the very end of the novel when, afraid that Amelia (who has confessed to having contracted syphilis in a lesbian relationship) will entice Guido from her, she makes a desperate bid to retain his affections by offering to pose nude for him in Amelia's presence. Guido, indifferent, accepts and she undresses. After a few moments she becomes aware that there is a fourth person in the room. She turns to find Rodriguez looking at her. He has been sleeping, as he does every day at that particular hour, on the bed behind the heavy red curtain which divides the room.[2] Mortified, she bursts into tears, seizes her clothes and flees behind the curtain. The others laugh at her prudery. She dresses hastily and runs away, inconsolable, convinced that she will never again be able to face her friends. Yet she comes to understand that her reaction has been childish and that she too ought to have laughed. Had she known how to laugh at herself her childhood would surely have been left behind her. When, after a time, she again meets up with Amelia, she humbly asks: 'You show me the way', for she has not yet attained that 'solitude which is self-sufficiency'.

La bella estate is a novel which is rooted deep within Pavese's own experience, and seems to have been written in response to many of the problems raised in his diary in the year before it was composed. Ginia's initial idealism is derived, perhaps, from the note written on 7 February 1939:

> the young do not know that others are others; a mature person is one who distinguishes between himself and others. How then can one explain the fact that civilisations at their birth believe in the objectivity of the world, and when in decline invent idealism?
>
> Like this: the *objectivity of the world* is achieved by animating the world, by believing in its mystical objective organised unity; *idealism*, by isolating the ego among empty formal appearances (the *others* of the mature man).

Ginia's ego is isolated, at least for a time, in the 'empty formal appearances' of the destroyed myths of her childhood. She experiences something like that 'terrible collapse' Pavese had known after his period of *confino*, and she too is conscious that 'nothing, for the moment, takes its place'.

The novel begins with a simple statement: 'Life was a perpetual holiday at that time', and childhood, the period of the long 'festa' in which sadness is only momentary, was for Pavese the time of illusion. Then there follows a long, breathless sentence which, in its very structure and delivery, captures the essence of that 'youthful enthusiasm' which was soon to crumble away:

> Just leaving the house and going across the street was enough to make us go wild, and everything was so nice, especially at night, so that even when we were on our way home we would still hope for something to happen, that a fire might break out or a baby might be born in the house or that night might suddenly even turn into day and all the people come out into the street and we could keep on walking and walking right out to the fields and even beyond the hills.

That sense of recklessness and endless discovery which had belonged to the children in *Lavorare stanca* is here also. The sense of limitation which the child gradually comes to experience is frequently not at first his own, but that of some adult observed as he goes about his daily work as, for example, in the poem 'Civiltà antica' (Ancient civilisation, *Poesie* p. 111). However, in *La bella estate*, that growing sense of limitation is the direct experience of the protagonist. Ginia's defensive idealism is subtly exposed in the following:

If there were any boys in the group, you could count on it that before nightfall some girl would lose her temper or even cry, if she were silly enough. They would tease girls like Rosa. They were always trying to get the girls to go off into the meadows with them. There was no arguing with them, you just had to be on your guard. But some evenings they would all sing and that was nice. They sang well, especially if Ferruccio came along and brought his guitar. He was tall and blond and was always out of work, but his fingers were still filthy and rough from the coal he had handled. It seemed incredible that those huge hands could be so nimble, and Ginia, who had felt them once go round her when they were all on their way back from the hillside, took care not to look at them whilst he was playing. Rosa had told her that Ferruccio had asked about her on two or three occasions, and Ginia had said: 'Tell him to do his nails first.' The next time she had been expecting him to laugh at her, but in fact, he hadn't even looked at her. (*Estate* p. 9)

We see the continual confrontation of Ginia's ideal world and reality; her false sense of superiority in that 'or even cry, if she were silly enough'; her rejection of the 'meadows' and what they might signify; her unwillingness to believe that the music which pleases her so much could be made by fingers which have dirty, broken nails; and her miscalculation over her influence with Ferruccio, who does not even look at her. The only answer she knows is to turn her head away and to close her eyes.

It is her friendship with Amelia which precipitates the destruction of the values which have already proved inadequate. Though Ginia begs her friend: 'You have to promise me you'll show me what to do', her attitude is ambivalent, and she steadfastly defends the ideals of the 'beautiful summer' which is slipping away from her. This ambivalence is usually indicated by some manifestation of fear – indrawn breath, a fast-beating heart, perspiration or, even worse, by headlong flight:

Amelia hadn't even put stockings on because it was so hot, so that when they passed a dance-hall, one of those with a muffled orchestra and shaded lamps on the tables, Ginia was afraid to go in with her. She had never been there before and she held her breath. Amelia said: 'Do you really not want to go in?'

'It's hot, and we're not properly dressed for it,' said Ginia. 'Let's walk. It's nicer.' (*Estate* p. 14)

We see her clinging on to her 'empty formal appearances' in her apparent belief in the convention of being appropriately dressed for particular occasions. Yet this is at best merely a pretext, for underlying her hesitation is her fear of the unknown, 'the muffled orchestra' and the 'shaded lamps' which suggest a luxury and a mystery which belong to a different world from her own.

Ginia's progress towards maturity is paralleled by a growing awareness of her own body, and that awareness is created by the continual reflection of her nakedness in a whole series of mirrors – shop windows, drawings, paintings, the attitudes of other people towards her, and so on. Nakedness represents that 'basic stratum', the object of Ginia's search. Ginia, like Ersilia Drei in Pirandello's *Vestire gli ignudi* (*Naked*, 1922), strips away the illusions in which she is clad, and should now – according to Pavese – attain that peace of mind which the period of transition denies her. She resists the growing awareness until, in desperation, she cries out: 'But why are we naked?'

The first time Ginia watches Amelia posing naked for the artist, Barbetta, things turn out differently from the way she has expected:

Her first thought was that Amelia must be cold and that Barbetta was hardly looking at her, and that she, having come out of curiosity, was the only one who felt uncomfortable ...

After a while, Ginia felt bored. She watched Barbetta paint bits out and then redo them; she saw his concentrated look; she exchanged a smile with Amelia, but she was bored. Her heart beat faster again the first time Amelia got up to stretch herself, and picked up her panties which had fallen down on the settee, but that was silly because she would have felt the same way even if they had been alone. The heartbeat was the recognition that we are all made the same and that anyone who had seen Amelia naked, it was as if they had seen her. Then she began to feel ill at ease. (*Estate* p. 23)

The naked body clearly does not have any sexual significance for either Amelia or Barbetta. The artist is engrossed in his work and Amelia is merely an object ('Do you think you are more important than a tree or a horse?' he has said to Amelia). Amelia too seems indifferent, so that the whole scene is devoid of any sexual content. Ginia has come to the sitting to confirm a prejudice, and comes away more perplexed than ever.

Awareness of a gap opening up between appearances and realities is hinted at through Pavese's use of 'mirrors' in situations other than those connected with nudity. Ginia seeks security in known situations, and in the following passage the girl, apparently secure in a familiar scene, points to the dichotomy between being and seeming, without being remotely aware of its implications or its relevance to the problems she is currently facing:

now Sundays and evenings were all boring, because on her own Ginia was no longer capable of making up her mind and she let herself be carried along by the others. Where she did enjoy herself, on occasions, was at the *atelier*, when the Signora called her over to pin up a customer's dress. She got a laugh out of some of the things that some of the silly customers said, but what was even funnier was when the Signora pretended to believe them and stood there, all serious-like, with the mirrors reflecting back her mocking looks. (*Estate* pp. 25–6)

The theme of nudity returns when, after making love with Guido, Ginia lies awake, alone with her thoughts:

Then she realised that Guido was asleep, and she thought they couldn't possibly sleep that way in each other's arms, and ever so gently she moved away and found a cool spot, so cool, in fact, that she became worried because she felt herself naked and alone. And again she was overcome by that sense of shame and nausea she had felt as a child when someone had washed her. She wondered why Guido made love with her, and she thought about tomorrow and about all those days she had waited, and her eyes filled with tears and she wept silently so that he didn't hear her. (*Estate* p. 75)

Out of love for Guido Ginia wants to offer her nakedness to him alone, because it is her most secret self, but he treats her gift casually, effectively rejecting it. And yet, what has he rejected if he still wishes to make love to her? Not her nakedness, merely her interpretation of it. Just as she senses that Amelia, posing naked for Barbetta, is being treated simply as an object, she realises that for Guido she too is nothing more than that. 'Love has the virtue', wrote Pavese much later, 'of stripping naked each of the two lovers, not the one before the other, but each one before himself' (*MV* 12 October 1949). This was Ginia's experience also. Her *inquietudine* comes from her awareness that she is her own body, and that Guido's refusal of that 'identification in love' condemns her to it, to the kind of separation which she experiences in a physical sense in the above-quoted passage. She is here on the threshold of the discovery that Guido has a destiny which has been shaped quite separately from her own, and in which she has only a superficial role to play, a necessary step in her passage towards maturity.

What we witness in Ginia is a re-enactment of the 'Fall', the loss of an innocence which is regretted but which is unredeemable. In the other characters, Ginia sees various possible lines of development once the sexual factor has asserted itself in their lives. Rosa will have greatly limited the horizons of her life because she is to become a mother at such an early age (it proves, eventually, to have been a false alarm), whilst, more seriously, the complicated Amelia has been led into lesbianism and disease. It is hardly surprising that the cautious Ginia should feel so afraid. Even the artistic idealism of Guido is not unaffected, for the time he insists he needs to devote to his painting can always be spared if the opportunity for making love arises. An experience similar to Ginia's had been outlined in 'A proposito di certe poesie non ancora scritte' (On poems which are yet to be written, 1940):

> Having defined *Lavorare stanca* as the adventure of the adolescent who, glorying in his native countryside, imagines the city as something similar, but instead finds loneliness there, which he tries to alleviate through sex and passion, which serve only to uproot him and drive him far away from both country and city, into a more tragic solitude which is the end of adolescence ... (*Poesie* p. 206)

The connection between the city and 'the end of adolescence' is important, for in addition to its significance in the two novels under discussion, it was soon, under the influence of Pavese's reading of Vico, Frazer, Jung and Freud, to become a prominent factor in his thinking on the nature of personal and social myth.

The world of art or pseudo-art, which forms the background against which Ginia's internal drama evolves, was to figure again in *Tra donne sole* (Among women only), one of the two novels together with which *La bella estate* was published in 1949. The dilettantish approach to art, for which Pavese had so severely upbraided himself after his return from Brancaleone, makes a brief appearance in *La spiaggia* also. For Ginia, it is inextricably bound up with nakedness, but nakedness which is gradually emptied of any sexual connotation. It represents for Ginia the 'other reasons', the mysteries of the adult life towards which she is blindly groping her way. The picture – which is a perpetual reflection – and the pose serve to make Ginia aware of her body and of her separateness.[3]

Technically, this novel represents a new departure in Pavese's writing. He was anxious not to fall into the 'traps' of Naturalism and, in any case, was by this time far more interested in 'the internal life' of the character than in the 'world outside him'. In *Il carcere* the story had been reported by the writer, someone who stood outside the events and yet had free access to Stefano's innermost thoughts and feelings. This was basically the method of Verga and of the Naturalistic tradition, notwithstanding an infusion of images which derived from the author's experience in *Lavorare stanca*. The most noticeable difference between *Il carcere* and *Paesi tuoi* was that in the latter the viewpoint changed and the narrative was now presented in the first person by Berto, the protagonist. Again we must refer to Pavese's diary in order to emphasise how conscious he was of searching for a style, and to highlight just what it was he sought to achieve by the change:

In the first person narrative one can be realistic, without, however, lapsing into *verismo*. Along with its greater realism, the first person narrative turns out to be more lyrical than that in the third person. (*MV* 13 November 1938)

Although the first person narrative opened up new possibilities for Pavese, particularly with regard to the kind of language used, it did not provide the kind of balance he was seeking. The partial failure lay, as Pavese himself later acknowledged, in his insistence upon the lyrical aspect of his story, for both *Il carcere* and *Paesi tuoi* lean heavily upon correlatives (in the 'external world') 'to clarify the internal reality' of the protagonist – obvious examples are the villa of Giannino's parents and the breast/hill image of *Paesi tuoi*. There are two passages in Pavese's diary at the time of the composition of *La bella estate* which suggest that he was beginning to understand the reasons for his dissatisfaction. The first comments on the work of Doeblin – and one of the characteristic features of Pavese's work as a novelist is his ability to clarify problems encountered in his own writing by analysing that of others:

Doeblin, Dos Passos, you yourself: if you want to escape from *verismo*, which is only skin-deep, you tumble into the abstract construction of Expressionism. What is lacking above all else is a sense of drama. (*MV* 16 June 1940)

Once he had perceived that *Il carcere* and *Paesi tuoi* were to some extent Expressionistic and that this was their weakness, it was only a short step to the following discovery – again made initially through other writers:

There is a connection between the naked, conversational sentence employed by Dostoyevsky and his clever, wholly rational invention. The strength with which he feels life is expressed not in live images but rather through dramatic, visionary qualities which are made up of everyday objects and events ... (*MV* 23 June 1940)

This entry continues:

Defoe is the greatest English novelist because he is the least Elizabethan. He has an *unmarred* [in English in original] voice. The others – even Dickens – hark back to the seventeenth century in both their poetics and their humour – they are imagistic, they speak through *images* which no longer have the instinctive and linguistic carnality (*wit*) [in English in original] of the Elizabethans, but which make rhetorical phrases and *do not arise from the character* and therefore are not dramatic.

Even a story with one apparent protagonist only can be dramatic (Defoe). But in this case there are a man and an environment confronting each other.

Two elements here are of significance with regard to *La bella estate*. Firstly, it is far less Expressionistic than its forerunners, and secondly, the relationship between the author and his characters is different. This second point had already been worked out some three months earlier than this diary entry, and yet again it was Pavese's study of Dostoyevsky and of Herman Melville which had helped him to clarify the point sufficiently to make it of practical value in the construction of *La bella estate:*

The balance of a story is located in the coexistence of two persons: one is the author, who knows how it will end, the other is the characters, who do not know. If the author and the protagonist merge (*Je*) [in French in original] and know how it will all turn out, it becomes necessary to increase the stature of other characters to re-establish the balance. Therefore the protagonist, *if he is narrating*, must be mainly a spectator (Dostoyevski: 'in our district'; *Moby-Dick*: 'call me Ishmael').

If one tells the story in the first person, clearly the protagonist must know from the start how his adventure will end; unless he is made to speak in the present tense. (*MV* 1 March 1940)

Although the method was first used by Pavese in *La bella estate*, it was not to be perfected until *La spiaggia*. Evidently he was aiming at the detachment of the narrator from the main events of the narrative and, as a consequence, from the central characters, without using the total detachment of the naturalistic novel. In *Paesi tuoi*, Berto, the first-person narrator, had been too involved in the action of the novel and was effectively its protagonist, even though his status was reduced to that of a helpless bystander in the drama of Gisella's death. In *La bella estate* it is established in the first paragraph that the narrator, who is unnamed throughout and undeveloped as a character, is nevertheless involved, if only marginally, in the lives of the main characters – 'even when we were on our way home we would still hope for something to happen ...'. Having established the distance which separates the story-teller from the main character, Ginia, Pavese is then able to proceed with the third person narrative as in the Naturalistic novel, entering whenever necessary into Ginia's thoughts, not merely to report them (as in *Il carcere*) but to present them in the first person, thereby retaining their form as well. The impression given is that the story is being told from the inside, from someone who is in the know (though we, the audience, do not know precisely how or why he/she should have such access), so that the artificial situation of the narrator of the Naturalistic novel, looking into a world of which he is not a part, is partially offset.

There are certain similarities between *La bella estate* and Svevo's *Senilità*, with which, as the diary entry for 17 September 1938 suggests, Pavese was certainly familiar. Both novels have, as a substantial part of their background, the world of the artist, and the jealousy and insecurity which Ginia feels with the knowledge that Amelia is posing for Guido seem to echo Brentani's when Angiolina poses for Balli. Ginia and Brentani attempt to deny reality in favour of a more palatable world of their own fantastic creation, while, for their respective authors, the two novels represent a conscious break with Naturalism in an attempt to explore the 'internal world' of their protagonists. Perhaps the most noticeable similarity is their lack of any detailed environment, and it could be that Pavese was, to some extent, influenced by Svevo when writing this novel. There is little description of the world of objects, and it is no accident that virtually the whole of the novel's significant action takes place indoors – in the café, in Guido's room, in Ginia's room, in Barbetta's studio and so on. Even when Amelia and Ginia are outside together it is only the fleeting glance, the occasional sentence which reminds us *where* we are.[4] This aspect of the novel, which is reminiscent of a series of close-up camera shots in which the background is blurred and indistinct, emphasises the closedness within herself of the beleaguered adolescent, Ginia. The city remains only atmosphere, and in this the break with Naturalism is extreme, and surprising too, considering that as recently as the November of the year preceding that in which the novel was written, Pavese had rejected Mérimée for a similar kind of omission:

He doesn't know how to live a drama of *man in his environment*; even where he is tragic, he is tragic by hearsay, by supposition, but he lacks roots in the background (*Carmen*). (*MV* 18 November 1939)

The characters in *La bella estate* are isolated under the gaze of the narrator as if under a microscope. Guido is a soldier, but we never see him as a soldier, just as we hardly ever see Ginia at work, nor Rosa, nor Severino. In its tight control over the world of the characters in it, *La bella estate* belongs more to the realms of the short story than of the novel. Only occasionally, and then only momentarily, does Ginia turn away from her inner world and its immediate environment, to glance from a window at snow-covered rooftops, to listen – when there is a lull in the conversation – to the sound of the rain against the window, or to hear the wind playing through the telephone wires. The objective world is transformed into sensations of warmth and cold, into impressions of light, and above all, into memory. It serves Ginia as a way of escape when the immediate reality becomes too intense. This absence of a developed environment, seen as a defect by some critics, stems from Pavese's current view that the surest way of finding a 'passage to other men' ('passaggio agli altri') was through self-analysis and self-construction. This attitude is reflected in Ginia who, nevertheless, remains inept in her dealings with others. Her final 'You show me the way' is an acknowledgement of her failure and of her need for people.

In the essay 'L'influsso degli eventi' (The influence of events), written early in 1946, Pavese made this comment about his own work:

> My most 'successful' work, the one which 'alone, is most typical of my art', is still *Lavorare stanca*. For what is *Paesi tuoi* if not a page from the same book, dwelt on at length and with particular relish? And *Feria d'agosto* [August holidays], the same book seen from a new angle and already accounted for? On the other hand, *La spiaggia*, my non-violent, non-proletarian, non-American novel, which fortunately very few have read, is not a chip off the monolith. It represents a diversion, albeit a human one, and indeed if it were worth the trouble, I'd be ashamed of it. It is what you might call a frank search for a style (*La lett. am.* p. 248)

Several interesting points are raised here: the 'new' importance of *Lavorare stanca*, which appears to deny the dissatisfaction which Pavese had previously felt with it; the admission that in the years preceding the war he had been looking for a style; but perhaps most important is his half repudiation of *La spiaggia*. It has been suggested that Pavese's denial of this 'non-proletarian ... novel' was little more than a sop to the Communist Cerberus, for he had only recently joined the Party when this statement was made. Certainly, 'proletarian' – as well as 'violent' and 'American' – could well be applied to *Lavorare stanca* whilst clearly not to *La spiaggia*. Yet, in what sense is the novel a 'diversion'? – if because of its setting and the bourgeoisie, with which it deals, then Pavese's judgement needs to be challenged. It is not much more of a 'diversion' than *La bella estate*, for that novel too had failed to present a picture of *man in his environment*. Severino, Rosa and Ginia, Pavese tells us, belong to the working class, but this is not demonstrated in the novel; indeed, the underlying viewpoint is as much 'bourgeois' in the one case as in the other. The linking of *Feria d'agosto* with *Lavorare stanca* but, by implication, not with *La spiaggia*, is indeed curious. Certainly a part of *Feria d'agosto* represents a return to the hills of the Langhe, and in that sense the connection with the earlier poems is real enough. Yet there is another side to *Feria d'agosto* in which Pavese pursues the enigmas of personality and being, and these questions are fundamental to *La bella estate* and *La spiaggia*. Pavese's preoccupation with the problems of personality in these two novels is defined in two consecutive diary entries made in October 1940. Firstly:

A person matters for what he *is*, not for what he does. Moral life is not actions; the way we treat others is only good or ill will. Moral life is the eternal, immutable being of the I – actions are nothing but ripples on this sea, which reveals its depths only in a storm, but not really even then. (*MV* 22 October 1940)

Secondly:

One significance of my presence in this century might be the mission of discrediting the Leopardian–Nietzschian myth that the active life is superior to the contemplative. To demonstrate that the dignity of the great man consists in *not* consenting to labour, to sociality, to *bourrage*. Without, of course, giving up living in a Dostoyevskian manner. Let all the passions come. But don't forget that one matters for what one *is*, not for what one *does*. (*MV* 23 October 1940)

The search, then, for the 'basic stratum' was for an entity which was absolute – 'the eternal, immutable being of the I'. In *La spiaggia* there is ample evidence to suggest that all of the main characters are *waiting* for their real selves to emerge and set them in motion again after the interlude of apparent stagnation which lies between adolescence and maturity. In this context the following passage seems particularly relevant:

One evening ... as we were walking towards the café where we had our aperitifs, and Doro was with us, their friend Guido observed slyly that in Doro ... the soul of an artist lay sleeping. 'Sleeping, yes,' said Doro, light-heartedly, good-humouredly. 'There are all sorts of things sleeping beneath the surface. What we need is the courage to wake up and find ourselves, or at least to talk about it. People talk too little in this world.'[5]

The revelation of one's 'I' is thought of in terms of 'waking up', of becoming conscious, but 'waking up' is an involuntary action and, as we see in the character of Guido, some people will 'sleep' forever. It is this passiveness which drains any sense of drama from *La spiaggia*. Characteristic of Pavese is Doro's faith in the power of talk as a means of salvation. What else is Pavese's diary, indeed, the whole of his work, if not an extended dialogue with himself? Whatever else they may be, the words of the writer are always a dialogue with himself; although one speaks to a public there is never any reply. It is perhaps this kind of belief and practice which Pavese felt as an embarrassment when he embraced the ideals of Communism.

The plot of *La spiaggia* is flimsy and uncomplicated. Doro has married Clelia, and has gone to live in her city, Genoa. As a consequence, the narrator and he meet very infrequently. The truth is that the former resents Doro's marriage (a motif which had figured in the earlier short story 'Amici' – Friends, 1937) and did not even go to the wedding. Despite a long-standing invitation, he has declined to visit his friend and his wife and spend a holiday with them at their house on the Riviera. However, he has visited them in Genoa, and has made his peace with Doro.

At the beginning of the novel, he has decided to accept the invitation and is on the point of leaving, when a telegram arrives from Doro telling him to wait because he is coming to him. In due course Doro arrives and at his request – 'Keep me company. I want to go back to the place I came from' – they go off to the countryside of the Langhe. During a brief interlude they relive their youth in the carousing, singing and horse-play beneath the windows of village Juliets; yet the experience is recognised to be devoid of meaning, for they have already lived beyond it and have changed too much.

This 'return to one's origins' takes on the character of a rite, a 'festa', an excursion into memory, and as such is a precursor of those 'feste' in 'Il mare' (The sea) and other stories in *Feria d'agosto*. The figure of the 'man in white who was doing somersaults' seems to be linked with the antics of the billy-goat in 'Il dio-caprone' (The goat-god) and the 'green mysteries' of the Langhe, and in this initial phase of the novel, at least, it is hard to see how Pavese could deny its claim to be 'a chip off the monolith'. There is an element of the bizarre, the exotic, running through this whole episode – an almost schizophrenic aspect of Pavese's writing which he found difficult to control.

This return to the Langhe is also a return in time, though

something more than a mere 'recherche du temps perdu'. Doro has gone back to find the source, the beginning of himself, because instinctively he feels the need to retrace his steps to pick up the 'right way' which he feels he has lost. The cousin of 'I mari del Sud' had already made a similar journey more than a decade earlier. In this sense too, *La spiaggia* would seem to be 'a chip off the monolith', because here, for the first time since *Lavorare stanca*, there is a renewal, which is at the same time a development of the theme of the countryside as the environment of childhood and memory. Conversely – and this was already present in *La bella estate* – the city evolves more and more as the environment of maturity and history, and at the end of *La spiaggia* it is the return of Doro and Clelia to Genoa which indicates their acceptance of a mutual responsibility, nothing less than maturity. In *Feria d'agosto*, which was written in the three years immediately following *La spiaggia*, this deepened contrast between city and country was to develop even further towards the mythological 'Titanic' (representative of the ever-present, primitive, natural urges in man) and the 'Olympian' (the civilised–rational aspect of man), which come to the fore in *Dialoghi con Leucò*.

After the brief interlude in the Langhe, Doro and the narrator travel together to join Clelia and her friends, the 'Genoese clique'. The life of the beach is characterised by the ephemeral, the superficial, the trivial, and the narrator, a teacher, rarely feels at ease there. To add to his discomfort is the growing suspicion that all is not well between Clelia and Doro. When questioned separately, they vigorously deny that anything is wrong and certainly there has been no quarrel between them. Only with the knowledge that Clelia is pregnant and that she and her husband are returning to the city does the 'mystery' seem to evaporate.

When Clelia and Doro married they were aware it would involve certain sacrifices for both of them. They were in love and believed that their love would be sufficient to pull them through. It is the sense of limitation, of environment and relationships, which each imposes upon the other, which is at the root of their apparent estrangement. They come from different backgrounds and environments and it is this difference, which has largely formed them, that they have not yet learnt to come to terms with in each other. They are not dissatisfied with their marriage, with what it includes, but rather with what it excludes. They have become aware, as does Ginia with Guido, that each individual has a whole secret life of his own which, perforce, excludes all others. In this context we should recall Pavese's observation that 'a sure sign of love is the desire to know, *to relive* the childhood of the other' (*MV* 5 August 1940). Love, in other words, wishes to possess its object completely, but this is impossible because, quite apart from the impossibility of possessing the past of the other, there is also usually a desire on the part of the other not to be totally possessed, and such possession is resisted, more or less consciously. It is this conflict of love which is variously misinterpreted by other characters as some kind of breakdown in the marriage of Clelia and Doro. With the realisation that they have created a responsibility *together*, in the coming child, there is an apparent cessation of 'hostilities', which is an acknowledgement that there is a whole area of each of them which will always exclude the other. It is in this context that the sea takes on a specific symbolic significance. The teacher, reflecting on Clelia's refusal to allow him or anyone to accompany her when she swims in the sea, informs us that:

She had explained to me that she did everything in public, but in the sea she wanted to be alone.
'That seems strange.'
'Strange it may be, but that's how it is.' She was a good swimmer, so it wasn't embarrassment. It was a decision she had made. 'The sea is enough company for me. I don't want anyone else. I've got nothing of my own in life. Leave me the sea at least.' (*Spiaggia* pp. 68–9)

For Clelia, the sea, which has always been an element in her life, is as much a symbol of her 'basic stratum' as is the countryside of the Langhe for Doro. Just as Doro is excluded from Clelia's sea, Clelia is *not* taken on the trip into the Langhe. However, Clelia's lack of curiosity about that trip seems to suggest that she, at least, has perhaps already realised that it represents something for Doro of which she is not a part. Doro, on the other hand, does not seem to achieve this kind of awareness until the very end of the novel. He seems to recognise the significance which the sea has for Clelia and attempts to possess it by painting it: 'Doro's seascapes – he did two of them in that time – were painted in pale, indistinct colours, as if the very intensity of the sun and the air, deafening and blinding, muted his brushstrokes' (*Spiaggia* p. 48). In this, Doro is putting into practice an idea which Pavese had held for quite some time, namely that 'to see human beings by means of a point of reference is the only way to get near them' (*MV* 26 April 1939).

The 'life on the beach' has been described as a limbo, a state of suspension, and it is certainly that for Guido, but for the rest a better analogy would be with the Dantesque 'ante-purgatory', which is a temporary state of suspension. Clelia's return to Genoa the teacher interprets as the end of her childhood. 'I was pleased', he says,[5] 'to have spent with her her last summer as a child'. The summer by the sea, the time of waiting, is closely akin to the 'beautiful summer', which Ginia, too, regretfully left behind her. Clelia and Doro with their coming child represent the *summum bonum* for Pavese, the defeat of loneliness.

One character, Guido, will never achieve the maturity and fulfilment of some meaningful purpose such as is in sight for Clelia and Doro, for his whole being precludes it. Guido lives the illusion that he has understood what life is all about a long time ago. '"You have to understand life," he said, winking somewhat uneasily, "understand it when you are young."' His adherence to the beach life is attachment to the anecdotal as permanence – 'if he left his car it was only to play a game of cards'. He lacks decision, purpose or any sense of responsibility, which fact becomes evident in a moment of confession about Nina, the mistress he keeps in the background because she is unacceptable to his other friends.

At my age, I can't change my ways, but if Nina wanted to amuse herself, to find friends and surroundings that suited her, it would be all right with me. (*Spiaggia* p. 101)

In response to the suggestion that 'all you have to do is tell her' he argues:

'No ... she feels she's on her own. You see, a man has friends, relationships to keep up. He can't always be spending his time with her.'
'Wouldn't a frank explanation do the trick?' I [the teacher–narrator] suggested.
'With other women, yes, but not with her. She's a friend, a long-standing friend, you see ... a woman who makes certain demands. Do you see what I mean?'

Vacillation, a failure of commitment, even hypocrisy seem to characterise his relationship with Nina. At the same time, he is effectively paying court to Clelia, but covertly, making no decisive move towards her. He is justly described as 'a forty-year-old who was too idle to grow up'. The ephemeral world of the beach is his natural element, for he is out of touch with any reality of the workaday world.

Berti, as a type, is not new to Pavese's writing. He has already made his appearance as the confused youth in 'La villa in collina' (The villa on the hill), one of the short stories written in 1938 and which has affinities with *La spiaggia*. He is also present in Ginia, whilst his problems have already been defined in the early poem 'Antenati':

> Stupefatto del mondo mi giunse un'età
> che tiravo dei pugni nell'aria e piangevo da solo.
> Ascoltare i discorsi di uomini e donne
> non sapendo rispondere, è poca allegria.

(Awed by the world, I reached an age when I punched at the air and wept alone. Hearing the talk of men and women, not knowing how to answer, is not much fun.)

He left school suddenly, and the narrator, his former teacher, meets him alone by the sea trying to find a way into the adult world:

> In effect he said he was bored, he had no friends, and would be very pleased to be able to talk with me and read a few books together – no, not lessons – but reading like I'd sometimes done at school, explaining and discussing, teaching him many things he was conscious of not knowing. (*Spiaggia* p. 55)

This desire to be taught by someone older was the point reached by Ginia at the end of *La bella estate*. The teacher, however, seems embarrassed, annoyed, by the presence of his former pupil, partly perhaps because he reminds him too much of his own insecurity; certainly he has no difficulty in understanding the boy's problems:

> What happens to everyone had happened to him also: his real nature had taken on the appearance of its opposite – like those gentle souls who aspire to being tough. (*Spiaggia* p. 45)

He listens to Berti's groping plea for knowledge and, not without a touch of cynicism, remarks that

> I envied him ... because, being young, he could still delude himself about his true nature. (*Spiaggia* p. 45)

Berti befriends a prostitute, recognising in her – as someone on the very margins of society – a kindred spirit:

> She was alone and bored at the seaside. They had met on the beach – she'd been the one who'd started joking and fooling around. – 'See,' he said, 'I didn't say no to her, because I felt sorry for her. She's got a handbag with a mirror in it that's all cracked. I know how she feels. She just wants company ... (*Spiaggia* p. 72)

Neither Berti nor his friend has achieved that 'solitude which is self-sufficiency'. Solidarity as a result of a common suffering had appeared in the short stories written in the period 1936–8,[6] and in *Il carcere*, from all of which it appears Pavese is convinced that if a 'passage to other men' is possible, it must always involve suffering – either mutually shared or mutually inflicted: 'Either with love or with hatred, but always with violence' (*MV* 25 December 1937).

Despite their bond of loneliness, Berti feels insecure with his prostitute friend, for 'She's like all women, trying to embarrass a man by ridiculing him' (*Spiaggia* p. 72). Perhaps for Pavese there is ultimately no real solidarity where a man and a woman are concerned, and this is not without significance in the achievement of that 'solitude which is self-sufficiency'.

Berti's attitude to women is Pavese's own – as his diary and many of his letters, particularly in the period after his return from Brancaleone, confirm. It is a love–hate attitude because Berti sees woman as possible salvation and possible destruction. He is captivated by the mysterious Clelia, and this attraction becomes yet another of the torments of his youth. When he discovers that Clelia is pregnant and has returned to Genoa he wishes to borrow the money for his fare in order to go and bid her goodbye. He persists in his love-fantasy and the teacher, perhaps in an effort to bring him back down to earth asks, rather bluntly. 'What are you thinking about? Do you honestly believe that she'll remember you?'

In this novel, there is amongst all the characters – with the exception of Guido – a profound dissatisfaction with the present. Berti

could not understand why people made out that it was nice to be young: he would have liked to be thirty already – with such a lot of things behind him – the years in between were just stupid. (*Spiaggia* p. 95)

Doro and Clelia, on the other hand, constantly look back wistfully to the very period of their own lives which Berti condemns in his:

Clelia grew thoughtful and said that if she hadn't been what she was – a spoilt child who didn't know how to do anything – she would have painted the sea herself, for she liked it so much, it was a part of her; and not only the sea, but the houses too, the people, the steep steps, the whole of Genoa. 'I like it so much,' she said.
'Maybe that's why Doro ran away. For the self-same reason. He likes the hills.'
'Maybe. But he says his place is only nice when you think about it afterwards. I couldn't do that. I've got nothing else that's my own.' (*Spiaggia* p. 75)

Not only in *La spiaggia*, but throughout the whole of his work,

Pavese's characters seek to escape the present which always signifies *inquietudine*. This necessarily implies a movement not only backwards or forwards in time (usually the former), but from the *real* – the world of action – to the *idealised* – the world of thought, memory or speculation. This shift is important for although it liberates it is also a measure of the alienation of the character (and indeed, of the author) from his own time. It is a retreat into subjectivity made in the belief that 'if you don't save yourself no one will save you' (*MV* 2 November 1940). In answer to Berti's rejection of the myth of youth, the teacher replies: 'But all the years are stupid. It's only when they're past that they become interesting.'

The most enigmatic character is the teacher–narrator. His function as an element in Pavese's *tecnica* has already been discussed, but he is more than a mere narrative device. The story he tells in ostensibly about other people, but as a character in his own right, involved in the lives of those around him, he is unable to escape the effects of the relationships he forms upon his own 'internal world'. He is compelled through those relationships to question his own values, and in so doing becomes more conscious of his own reality and limitations; speaking of Doro, for example, he observes:

But now I felt that his silences – like mine – were distracted, estranged, in short, unusual. I had been at the sea for just a few days, and it seemed like a century. And yet nothing had happened. But when I came in at night, I had the feeling that my whole day – the ordinary, banal beach day – demanded some sort of clarification on my part, if I was to get my bearings. (*Spiaggia* p. 79)

However, as a character he does not develop visibly within the novel, for the 'new awareness' he achieves is never succeeded by any positive action. He remains aloof, the guardian of his own 'solitude', the observer. His limited and limiting perspective is Pavese's own. He takes the view – perhaps an excuse for his own reticence – that 'as luck would have it I was at the sea, where the days have no meaning'. The opposition between 'being' and 'doing' already noted (p. 83) comes to the fore in this character: 'As usual, I took a perverse pleasure in keeping a little apart, knowing that a few steps away in the shadows the others were milling about, laughing and dancing' (*Spiaggia* p. 40). Nina, Guido's 'friend', has observed the same traits in him from a distance. She also questions his motives for being there at all, and taunts him with her suspicions:

'You don't dance, you don't sunbathe, you don't eat with anybody. Why don't you come with us? Oh, those friends of Guido's, what is it about that woman [Clelia] that seduces you all? You're not going to tell me it's her husband you've come to see.' (*Spiaggia* pp. 106–7)

There are occasions when it is hinted that the teacher is also captivated by Clelia, yet he invariably pleads 'I was at the sea for Doro.' Nevertheless, once, before the suggestion has ever been made, it occurs to him that 'Anyone who didn't know Clelia very well, seeing us walking along and laughing together, would have said there was something more than friendship between us' (p. 73).

Is this wishful thinking? Is the apparently self-sufficient teacher prey to a half-conscious urge towards his friend's wife? In his essential characteristics he is perhaps not so very far removed from Berti, or indeed, Guido, as he would prefer to believe. Knowledge of Clelia's pregnancy and departure disturb him, yet he resists the temptation to follow the couple to Genoa, though not without misgivings:

I was thinking what a strange thing it was: I had the fare in my pocket and I didn't go ... I was beginning to realise that there is no place more unliveable than one in which you have been happy. (*Spiaggia* p. 115)

The question of time returns forcefully. He claims to have been happy there, but has not shown himself to be so whilst living the experience. The experience past, the memory of it sweetens – Stefano's experience, precisely, in *Il carcere*. Doro's 'escape' has been an excursion into memory, into a time and a place where he has known – or thinks he has known – happiness as a child. But 'all time is unredeemable' and there is no real, lasting escape from the present. Doro learns the lessons which he passes on to Clelia, who, in her turn, tells the teacher: 'he [Doro] says that his place is only nice when you think about it afterwards'. Without the people who have made up that happiness, the place becomes intolerable and the narrator hastens to leave it, to return to his 'destiny' of 'solitude–maturity'.

This bizarre summer by the sea is symbolised by 'a great, twisted olive tree, which had grown – goodness knows how – right there in the middle of the cobblestones', of which the narrator says, 'It gave me a feeling of being in the country, an unfamiliar countryside, and I would often sniff to see whether it smelt of salt' (*Spiaggia* pp. 33–4). The tree is out of its element, isolated and, perhaps for these reasons, is full of suggestion for him. One critic, Leinhard Bergel, has suggested that it is the 'paradigm for all rustic nostalgia' and as such balances the significance of *città* for the majority of the characters in the novel.[7]

Throughout this chapter, the intention has been to refute the judgement which Pavese made about *La spiaggia* in that statement of 1946, and to show that it is in many ways typical of his mode of writing and has many links with earlier and later works.

Typical motifs abound; for example, Doro, in an anecdote about an old peasant he had known as a boy, tells his friend that that peasant had never married but rather 'kept one of his sisters at home, the sturdiest one. She had his children for him and took care of his vineyard' (*Spiaggia* p. 19). This motif recurs in Pavese's last novel, *La luna e i falò* (The moon and the bonfires), in the peasant Valino. Incest in a rural setting was perhaps carried over into this anecdote from the more central position it had occupied in *Paesi tuoi*.

Early on in *La spiaggia*, there is an echo of some lines from 'I mari del Sud', and in yet another sense Doro's 'escape' represents – in poetical terms – an artistic return for Pavese. In the novel we find:

M'indicò con gli occhi la costa ripida della più alta collina e non rispose. Salimmo taciturni fin che ci fu luce, e di lassù ci fermammo a dare un'occhiata alla pianura. (*Spiaggia* p. 20)

(With a glance he indicated the steep slope of the highest hill, and did not answer. We climbed without speaking as long as the light held, and at the top we stopped to look down on the plain.)

The motif – that of climbing a high hill in the evening then looking back at the plain – is common to both the novel and the poem, but there is no significant reworking of the language in the prose version.

The image of drunken men singing, encountered as a memory sequence in *Il carcere*, reappears in *La spiaggia* (pp. 22–3), whilst Doro's 'cry' (*Spiaggia* p. 27) is taken up in that of Oreste in *Diavolo sulle colline* (The devil on the hills). The indolent, superficial life of the *borghesia* was to emerge strongly in Pavese's novels after the war. And finally, though not exhaustively, the friendship made up of silences, which we saw in *Il carcere* (Stefano–Giannino), returns with Doro and the teacher–narrator:

Doro knew my way of breaking off momentarily during a conversation, turning my eyes away to follow a sudden thought. He used to do the same thing, and in the past we had done a lot of walking together, each brooding in silence. (*Spiaggia* p. 79)

It has been pointed out – again by Bergel – that *La spiaggia* is a

The 'search for a style' in 'La bella estate' and 'La spiaggia'

story which is told in dialogues,[8] and this is so. However, equally important is the contribution of the teacher–narrator, who reports not only the words of his friends, but their expressions and gestures, and even in conversations where he is, for the moment, taking no active part, he is nonetheless felt as a presence. There is a definite pattern to the prose structure of the novel. Patches of dialogue and brief précis of the words of others are followed by paragraphs of summarised action in which the short, simple sentence predominates. The following passage is typical:

They were talking about some scandal or other – I don't remember much about it – but I recall that the girl was defending the case and appealing to Doro, interrupting him every now and then, whilst Clelia kept repeating sweetly that it wasn't a question of morals but one of taste.

'But they're going to get married,' said Ginetta.

That was no solution, retorted Clelia, getting married was a choice, not a remedy, and a choice that ought to be made calmly.

'What the Hell, it's got to be a choice,' Guido cut in, 'after all the experience they've had.'

Without smiling, Ginetta replied that if the object of marriage was a family it was just as well to get started right away.

'But the object isn't just a family,' said Doro. 'It's to prepare an environment for a family.'

'Better a child without an environment than an environment without a child,' opined Ginetta. Then she blushed and her eyes met mine. Clelia got up to serve the drinks.

Then we played at cards. Late at night, Guido took us home. Having left Ginetta in front of the garage, we walked back towards the hotel. I should have preferred to do the walk alone, but Guido, who had talked very little all evening and played distractedly and aggressively, wanted me to keep him company. I talked to him again about Mara. Guido replied without enthusiasm: Mara was in good hands and out of danger. When we got to his hotel he kept straight on.

We arrived, in silence, at the end of my street, and I made as if to stop. Guido went on a few steps, then he turned round casually. (*Spiaggia* pp. 81–2)

At that point we enter, yet again, into another conversation. This is Pavese at his best in prose. There is nothing gratuitous here, nor pretentious. Each word in each sentence has its precise function and his 'frank search for a style' had borne fruit in this prose which is 'stark and discursive' in the best Dostoyevskian tradition. He does not explain, but rather demonstrates what the characters are by their own words and actions.

Immediately before this passage the teacher has been giving his own impressions of the girl, Ginetta, and has concluded that '[w]atching her talk, you had the distinct impression that nothing of her remained concealed'. The passage with which we are concerned implies, therefore, among other things, an invitation to judge the rightness of that view. Sure enough, Ginetta's lack of guile leads her to make that tactless remark about the child and the environment, so that the teacher's opinion seems to be vindicated. Once again, Doro's and Clelia's childless marriage is indirectly brought to our attention. It is interesting to note the reactions of the couple to Ginetta's indiscreet, if ingenuous, raising of the question. Doro speaks of marriage as a preparation for children – which could be interpreted as hesitation to accept the responsibility of a child – whilst Clelia avoids the issue altogether by busying herself with serving drinks. The conversation, which has centred on other people outside the novel, and has begun to evolve as the various expressions of fixed views on a given state of affairs, suddenly, without any warning, swings violently inwards and becomes highly personal. In this sequence, the character of Clelia seeps through every word – persistent in her opinions ('[she] kept repeating') but genteel to the ultimate degree ('sweetly'), and concerned, like the sophisticated *borghese* she is, more with 'taste' than with 'morals'. And then, in response to the suggestion that a timely marriage would tidy up the scandal they are discussing, Clelia, falling back on her own personal experience, upholds marriage as a calm, rational choice, not as an irrational obligation brought about by force of circumstance.

The vulgarity of Guido, with whom Clelia is continually on the defensive, appears yet again in his brief contribution, whilst Ginetta, ignoring Guido's attempt to lower the tone of the conversation, presses right on with her argument and ultimately causes Clelia greater embarrassment than the coarseness of Guido had done. It is only a moment of the novel, but brilliantly executed. The rest of the passage condenses what remained of that particular evening into two short sentences and then prepares the way for the next significant development in the conversation between Guido and the teacher.

By the time he had completed *La spiaggia* Pavese had perfected his use and construction of dialogue and had effectively banished the ornamental adjective from his writing. However, as his diary and letters indicate, he had already begun to develop that interest in anthropology and ethnology which was shortly to lead him to a theory of history based on myth, and his next excursion into prose, the short stories, essays and 'mezzotints' of *Feria d'agosto* (1941-4), was to herald a revival of many of those features which, momentarily in *La spiaggia*, had been purged from his writing.

6

The 'once and for all' event: symbolic reality in 'Feria d'agosto'

The closing months of 1943 were critical in Italian history. The royal *coup d'état* which unseated Mussolini, after almost twenty years as dictator, shocked and divided the nation. The situation was further complicated by two other factors. Firstly, though technically still allied to Nazi Germany, Italy, on the initiative of the king and Marshall Badoglio, was making representations to the Allies about the cessation of hostilities and the possibilities of a separate peace. Secondly, during this period of uncertain direction, Mussolini was rescued from his prison on the Gran Sasso by a German commando unit, and this event was shortly followed by the establishment in the north of the puppet republic of Salò (Repubblica Sociale Italiana), with Mussolini nominally at the helm. It was in these conditions that the Italian people behind the Nazi–Fascist lines decided to take matters into their own hands, to attempt to speed the departure of foreigners and Fascists alike. Many became partisans and took to the hills, and Turin, always a centre of opposition to Fascism, even in its most triumphant years, saw the rapid exodus of many of its young and even older men and women, workers and intellectuals, all bent on direct action in determining the future of their own lives and that of their country.

Early in September of that year Pavese, who had been in charge of the newly established branch of the Einaudi publishing house in Rome, returned to his home in Turin. The city was in a state of turmoil, not least because of the continued aerial bombardment of its factories by the Allies. Pavese's sister, with whom he had made his home since his mother's death in 1931, had fled the city with her children to stay with her sister-in-law at Serralunga, a village near Monferrato, in Piedmont. Pavese, unable to locate any of his friends – the majority of whom had either gone off to join the fight or were in Fascist prisons – found nothing at all to keep him in the city, and very soon joined his sister at Serralunga. It was in this vicinity that he was to spend most of his time until the end of the war.

Since his death in 1950, Pavese has been the centre of much controversy in Italian literary and political circles with regard to his conduct at the time of the civil war. At Serralunga, he was very close to much of the bitterest fighting and yet he apparently made no attempt to join the struggle against oppression. This failure to act at the crucial moment was resented by many and in October 1953 this very point was being debated on the 'third page' of the Communist daily *L'Unità*, by Massimo Mila and Valentino Gerratana. In that exchange of views, which centred around Pavese's recently published diary, Mila defended his friend's 'claim to privacy'[1] but Gerratana, calling on the example of Pavese's friend, Giaime Pintor, rejected the view that an individual has the automatic right to decide for himself at all times, asserting that he must be prepared – as Pintor had been – to subordinate his personal wishes to those of society in certain circumstances, such as the civil war. Gerratana cited the following opinion, and as a blanket statement it perforce included Pavese:

I do not believe the present generation has a thirst for transcendence, for struggle against demons, for heroic myths and sublime horrors. It leaves all those confused ideas, along with religious conversions and retreat from the world, to the old, disillusioned intellectuals. Confronted by real problems, having grown up amidst precise and palpable differences, this new generation has no time to create an interior drama for itself: it has found an exterior drama perfectly constructed.[2]

What Pavese thought about the war in Piedmont, as it was actually taking place, is little indicated by his diary. The entries for 1943, 1944 and early 1945 deal, for the most part, with his thoughts on the books and studies he was absorbed in and only very occasionally is there any hint of anxiety. There are no comments on specific events other than a reference to the death of Leone Ginzburg, under torture in the Regina Coeli prison in Rome, and even that is immediately interiorised, for what is recorded is its effect on him personally. From this almost total silence it is easy enough to assume that Pavese sat out the war in relative unconcern as one of Pintor's 'old, disillusioned intellectuals', yet it was not in Pavese's nature to find contentment and peace with himself in that or any other situation. In his own terms, mistaken though we may judge them to have been, Pavese had been at war within himself long before the Second World War or its Piedmontese phase had overtaken him, and was to continue so long after the fighting had ended. His perspective may have been mistaken – perhaps he might even have found the salvation he desired had he taken that vital step 'towards his fellow men' and seen his own problematical self in the larger context of a problematical world. But he did not. The barriers in his own mind, whatever they were, proved unsurmountable. Our job, at this distance in time, must be to attempt an evaluation of what he did in those years, not of what he 'ought' to have done, for recriminations are by now useless – as indeed they were even in 1953.

An examination of Pavese's diary for the years 1943–5 reveals almost continuous concern with the problems of ethnology, psychology, anthropology and myth and their links with his own life and writing. In this period of probably total intellectual isolation in the hills of Piedmont,[3] the various strands of Pavese's own cultural background – Italian, Piedmontese, American, Shakespearian–Elizabethan and classical – were gradually worked into a theory of history based on myth, and in this theory Pavese was convinced he had found the key to his own personality and his 'passage to other men'. His writing, which, ever since the days of his discovery of Anderson and the other Americans, he had maintained must have some practical end, now found a single, all-embracing purpose, that of 'clarifying his own myths'. Even before the disruptive experience of Brancaleone, some seven or eight years previously, Pavese had been aware of the powerful bond between himself and the countryside of the Langhe. In the poems of *Lavorare stanca* the Langhe had been pre-eminent and this fact had been complemented by a strong sense of disorientation experienced by a succession of *langheruoli* who, for various reasons, moved away to the city. When Pavese's own experience compelled him to broaden his horizons and include the Italian South in his work, he became acutely aware of a sense of personal alienation. The opposition, in his poems, had been between city and countryside, but appeared, as a result of the Brancaleone episode, in a new guise, that between North and South. He began to realise that not only was he experiencing the clash of two significantly disparate ways of life, but because of that clash a sense of belonging or not belonging to the region in which those cultures had evolved. In his diary he made the following observation:

This evening under the red lunar rocks I was thinking what great poetry could be written to show the god incarnate in this place ... Then I realised with surprise that the god isn't there ... and therefore someone else might write that poetry but not I.

Why can't I write about the red lunar rocks? Just because they don't reflect anything of my own, except the bare emotion of the landscape itself, which is never enough to justify a poem. If these rocks were in Piedmont I could very well absorb them into an image and give them a meaning. Which goes to show how the first condition for poetry is the obscure awareness of the value of relationships, even biological ones, that already live as embryonic images in the pre-poetic consciousness.

Certainly it must be possible, even for me, to write poetry based on material that does not have a Piedmontese background. It must be, but up to now it hardly ever has been. This means that I have not yet passed the stage of simple re-elaboration of the image, represented in material terms, of my original bond with the environment. It means, in other words, that in my poetic activity there is a gratuitous dead centre, an implied material basis, which I cannot seem to make sense of. But then, is this actually a residue of the objective world, or is it an indispensable lifeblood? (*MV* 10 October 1935)

What he discovered to be true for him as a poet was soon to become fundamental to the personalities of his characters in his prose. The narrator of 'Terra d'esilio' (Land of exile), a Piedmontese engineer in the South, and Stefano, the central character of *Il carcere*, both experience a strong sense of alienation in their new, temporary environment. Both of them see the South as bizarre and meaningless and feel repelled by its way of life and its natural, physical character. This same reaction is found in Berto in *Paesi tuoi*, the city-dweller who was 'lost' in the Piedmontese countryside; while in *La spiaggia* it is there in Doro's desperate 'escape to his origins' occasioned by the sense of disorientation which has been growing in him ever since his marriage to Clelia took him away from the mountains to Genoa and the sea.

The emphasis up to 1941–2 had been on that sense of alienation caused by the temporary exile of an individual in an environment which was not his own, an abstraction which implied the interruption of his established rhythm of life. However, with *Feria d'agosto* (August holidays, 1941–4),[4] Pavese began to explore in depth what had hitherto been taken for granted, the meaning and nature of the individual's relationship with the environment in which he had spent his formative years. Pavese had an eye for the bizarre or the unusual in life and made use of this in his writing in the characteristically Romantic belief that it is a man's confrontation with what was hitherto unknown to him that reveals both his real self and the world as it really is to him and makes for the most satisfactory art. Putting a man in an unfamiliar situation to see what happens to him is Pavese's basic formula in his early novels and short stories. Yet, in his degree thesis, he had strongly criticised writers who sought 'material that was new in terms of names, places and voyages of adventure'; however, after *Lavorare stanca* he had seemingly forgotten this lesson. He had not fully understood perhaps that one does not have to set a story in the frozen North or the South Seas or in some remote century to warrant condemnation under the terms of this statement. For his protagonists the South, the Riviera beach, even the Piedmontese countryside, though all 'Italian', nevertheless represented the abnormal and the bizarre. All of them told the individual what he was not and where he did not belong. *Feria d'agosto* takes up the long-suspended thread of 'I mari del Sud' in an attempt to define the individual's reality in terms of an environment which is most properly his own.

Thus, in the early years of the war Pavese returned to his 'origins' in the Langhe in an artistic as well as a physical sense. This return involved not only spatial movement – Rome to Turin to the Langhe – but also temporal, for only in early childhood had he spent any appreciable time in the country. However, though that time was comparatively short, it was to Pavese's mind a crucial time, that of his most impressionable years, for 'at more or less ten years old for each one of us', he claimed, 'the die is cast'. Besides, 'origins' implied a good deal more than simply 'childhood environment'. It involved a whole culture, a traditional way of life to which his family had belonged for many generations and which came to him 'in the blood'. *Feria d'agosto*, therefore, becomes a kind of 'recherche du temps perdu' in order to arrive at the essential self that lies hidden beneath layer upon layer of experience which separates the individual's present from his childhood past. The tone and purpose of that journey, which begins in the present and goes back through memory into the past, are set by the following observation, taken from 'Fine d'agosto' (End of August):

In those summers, which by now have a unique colour in my memory, moments lie slumbering which a sensation, a word even can suddenly reawaken, and I am at once bemused by a sense of distance, incredulous at finding so much joy in a vanished, almost annihilated time. (*Feria* p. 12)

Much of Pavese's early theorising about myth in *Feria d'agosto* is often confused and even contradictory. What is essential to the theory was eventually set down in an essay entitled 'Il mito' (Myth), which Pavese wrote early in 1950 and published in the periodical *Cultura e realtà* (Culture and reality), later in the same year. In the essay he argues that the history of any people always reveals that

The various traditional practices of everyday life and festive observances – language, techniques, institutions and emotions – all are modelled on events that happened once and for all time, on divine patterns that lie – not only in a temporal sense – at the root of every activity: in order to happen a thing must already have happened, it must be rooted in something outside time. (*La lett. am.* p. 345)

The language which Pavese employs here and elsewhere in his discussion of myth belongs perhaps more properly to theology or metaphysics than to literature, and it is this apparent connection with mystery and metaphysics which has repeatedly brought the theory under heavy fire from critics. And indeed, Pavese *is* arguing for the existence of absolutes which stand outside time but which recur from time to time within the flow of time. It is to these absolutes, which are either social or particular to an individual, that he gives the name of myth. The passage just cited states uncompromisingly that these 'events ... happened once and for all time', that these absolutes have their origin 'outside time', so that if reality is created in the way he suggests, then apparently neither man as an individual nor mankind as a whole can have much control over that reality. It is not surprising that Pavese fell foul of the Italian Communist Party (to which he belonged from 1945 on), positing such a theory as this.

However, the theory is not as preternatural as it at first appears, for the myth, before it became such, was firmly grounded in materiality, and the expression 'outside time' has – in the context of the theory – a metaphorical and not a literal connotation:

Before it was a story, a miraculous event, every myth was simply a norm, a meaningful form of behaviour, a rite that sanctified reality. And it was also the impulse, the magnetic charge, which alone could induce men to do things. (*La lett. am.* p. 346)

If, in the development of a people's history, 'a norm' took on the aspect of 'a miraculous event', it was because men, for reasons probably not known even to themselves, made it so. For a people, a tradition of any kind, handed on from one generation to the next, especially where there were no written records, would indeed seem to celebrate or revive an event, an attitude, whose origin was 'outside time'. But it is not time as an absolute entity which is indicated, rather that which is relative to the whole span of time which represents the history of that people. Again though, we notice the terminology – 'sanctified reality' – and the reason for it is that a heightened significance given to such a 'norm' amongst primitive peoples invariably implied those values which Pavese acknowledges as 'none other than a religious attitude'. It is at this point that Pavese indicates his debt to Vico, and in particular to the following passage from the *Scienza nuova:*

> The first men, like children of the human race, being unable to formulate intellectual categories of things, had a natural urge to invent poetic categories, imagined universals, so as to be able to assign each particular species to its proper category, as to an idealised model or picture.[5]

What Vico called 'imagined universals' are substantially the same as Pavese's myths. The analogy made by Vico in passing between 'the first men' and 'children' was of the utmost significance in the development of Pavese's theory, and he extends it to include poets and 'all those who still do not live by reason, "human philosophy", or not wholly by reason'. Starting from Vico's pronouncements on the nature of the development of the history or character of a whole people, Pavese sets out to explore the development of the individual's reality (or personality) by applying more or less the same formula. The myths, whether at the individual or the collective level, are a spur to action, to the creation or extension of reality simply because they are believed in, accepted without question, precisely because they are not consciously recognised for whatever they are. When we, whether poets or not, endeavour to 'know ourselves' we are in effect attempting to do what Pavese claimed was the sole purpose of his writing, that is 'to clarify his own myths'.

First, however, we need to understand what Pavese took to be the significance of the myths to the development of individual personality. He explains it in the following terms:

> From our earliest years, from our childhood, from all those moments of our first, essential contact with things and with the world which are liable to catch a man off guard with their immediate, emotional impact, from all the 'first times', irreducible to rationality, from the auroral moments when an image, an idol, a prophetic tremor took shape in the mind as it confronted the amorphous, there comes a giddy sensation, as if rising from a whirlpool or rushing in through a door thrown wide open – a promise of conscious awareness, an ecstatic presentiment. (*La lett. am.* p. 348)

Again the language, at first glance, seems hieratic, but we must be clear why this is so. Pavese is attempting to describe the beginnings of the individuation process, and at the beginning the rational faculty is as yet totally undeveloped – one is aware of experience but is unable to give it a name, and so it is with almost all of those 'moments of our first, essential contact with things'. Those 'contacts' are retained by the memory not as words but as pictures or sensations and only much later does one come to give them a name, that is 'clarify them'. 'Image ... idol ... prophetic tremor' are thus representative of what, for the individual concerned, as yet has no name and, because he is still unaware of the significance of time, is not, from his point of view, located in time. The majority of our 'first, essential contacts' occur in very early childhood but the process continues perhaps even into our early teens. However, as rationality develops, the order of the process can even be reversed in the sense that we can know the names of objects or experiences before we meet them in reality, and having only the form (the name) without the content (the experience) only our imaginative faculty can come to our aid and provide a content. That imagined content will in some way colour the experience for us when we finally consciously possess it and thus make it something unique to us personally. When all or nearly all the 'first, essential contacts', which belong to the social environment in which the individual finds himself, have been made, then the first part of the individuation process, that of the assimilation of experience, is completed and the second part begins, the rediscovery and categorisation of each 'moment' or myth as it *recurs* in our subsequent life as – according to Pavese – it most surely will. When it does so we meet, in the flow of time, something which for us, individually, is essentially timeless, and that encounter, be it person, event, sensation or any other experience, is symbolic of that absolute reality which occurred *when we were unaware of what time was.*

To abandon oneself to the contemplation, the excavation of that moment, means to move outside time, to make contact with a metaphysical absolute, to enter a sphere of travail, of quest for a seed which cannot lose its immobility without becoming something else – conscious poetry, unfolded thought, responsible action – in other words, *history*. (*La lett. am.* p. 348)

The process is one of drawing the unknown or half-known into consciousness, from shadow into light. Whilst ever they remain undisclosed the myths 'radiate so much life, warmth and promise of light', for what is unknown has infinite possibility. Pavese, in his espousal of this view, is linked with Leopardi for whom life was always the implied promise of the not known, the unexplained. However, both accepted the rationalising process as inevitable, though regrettable, and both warn in no uncertain terms against the man or the poet who attempts in some way to evade it. These myths

disturb the mind in the same way as an important word which is only half remembered; every bit of spiritual energy is needed to clarify and define them, to possess them entirely. But to possess means to destroy, as we know. This destruction – which is, of course, a transformation – robs the violated myth of its uniqueness, the mysterious power of a symbol which is *believed in*. When a myth becomes poetry it loses its religious aura. When it goes on to become a concept ('human philosophy') the process is complete.

Then comes the warning,

Which is not to suggest that one's myths ought to be kept in cotton-wool. The overwhelming initial faith is sincere in so far as it spares no effort to better penetrate and possess its object. And there is no use pretending, for aesthetic reasons, that a mystery persists when in fact it has already been resolved into a clear image or a lucid concept.

Pavese is most emphatic in his condemnation of any attempted artificial preservation of the myth:

The law of the spirit is this: to bring one's own myths incessantly into conflict with reality and strive to resolve them into poetry or theoretical knowledge. Anyone who goes on tinkering with a myth after it is explained, penetrated, violated, is neither true believer nor poet nor scientist. He is a mere aesthete and nothing more. (*La lett. am.* p. 349)

Adverse critics of Pavese's theory and the novels and poetry which were influenced by it all too readily overlook the uncompromising position he took up with regard to the personal myth. Undoubtedly, it is possible to reason well but to contradict one's own rational beliefs in practice – Pavese himself was aware of this and admits as much, recognising that it is easy enough to be distracted from one's purpose and to be seduced by one's own myths, even for motives which he expressly condemns. There are instances in his work where one can argue that this has happened – but to see only that, with a sense of triumph, is to fail to recognise the nature of Pavese's problem. His whole makeup tempted him towards non-communication and withdrawal, towards the mysterious, the *selvaggio* (inhuman), so that that theory of myth took on the semblance of a life-line for him; it represented his struggle towards the rational, the essentially human and the rejection of his innermost self which, as early as 1936 he had seen as *voluttuoso* (self-indulgent) and condemned as such. But it is one thing to be convinced with the head and quite another to be convinced with the heart, and the inner conflict in which Pavese engaged was heavily weighted against him. In self-analysis it is always difficult to know whether or not one is being scrupulously honest, and if Pavese's work deviates from that 'law of the spirit' it is not necessarily because he is being deliberately self-indulgent or dishonest. Condemnation here – or, for that matter, approval – seems out of place.

The myth ultimately denies itself: it becomes its opposite – history – that which has a name and takes its place in consciousness. It is measured and sounded, its limits are known and it becomes, as a concept, a guide to action, a part of our *savoir vivre*. This process is continuous whether for the individual or for a whole society, but neither the one nor the other acts solely according to the dictates of reason (resolved myths). The irrational (our unresolved myths) spurs us to action but also to the comprehension of our acts, because it is the cause of a historical effect, a significant change. Pavese is insistent upon this connection between the myth and history, and upon the individual myth's potential contribution to historical change:

a myth worthy of the name can only arise on the ground of all existing culture, taking it for granted, and yet pointing beyond it, manifesting itself as an image which is mysterious and full of promise because it cannot be reduced even by the white-hot flame of our most rational theory. (*La lett. am.* p. 350)

What Pavese is saying here is that while our minds are in the grip of the irrational all rationality is abolished, time – a rational dimension or category – is abolished, and we are lifted out of time and brought face to face with that nameless entity, the myth, which began for us before that dimension of time had any meaning in our individual life. This process, it must be emphasised, is purely a function of memory, for, argues Pavese, 'It is precisely the repeatability of these myths, their ever-renewed uniqueness, that is celebrated in memory.'

If we allow that this is so, what is the function of the poet in relation to the myth? Pavese gives us his answer in the following terms:

The poet – creator of tales – jealously guards and studies these auroral glimmerings which are the starting-point and nourishment of every good tale. To write poetry means to show forth and give imaginative completion to a mythic seed. But it also means reducing this seed, by giving it concrete form, to an object of contemplation, detaching it from the maternal twilight of memory, and in fact ceasing to believe in it, as a mystery which is no longer mysterious. (*La lett. am.* pp. 350–1)

The theory of myth, despite its esoteric terminology, has no supernatural element in it. What Pavese has done is to bring a whole range of metaphysical concepts within the bounds of materiality and applied them to those realities whose existence is undeniable, but to which we can temporarily give no name. Individual myths have a social or cultural origin and when they are eventually clarified they re-enter the history from which they began, although changed in themselves as well as being the agents of change and discovery. Whether we accept such an interpretation of the individuation process or not we cannot condemn it on the grounds of mysticism, for Pavese posits no spirituality which transcends the material. In arguing that at a certain age the myths, which constitute an individual's core of essential reality, have all been assimilated and that after that nothing new will be added, Pavese seems to be denying the validity of direct action in bringing about any kind of change. However, we must bear in mind that he is here expressing an opinion about individuality, not about the collective. When this assimilation process is completed the individual is already engaged in that process of the clarification of those myths (though more often than not *unaware* of what he is about) and, theoretically, he may indeed exhaust them all – that is, come to a complete awareness of what he himself is. That the individual is limited is what Pavese is arguing and attempting to explain. However, the consequences of this process for the collective are significantly different:

a myth is obviously a revelation, an absolute, a timeless instant. But by its very nature it tends to become history, to happen among men: that is, by taking the form of poetry or theory it ceases to be a myth outside time and becomes subject to genetico-causal investigation by historians. (*La lett. am.* p. 349)

The myth which becomes 'poetry or theory' adds to the knowledge and therefore to the possibilities of change and progress within a society. What Pavese seems to envisage here – and he explicitly states that 'the experience of myth' is not just 'the privilege of the poet and of the thinker' but rather 'a universally human gift' – is a continuous process of clarification going on amongst all the individuals who comprise a given collective in a particular place. The 'pool' of knowledge, of conscious experience, which a society represents, is constantly being enlarged and thus the conditions in which succeeding generations will form their myths are always being changed. For the individual who, unlike the society, is bounded closely by time and limited possibilities of experience, the theory leads towards self-definition – the self being a unique absolute – whilst for a society, which is subject to a continuous process of change, its effect is dynamic.

During the war, Pavese does not seem to have been fully aware of these different implications of his theory; his failure to act at the crucial moment suggests that he made no distinction between its effects on the individual and on the society as a whole.[6] Later, he joined the Communist Party because – it has frequently been suggested – he felt guilt and remorse at having 'missed the boat'. Perhaps this is the explanation, or part of it. It is also possible that the success of the Resistance movement convinced him that action *could* bring progressive change for a society and that even writing could be an agent of such change, particularly if it concentrated on the task of bringing to light the myths of contemporary society. Pavese's thought did not remain static – a fact which is sometimes overlooked – and in his attitude to the business of living as well as to the business of poetry he was continually searching for new answers, new techniques. A failure to recognise this is to run the risk of falsifying the complex picture of his development. He was perpetually assailed by doubts which led to revisions and new revisions – the many corrections indicated in his diary bear witness to this. The significant breakthrough came with the theory of myth, yet even that took several years of trial and error to develop and perfect, as again his diary reveals.

What Pavese sought was some measure of certainty, that is, of fixity. Failing continually to locate it in relationships with women, in orthodox religion, in work, in politics – the more obvious sources of security in society – he believed, with the gradual evolution of his theory, that he had found it in his myths. One of the most revealing entries in his diary in this context is the following, written in 1939:

The worst misfortune of all is loneliness, and in fact, the supreme comfort – religion – consists in finding a companion who never fails, God. Prayer is an outlet, like talking to a friend. Art is equivalent to prayer, because it puts one, on the plane of ideas, in contact with someone who will benefit from it. Thus the whole problem of life is this: how to break one's own solitude, how to communicate with others. This explains the persistence of marriage, fatherhood, friendships. But why happiness should lie in these things, why one should be better off *communicating with another person* than on one's own, is a strange thing. Perhaps it's only an illusion: being alone is quite pleasant most of the time. Now and then it's nice to have a goatskin to pour yourself into then drink yourself out again: seeing that what we ask from others is what we already have within ourselves. The mystery is that we are not satisfied to look into ourselves and drink there, that we need to be given back to ourselves by other people. (*MV* 15 May 1939)

It was this link between God, paternity, marriage, and so on, which led Pavese to the suspicion that what he was looking for was a religion substitute. During the years in which he was writing *Feria d'agosto*, evolving his theory, he sought refuge and comfort for a time (see *MV*, 1944) in Catholicism. However, he found he was incapable of a sustained faith for, by definition, it was a contradiction of the rationality which, ever since 1936, he had striven so hard to make the guiding principle in his life. When he had eventually sufficiently clarified his theory of myth to be convinced that it would provide him, through poetry, with a way into his own reality and that of others, we find him wondering whether 'this will suffice as a substitute for the religious urge' (*MV* 17 September 1943). Even before it had taken shape in his mind, the theory was destined to be thought of in religious terms, even though it is a religion devoid of transcendental mystery.

Pavese's concern with childhood in *Feria d'agosto* constitutes both an exploration of his theory and an escape, through memory, into a lost paradise in which there was a sense neither of limitation nor of anxiety about future and past. He sees the child as living only for the present moment, unaware of any significance in his actions beyond the immediate one, even though, in reality, he is in the process of constructing his own destiny. It is the freedom of that unconsciousness which Pavese regrets losing as a mature man. For the child the *voluttuoso* is the norm, whereas for the man, whose destiny is to all intents and purposes fixed, there is so much outside him which he no longer has any hope of attaining, for it did not become a part of his myths when he too was at the beginning. In 'Mal di mestiere' (Missed vocation) he explains that

in childhood we were something else. Little unconscious brutes, and reality gathered us up as we gathered seeds and stones. We were in no danger then of admiring it and wanting to jump into its whirlpool. We were the whirlpool itself. But the secret story of everyone's childhood consists of those shocks and ruptures that uprooted us from reality, whereby we set ourselves against things and learned to appraise and contemplate them through language – today a shape, tomorrow a colour. What we hold most dear, then, will be this discordant concord of encounters, discoveries, development. (*Feria* pp. 186–7)

In many of the pieces in *Feria d'agosto* Pavese tries to view the child's expanding experience of the world through the eyes of a child narrator, in an attempt to get beyond the nostalgia and possible sentimentalism which might very well be the adult's reaction to the memory of his own formative years. Pavese is interested in the accumulation process itself and explores different aspects of it. In 'Primo amore' (First love) it is the traumatic discovery of sex by two young boys which is portrayed; in 'La giacchetta di cuoio' (The leather jacket) the destructive effect of a woman on the life of a man who is much admired by the child narrator; whilst in 'Le feste' (The festivals) violence and greed are closely observed. However, it is 'Il mare' (The sea) which perhaps gives the roundest picture of any of the accumulation and significance of myths in the life of the young child.

'Il mare' tells the story of two boys who set out, one evening, from their home deep in the Langhe, to walk to the sea. The grandfather of one of them, Gosto, once climbed to the top of a hill and, so the boy claims, from there saw the sea. For a long time the idea of a journey in search of the sea gradually takes shape in the minds of the two boys. The narrator tells us that 'I have always imagined the sea as a clear sky seen behind water' (*Feria* p. 75), and it is with this vague image in mind – an image which has been unconsciously culled from the words of those about him – that he sets out. After walking for a whole night and a good part of the following day, after various encounters, including one with a strange tramp-like character called Rocco, Gosto decides to go back home. He senses that they will not reach their objective and for him that is all that matters. The narrator is different in temperament and continues alone; for him the journey is everything, the sea only a pretext, a myth which will remain intact for him for years to come:

Now [he explains] it no longer mattered if I couldn't see the sea beyond Cassinasco. It was enough to know the sea was there, beyond the hills and the villages, and to think of it as I walked along between the hedges. (*Feria* p. 88)

This solitary journey has about it an atmosphere which is magical. So much that is only hearsay is accepted by the child as fact; so much depends on the workings of his imagination. At one point he falls asleep and dreams and the dream merges into reality when he awakes. 'The sky was full of stars,' he says, 'and I thought that Gosto was under the trees.' Yet he remembers he is alone, that Gosto had already gone back. There is a huge bonfire, and men and boys milling about it in the flickering shadows, and he shouts Gosto's name out loud. In the confusion and the darkness there are sounds and figures, but to the child all is obscure, and in order to give a meaning and a name to his experience he, true to Pavese's understanding of Vico, populates his dark world out of fantasy. It is this continuous groping for reality which Pavese evokes so well, as in the following passage:

Now and then you'd hear a voice from the road screaming in fright. The men would run over and start laughing, because the girls would be there waiting for them. A man grabbed me as I was about to pull out a branch. 'You fool,' he said, 'what if you fall in the fire?' He tore the branch out of my hands and ran off in the dark with some others, and they threw it down from the road, still burning. There was a lot of shouting and a woman's voice, then laughter and they began punching each other. If only Gosto were here, I thought. The flames were so high they lit up the whole valley. 'I wonder if they can see it from the sea,' I said, and whenever someone threw in a bunch of sticks I would look down the valley to see if the Belbo at least was lit up. I had a longing for clearings among the trees; I wanted to dance and to see all around from up there. (*Feria* p. 90)

The interplay between reality and the child's thoughts, the association of ideas and objects which occur in the flow of the narrative in this passage, show Pavese at his most sensitive. Straining to hear, to catch sight of, to understand – to clarify, in fact; that is the essence of 'Il mare'. But this is the time before understanding – which will come much later – and for the child only the vague, the imprecise, indistinct, the half-known, half-heard – in short, the myth – must fill the void. The story is full of parties, music, wine, food, bonfires, dancing, trees, the normality of the Langhe; and yet, for the child, they are electric, vibrant, suggestive, and all contribute to that atmosphere of magic in which, for Pavese, the child accumulates his own destiny.

'La città' (The city) constitutes yet another attempt on Pavese's part to illustrate and perhaps further clarify that fundamental conflict which he posits between town and country. Two students, both from the country, share a flat in the city. The elder of them, Gallo, though popular enough among his friends in the city, never attempts to sever his roots, which remain deep within the countryside of his origin, and he returns there quite contentedly after completing his studies. The narrator, however, experiences a growing sense of shame for his country origins, and even for Gallo, on whom he had previously looked with admiration. He tries to adapt himself to the ways of the city. He is strongly attracted to the sister of one of his city friends, Sandrino, and one summer, mainly in the hope of being able to be near her, he decides not to return home for the long vacation. He remarks on the sense of 'new life' which came to him as a result of that decision:

In the clear air the dark, corrugated rooftops struck me as an image of my new life – ephemeral hopes on a rough foundation. In that calm, that expectancy, I felt a sense of rebirth. (*Feria* p. 141)

Unfortunately, those 'hopes' are shortlived, for after only a few short weeks the girl goes off to the sea with her family and he is left disconsolate and alone in the half-empty city. It is in these circumstances, during this period of depression, that he meets up with Giulia, a former girl-friend of Gallo's, a girl to whom he himself had never felt particularly attracted. However, they drift together out of a mutual sense of loneliness and boredom and frustration. Then suddenly, one morning, Sandrino and his sister, Maria, turn up at the flat. At a glance the girl 'understands' the situation and she and her brother leave at once. Explanations, even if possible, would have been pointless. There is a cruel irony in this turn of events, for Maria has been the cause of his decision to stay in the city and then of his subsequent loneliness. Giulia fills a need for warmth and affection, as he does for her, but the rigid, conventional morality of the girl cannot admit this even as a possibility. Once again, a Pavesian character had foundered in the city, which is essentially alien to him, and again we are reminded of those words in 'I mari del Sud' which have such a long echo in Pavese's writing:

> La città mi ha insegnato infinite paure:
> una folla, una strada mi han fatto tremare,
> un pensiero talvolta, spiato su un viso.
> Sento ancora negli occhi la luce beffarda
> dei lampioni a migliaia sul gran scalpiccio.

(The city has taught me countless fears: a crowd or a street have made me tremble; sometimes even a thought glimpsed on someone's face. In my eyes I still feel the mocking light of thousands of street-lamps way above the great shuffling of people in the streets.)

Later, in *Il diavolo sulle colline* (The devil on the hills), a similar situation arises when Oreste, a *compagnuolo*, becomes infatuated with the indolent, dissipated wife of a drug addict. He too suffers because his relative purity is tainted by the relative corruption of the girl. However, neither here nor in 'La città' is Pavese taking a moralistic stand. He is concerned to show that city and country represent not merely two different ways of life but two different stages of civilisation and that the more 'advanced' values of the former will always leave the man from the country in a state of bewilderment. The converse is also true, however, as we have already seen in the case of Berto in *Paesi tuoi*. The myths of town and country are perforce different, and since (according to Pavese), they operate at the instinctive and not the rational level, they will always be a hidden source of conflict in a relationship such as those described above.

The search for one's self, for one's destiny, is carried on always on the frontiers of the unknown, or the half-known, and the poet, as interpreter of himself and of the world, is a pioneer who does battle with many chimeras, attempting to lure them out into the open to be recognised. Sometimes, however, the myth presents itself unexpectedly, in the shape of a symbol, in the normal run of events in the individual's life. In 'La vigna' (The vineyard), for example, the vineyard is just such a symbol which immediately connects the narrator, through memory, with something which occurred at some remote time in his past, probably in his childhood. This and any other such symbol is 'a magic door' out of time to the timeless moment. In 'Il campo di granturco' (The field of maize) we discover that the symbol

> that day was a field ... [however,] it might have been a rock overhanging a road, a solitary tree by the curve of a hill, a vine at the edge of a cliff (*Feria* p. 15)

and that for the narrator, the timeless moment is always recreated in time in 'natural forms'. It is these 'natural forms' which are both the objective manifestations of an internal landscape and the symbols in the flow of time of those absolute realities, the formative myths.

The journey back through memory always brings the poet, the clarifier of myths, into the twilight zone between consciousness and unconsciousness, and it is in 'Nudismo' (Nakedness) that Pavese gives us an allegory of the poet's descent to the level of the unconscious. Here we realise just how much Pavese had absorbed of the theories of Carl Gustav Jung, without actually committing himself to faith in the existence of a transcendental reality. In this piece the narrator reaches the *selvaggio* (the 'natural' in an essentially non-human sense), that which lies beyond consciousness, by discarding the trappings of civilisation, symbolised by clothing and language, and by locating '... just one patch of ground that has not been dug and cultivated by human hands' (*Feria* p. 196), in which to immerse himself physically. The nakedness of the body, the natural, non-rational part of man, is brought into contact with the rest of nature. 'In exceedingly rare moments,' he admits, 'I lose my self-awareness and forget my body.' He lies there surrounded by stones, roots and grasses, his eyes riveted on the sky above, cut off from all that is human:

The shadow grows and I watch the wood and the still water. I couldn't express what I see and what I am thinking. Words are grass and roots, they are stones, mud, brightness – there aren't any others – but my body does not accept them. (*Feria* p. 190)

Language, which separates man from reality, is rejected by the body in its descent from consciousness:

Enter into the grass, enter into the stone: that's what my body would say, but it is not enough. This hollow is a piece of matter without a name; I must move, hear it, touch it. I have to force myself not to clutch the roots, climb up into the forest among the thorns and green trunks, and walk there. I contain myself, touching my body. (*Feria* p. 191)

There is a mental struggle, the assertion of rationality over the irrational, instinctive call of nature; but it is a struggle. Like Leopardi, Pavese realises that nature is still man's greatest enemy, but as the enemy within, always tempting him away from what is essentially human. Pavese's failure to act in the armed struggle against Nazi–Fascism represented his refusal to capitulate to the irrational and inhuman, the degradation of war. The bestiality which the war brought to the surface once again in the history of man makes it impossible to disagree with Pavese's analysis, whatever we may think about his refusal to participate. It is in rationality that man's future lies and in acknowledging this Pavese is endorsing the Enlightenment view:

Everything is marked by the eye and the words of men, which come from the fields like a quiet breathing; yet they do not penetrate down here where the water and slime and sweat stagnate and say nothing. (*Feria* p. 196)

This is Pavese's true position. Refuge is found ultimately not in myth but in the rational and human, the 'quiet breathing' which is surrounded by the stagnant, meaningless world of the *selvaggio*.

The passage, which concludes 'Nudismo', continues: 'Here every day I find life, but then I stretch out my black body and lie like a dead man'; and the poet's position 'between the human and the non-human' is defined. However, unlike the 'religious' mediator, the poet is concerned to destroy, not to preserve, the mystery, to give it meaning and possess it for himself and his fellow-men. It was this position, defined to Pavese's satisfaction in *Feria d'agosto*, which led him to re-examine many Greek myths in the highly schematised *Dialoghi con Leucò* (Conversations with Leukothea) in order to demonstrate how the gradual encroachment of rationality upon the *selvaggio* heralded a humanisation and yet an ever-growing sense of limitation for mankind. Yet for Pavese, just as for the Leopardi of 'La ginestra' (The broom-flower), where Vesuvius symbolises the tremendous physical power of nature, the *selvaggio* is never really destroyed but is always ready to reassert itself at any moment. The myth may be rationalised at one stage in history, but may well return again at a later point in time, so that man's accumulation of knowledge throughout history is a process of ebbing and flowing rather than an unbroken forward movement. Let us be clear at this point what Pavese means by 'clarifying' in relation to myth. It is the possession through the recognition and naming of experience; but the mythical substance is indestructible, and will return again and again. Every age has its myths, and although the overall evolution of civilisation reveals a slow, steady gain of reason over the irrational, it is impossible to foresee a time when that triumph will be absolute. The individual, in his short span of time, may add something of value from the rationalisation of his personal myths, but there is no guarantee that what has been gained will not again be lost. The light, then, is at best only ever partial and is forever surrounded by darkness.

7

The Language of Myth in *'Dialoghi con Leucò'*

Of all Pavese's works that which has met with most antagonism (and generally continues to do so) is *Dialoghi con Leucò* (Conversations with Leukothea).[1] We have long grown accustomed to reading the disparaging and dismissive comments made about it on grounds which range from the 'purely' literary to the political; the following indicates the shortsightedness of even a normally sensitive critic, when dealing with this particular work: 'The adolescent's destiny is ... self-pityingly mythologised and generalised in the *Dialoghi con Leucò* ... '[2] It is not that the judgement is wrong but that *Dialoghi con Leucò* is much more than just that.

On the negative side, its style appears pretentious, the genre anachronistic, and this was no less so when it first appeared in 1947, for at that time Italians had in their immediate past been made aware of the apparent efficacy of united action in changing the course of their own destiny, and were in no mood for either literary *passatismo* or a fatalism which seemed to belong with the stagnation of the Fascist *ventennio* rather than with the present and future. It contrasted starkly with the *neo-realismo* which was just beginning to emerge as both a literary and a cinematographic style. Pavese, in that he saw the present as merely a brighter, albeit temporary aspect of a total human experience which was much more gloomy, was writing very much against the tide of hope and opinion. It was in the euphoric climate of the Italy of 1945-6 that Pavese attempted coolly and rationally to take stock of the human situation. This is not to suggest that he was not affected by that highly contagious optimism which, for a time, dominated the Italian political and social scene. As we have seen, he was a man of strong emotions and indeed one of the main, conscious aims of his writing was always to temper the heart with the mind. It was a part of his ascetic self-discipline. Yet he joined the Communist Party; he wrote political articles for *L'Unità*; and he quickly composed his one overtly political novel, *Il compagno*. In all of this, it is hard to believe that the determining factor was simply and solely a cool rationality.

There appears then to be some contradiction in Pavese's behaviour as man and writer at this time, and by this I do not wish to imply that the *Dialoghi* is not a 'committed' book (indeed, on Pavese's own terms it is his *most* 'committed' piece of writing), but simply that he appears to have tried to run with the hare and hunt with the hounds – a sure indication that he had formed no conclusive views about the human condition – indeed about whether there even *was* a human condition. So, although the *Dialoghi* presents a tightly schematised, more or less pessimistic view of man and the possibilities open to him, Pavese was still prepared to discover that he was wrong, and in writing this book he took steps – the only sort of steps he knew – to prove himself wrong. If this was so, it must have considerable bearing on the book the *Dialoghi* turned out to be. In reading it, we do not have to go very far before we encounter contradictions and apparent loss of direction, and this is primarily because the book is as exploratory in its perspective as the novels and poems which preceded it. We have some hint of this in a letter which Pavese wrote to Mario Untersteiner, in January 1948, when he observed that:

You have read the *Dialoghi* just as I dreamed they would be read, unravelling their motifs, *interpreting* them. In short, you have treated these *Dialoghi* precisely as you would treat a mythological document ...

Without any doubt, the meaning of this tangle that the *Dialoghi* are, even for me, is located in the search for human autonomy. (*Lett. II*, p. 211)

There is, I think, a suggestion in the words 'tangle' and 'unravelling' that the collection probably contained much more than he had consciously put there, possessing all the tension and anticipation of the coiled spring. It is as much a series of questions as of answers, and it is this feature which causes its unevenness. Dogged always by pessimism, Pavese nevertheless struggled against it continuously, and the *Dialoghi* represent yet another, indeed major battlefield in that war.

Of the critics who have given more than just a passing consideration to the *Dialoghi*, only Eugenio Corsini has taken the trouble to bring out its positive aspects and, in so doing, to promote a more balanced critical perspective. However, even he approaches it obliquely, for the main concern of his essay is to attempt a definition of Pavese's classicism[3] by identifying and classifying his sources. Here, I am not concerned with those aspects of his researches, but rather with his understanding of Pavese's *Weltanschauung* in the work. The following seems particularly helpful and encouraging:

Men, therefore, are the true protagonists of the *Dialoghi con Leucò*. It is they who have within them, in their all-embracing nature, the chaotic, titanic world of monsters from their origins as well as the serene cosmos of harmony, order and peace. It is between these two opposite poles that the life of man is stretched, not flowing like an unruly flood towards the eternal nothingness of death, but coming to the threshold of a new immortality, even though it is conceived in terms which are entirely earthly and immanent. The insistence on the demiurgic function of the word – in its full, original sense of *logos*, the articulated word-thought – brings us to an understanding of what it is, even for Pavese (and it is here that we have the highest point of his classicism), the creator of this new immortality: the word, which gives a name to all things, creates order out of chaos with its perennial myths, it stimulates life in the mysterious with its stories which seek out the original event, it evokes the immortal harmony of poetry from the womb of the indistinct and the irrational. Here too, therefore, the Muses 'stand guard' over time and eternity, and this is the most important message, though misunderstood, of *Le muse* [The muses] and of *Gli dèi* [The gods], which bring the *Dialoghi con Leucò* to a memorable and resounding close.

The *Dialoghi* explore and chart recurring themes in the history of man's struggle with his environment. Those themes are representative of quintessential human experience which, because never quite managing to break free from its own intrinsic limitations, is by its nature tragic. Pavese manipulates the body of myths with which he was most familiar, the Greek, with the aim of creating universal paradigms of those themes – and in this was probably influenced by the work of Jung and Kérényi in their attempts to establish a scientific connection between the so-called archetypes of the collective unconscious and myths common to different cultures.[4] The myths already testified, in their original forms, to the limitations set on mankind (by the gods) and to man's inevitable defeat in his unequal struggle. Pavese is thus in harmony with the spirit of those myths when using them as a medium for his own more or less fatalistic suspicions about the nature of human endeavour. And here it is worth recalling Pavese's aspirations with regard to the *Dialoghi*:

I shall not try and conceal from you the fact that in composing this little book I was, if you like, seeking to make a place for myself in the illustrious

Italian tradition – humanistic and speculative – which stretches all the way from Boccaccio to d'Annunzio. (*Lett. II*, p. 218)

If, in certain of its aspects, *Dialoghi* seems to belong with the more recent, decadent exponents of that tradition, we should not lose sight of either its humanism or its speculative character. To see only a 'Pavese decadente' is to fail to appreciate the singular contribution which he made through that book to the furtherance of 'the illustrious Italian tradition'. Corsini reopened the prematurely closed case of *Dialoghi*, revealing a great deal more than merely multiple illustrations of Pavese's 'what has been determines what will be', and thus emphasised the need to look again at this work, which Pavese himself prized more highly than anything else he ever wrote.[5]

The underlying assumption in *Dialoghi* is that at some point a fundamental change came about in human consciousness, a shift from instinct as the dominant motivating factor in behaviour to the predominance of rationality. With that shift man's self-awareness set him apart from all other living things. This is a view Pavese shared with two writers of that 'illustrious Italian tradition', Vico and Leopardi. As has already been shown, he made use of the former's analogy between 'the first men' and 'children of the human race',[6] while in a reference to the latter, he claimed for the *Dialoghi* that 'with that book, I had wanted to try and write my *Operette morali* (Little moral essays)' (*MV* 10 July 1974).[7]

The Titan–Olympian conflict, which is central in *Dialoghi*, is symbolic of a variety of dialectical processes. It is the movement from pre-history to history, from darkness to light, from childhood to maturity, from *selvaggio* (the untamed) to the civilised, even perhaps from 'feudalism' to 'capitalism'; whilst it also reflects the different levels of consciousness posited by the psychologists with whose work Pavese was most familiar – Freud and Jung – in particular the Freudian thesis of Id, Ego and Superego. Whatever its configuration, however, it is always accompanied by struggle, suffering, violence and the shedding of blood. If the general trend is towards a more rational world, the process is continually frustrated, even, at times, reversed. Pavese, unlike Leopardi, did not see the onslaught of reason as progressive or even inevitable; the rate at which it occurs is well-nigh imperceptible. Each generation has its myths, as does each individual – some disappear, explained away by reason (or new myths), but many return at some future 'season', for the essential myths are indestructible.

On 4 August 1947, Pavese wrote in his dairy – apparently

contradicting, the claims made in the Preface to *Dialoghi*:

(From Harrison *Prolegomena* etc. p. 650.[8]
The Olympians are equally unconcerned about the Before and After; they are neither the fountain of life nor its goal. Moreover, another of their characteristics is that, with the strictest limitations, they are *human*. They are not one with the life that is in the beasts, the currents and the forests, and which is in men. Eros 'who has his feet on the flowers' and who 'sleeps in the hollows' is a part of all life, is Dionysos and Pan. Under the Athenian influence Eros is enclosed in purely human form, but the *Fanes* of Orpheus was polymorphous, a god-beast wrapped in mystery. – Without being aware of it, you applied this idea in the *Dialoghetti* by taking up cudgels for the bestial world of the Titans against that of the Olympians.)

Quite apart from the information about the nature of the Olympians – to which we shall return shortly – this passage suggests Pavese's antipathy towards whatever it was they represented, as well as ranging man on the side of 'beasts', 'currents' and 'forests'. A little less than a month before he made this discovery in Harrison, Pavese had noted with reference to the *selvaggio* (the principle of blind, instinctual motivation) that in his 'favola perenne' (perennial fable) 'the untamed, the Titanic, the bestial and the reactionary are overcome by the urban, the Olympian and the progressive ... You exalt order by describing chaos'. Clearly, there is a contradiction between the one conclusion and the other, as Pavese himself seems to recognise in the paragraph which precedes this statement: 'You dream of the countryside, the Titan – *the untamed* – but you appreciate the good sense, the order, the understanding ... of the city sidewalks.' It is this hesitation which makes of *Dialoghi* – and not only for Pavese – 'a tangle'. Some clue to the causes of this apparent equivocation is suggested in *Le streghe* (The witches), which, incidentally, was probably the first dialogue to be written, despite its position in the collection.[9] What it does is to seek to differentiate between the worlds of 'beasts', 'gods' and 'men', and it is in their individuation that the contradiction is perceived. Speaking of Ulysses, Circe explains:

he didn't know why I smiled. Often, he didn't even know I was smiling. Once I thought I had explained to him why beasts are nearer to us immortals than is man with his intelligence and courage. The beasts which feed, mate and have no memory. He answered me by saying that in his own country a dog was awaiting his return, a poor dog which was perhaps already dead, and he told me its name. Do you realise, Leukothea, that dog had a name. (*Dialoghi* p. 145)

What is significant here, despite Circe's assertions about the relationships of the three orders of being to each other, is that Ulysses, the real, human hero of *Dialoghi*, though not able to refute the assertions outright, illustrates how man attempts to possess the 'beast', by giving it a name and human attributes ('a dog was awaiting his return'). We learn a little later that Ulysses had sought to possess the goddess herself, by the same technique:

> In my bed, Ulysses called me by many names. Every time there was a name. At first it was like the cry of a beast, of a pig or a wolf, but he himself gradually realised they were all syllables of a single word. He called me by the names of all the goddesses, of our sisters, by the mother's names, by the names of living things. It was like a struggle against me, against Fate. He wanted to give me a name, to hold me, to make me human. He wanted to break something. He put a lot of intelligence and courage into it – and he had plenty of both – yet he never knew how to smile. He never realised what the smile of the gods is – we who know what Destiny is.
> (*Dialoghi* p. 145)

There are several points worth nothing here; perhaps of greatest importance is the struggle of the human to possess the divine, albeit in wholly human terms, for Ulysses has no aspirations towards immortality. Earlier we learnt that he 'did not wish to become a pig' and 'did not wish to become a god, either' (p. 144); it was as though (Circe surmises) 'He wanted ... to hold me, to make me human.' The struggle 'against me, against Fate' was identical with that which had begun for man 'like the cry of the wild beast', his long struggle towards humanity through rising above the merely instinctive, driven on by 'intelligence and courage'. Ulysses had already refused the soft option of becoming 'a god'. 'You know how much that silly Calypso begged him', says Circe, reminding us of Ulysses' other dialogue *L'isola* (The island), for 'He wanted to break something' – the wall of incomprehension separating him from the 'beasts' and the 'immortals'. But why? Merely curiosity or perhaps the urge to dominate? The former certainly loomed large in his attitudes, whilst the latter must be discounted altogether when we remember that by becoming a god he could indeed have achieved such dominance. There was a more important reason, the desire for wholeness, however dimly perceived. Man had his distant origins amongst the beasts (and here we should recall the grouping together of 'beasts', 'currents' and 'forests' with 'man' which Pavese had found and presumably approved in Harrison, whilst composing *Dialoghi*) and retained many of their characteristics ('the beasts which feed and mate' as Circe puts it), whilst through the growing power and sophistication of his reason he was moving towards the privileged position of the gods (of 'we who know what Destiny is'). The desire to possess the world of the superhuman and the animal was nothing less than the desire to possess himself, in his entirety.

Pavese's clearest statement about man's relationship to the other two orders of being appears in his diary on 24 February 1947; in pointing to the outcome of the war between the two orders of gods, it emphasises the fragmentation of reality for man, resulting from the fragmentation of his consciousness, inevitable concomitant of the dominant intrusion of rationality into his daily decisions. Differentiation and organisation into categories and hierarchies had been the most obvious manifestations of this change in his consciousness:

Kronos was a monster but his rule was the Golden Age. He was conquered and from his defeat Hades (Tartarus), the Blessed Isle and Olympus were born – unhappiness and happiness opposed and institutionalised.

The Age of the Titans (monstrous and golden) is that in which no distinction was made between men, monsters and gods. You regard reality as being forever Titanic, that is, like a human–divine chaos (=monstrous), which is the perennial form of life. You present the Olympian gods, who are superior, happy, detached, as the wreckers of this humanity, towards which, however, the Olympians are in the habit of doing favours which derive from a nostalgia for the Titans, or from caprice, or from compassion rooted in that Age.

The Olympians are not the creators, nor will they have any effect upon the final outcome of the created world; their function is merely organisational that of imposing temporary law and order upon mankind. They, because representative of the rational principle in man, largely dictate the conditions of the relationships between the three orders in the current phase of history. The supervention of the rationalising–organising principle in the life of man is mythologised in *Gli uomini* (Mankind), where Kratos (who, according to Hesiod, had assisted the Olympians in their struggle against the Titans), in speaking of the new order and its leader, Zeus, observes:

There is something which is not as it was before. Our mother told of it: 'The storm will come and the seasons will change.' This son of the Mountain, who commands with a nod, is not like the old lords were – the Night, the Earth, the old Sky and Chaos. You could say the world is divided. At one time things used to happen. Everything came to an end, and it was something whole which lived. Now, however, there is a law and a mind. (*Dialoghi* pp. 181–2)

These characteristics of the observed change are those already mentioned – a sense of difference and division, of hierarchy with an attendant authoritarianism, of the imposition of an absolute law which, paradoxically, has destroyed the 'something whole which lived'.[10] This theme of division and alienation is also the subject of *La nube* (The cloud), the dialogue with which *Dialoghi* begins. In response to Ixion's 'And what is it that is changed ... on the mountains?' La Nube explains:

> Neither the sun nor the water ... it is the Fate of man which is changed. There are monsters. Limitations are set on you men. The water, the wind, the rock and the cloud are no longer yours, you can no longer clasp them to you, begetting and living. Other hands now hold the world. There are laws, Ixion. (*Dialoghi* pp. 11–12)

The 'laws' are those generated by the rationalising consciousness of man in his new phase of awareness, those of division and hierarchy. 'There are monsters' in the sense that they are now *seen as such* and called such by a differentiating and categorising consciousness, whereas previously they had existed on an equal footing in the same world as man. The defeat of the Titans is the allegory of this significant change in man's view of that world and of the relationships within it.

However, it is in his changed view of death that the supreme limitation is placed upon man by the extension of his rationality and knowledge. Previously, La Nube explains, 'death' was 'something which happened, like day and night', inevitable and unquestioned by man, of which he had no fear and to which he gave no thought. Under the new order its significance has undergone a real transformation, which is explained in terms of the meaning of the actions of the individual. Under the old dispensation each act performed was thought of (if indeed it was *thought of* at all) as complete in itself and had no significance beyond itself, whereas under the new, La Nube insists, 'your actions have a meaning which goes on into the future'. Each action, that is, has positive or negative value for the gods: 'The things that you do or don't do, what you say, what you seek – everything pleases or displeases them'. Everything is recorded on the balance sheet which, ultimately, will determine whether or not the individual will be allowed to share in the imagined eternal bliss of the gods after his physical death. Here, La Nube spells out what life after death *really* is:

> And if you upset them – if, by mistake, you disturb them on their Olympus

– they hurtle down upon you and they give you death, that death they know so well, a bitter taste which goes on and which you suffer (*Dialoghi* p.13)

but the eternal death (or eternal life – for the one is as negative as the other, as the *whole* of *Dialoghi* makes plain) that the gods bring to man is not the oblivion of absolute unconsciousness and reunification with the earth, as it had been under the Titans; nor is it the best moments of this earthly life eternally prolonged, as men might wish. Indeed, La Nube warns, 'They will turn you into a shadow, but a shadow that wants life again and never to die again.' And this is the experience of Sappho in *Schiuma d'onda* (Sea-foam), notwithstanding that her earthly life had been so unhappy that it had led her to seek death by her own hand; and it is so because 'that death which they [i.e. the Olympian gods] know so well, a bitter taste which goes on', is the state of their own petrified existence, that is of an absolute security, of omniscience, of – in short – eternal *noia* (tedium). Their fixed smile, whatever else it may be, is also an ironical comment on their own unenviable condition. This condition (which men, in their ignorance of its true nature, long for all their earthly lives) permeates and distorts the life of the individual and consequently of whole societies, with its ever-present fear of death, which was previously accepted as was any other natural event. Death is now also life-in-death, the fake promises and threats of eternal existence; but, equally, it is death-in-life, a source of continuous *inquietudine*, which takes man away from the moment as it comes to the after-life and its consolations: a shift from the natural-present to the supernatural-future.

The trick of immortality is discussed in *Il mistero* (The mystery) by Demeter and Dionysos; Demeter suggests it as a way of preventing human bloodshed, which derives from fear of the emptiness which death now is for man. The 'trick' is 'constructed' almost cynically, even though its motivation is pity for suffering humanity, for it is merely 'a story', which men will be induced to accept as truth, and live out according to its precepts: 'What is it you want to do?' Dionysos asks. Demeter replies:

To teach them that they can be our equals the other side of suffering and death. But I want us to tell them. To teach them just as the corn and the vine go down into Hades to be born, so too for them death is new life. To give them this story. To teach them a destiny which is entwined with ours. (*Dialoghi* pp. 190–1)

To which the incredulous, uncomprehending Dionysos rightly suggests, 'They'll die just the same'. So they will, agrees Demeter, but they, being dead, will never know that: 'They will die and they will have conquered death.' It is not the fact of dying which is of significance but the frame of mind in which one dies. 'They'll no longer fear death nor will they need to placate it by shedding the blood of others.' At last Dionysos understands (as in Plato's dialogues, this common, if crude device of one who is 'in the know' explaining ultra-graphically to some conveniently slow-witted companion becomes irritating): 'It will be the tale of eternal life ... They will not know Destiny and they will be immortal.' But then comes a cautionary note, countering her optimism as to its effects on the tenor of human life: 'But don't hope to staunch the flow of blood.' Not quite understanding, perhaps, the thought behind the words, Demeter admits that with the prospect of eternal life, men may possibly neglect their earthly one ('these fertile fields'); which was precisely the danger discussed in *La nube*. However, this is not quite what Dionysos has in mind:

In the meantime, yes – he in turn concedes, though with a hint of the secondary importance of the observation – But once the corn and the vine have the significance of eternal life, do you know what men will see in the bread and the wine? Flesh and blood, as they do now, as they always do. And flesh and blood will gush forth, no longer to placate death, but so as to reach the eternal which awaits them. (*Dialoghi* p. 191)

Demeter is amazed by this confident assertion: 'One would think that you see into the future. How can you say that?' It is in Dionysos' reply, the closing words of the dialogue, that the cautionary – and in 1945, unfashionable – philosophy of the author surfaces: 'It's enough to have seen the past, Demeter, believe me. But I'll go along with you. It will be just a story.' In Pavesian terms, 'reality' is 'just a story', the creation of the mythologising human imagination in response to some deeply felt necessity. It usually has no bearing on 'truth', the way things are in fact; it corresponds, as panacea, to 'illusion' in the poetry and thinking of Leopardi. As Pavese was to write somewhat later than *Dialoghi*: 'The *selvaggio*, as such, has no reality. It is what things *were*, in the degree that they were not human. However, in as much as things interest us, they *are* human' (*MV* 10 July 1947): the *selvaggio*, as the natural rhythms and forms of all life, presents man with the 'raw material' from which he creates the myths he believes in as 'reality'. Emphatically, however, there *is* an order of existence outside the orbit of 'things in as much as they interest us' – the 'non-human', the *selvaggio*, from which *homo rationalis* has long been severed but which is the condition of his very existence. It is that stratum which, for Pavese, is 'truth', the irrational, driving forces and rhythms in nature and human nature, that which has no name but nevertheless exists as the pre-condition of all other existence, as an inescapable superstructure, the Titan.

The great change which came about in human consciousness is identified as a propensity for interpreting the world rather than merely living life as animals and other living but inanimate forms appear to do. This theme is central not only to *Il mistero* but also, in particular, to *Gli dèi, Le streghe* and *Gli uomini*.

Gli dèi differs from all the other dialogues in that it takes place at a time after the human race has vanished. The two speakers are not named, for men, who gave the names and kept them alive, are no longer there. In an absolute sense, it is the realisation of Pavese's 'what has been determines what will be', for the earth has returned to its pre-Olympian state. One of the speakers, referring to the wonders which constituted human 'reality', contemplates 'whether they really did see such things', and the answer is: 'Who can say? But yes, they saw them all right. They told their names in stories, nothing more – and that's the whole difference between fable and truth' (*Dialoghi* p. 211). It is by giving a name to the hitherto unnamed that man 'creates' reality and the *favola* (fable) thereby replaces *il vero* (truth) in his mind; he possesses, but what he possesses is the name, not *il vero* – as one of the speakers insists: 'Without doubt, they saw what we hardly know ... They saw tremendous, unbelievable things, and didn't even marvel at them.' What becomes eminently clear in this final dialogue is that existence for the speakers – who or whatever they may be – has been greatly impoverished by the disappearance of man, and that whatever they now know and possess is what men taught them and created for them, in the mistaken belief that it was their gods, not themselves, who created and extended possibility. The title of this dialogue is ambiguous; we begin reading believing that it refers to the speakers, but when we have heard it, we suspect that it may, after all, refer to man himself, so clearly the greatest of all creators. One of the speakers, asked whether he believes in the reality which men created, replies emphatically:

I believe in whatever any man has hoped for and suffered for. If at one time they climbed up on to these rocky heights or searched about in the marshes of death beneath the sky, it was because they found there something that we don't know about. It wasn't bread or pleasure or that health which is so dear to them. These things have their place, but not here. And we who live far off along the margins of the sea or in the fields, we have lost this other thing. (*Dialoghi* p. 213)

Urged to specify what they have lost, he explains that it is the capacity for belief in, and therefore invention of, the supernatural, the 'incredible encounter', which burst through the limits imposed by *il vero* and constructed a whole order of reality whose existence was only in the mind, but was so successfully projected into the objective world that it profoundly changed its character, complicating yet enriching it. It is Bia, in *Gli uomini*, who expresses the admiration and envy of all the immortals for man, when she argues that:

Poor worms they are but everything among them is unforeseen, a discovery. We know what beasts are like, we know the gods, but not even we know the depths of those hearts. Amongst them, there are even those who dare to set themselves against Destiny. It is only by living with them and for them that you can savour the world. (*Dialoghi* p. 184)

This admiration, whilst centring on man's ability to create a new vision of life, which for the immortals is ever the same, goes beyond that of the speaker in *Gli dèi* for it includes 'anyone who dares to set himself against Destiny'. Here, we must return to *Le streghe* for Circe's experiences with Ulysses bear on the question of Destiny and human attitudes towards it, but particularly Ulysses', for he is the type of those 'who dare to set themselves against Destiny'. The gods know that both they and mankind are living out a destiny which is determined by *il vero*, by what Leopardi had termed 'l'infausta verità' (the unfortunate truth). Men in general, however, do not have such knowledge, except sporadically, exceptionally (as in the case of some poets). 'They don't feel themselves to be acting a part as we do', Circe explains, 'their lives are so short that they cannot bear things which have already been done or which are already known.' Most men live by their own created myths and even death, which they must recognise as an inescapable destiny, 'they delude themselves into believing ... will change things for them'. Yet, occasionally, they have an inkling of Destiny even as they are living it, so that particular myths no longer serve, and so it is with Ulysses, for, says Circe, 'he wept that day when I told him of the long journey which lay ahead of him and the descent into Avernus and the pounding darkness of the Ocean' (*Dialoghi* p. 146). Nevertheless, the knowledge is ultimately strength to him, a hardening of his will and determination, for 'These tears ... clear the vision and give strength.' Tears not of fear, we learn, but of anger and disappointment that 'his last voyage was imposed on him by Fate, it was something already known'. The adventure of the voyage always into a new unknown is lost in this knowledge, and he becomes an actor, a mere marionette, in a series of mechanical actions. And yet, even as he asks, 'Then why do it?' we learn that he is buckling on his sword and walking towards the shore, and it is this boundless courage – 'he ran towards death knowing what it was, and enriching the earth with his words and his deeds' – which has such a profound effect upon Circe, for she admits, 'That was the only time that, without smiling, I looked into the face of my destiny and lowered my eyes' (*Dialoghi* p. 147). Circe too has learnt the art of living by illusion, pretending she does not know her destiny, even forgetting she knows it:

Sometimes I forget what we know, and then I amuse myself as if I were a girl. As if all these things happened to the great ones, to the Olympians, and happened like this, unavoidable, yet all absurd and unforeseen. What I never foresee is precisely having foreseen, knowing every time what I shall do and what I shall say – and what I do and say is thus always new, surprising, like a game. (*Dialoghi* p. 148)

This 'game' is what man's mythical interpretation of his life amounts to, and Ulysses has understood this and defined it for her. He knows that there is a destiny, though not its content (except when she reveals it to him); nor does he wish to know it; life for him is 'like that game of chess', which he has taught her, 'all rules and conventions but so beautiful and full of surprises, with its pieces of ivory' – and the suggestiveness of the 'pieces of ivory' is significant. He insists 'that game is life itself ... a way of conquering time', and she, too, far from reducing him to 'a pig', 'a wolf' or, for that matter, 'a god', in the face of a revealed destiny, is herself infected by the only immortality that human beings ever know, that of 'the memory they bear with them and the memory they leave behind'; for that is what Ulysses has become for her, obsessive memory, and it is memory – along with rationality – which distinguishes man from all other forms of life, and which is the great source of his myths and created reality. In this dialogue, the myth is indeed fertile, for there is more than just a hint that man, through being true to his own best nature, has begun to reach out and move towards his own concept of the divine – and wholly on his own terms. Circe is not one of 'the great ones ... the Olympians', yet she *is* an immortal and shares with 'the great ones' many of the attributes which are denied mankind. If man can make conquests such as this made by Ulysses, he may yet reach the tremendous heights which, in other circumstances, Leopardi and a whole tradition of Enlightenment thought had considered might possibly be within his capabilities. Not so, it should be urged, is the possibility of achieving happiness, for with both Leopardi and Pavese the growth of rationality and a steadfast opposition to the natural determinism it inevitably revealed could only lead in the other direction; rather a growth in dignity, magnanimity and human brotherhood. Quite apart from this reaffirmation by Pavese of his faith and belief in man, there is in the figure of Circe herself an interesting reflection of an attitude which, to a greater or lesser extent, was Pavese's own. As a poet (an 'unacknowledged legislator', as Shelley puts it), Pavese believed he had greater insight into life's processes and rhythms than the average man, that he was, in effect, one of the lesser gods – like Circe. However, also like Circe, he would often rather have been without the knowledge (and its consequences) that his 'privileged' state afforded him, and he too, on occasions, tried to behave as though there were no Destiny, so that – in the words of Circe – 'whatever I do and say becomes, as a consequence, ever new, full of surprise, like a game ...' (*Dialoghi* p. 148). Oedipus, who in Greek mythology was clearly 'marked by Destiny', reveals, in *La strada*, the inevitable sense of futility which grips any man once he has realised that the decisions he makes, the actions he performs, are imposed on him, as if from outside. The knowledge that destiny exists brings with it a state of acute anxiety, as he explains to his interlocutor:

I was born to reign among you. For anyone who is sick even the best of fruit can only cause discomfort and nausea. Well, my sickness is my destiny – the fear, the ever-present horror of fulfilling what is already known. I knew – I have always known – that I was like the squirrel which thinks it is climbing and is merely rotating its cage. And I wonder: who was Oedipus? (*Dialoghi* p. 85)

Even experience, which in a state of 'unknowing' can provide real pleasure, is to the man who knows he is fettered by Destiny merely further proof of his burden. The question then arises whether the sentient, rational, recording part of us has any reality which is apart from, not governed by, that destiny, or are we merely 'a game' – 'shadows, a nothingness' – as Hermes suggests to Meleager (p. 71)? Oedipus begins by believing that he alone has been specially selected for a specific role in history. The Mendicante (Beggar), however, shows him that although his particular destiny is indeed unique, it is so only in terms of content, for a destiny, always unique, is the lot of every man. Oedipus speaks of the 'mountain of childhood', image of that period in which, quite unwittingly, we were creating our own destiny, and it is this image which is taken up by the Mendicante and expanded as a symbol of the predestined life: 'But all of us have the mountain of childhood', he argues. 'And no matter how far we wander, we find ourselves back on its pathways. It is there that we were made what we are' (pp. 86–7). But, as Oedipus emphasises (for he comes back to it more than once), it is not so much the *fact* of Destiny as the knowledge of it which destroys the spirit – 'Is there any point in doing something when it is as if it had already been done even before you were born?' Yet, what is of significance, in the last analysis, is whether or not our *actions* (predetermined) and our *wills* are in tune with one another:

You will never know if what you have done was what you really wanted ... Yet, without doubt, the open road has something human about it, something uniquely human. In its tortuous solitude it is like the image of that pain which gnaws away inside us. A pain that is like a respite, like rain after the sweltering heat – silent and peaceful, it seems to flow out of things, from the depths of one's heart. This tiredness and this peace, after the clamour of Destiny, are perhaps the only things that are truly our own. (*Dialoghi* p. 86)

The association of freedom and that which is 'uniquely human' reminds us of the paradoxical hope implicit in that earlier 'who was Oedipus?' – that is, that what is essentially human, essentially 'us', has nothing to do with Destiny, which is mechanistic, a denial of humanity. Yet, the very image used – 'the open road' – is blighted, for 'road' suggests determinism, little possibility of choice to those who are already on it – and Oedipus seems to have surmised it even before he speaks. The liberty it affords is only momentary relief from grief in the shape of a lesser 'grief' which thus 'is like a respite' – a question merely of intensity. There is no possibility of a fundamental change of state, even though 'this tiredness and this peace, after the clamour of Destiny' seems to suggest that Oedipus sees the moment of relief and the destiny from which it is an escape as being somehow qualitatively different, even perhaps two different orders of experience. At least in these moments 'like the rain after sweltering heat' will and experience are in harmony. Yet doubt is immediately reawakened by the Mendicante:

> One day we didn't exist, Oedipus. Therefore, even our heart's desires, even our blood and our reawakenings have come out of nothingness. I am almost at the point of saying that even your desire to escape your destiny is itself Destiny. It's not we who have made our blood. It's enough to know it and to live honestly, as the oracle says. (*Dialoghi* p. 86)

The message is clear enough: nothing lies outside Destiny's control, not even our desire to escape it. Moreover, we are in no sense responsible for the factors which control our own particular destiny, for they were transferred to us 'in the blood', a parental legacy. Thus we are left with no alternative but acceptance, a willed attuning of Destiny and desire. Sound enough advice, Oedipus acknowledges, whilst ever one is still in the process of discovering what that destiny is, but once it is all laid out before us, and experience becomes mere repetition of what has gone before, 'everything crumbles' – and here we are reminded of Stefano's experience in *Il carcere*. 'Everything crumbles' in the sense that one's life becomes predictable and the horror of seeing the prediction verified in practice takes away any sense of purpose or meaning. It is when one finds it impossible to fall back on some old or newly created myth, as consolation or hope, because the evidence in favour of the existence of a specific destiny is so overwhelming, that 'everything crumbles'. Here, Oedipus' question 'Is there any point in *doing*?' becomes more urgent in tone and ushers in even the possibility of suicide as a resolution of the impasse. It is not suggested in this particular dialogue but it is nevertheless a logical enough concomitant. When the possibility of new experience, real discovery, is removed, what alternatives remain other than cynical acceptance or self-inflicted death? It depends on the depth of conviction one has about the absoluteness of the Destiny theory. It seems that for Pavese there was no doubt at all – at least, not by late August 1950. Yet, in *Dialoghi*, not even suicide is seen as relief from the futility of destiny, for Sappho, in *Schiuma d'onda*, questioned as to why she had sought death, which she finds to be 'monotonous', replies: 'I didn't know that it was like this. I thought it would all end with that final leap, that the desire, the anxiety, the tumult would all be spent. The sea swallows us, I thought, it obliterates us' (*Dialoghi* p. 59). If death is not an escape, merely an intensification and eternal confirmation of Destiny, then the human tragedy is indeed complete. Life and death are no different if, in the former, one has reached the terrible awareness that absolutely nothing is under our control.

In *La madre* (The mother), yet another determining factor is explored when Meleager complains that 'when I was born my destiny was already sealed in the burning brand that my mother stole. I had only a few companions – the beasts and my mother' (*Dialoghi* p. 67). The god Hermes tells him that the formula is the same for all men: only the circumstances and therefore the details are different. 'There was never anyone who was master of himself or who had other companions.' Meleager then puts effectively the same question as Oedipus:

Have any mortals yet existed who lived their lives to the full, without anyone controlling their days ...?

The reply is explicit enough:

Do you know of any, Meleager? They would be gods. There are some wretches who've managed to hide their heads, but even they had their mothers' blood in them, and then hatred, passion or fury have flared up in their hearts and they have been all alone. Some of them, in the evening of their lives, have even felt the flame rekindling inside them. Not all of you, it's true, have died of this. Every one of you, when you become aware, live like the dead. (*Dialoghi* pp. 70–1)

Even the recluse, sooner or later, feels himself controlled by the inherited characteristics of the mother within him – 'In the flesh and the blood of each one of us the mother roars.' It is, perhaps, in keeping with Pavese's own difficult relationship with his mother that the traits of character cited here should be negative, destructive even – 'hatred, passion, fury' – and that they should be expressed in terms of fire – 'flared up', 'burning' – partially determined by the original myth (the 'burning brand') but also by established tradition in Pavese's own writing, going back to *Paesi tuoi* – the uncontrollable, irrational burning from within. The fire imagery is maintained throughout this dialogue:

Your lives are always in the burning brand, and your mothers have snatched all of you from the fire and you live half burnt by it. And the passion which finishes you is still that of your mother. What else are you if not her flesh and blood? (*Dialoghi* p. 68)

Here it is extended to include the chaos from which the individual comes into life; in *Schiuma d'onda*, the sea had had the same symbolic function, fire and water being traditionally regarded as fundamental elements of creation both having their specific rhythms and age-old effects on human personality.

The mother is also a woman: 'No mortal', Meleager is reminded, 'ever manages to think of his mother as a girl'; and the mystery, the irrationality which she seems to represent is in all women, all of them potential mothers, which, in Meleager's experience, means creators and destroyers.[11] They are merely instruments of the *selvaggio*, the *inumano*, yet – Hermes suggests – 'Without men women are nothing.' The theme goes back to the poems of the first *Lavorare stanca* and the youthful misogyny of the author, but there, women were mere shadows, and to be a man was to be the master. The image had changed over the years, and by the time Pavese came to the *Dialoghi* she had become the 'donna–mago' (enchantress) who reduced man to a state of abject, humiliating bestiality – the type is Circe – but there are others in *Dialoghi* and they were to appear frequently in the poems and novels which followed that book: Linda in *Compagno*, Gabriella in *Diavolo*, Santina in *La luna e i falò*.

Taken together, *Feria d'agosto* and *Dialoghi con Leucò* posit something like a theory of man in which all the essential formative factors have been decided for him before the individual is aware of the significance of what is taking place. The process begins before birth and terminates at about the time adolescence begins when, according to Pavese, one begins to move towards self-awareness. Life becomes, from then on, consciously or not, a search for one's 'self', that nucleus of personal myths which predetermine the paths our whole life will follow. The desire to know ourselves is one of our most fundamental drives and whilst ever our rediscovery of our myths continues to bring new knowledge before our consciousness we have the illusion of the growth of our personality and all is well; it is when – if – we begin to discern a pattern, and try as we may we are unable to change it, that the despair which Pavese expresses, particularly in *Dialoghi*, becomes the tragedy of man.

'I, like, I believe, many others,' wrote Pavese in March 1948 'am not searching for what is true in the absolute, but for what we are' (*MV* 27 March 1948), and in *Dialoghi con Leucò* the journey back to Ithaca, for Ulysses, and the descent into Hades, for Orpheus, are both powerful myths of that search for 'what we are'. In *L'isola*, Calypso offers Ulysses a comfortable escape from the trials and sufferings of his wanderings:

We are both of us tired of our huge destinies. Why go on? ... Nothing ever happens here. There is a bit of land and a horizon. Here, you can live for ever ... rest your head and be silent. (*Dialoghi* pp. 131–2)

That renunciation consists in accepting the limitations of time and space; it is tantamount to becoming an immortal, for, 'Whoever accepts the moment only is immortal. Anyone who no longer recognises a tomorrow.' It is a state in which the future (and its aspirations) and the past (with its memories) no longer exist, similar to that of the gods, and also of the beasts. *Inquietudine*, which always accompanies the journey into the unknown which is life, is dissolved in familiarity and results in peace. But the price is too high for Ulysses. Ithaca, the goal, is also the Ithaca of all his dearest memories, that past which gives his life its meaning, and, as both future and past, expresses ideally Pavese's conviction that life is never lived in the present, but is savoured as memory or anticipation. It is the search and the question which are the driving motives in life, not the achievement and the answer, for these latter only take on real significance when they have passed into memory; the moment of achievement, of triumph, is followed inevitably by the moment of emptiness. Man, in Pavese's eyes, is one of Rilke's 'things that live on departure'; for him, truly, 'staying is nowhere'. To seek to break with one's destiny is to become less or more than human, and Ulysses rejects it absolutely; 'I am not immortal', he points out, and it is here that Calypso offers what amounts to a definition of 'eternal life' when she asks: 'What is eternal life if not this acceptance of the moment which comes and the moment which passes? Inebriation, pleasure, death have no other purpose than this' (*Dialoghi* p. 134). The inclusion of death amongst these other moments of unconsciousness (the 'istante–eternità'), the escape routes from *inquietudine*, is significant, for whilst 'ecstasy' is not rejected out of hand, as momentary relief, the implication would seem to be that all forms of 'ecstasy' have something of death in them; they lead, that is, to nothingness, the absolute negation of all life. However, as Ulysses affirms, in *L'isola*, it is one thing to be tired of one's destiny and quite another to want to put an end to it. Calypso makes the mistake of believing that the one follows automatically from the other. Here Pavese's own view is corroborated – 'We never free ourselves from something by avoiding it, only by going through it' (*MV* 22 November 1935) – so that life, not death, is Ulysses' unequivocal choice.

Orpheus, in *L'inconsolabile* (The inconsolable one), makes the same decision. Returning from the Underworld, with Eurydice close behind him, he realised that her death has made him lose his sense of direction in life. His descent into Hades, the realm of nothingness, had the aim of recapturing an area of his past (Eurydice is described as 'a season in my life') and making it live again. However, if he succeeds he – and she – would have to live through the trauma of her death all over again – 'what has been determines what will be' – and he suddenly realises that the past did not need her physical presence, for it was in him, was his, 'a past of which Eurydice is unaware', his myth of her and of their life together. Eurydice was, in this sense, Orpheus' Ithaca. The realisation has far-reaching consequences for Orpheus; formerly the creator of 'ecstasy' through his music – that is, of moments of 'not-life' – he has now, as a result of his journey to the Underworld, become the advocate of self-discovery entirely within the realms of the conscious and sentient:

Every time you invoke a god you experience death, and you go down into Hades to snatch something away, to break a destiny. You do not conquer the night and you lose the light. And you struggle there as though obsessed. (*Dialoghi* p. 103)

The moment of 'ecstasy', whatever form it takes, whatever its intention, is an invocation to 'a god', which means death. The intention, whatever its specific colouring, is also always an attempt to escape a destiny, which has become intolerable. But the message is clear enough from one who, like Dante, has been in Hell and experienced its futility: 'We do not conquer the night', for even the ultimate 'ecstasy', death, is no escape, is, in fact, 'the night'. This is Sappho's experience too and her eternal complaint in *Schiuma d'onda*. By embracing 'ecstasy' – inebriation – whether through a descent into Hell, choosing to stay on Calypso's isle or a leap into the sea, 'we lose the light', where 'light' is life and reason. Orpheus admits: 'I was almost lost, and I sang. In coming to that realisation I found myself' (p. 103). The juxtaposition of 'I sang' and 'coming to that realisation' is no accident; for all the moments of pleasure and happiness his singing could create and for all the pain and suffering the acceptance of a destiny could bring, he recognises the former as evasion of the main task in life, that of knowing oneself through understanding one's destiny. *L'inconsolabile*, like *L'isola*, is thus an affirmation of life, a rejection of the poetry of evasion. Nevertheless, it does have its negative aspect, and one which, in part, may help to explain why in *Dialoghi* and later (the continuing affirmation notwithstanding) Pavese finally chose 'the night'. Orpheus admits that 'She who was following me was of no consequence to me. My past was a shaft of light, a song and the morning' (*Dialoghi* p. 101), and whilst in its context this merely points to life and away from death, it has wider implications in that the very myth of Eurydice which makes this affirmation possible at all is also indication of the individual's seemingly inevitable, tragic isolation within himself. The Eurydice Orpheus *knew* was the one he had created for himself, not the Eurydice who existed for herself. In Pirandellian terms, whether consciously so or not, Pavese is pointing to the myth as *necessary* substitute for the truth we seem to be incapable of grasping even in our most intimate relationships. Ultimately then, this is a statement about the human condition; at best, others are but mirrors of ourselves. If the long-sought-after 'passage to other men' did not exist – and here we recall Oedipus' words, 'It is indeed strange that to understand the one who is nearest to us, we have to get away from him' – was not the search for 'what we are' all that remained if a man was to try and make some sense of his existence?

Despite the isolation Orpheus' discovery implies, 'the law of Destiny' ensures that whilst each is living out and seeking to understand his own destiny, he will necessarily be involved in the destinies of others, so that, effectively, 'Each of us works for everyone else' – as Prometheus explains to Hercules in *La rupe* (The rock) (*Dialoghi* p. 93). Where a destiny involves suffering – symbolised by the rock to which the former was chained in punishment for his theft of fire from the gods – release will come only at the expense of another: 'It is the law of the world that no-one may be freed unless blood is shed for him.' This law of cosmic retribution is asserted and even demonstrated in *La rupe*, although nowhere is there any convincing explanation of why it should be so. Hercules, in living out his own destiny, sets in motion the chain of events which will lead to Prometheus' release, but that involvement includes the death of 'Chiron, the compassionate one, the good friend of the Titans and of mortal men'. The remorse which Hercules begins to express when his deed is revealed to him is waved aside by Prometheus – 'Do not grieve about it, Hercules. We are all as guilty as one another.' Besides, 'the law of Destiny' will demand much more of him than remorse, nothing less than an ironical-seeming nemesis – as Prometheus further explains:

I could be set free only if another took my place. Chiron was transfixed by you who had been sent by Fate. Yet in this world, born out of chaos, there is a justice. Compassion, fear and courage are only a means. There is nothing you do which does not come again. The blood you have shed and will shed will drive you on to Mount Oeta to die your death. It will be the blood of the monsters which you live to destroy. And you will climb up onto a pyre made from the fire which I have stolen. (*Dialoghi* p. 94)

'Pietà' – the compassion which spurs man to action ('Man is compassion and fear,' says Prometheus) – whether expended on others or on self through others, leads inevitably, it seems, to taking the suffering of another upon oneself, so that what began as compassion for another ends as pity for oneself. Even fear of the unknown, which urges man to an understanding of that unknown, thereby destroying the fear which had moved him to action, has its nemesis, for when all is known, when a god-like omniscience is attained, what was formerly active life becomes static existence – a death-in-life – a state of perpetual *noia*.

Figuratively, however, the killing of 'a monster' signifies the giving of a name to previously less-than-conscious experience, bringing it within the bounds of human understanding. This passage from darkness to light means that the mystery and the fear inherent in it are dissolved, though the 'monster' remains, albeit submerged beneath our consciousness. 'The monsters do not die. What dies is the fear which they arouse in you. That's how it is with the gods. When mortal men no longer fear them, the gods will disappear' (*Dialoghi* p. 95). However, for Pavese, this acquisition of experience through the giving of names, though continuous, is by no means irreversible. Just as, at the individual level, certain experiences fall out of our conscious memory or, for whatever reason, cease to be important for us, so too at the level of a whole culture, so that Pavese, like Eliot, seems to recognise that

> There is only the fight to recover what has been lost
> And found and lost again and again.[12]

Names change or are forgotten in the passage of time, so that eventually the 'monsters' they once covered and held in check ('with such permanence as time has' – Eliot again) may re-emerge as the unknown, as fear. Theoretically the total content of collective consciousness may be subject to this lability over a great enough span of time, though Pavese is nowhere explicit on this point. In practice, such change may affect only a small proportion of total human experience, so that there is, in effect, a steady and continuous gain of rational knowledge. In *La rupe*, however, Pavese takes the total view in that Prometheus explains to Hercules, who is the type of human self-assertion through action, that:

We are a name, and nothing else. Do you see what I mean, Hercules? While the world has seasons like the fields and the earth. Winter comes round again, summer comes round again. Whoever can say that the woods perish? or that they stay the same? You will be the Titans, before long. (*Dialoghi* p. 95)

Hercules, not surprisingly, given that it is his symbolic labours which raise man above the rest of nature, is shocked to learn that men 'before long' will be 'the Titans' – 'the monsters', in fact. 'We mortals?' he asks incredulously, to which Prometheus replies: 'mortals or immortals, it doesn't matter'. It is in the context of this cyclic flux, in which *il vero* is unknowable as the *thing-in-itself*, merely as the nucleus around which innumerable myths or fanciful interpretations are constructed, that one has to understand Pavese's tragic conviction about the impossibility of 'a passage to other men'. Experience, as the individual assimilates and rationalises it, is always, only, an expression of a particular need that is in him, and, in Pavese's view, this would seem to be the case at the level of a whole society. For Orpheus, Eurydice is the expression of his own specific needs, whilst for succeeding centuries she has represented many things for many cultures, and will continue to change in this way perpetually, for *she-in-herself* remains ever the incommunicable mystery.

Orpheus' myth of Eurydice was one of joy and mutual happiness, but there are many in *Dialoghi* for whom a woman is a negative, even a paralysing experience; her impenetrable mystery, as the unattainable object of desire, becomes a prison for her hapless victims. We have already encountered something of this in the magic of Circe, which turns all men into grovelling animals, or of the mother who, whether she would have it so or not, holds the life – and death – of her son and victim, Meleager, in the palm of her hand. In general, then, woman is regarded as an aspect of the *selvaggio*, and her ultimate associations are always with the 'bestiale' – as we see in both *In famiglia* (In the family, *Dialoghi* p. 155) and *La belva* (The she-beast, p. 47).

Castor and Pollux (*In famiglia*) discuss the fortunes of their sisters, Helen and Clytemnestra – though chiefly the former – in their relations with the Atrides. The traditional violent nature of the Atrides is emphasised – 'They're a family which, in times past, even devoured one another' – and Castor suggests a possible link between this violence and the personalities and behaviour of the women they marry: 'Have you ever wondered, Pollux, why their women – even our sister – after a while, become wild, crazy, they shed blood and have it shed?' (*Dialoghi* p. 153) Pollux is sceptical at first, pointing to 'our other little sister, Clytemnestra', wife of Agamemnon, who – he reminds his brother – 'is managing well enough'. Castor takes the view that 'Everyone finds the wife he deserves' and that, in effect, the Atrides 'have always married the same woman'. It is this belief, set against the background of violence and the already seemingly far from uneventful career of Helen herself, which predisposes us to the havoc which Helen (and Clytemnestra) will create. The mutual attraction of certain types of men and women suggests some cosmic law – 'is it likely that it's all just chance?' asks Castor – as well as the suspicion that, for all she is their sister, 'Perhaps we, her brothers, don't yet really know who Helen is.' Yet, the behaviour of the women who have been closely associated with the Atrides in the past is explained in terms of self-assertion, indeed of self-preservation. However, if the violence of the Atrides represents provocation it is because they themselves have a need to suffer as well as to cause suffering – 'They need a woman who will scourge them.' Hippodamia, who 'treated men like horses', is called in evidence, but Pollux sees no connection between her bloody career and Helen's seemingly gentler behaviour: 'Helen doesn't kill, nor does she have people killed.' Castor is much less certain. His brother thinks of violence only in overtly physical terms, but Castor knows it can take on subtler forms – a look, a word, nothing more is needed, he suggests, citing further examples. Given the past record of the Atrides and their apparent predilection for 'cold, murderous eyes', it is difficult to resist the conclusion that Helen, however unlikely it may now seem, is just such a woman: 'They need the cruel virgin, she who goes by on the mountains.'

This picture of Helen is substantially that which Sappho presents in her conversation with Britomartis; she speaks of her 'sowing fire and carnage' (*Dialoghi* p. 63). Moreover, she is linked, by inference, with her who 'sprang from the foam ... the sorrowing, restless one who smiles alone' – the goddess Aphrodite, who is not named, and of whom all go in fear: 'everything which is worn away and tossed about in the sea, is her substance and her breath'. Aphrodite, the principle of love and therefore of anguish, is the myth of the great destroyer, faithfully reflected in Helen, her proselyte.

In his last letter to Lajolo (25 August 1950), written only hours before his death, Pavese suggested that he himself was to be found in *La belva*, so that it is difficult to discuss this particular dialogue without thinking of it in terms of autobiography. Endymion, in his anguished conversation with the Straniero (the stranger, who subsequently proves to be 'a wandering god'), recalls that in dreams 'it happens that ... you listen to the murmuring of the wind, to the birds, the water and the murmur which is the voice of the water', and that 'it seems, when you are sleeping, that you are never alone' (*Dialoghi* p. 50). In that less than conscious state, one regains something of that sense of oneness with all nature which reputedly existed in the Golden Age of the Titans. However, as Endymion reveals, he no longer finds that comfort, for he has been 'awakened' once and for all from 'sleep' (where 'sleep' signifies the illusion of open possibility). He too is the victim of that dreaded encounter with 'the cruel virgin, she who goes by on the mountains', she who 'has no name', or rather 'has many names'; and again the motif of woman as the darkness, incommunicability and horror of the *selvaggio* returns:

Have you ever known anyone who was many things all in one, carrying them within her, so that her every single action, every single thought you have of her had so much of your land and of your sky, and words, memories, days gone by that you will never know, days yet to come, certainties, and another land and another sky which are not yours to possess? (*Dialoghi* p. 51)

Endymion is possessed without possessing, and worse, is in a sense damned, for 'she' is 'the untamed, impenetrable nature, which has no name'. 'She' is encountered on the mountain, Latmos, the place of aspiration and hope, which are fed by imagination and desire, and she has commanded: 'You must never wake again ... you must never act again.' Endymion should never wake to life as he had hitherto known it (characterised as it is here, by action) but live on, the prisoner of his own vision of this goddess – 'of that slightly hoarse voice, which is cold and maternal' – realising 'that never again would I live among men. I was no longer one of them' (*Dialoghi* p. 53). The closedness and incomprehensibility of woman, for Pavese, as exemplified in his mother and 'the woman with the hoarse voice', and the partial substitution of the one for the other at a moment of crisis in his life, and thus also the fusion of the one with the other in his imagination, is remembered here, as it is so often after *Dialoghi*, in the corrosive influence of this 'familiar compound ghost' upon his male protagonists. The *selvaggio* is manifested in many different ways, and Endymion enumerates some of them, but 'for her [the goddess], the savage is loneliness. For her the beast is loneliness. Whenever she caresses it is as though she were stroking a dog or a tree trunk'. (*Dialoghi* p. 53). She is both woman and goddess, which for Pavese means 'belva' and 'divina', and Endymion, seeming to understand that man is a finely balanced combination of these two extremes, is in no doubt that 'unfathomed nature and the divine eliminate man between them' – as indeed they must if either gains the upper hand, or if, as in this case, the two prove to be one. The mountain and its goddess are the cause of his perpetual *inquietudine* – 'Whilst ever that mountain exists' – he believes – 'I shall have no peace in sleep.' The 'wandering god', however, reminds him that he is living out a destiny which 'is an eternity of voices, of cries, of earth, and sky and days' and that mankind has only this – the dream, the myth, the illusion, for 'this impenetrable loneliness is yours. Love it as she [the goddess] loves it.' It is, once again, the Leopardian plea for acceptance of Destiny, because life, for all its unhappiness is also richness and 'being here is much'.

The elements and the process of the theory of human destiny which Pavese avers, once recognised and understood, become also the basis of a theory of art which is itself mimetic of those determining forces and rhythms in life. Such a theory, he was aware, had existed for a long time:

The character is a theatrical conception, not one which is peculiar to narrative. Telling a story doesn't necessarily require characters. The greatest of the Greek story-tellers is Herodotus, not Homer – whose work is really theatre *ante litteram*.

The nineteenth century aspired to theatre but didn't achieve it – instead it created a great novel, which was theatre, that is, characters. Now there is a tendency to be interested again in pure narrative. One doesn't bother with characters, it's a banal occupation, anybody can do it. Discovery abides in the sense of rhythm, in the animated reality of Herodotus. (*MV* 22 March 1947)

It is a theory of art in which the 'how' is of much greater significance than the 'who' and the 'what', for the latter are merely an accident of the process itself. It is a theory in which 'ideally the myth comes before form, even if it is the animus underlying all forms; poetry is the form which fantasy gives to reality' ('Il mito' in *La lett. am.* p. 357) and thus represents the conscious application by the poet of what, in the vast majority of human beings, is largely an unconscious process in their day-to-day lives. Why does Pavese pursue this process? I think because he is convinced that what happens at the socio-historical level is reflected in the individual – who, incidentally, reflects much of the contemporary 'mythology' – and if the individual's pre-conscious origins (i.e. his individual motor factors) can be located and the patterns ('myths') they have set up in him be discovered, he can then come to self-knowledge which allows him to accept, modify or perhaps even reject his own destiny and become truly 'master of himself', instead of merely the chance creation of circumstance. In general, after *Dialoghi*, Pavese consciously applied an imaginative *rationality* to provide *theoretical* answers to personal problems. The *detachment* of his art – implied in the diary entry quoted above – thus becomes a surrogate for *attachment* (i.e. relationships) in his day-to-day living, the only level at which *practical* solutions can, in reality, ever be worked out. The danger is that although art may indeed occasionally instruct life, it can never become a substitute for it. Pavese, operating at this theoretical level, took in *Dialoghi* another step in the direction he was already taking in *Feria d'agosto:* he posited 'certain inflexible laws unalterable' (to evoke, yet again, the closeness of Pavese and Eliot in much of their thinking), which he then assumed not only as the basis for his writing, but as the fundamental condition of his own life. The theoretical – because devoid of historical context – nature of *Dialoghi* is emphasised in the following:

The *Dialoghetti* preserve the elements, actions, characteristics – the nuclei of the myth, but they do away with its cultural reality which is rooted in a history of graftings, mouldings, derivations, and so on – that which makes it comprehensible. They also get rid of its social environment – that which made it acceptable to the ancient peoples. What remains is the problem, which your fantasy resolves. (*MV* 28 July 1947)

However, having set up this theory of the seemingly mechanistic imposition of a destiny upon each individual, Pavese's writing becomes a search for a means of liberation from it by understanding it as fully as is possible and coming to terms with it so as to harmonise two contradictory needs in man's nature: the need for security, which is achieved precisely through that full understanding (the principle of absoluteness, which characterises the Olympians), and the need for all things new, for endless discovery – the condition of 'labilità', which characterised all lives and relationships, human, animal and vegetable, during the age of the Titans. The difficulty of such reconciliation is suggested in *La rupe* when Prometheus, on the point of release, admits that he is afraid to pass from a seemingly endless state of fixity to a state of freedom:

My experience is like that of the man who has suffered greatly in a particular place – in prison, in exile or in some dangerous situation – and when the moment comes for him to leave it he doesn't know how to decide to go beyond that moment, to put the life he has suffered behind him ... just as that moment weighs heavily on such a man, so it is with me also. (*Dialoghi* pp. 91–2)

Without explaining why it should be so, Pavese here points to a difficulty which he certainly experienced himself – not only in coming out of prison, but in any circumstances which involved passing from certainty to uncertainty – the fear at the root of all conservatism. It is this fear which suggests continually that the aim of his writing, that of 'clarifying his own myths', is folly, and sets up an undercurrent of resistance to it within him.

Liberation via the 'clarification' formula is, as Pavese indicated in the already cited letter to Mario Untersteiner, 'the search for human autonomy'.[13] This implies a state of mind in which *inquietudine* will be significantly reduced, if not altogether eliminated, if the will achieves some degree of harmony with Destiny, which is now known and approved.

In *Il diluvio* (The flood), the terms of the contradiction are clearly expressed by the Satyr who, in describing mankind, explains:

They know how to tell stories, these mortals. Their future lives will depend on how much their imagination has been set to work by the terrors of this night. They will be wild beasts, rocks and trees. They will be gods. They will have the courage to kill the gods so as to see them reborn. They will create a past for themselves so as to escape from death. There are only these two things – hope or Destiny. (*Dialoghi* p. 198)

'Hope' is 'labilità', which depends on ignorance of Destiny; 'Destiny' is the 'certain inflexible laws unalterable'; the one, in its absolute state, is life in the Golden Age, the other is the death-in-life of the Olympian gods. Both are desired by men at different moments of their lives, but momentary attainment of the one continually becomes desire for the other, that is, becomes the cause of *inquietudine*. 'Favoleggiare' (lit. 'creating fables'), which is often panacea, is also, as the Hamadryad notes, a 'self-creation' and a 'caprice' (*Dialoghi* p. 198). However – as the Satyr is quick to suggest – men themselves are unaware that it is so; in fact, 'they stumble across the most extraordinary kinds of salvation, when they are already in the clutches of Destiny and being crushed by it' (Ibid.). In this sense, art (i.e. 'favoleggiare') – which means applying memory–imagination to the resolution of a practical problem – is always a groping after a form of liberation. The liberation – or more accurately, the imagined formula for it – always comes too late to be of practical value in the sense of affecting the objective situation, but not in the sense of helping one to come to terms with it. The capacity for creating myths in any *present* situation ensures that the future ('the new world') 'will have something of the divine in its mortals who are transient in the extreme'. It amounts to another order of being which exists parallel to that of *il vero* – of Destiny, in fact – and man lives always between the two, being both mind–spirit and body–instinct: 'they who live unlooked-for moments, which are unique, are unaware of their value', the Satyr remarks. 'They would rather have our kind of eternity. That's how the world is' (*Dialoghi* p. 198). In *Le muse* (The muses, *Dialoghi* p. 201), a conversation between Mnemosyne (one of the twelve original Titans and mother of the nine Muses) and the poet Hesiod, it becomes apparent that the sweetness of life is never actual but rather the memory of past experience. Mnemosyne, the source of that pleasure and, as the mother of the Nine, of the celebration of it in artistic form, explains that she may be found anywhere, but that especially 'I love to be where men are, though a little way off. I don't seek anyone out, but I talk with anyone who knows how to talk' (p. 204). In this explanation there is something of the image Pavese had of himself as the artist – the lover of mankind who is never quite involved with his fellow-men, presumably because his function of observer and recorder will not permit it (here we remember the words of Oedipus, in *La strada*: 'It is indeed strange that to understand the one who is nearest to us, we have to get away from him'). There is also something of the long-sought-after elusive ideal of 'solitude which is self-sufficiency', together with the suggestion – in that 'I talk with anyone who knows how to talk' – of belonging to an élite. Curious to know why Hesiod believes himself contented only when he is talking with her, Mnemosyne elicits the following reply, which goes a long way towards clarifying Pavese's own passion for, and belief in, poetry as a process not only of clarification of myth (self-knowledge) but equally well of its creation (self-construction):

The things you say don't cause annoyance as do everyday events. You give names to things, which make them different, unheard-of, and yet dear to us and familiar, like a voice long silent. Or it's like suddenly catching sight of yourself in the water, which makes you ask, 'Who is this man?' (*Dialoghi* p. 205)

This answer is worth examining, concerned as it is with transforming banality into something exciting – 'different' and 'unheard-of' – but at the same time, into something known and therefore secure – 'dear' and 'familiar'; in other words, the poet, in his attempt to give a name to experience, is always seeking to overcome the great contradiction: his desire for all things new, and at the same time, for all things to be familiar. In poetry, which for Pavese is the manipulation of affective memory, the modification of a past, the sense of discovery and yet of familiarity is possible, for the 'discovery' is always 'rediscovery' ('a second time') which, because made in new circumstances, always contains some new element. It is also centrally concerned with 'seeing oneself all of a sudden': with a *reflected* self (in both obvious senses of the word) which continually reveals its many facets: in other words, a 'clarification'. However, the heightened awareness and sense of pleasure in the memory–discovery, Mnemosyne reminds Hesiod, are also there in objects or experiences which lie outside his own subjectivity. Though similar to others he has known in the past, their effect is startlingly different, so that 'for a moment, time stands still, and you feel the commonplace in your heart as though before and after no longer existed' (*Dialoghi* p. 206). This sort of experience, the 'istante-eternità', the moment of ecstasy, 'has turned *the object* into a memory – a model', linking it irrevocably with his whole being, which, in possessing the object, possesses, or rather repossesses, something more of itself.

Mnemosyne speaks of her own existence as 'a life made up entirely of such moments', and in this there is something of the Neoplatonic idea of all artistic form already existing, simply awaiting discovery by the artist. Hesiod is not convinced, however, because 'mortal moments do not constitute a life', he argues, for 'the tedium always returns'. He does not readily recognise the possibility of discovery–eternity in the moment which is repeated – 'If I were to repeat them', he reasons, 'they would lose their savour.' A memory, counters Mnemosyne, is always 'emotion re-lived', a nucleus of emotion which in its origin was 'mortale', but which, inexplicably, is transformed by that all-important moment, after which its repeatability is a sure sign of its 'eternal' nature. Thus it follows that the entire objective world is, in effect, merely awaiting the moment (just as the artistic form is awaiting the artist) – as Mnemosyne suggests, 'things immortal are but a couple of steps away from you' – for the origin of all 'immortality' is the 'mortal'. Hesiod remains sceptical: it is one thing to have a theoretical awareness of the process, quite another to experience it and thereby come to believe it: 'Knowing it isn't difficult. It's touching them [i.e. 'things immortal'] that's difficult.' Here, the idea of poetry as the religion substitute returns, the poet becoming what he perhaps was originally, the priest–custodian of the transforming word (the spell, the incantation): 'You have to live for them [things immortal], Hesiod,' Mnemosyne urges, adding significantly, 'which means having a pure heart.' Thus poetry becomes also self-sacrifice, alienation ('though always a little way off'), even though, paradoxically, its ultimate object – so far as Pavese is concerned – is knowledge of self. Still Hesiod remains unmoved. It is easy enough for Mnemosyne to talk for she is, after all, immortal; even nature, in all its manifestations, has the power of self-renewal, but for mortal man life is 'endless toil' whilst ever it lasts. At this juncture, Mnemosyne reminds him that she herself came originally 'from places which are entirely barren, from misty, inhuman pits where, *however*, life had its origins', in comparison with which 'these olive groves ... and ... this sky', amongst which he lives out his 'endless toil', may be considered a veritable paradise. Only now does Hesiod begin to understand. She has transformed her place of origin, despite the horror of it, by giving it a name (i.e. not as Pavesian 'truth' but as 'reality' – 'by speaking about it ... you have made a divine destiny for it. Your voice has reached it, and now it is a terrible and sacred place' (*Dialoghi* pp. 207–8). He at last comprehends the analogy. A particular time and place and their attendant experiences are not everything, yet it is man's nature always to lose sight of this fact, being constantly the prisoner of the moment as it comes. Man also, she reminds him, 'is born in that swamp of blood' from which she came; that is, mortal and immortal have the self-same origin, so that 'your every action repeats a divine model. Day and night there is not a single moment, not even the most futile, which does not flow from the silence of those origins' (p. 208). It is the moment of reception, the predisposition of mind and emotions, though chiefly the latter, which makes *all* the difference; we each create our own immortality by the same process by which we create our own reality. In this 'colloquy' between the poet and his affective memory (Mnemosyne), there is the great danger of, indeed the expressed desire for, introversion: 'You speak, Melete, and I cannot resist you. If only it were enough simply to revere you' (p. 208). But veneration is not enough, she warns, for it is of much greater value to 'say to mortal men these things that you know', implanting in him, therefore, the idea of a mission which will inevitably be self-sacrifice. Here, I think, Pavese was recognising the contradiction between his public and private self, the struggle, that is, between the natural–instinctive and the rational, between Titan and Olympian. What has tended to happen since Pavese's death is that the 'defeat' which his suicide represented has continually been allowed to overshadow the 'struggle' to avoid it—a struggle which is central to *Dialoghi con Leucò*, and which is in itself an affirmation, an optimism; as the refusal to be defeated always is.

Perhaps the key question in *Dialoghi* is that concerning human autonomy: how much *conscious* influence does the individual have in determining the course of his own life? All the evidence, so far as Pavese is concerned, seems to point to the essential formative choices being made without awareness of their true significance; they are for us, and of us, but not really by us. We give those choices and their continuing effect in our lives a rational gloss, which is presented as the choice itself. Yet, so long as one lives in the illusion of being 'master of oneself', the failures to attain one's objectives are seen as isolated instances of bad luck, errors of judgement and the like. It is only when a pattern is discerned, through the repetition of types of experience, that one begins to suspect one is not – and never has been – in control, and this can be the top of the slippery slope which leads – though not necessarily – to depression and ultimately disintegration of personality. The point is that, for Pavese, life was lived primarily, and as he grew older, increasingly so, in the mind, so that interpretation ceased to be linked to individual events, but rather to a rationally worked-out formula, and the events always, it seemed, confirmed the formula.

In *Dialoghi*, individuals appear to be singled out by the gods to play a specific role in history, and this is raised to the level of a universal law. The syndrome is common enough, that of the individual's personal condition projected as a universal condition, particularly when it is a case of personal unhappiness or tragedy, for there is some little comfort to be derived from the knowledge that one is *not* alone in one's suffering, that one has *not*, after all, been singled out, that the only difference between individuals is one of *awareness*.

The ideal condition is one of unawareness, in which the individual will is continually adjusted to be in harmony with individual destiny; this is the only formula for happiness, self-satisfaction and a sense of personal fulfilment. Pavese decided that the only possibility of liberation from Destiny lay not in evasion but in embracing it completely, seeking to understand its countless manifestations and its origins. Only thus might there be any possibility of change, through the exertion of the rational will;

hence the formula of 'clarifying his own myths'. However, this was like riding the tiger. *Faith* in rationality as a force for significant change became suspect – irrational in itself – possibly another facet of the all-embracing Destiny. Perhaps the rational will could change nothing, merely destroy the illusions which myth provided as a shield, so that with that gone there was only the endlessly repeating experience of Destiny, known as the gods know it in *Dialoghi*, without surprise, contingency, vitality or even hope for change. Pavese's developing awareness followed a curve similar to that experienced collectively in the eighteenth century, which led to an emphatic reaffirmation of the power of nature over reason in certain Romantic interpretations of human experience. His confused 'philosophy', as it unfolds in *Dialoghi*, is a mixture of Romanticism and Platonism. It recognises a power in mystery, it uses a hieratical, mystical language, which seems artificial, even irritating at times. His style is aphoristic, he makes vatic pronouncements in solemn tones which often cause uneasiness. He tinkers with ambiguity and obscurity, and whilst this is understandable to a degree, if one accepts that even when complete *Dialoghi* still remained 'a tangle', yet there is the possibility that it was also a deliberate choice. Why was it so? Was Pavese naive enough to believe that such a style would give him the aura and authority of a poet–seer, with the memory of d'Annunzio still fresh in Italian minds? Despite his self-confessed desire to 'slot into the illustrious Italian tradition', this is difficult to accept. A more likely explanation is lack of confidence – not in the validity of the inquiry in *Dialoghi*, but in its likely reception at that particular moment in Italian history.[14] The esoteric style was a way of commanding attention.

Yet, like Leopardi before him (and the parallels are many), Pavese recognises no supernatural powers, only natural ones, the strength of which, in our contemporary arrogance, we have grossly underrated. The gods in *Dialoghi* are a literary convention, a myth existing only in the collective mind of an earlier age of men, and continually demonstrate the failure of the supernatural, as well as the rational, to dominate the natural forces, both internal and external, which are the inescapable condition of all human life: the forces of Destiny, in fact.

There are many levels of awareness, however (just as there are innumerable destinies), and anything less than total awareness of the workings of Destiny can be a source of richness, happiness and fulfilment. The richness and variety of human life, so much envied by the gods, is entirely the product of the imaginative interpretation of experience and that, so long as it is believed in and is believed to be changeable, is the only freedom man can ever know, according to Pavese. And this *is* the whole point for Pavese: reality is what is believed to be, which is not necessarily what *is*, and we cling to that reality which promises happiness, just as we reject that which threatens its opposite. We live, in fact, by our own created myths. Though Pavese failed to find a 'passage to other men', *Dialoghi* is full of exhortations towards human solidarity as an ideal. The book explains obliquely, but powerfully, why Pavese himself was unable to follow that ideal. He speaks continually of the richness and beauty of life, and it is only if *we* understand his theory of Destiny as he came to interpret it that we, too, are compelled to see *Dialoghi* as entirely negative.

8

'Not fear, not the usual sort of cowardice'

Dialoghi con Leucò was Pavese's attempt to graft his theory of myth on to the myths of an ancient culture so as to invest them with a new significance which would be wholly relevant to the contemporary world. Their consequent esoteric nature has impeded their acceptance by that world. However, the novel which Pavese was writing contemporaneously, *Il compagno*, though constructed around several of those myths (particularly those of violence, love and self-determination), nevertheless dealt with them in the concrete terms of Italy's most recent past. In the novel, the myths are put back into a historical context, functioning as a kind of superstructure in the life of Pablo, its central character.

The conscious use of the theory of myth in a structural sense, to provide what Pavese called 'the rhythm of events', was to become one of the most distinctive features of his writings in the post-war period.

Both *Il compagno* and the novel which followed it in 1947, *La casa in collina* (The house on the hill), explore the response of their protagonists towards Fascism, and for that reason the two are considered together in this chapter. The first, though drawing on the author's experience of the mid nineteen-thirties, has an added dimension in the growing political awareness of its main character, an awareness which Pavese himself did not share at that time. Since *La casa in collina*, a later statement than *Il compagno*, is broadly humanitarian, not politically sectarian, in its point of view, this would seem to lend weight to the argument that the earlier novel was written in a moment of euphoria, as Pavese's 'entrance ticket' to the Italian Communist Party, which he joined shortly after the end of the war. An apparent lack of conviction in and about *Il compagno* certainly encouraged this view (see his letter to Pietro Pancrazi of 22 August 1947). It is a futile exercise to blame Pavese for the experience he did not have (and the second of these two novels goes a long way towards explaining why he did not have it), and yet much criticism of *Il compagno* has implied just such a standpoint by suggesting that the novel was written merely out of a sense of duty and possibly even of guilt. Whether this is so or not is largely irrelevant to our purpose, and has only minimal bearing on an evaluation of the novel as such.

In reality, the fundamental weakness of *Il compagno* lies in the contradictions surrounding its hero, who belongs to the lower classes and yet who, in his thoughts and actions, strongly reflects the middle-class intellect which created him. It is precisely here, in the person of the main character, Corrado, that *La casa in collina* is most persuasive. He is an intellectual who, faced with the reality of war, is unable to resolve the dilemma which his very humanity creates: whether or not to act, to take sides, to ignore the contradictions which, his intellect tells him, ought to be resolved before he can be sure that his irrevocable action and its consequences can be justified. These were Pavese's own doubts at the time of the civil war in Italy, and although *La casa in collina* may well be interpreted as a personal apologia for not having taken to the hills, it is much more than just that. Corrado's hesitations and procrastinations were shared by innumerable Italians, intellectuals and non-intellectuals alike, when called on to decide for participation and possibly even death in the struggle against Nazi–Fascism. In this sense, *La casa in collina* probably spoke for a far greater number of Italians than did *Il compagno*. Quite apart from its technical and aesthetic superiority, it conveys a sense of historical authenticity that the earlier novel sometimes lacks. Whilst Pavese's novels are never without compassion, it is perhaps deeper in *La casa in collina* than in any other because this novel represents felt rather than merely observed experience. In *Il compagno*, Pavese is at cross-purposes with himself, for although Pablo and his friends, in both Turin and Rome, are said to belong to the lower and working classes, the reader seldom has the feeling that he is in the working-class world, looking at a historical situation whose resolution will come about only when the brutality, the cynicism and the deprivation have become so unbearable that there is nothing left but direct action. The emphasis of the novel is on thought as the spur to action, not on suffering, and thus a vital distinction between the attitudes of the working classes and the middle-class intellectuals to the developing historical situation is lacking. If *Il compagno* may be adjudged a partial failure, it is considerations such as these which make it so.

Corrado's continued though (as he admits) weakening resistance to active involvement in the struggle is only in part due to that habit of solitude to which he has long been accustomed, even before the outbreak of the war. If, at the beginning of *La casa in collina*, he is simply trying to defend his precious detachment in much the same way as Stefano in *Il carcere*, this is hardly the case at the end. His reflections on the experiences related in the novel lead him to a rationalisation of his refusal which is wholly in keeping with the *Weltanschauung* demonstrated in *Dialoghi con Leucò*: the rejection of the *selvaggio*, represented in this case by the carnage of war. 'The great problem in life is to justify oneself,' argued Pavese (*MV* 27 August 1944), 'and only *uniqueness* justifies, the absolute value which raises us above all contingencies' (29 August 1944). Something very like this is at the root of Corrado's inaction as it is explained at the end of *La casa in collina*:

I have seen the dead who were unknown to me, the Republican dead. It is they who have roused me. If someone we don't know, an enemy, becomes by dying a thing like this, if he stops us in our tracks and we are afraid to step over him, it means that even in defeat an enemy is a person. It means that after having shed his blood there is a need to appease it,to give it a voice, and to justify the one who shed it. Looking at some dead people is humiliating. They are no longer somebody else's business, nor do we feel that we came across them by chance. We have the impression that that self-same destiny which stretched them out on the earth holds us riveted there so that we see them, so that we fill our eyes with them. And it is not fear, not the usual sort of cowardice. We feel humiliated because we are aware – we sense it as we watch them – that we could be there in their place and there would be no difference, and that if we are alive we owe it to that sullied corpse. That is why every war is a civil war; each one who has fallen resembles those who remain, and demands a reason for it from them.[1]

This passage gives a perspective to Corrado–Pavese's refusal of participation, which has nothing at all to do with cowardice. Mere self-justification? Perhaps; but that would be a fault only if it were fabricated in order to hide a truth. In Pavese's case this hardly seems likely in the light of both earlier and later actions and statements. Without wishing to digress too much in a defence of Pavese, we might nevertheless remember such statements as the following, made not for public consumption, but for himself alone:

War brutalises us because, in order to fight it, we have to harden ourselves against all regrets for, and attachment to, finer values; we have *to live as though those values did not exist*, and once it is all over, we have lost the resilience necessary to return to those values (*MV* 9 September 1939; Pavese's italics) and

> To have courage and to be right – these are the two opposing poles in history, and in life. In general, the one denies the other. (*MV* 20 October 1944)

It was Pavese's 'attachment to finer values', and to the side of 'right' rather than 'courage' (reason rather than instinct), which made it impossible for him to take up arms and kill in the fight for the liberation of Italy. Such an action would have implied a rejection of the deepest human values and a capitulation to the emotions and barbarism of the historical moment. Corrado, in Pavese's terms, is expressing a fear, not a hope, when he explains that the war

> will end up forcing us all to fight, tearing active consent out of us. And the day will come when nobody will be outside the war, neither the cowardly nor the unhappy nor the lonely. Since I've been living here with my family, I've thought about it a lot. We shall all have agreed to make war – and then perhaps we shall find peace. (*Casa* p. 253)

There is an apparent contradiction here, but it is only apparent. The 'peace' to which he refers is the peace of mind which comes with the submission of the will and the removal of psychological and social pressures implied in the refusal to participate. Much earlier, in his diary, Pavese had remarked on the psychological and social effects of war, and his words are worth recalling at this juncture:

> War raises the whole tone of life because it organises the internal life of everyone around an extremely simple plan of action, that of the two sides; and by implying that death is ever ready and waiting it lends to even the most banal of actions its hallmark of a gravity which is more than human. (*MV* 12 June 1940)

Whether or not Pavese welcomed the idea of war because of its potential ability 'to break his solitude' when he wrote this is uncertain, but by the time he had finished *La casa in collina*, having experienced war as a reality, it could no longer have seemed so attractive. Its price would have been considered far too high. Pavese did momentarily 'capitulate' when he joined the Italian Communist Party and turned his hand to political polemic in *L'Unità* and *Rinascita*; but after a time he came to realise that such action was tantamount to support for the *selvaggio*. The Communist line turned out to be far too narrow, another form of dehumanisation. Pavese ceased to believe not in its ideals, but rather in its methods. The choice was between a short-term class solidarity based on hatred (the *selvaggio*), whether in war or in cold-war politics, and a longer-term search for a human brotherhood based on the most human of all human attributes, reason. Pablo – the Pavese of the euphoric moment – chooses the former, Corrado the latter. In making this distinction Pavese ran the risk of criticism and even vilification by his fellow-Communists, who were quite content to continue the struggle on the terms dictated by the perpetrators of social and political injustice and, as time has shown, to sacrifice ideals for some share in power. In the ideological sense, Pavese was perhaps a better Communist than many of his Stalinist comrades, but this had little meaning in the practical struggle for power at the end of the war.

Pavese had rejected physical violence (or political expediency) in the resolution of human differences and this, in effect, placed him outside the history of his own times. The dilemma he faced was whether to 're-enter' history by accepting its mistaken perspective or remain aloof in what amounted to Utopianism. In *La casa in collina*, Corrado makes it clear that the pressure to 're-enter' history may become so great that he will no longer be able to resist it: there will be no choice, but a decision imposed by forces which are in essence anti-rational and therefore anti-human. *Dialoghi con Leucò* analyses the struggle against the inhuman within us, as does *La casa in collina*, whilst *Il compagno*, though recognising the need for widespread political education as the surest base from which to conduct the struggle, nevertheless points towards eventual armed conflict as, if not the only way, certainly the quickest way of ridding Italy of Nazi-Fascism. In Pavese's terms, only if the shedding of blood represented a real step forward in man's liberation from the *selvaggio* could that blood be justified, and in post-war Italy it quickly became apparent that it did not. Pavese, it appears, had briefly supposed that the fight against the *selvaggio* could be conducted at the socio-political level, but the many setbacks and disappointments, both personal and social, of the years immediately following the Liberation persuaded him that he had been wrong. There were no short cuts and no revolutions, and this is the principal message of *La casa in collina* and of all that Pavese was to write after it.

Pavese's active participation in politics, through his post-war articles, was inspired by a belief which proved to be illusory: that in the new mood of optimism and solidarity which came with the Liberation, he, too, would be able to 'break his solitude' and belong to the cause of humanity now widely recognised at last. This desire for a sense of community, equality and justice is the motivating factor in those articles which now seem so naive, even childlike. His specific aim seems to have been to educate the workers, who at that time formed the backbone of the Party, to the need for the writer and the sensibility and communication he could offer. His writing is self-conscious, and not infrequently falls into the trap he so desperately wanted to avoid, that of condescension. He attempts to convince his readers (and, one suspects, himself) that as an intellectual he is not really so very different from them: 'We shan't move towards the people,' he exclaims, taking up one of Mussolini's slogans, 'because people is what we already are and all the rest is without meaning',[2] and the solitude he had long recognised in himself becomes, for a time, identified with that sense of alienation which twenty years of Fascist rule had imposed upon so many: 'If anything, we shall move towards man. Because this is the obstacle, the real nut to crack: alienation – our own and that of others' (*La lett. am.* p. 218). Pavese did not – could not – belong to the proletariat, despite his self-designation as 'a workman of the imagination,' so that, in effect, his words represented what he had denied they were, an attempted 'move towards the people.' His diction, his style, particularly in the 'Dialoghi col compagno' (Conversations with a comrade), are symptomatic of that same lack of identification with the proletarian *forma mentis* which was to characterise *Il compagno*. He is patronising, self-conscious, idealistic to the point of Utopianism: 'Writing well means this. Telling about something you would like and haven't got. What you already have you don't talk about.'[3] Whilst he talks to the 'comrades' about the way books are written and why, Pavese is talking primarily to himself, about himself. He, the professional writer, tries to appear accessible to all, as though there were no social or cultural gap between himself and his hoped-for working-class readership. 'Some of us comrades were talking about you and the things you write – Masino told me the other day in the street.'[4] In the Italian, the familiar 'tu' form is used; however, the familiarity is emphasised in other ways too: 'Masino knows when I'm pulling his leg. He knows I do it only to make things clear and it doesn't annoy him,'[5] and 'I saw him wink like you do when you're in on something' ('Le parole,' *La lett. am.* p. 254). None of this is very convincing in the harsh world of political manoeuvre and chicanery and its impact was almost certainly negligible. The attempt to convince Masino that he too could sit down and, by taking thought, become a reader of books, an intellectual (even supposing, of course, that Masino saw any point in doing so), and that all that is required is patience and the will to learn is a fair enough measure of Pavese's failure as a political writer. This very motif is a weakness in *Il compagno*. For the moment, the rule of 'what has been determines what will be' is forgotten, and the lower-class hero – be he Masino or Pablo – is consciously able to reshape his destiny, if only he will. Pavese apparently seeks a self-justification which will be wholly acceptable to the Party representing the long-downtrodden masses in Italian society. Nevertheless, in the last analysis, he will not compromise his autonomy and integrity as a writer for reasons of mere political expediency. The following passage is a fair indication of the straining of his habitual style to fit a mould for which it was never intended:

I'll tell you something else, comrade. We don't *make contact* with the people, because we are the people. In our business it's not as though at a certain moment you can decide to write from then on in a particular way, or speak for a particular class or for particular interests. Of course, you can do it, but if you do then you've sold yourself, even if the ones who buy you are the workers. In our business we don't *go towards* something, we *are* something. Using out-of-the-way expressions or talking even like the peasants counts for very little; what you are is in your blood, in the life you've lived, in the way in which thirty years of living have moulded you. Whoever feels now, and I mean right now, he has a duty to write for everybody and to talk like everybody, and yet who before, when times were bad, didn't feel like that ... You see what I'm getting at?[6]

The passage is full of contradictions when set beside Pavese's actual conduct, and in it already appear some of those opinions which were before long to bring him into disrepute with the Party. Politically, Pavese was naive; he seems to have assumed that personal sincerity and openness and a sharing of ultimate common aims would be sufficient to bind him to the cause. Yet he was temperamentally unsuited to deal with the frequent changes in tactics which the post-war political situation imposed on the Communist Party. For Pavese, means and ends had to be morally commensurate, and he could feel only repulsion for the intrigues and political deals in which the Communist Party increasingly indulged in order to become a party of government. The continuous need for compromise, which in turn called for tactical rejections, revisions and opposition to positions defended but a little while before, was wholly foreign to Pavese's essentially moralistic mode of thought, and, remaining aloof, he came under attack ever more frequently during the last few years of his life. Pavese sensed the need for a radical break with the political and social systems of the past, reimposed at the end of the war through the collusion of the 'Court' parties and the Anglo-American Allies, but he saw the Party which was ostensibly committed to social and political revolution compromise itself ever more deeply with those systems. The result of all this for Pavese was a growing sense of disillusionment and a gradual return to the habit of solitude; he was more convinced than ever that 'self-sufficiency' was the only safe condition.

The action of *Il compagno* falls into two distinct phases. The first, which evolves against a background of bars and dance-halls in Turin, shows Pablo's lonely struggle towards an understanding and articulation of his own brooding dissatisfaction, his lack of purpose and direction:

Going back home at night, I would think about all the talking I'd done with everybody, but that I'd never told any of them that I was as lonely as a dog, and not just because Amelio was no longer around – he too was a part of that loneliness. Perhaps I might have told him that summer was my last, for what with the bars, the shop, the guitar and everything I was fed up to the teeth. He understood about that sort of thing.[7]

This *inquietudine* is reminiscent of most of the earlier novels, whilst the following motif echoes as far back as *Lavorare stanca*, as far forward as *La luna e i falò*:

Could I tell him I was fed up with my life as it was and that I would rather have played the guitar for a living? That the world was a big place and I wanted a change? To go all round it and change everything? That morning all I knew was that I had to do something. Everything had still to happen. (*Compagno* p. 13)

Pablo, however, is indolent and apathetic, and in this respect seems an authentic enough product of his social milieu, and for a time we see him continually compromising himself, failing to take the decision which will lead to change. It is his meeting with Linda and the tormented love affair with her that spur him towards the revolt that leads him to Rome and new awareness in his *vita nuova*.

The atmosphere of the first part of the novel is heavy and turgid, and critics have taken exception to the flatness of much of its dialogue. Gianni Venturi observes:

In *Il compagno*, the characters talk in a style that apes Hemingway's in that it is made up of sophisticated terms and a dialectal structure, and this becomes irritating, boring even.[8]

There is, undeniably, some similarity with Hemingway. Yet to note only this is to fail to appreciate Pavese's artistic purpose in this, his most 'conversational' novel. To the majority of Italians, and especially to the working classes, resistance to Fascism was communicated orally in the main; the clandestine press had little effect, and there were times – such as the period of the Fascist 'triumphs' in the Spanish Civil War – when it was almost totally silent. It seems not unnatural, therefore, that it is largely through conversation that Pablo's anti-Fascism evolves. But there is something else: the flatness of the conversation is a key component in that atmosphere of stagnation already alluded to. This same 'fault' had already been most successfully used by Moravia in his first novel *Gli indifferenti* (*The time of indifference*, 1929), and whilst it does not make for entertaining reading, it does add an authentic dimension to the novel. The following is typical of *Il compagno*:

She told me about when she went to the sea at San Remo, how she'd gone swimming on her own in a boat, and, when she was far enough out, she'd taken off her costume and got sunburnt all over. 'It's lovely,' she said, 'we ought all of us to go naked all the time. If people went out in the street naked, it would be a lot better.'
'Don't you ever go to the pool?'
'No,' she said, 'the water's dirty.'
Then we went outside. It was all white and frozen over among the trees, and we looked at the cars to see if the Lancia was there. We had to go back on the tram. When there's the snow I like to smoke and we walked about under the porticoes finishing our cigarettes, then we went into a bar.
'What do they say at home about you always being out?'
'What bit I am there I drive them crazy playing the guitar. I work at it all the time. Some evening I must play it to you.' (pp. 72–3)

Whilst conveying little which contributes to the forward movement of the action of the novel, there is little that is gratuitous here; this dialogue transmits an all-pervading sense of stagnation, of the banality of Pablo's life; it sheds light on the quality of Linda's mind and, at this point, on Pablo's own frame of mind, whilst at the same time constructing a picture of the essential framework of that life, against which Pablo is eventually to rebel. We are told that 'the days passed like that': everything – the conversations, the locations, the sense of aimlessness – is calculated to slow the pace of the novel, encapsulating that sense of inescapable triviality so typical of life in Fascist Italy.

Pablo gropes painfully towards a sense of identity and purpose through his relationships with Linda, Lubrani and Amelio. In Linda there is the hoped-for salvation through a woman; but, as ever with Pavese, she is the false path, though necessary, if a frequently gratuitous emotionalism is to become rational self-discipline. Nor is Lubrani a stranger to Pavese's fictional world:

Lubrani was always elegant. With the fifty years he had on his back and his great need for eating and boozing, if he hadn't gone in for massage and been well dressed and hadn't bathed in perfumed water he would have looked like a baggage porter. 'Turkish baths', he was always saying, 'get rid of it all through your pores; that's the answer. Mine are all in order.' ... So as to go out with Linda I even put up with him. (*Compagno* pp. 78–9)

Pablo is willing to compromise himself with this man whom he abhors, as so many Italians were willing to compromise themselves with Fascism. Yet there is a reluctance, a conscious refusal of what Lubrani represents, an unwillingness to prostitute his Seepest values by seeking approval – and even employment – from such a boorish, ignorant man.

Amelio is more complex: not as a realised character, for we see little of him, but in his influence on Pablo, which persists long after he himself has been left behind by Pablo's story. It is rumoured that he is politically active against the Regime; he is a reader and a thinker – an intellectual in the Gramscian sense – and Pablo, without really understanding why, respects him more than any other person he knows. His relationship with Amelio is lost in his sense of guilt at having 'stolen' his friend's girl, the more so because his friend, crippled in a motor-cycle accident, is entirely helpless. Friendship destroyed by a woman is a recurring motif in Pavese's writing. He deeply resented the marriage of one of his closest friends and it seems not unlikely that this was reflected in the attitudes of his male protagonists towards Linda and other of his female characters. It is ironical that Linda is with Amelio when the accident occurs, that she is instrumental in destroying the friendship, and that finally it is she who brings Pablo the news of Amelio's arrest for his part in clandestine activities against the Regime. She destroys whatever she touches; yet without his relationship with her, Pablo would never have taken that decisive step into a new life which involves him in a purpose which is collective and not merely individual. It is this interaction of relationships, rather than the careful delineation of character, which is fundamental to Pavese's realism.

Subtle shifts in personality and consciousness – and consequently in the direction of the individual's life – are observed almost incidentally, for Pavese has a habit of presenting the highly significant in very low key. The following is typical:

> Then I told her about the encounters I had at night time going along Corso Inghilterra. 'Goodness knows what you men are,' she said, 'you buy a woman in the streets just like buying chestnuts. Where do you take them?'
> 'I buy nothing,' I told her.
> 'Yes, but you're glad that they're there on the street. You're all right while you have your girl-friend, you don't need them then. But when it's over you wouldn't think twice about going with them.' Linda was talking in that sulky way of hers so that she seemed to be making a joke of it. 'You went there at one time, I know. What is it they say? "Gimme a fag"?'
> I would see them every evening on my way home, after being with her. It wasn't like it had been in other years when I used to walk right through the middle of them and say, 'Well, it takes all sorts to make a world.' Now I felt real pain. They would be walking around in the snow and the glowing tip of their cigarettes hid their faces.
> 'Any woman who goes in for that sort of a life is a fool.'
> 'It's hard to say. They do it out of necessity.'
> 'Gimme a fag,' said Linda, laughing. 'They're just stupid.'
> I was thinking about the one that Milo and I had met on the road. We were on our way back to Turin after delivering a load at Pianezza. She got us to give her a lift on the wagon and when she was getting in she had let us see her legs. 'You drive,' Milo had said. I drove all the way back. They were thrashing away in the back there as though they were draining each other dry. 'Mind what you're doing,' she had said to him, 'or you'll have me out.' But she wasn't one of those who are dressed to kill. She wasn't even wearing makeup. She looked like a housewife, maybe thirty or forty she was, thin-faced, with those hungry eyes of hers.
> 'Your friend's not a bit like you,' she said to him. I was driving along and thinking: 'Even you will have been somebody's Linda.' (*Compagno* pp. 86–7)

This change in attitude, this empathy, has its origins in his own suffering with Linda, which makes him more sensitive to that of others. A little later Pavese returns to this theme:

> There were three or four faces I didn't know. But I didn't bother about that and stayed listening to what they were saying. Gilda was talking about a couple who'd gone to the Valentino and sat down on a bench and fired a couple of shots. 'She's dead, but he isn't.' What's the world coming to, I thought, at one time I'd've said, 'Good health!' (*Compagno* p. 95)

These are small details but they are indicative of a growing self-awareness and humanity, which bring Pablo to political 'take-off' in the realisation that one's own personal history, bound up as it is with that of others, does not have to be suffered passively, but can be created within the limits of contemporary social reality. This realisation, which he achieves shortly after his arrival in Rome, is crucial in his political (and individual) maturation, because from it is derived the belief that directed collective action can change even those limits and thus possibly even the course of history itself.

The rejection of Linda, when it comes, implies the rejection of a whole way of life:

> I now knew that Linda was for me. All I had to do was to think of Lilí in order to understand – Lilí who would go with anybody at all and whose only thought was dancing shoes. It would have been easy enough to take her and fall in love with her. It would have been like a game. There was nothing in Lilí. (*Compagno* p. 108)

Lilí's (and by implication, Linda's) inability to differentiate between person and person, and her obsession with objects which, she believes, will enhance her in the eyes of those about her, making her, in her turn, an object (of veneration), are indicative of the quality of life and the relationships which are possible in the world in which Pablo moves. There is no commitment of person to person, no satisfaction, because there is no sense of participation in anything more serious than a game. It is tempting to argue that Pablo is merely unfortunate in his choice of friends, and that this 'set', whilst typical of a certain social milieu, is not typical of the society as a whole. Yet even before Amelio's accident Pablo has confessed to being 'fed up with that life', and the same sense of futility and frustration gripped him even then, when his companions were of a different sort. Only in Amelio does Pablo glimpse something more positive, and, despite the distorting sense of guilt which dominates his thoughts towards his former friend, it is he who remains Pablo's paradigm of meaningful experience. 'It was good to know that Amelio had never been down here,' he reflects, whilst en route for Rome.

Pablo's escape to Rome (traditionally a symbol of spiritual regeneration) is an act of desperation, and from it develops a sense of purpose which the author sees as transcending egotism in a collective faith that flows into Communism. Ironically, as Pablo's political awareness evolves he again becomes involved with a woman, his employer–landlady, Gina. Yet, it is necessary that the dual domination which she represents in Pablo's life – economic need and captivating femininity – should collapse before the onslaught of a rationally based (Marxian) process of self-determination. The rejection of a woman – Elena in *Il carcere*, Cilia in 'Viaggio di nozze', Carlotta in 'Suicidî' – is repeated here, but whereas in these earlier works that rejection was simply a conscious act of self-preservation, in *Il compagno* it is presented as a sacrifice to a higher purpose, a motif which recurs dramatically in the death of Santina in *La luna e i falò*. Failure to form a deep, lasting attachment to a woman had a paralysing effect upon Pavese, especially at the time of *Compagno*. He sought liberation from it through liberation from self, yet he never progressed beyond a crude, total rejection of Woman as a solution, in what seemed an all-too-obvious imaginary vendetta. However, in *Compagno* there is perhaps something more. Fascism had consistently made its appeal to the emotions of Italians, initially in a situation of near social and political chaos, and the choice which Italy had made in that combination of circumstances had resulted in the disastrous twenty-year rule of Mussolini's Regime. Pavese's own earlier suspicion and rejection of the *voluttuoso* (gratuitous emotion, sentimentality) return again, not only at the personal but also at the collective level, in *Compagno*. Pablo refuses to be captivated by the situation or the emotions which it generates, and begins his 'constructing in life' through commitment to Communism. The dismissal of Linda and Gina thus partly represents a rejection of the old Fascist Italy, and Pablo is raised to the level of the 'new man', the 'new prince' in the Gramscian mould who, supposedly, was to emerge from the Resistance to regenerate Italy according to the formula of a reasoned altruism.

Pablo, however, falls into the same trap as the earlier Stefano. His commitment to anti-Fascism does not extend as far as the humanity that it must embrace if it is to have a truly progressive meaning in the history of mankind. The idea which claims Pablo detaches him from real people and their deepest feelings, which he mistrusts because of his own experience, and there is evidence enough that he is aware of this distancing: 'What Linda had shouted at me – that for me a woman was only a plaything – was true enough' (*Compagno* p. 180). Towards the end of the novel, Linda again makes a brief appearance when she comes to Rome with Lubrani, but she finds that she no longer has any hold over Pablo. Almost as soon as they meet again Pablo informs us that 'I told her I was fine because there wasn't anybody or anything that mattered to me' (p. 165). It is ironical – though typical of Pavese's artistic integrity – that Pablo, in discovering and working for the realisation of the political myth of collectivity, should withdraw from people, employing a stoical rationality to repress his strongest feelings. When Linda reappears she momentarily disturbs the poise at which he has arrived through his suffering and reasoned reflection on his past, for he admits: 'When I was alone and Linda had disappeared down the street, the whole of Rome had become something else for me' (p. 166). Yet the uncertainty is shortlived:

Just for a moment I felt that my heart was beating faster all over again and I was almost on the point of believing her and telling her: 'You're wrong.' But if all those nights and all that suffering had been for nothing, then I really would have done better to have thrown myself into the Po. But my heart-flutter didn't come back – I'd thought about it far too many times. (*Compagno* p. 167)

Here, the perspective remains substantially that of the Pavese who had returned from Brancaleone, and who had believed that an ascetic self-discipline could purge him of those personality traits which, if given free rein, would condemn him to dependence on the caprice of another, and expose him to such suffering all over again. 'I knew that women counted for nothing,' Pablo says at one point (p. 170), for they represent an irrationality which can so dominate a man that he becomes incapable of meaningful action. For the Pavese of the post-war euphoric moment, only commitment to such action could create a better world. Once again, therefore, a woman is humbled by the stronger rational will of a man. Linda can only hurl abuse at Pablo; her magic dissolves into petulance. Pablo tells her: 'I know what you're worth and what you cost. You are what you were, but I am not' (p. 173). He has not only understood the terms of a fundamental contradiction in his life, he has found the means of going beyond it. The formula is that distilled from *Dialoghi con Leucò*; the *selvaggio* is transcended by the rational.

Pablo's purgatorial journey is by no means over with this triumph. No sooner has he achieved his new perspective than he finds himself in prison, so that the logical continuation of that awareness, political action, is thwarted. In prison, it is the uncertainty in the waiting which tortures him. In the vacuum prison represents, it is the normally insignificant actions and situations of everyday life which Pablo misses most of all:

To be able to move about, have my say, not always to be thinking about questions and answers. I would remember the girl with untidy hair on the bridge, and fantasise about what she would be doing just then, what she would be thinking about, where she came from. I would set off on an imaginary walk – the Flaminio, the Tritone – I would imagine the people, know their faces; it seemed then as though I had always wasted the finest moments in my life. (*Compagno* pp. 202–3)

He takes refuge in fantasy, but it brings him back to his own past and to the realisation that experience and the meaning of experience never coincide. In Rome he has found 'new life', but ironically it has been snatched away even as he is beginning to realise its implications for him. It is at this point that he identifies fully with Amelio (the 'invalid' sequence, pp. 202–3). Prison and the paralysis of his sometime friend are essentially the same experience – the physical limitation of possibility – and it is worth remembering that, whilst Amelio has persisted in his anti-Fascism despite his condition, Pablo lapses into doubt and a crisis of confidence.

In the novel, Turin and Rome have an atmosphere which reflects Pablo's varying states of mind. The former is seen in its pleasure-seeking indolence in the glittering, sordid little night world which revolves around Lubrani; but there is also the escape into the *periferia*, which Pablo experiences in the mornings like the promise of a new beginning. It is a world of mist, open fields, the hillside where Pablo could walk 'for half an hour' and meet 'only horse-drawn carts' along the road. It is simplicity, honesty, purity, and Pablo 'was content to be alone there' (*Compagno* p. 38). It is this Turin, the 'città in campagna', which he is frequently to remember in Rome:

What I liked about Rome was precisely that indifference towards time that you can feel in the air. If I went for a drink it wasn't anything like in Turin; I wasn't drinking out of anger, trying to get my blood going. The people, those houses, the clear wine, indeed everything about it – I felt it getting inside me, creating me all over again. I was aware of living there and that I would find work, that the long road and the mountains were behind me. Each day it was as if I had just climbed down from the wagon for the first time, and if I'd had any say in it, the whole world would have been a road like Rome. If ever the anger that had gripped me in Turin came back I would clench my fists, look around me, move about and think that Pablo was in Rome. That was sufficient. This time, I was somebody else. (*Compagno* p. 119)

Here, the city is described not in terms of streets and piazzas but rather in its effect and its meaning in Pablo's life. It is comparable with the *periferia* in Turin, though that suggested possibility only, whereas this is realisation. Differences are noted with that air of wonder found previously only in Pavese's child characters:

> I looked at the streets and the buildings, and there were some of them that were so old and unusual that only the Romans could have built them. I could hardly believe that people like me had had a hand in it. Even the air you breathed there was different. I would stop on a bridge, look about me and listen to people talking. There were hills and certain kinds of trees such as you never see in our parts. That old Marina just talked for the sake of it. If I felt good in those streets it was only because everything seemed so different. (*Compagno* pp. 120–1)

Rome by no means implied a romantic rejection of Pablo's past. In the following passage there is a certain wistfulness, as well as an affirmation of continuity:

> And yet there were times, when I was crossing the Milvio Bridge on a moonlit night, that that stretch of hillside up above the Tiber and those woods in the distance resembled the woods on the Po and the Sassi escarpment. All bits of countryside below a hill look alike. I liked that bit more than all the buildings in Rome. There was an avenue of plane trees at the end of the bridge which was just like the Valentino or Stupinigi. Lots of lorries went that way, leaving the city. (*Compagno* p. 121)

Prison reminds him that while living through an experience we are hardly ever aware of its real meaning; only later, in memory, do we realise what it could have been, but then it is too late. Pablo's last few hours in Rome (perhaps because he knows them to be his last) give him a curiously heightened awareness of this tragic inability to possess the moment as it comes:

> Seeing the streets had a strange effect on me. What with being in prison and the fact that I was leaving that evening, it was like a new city for me, the most beautiful city in the world, where the people didn't really appreciate how content they were. It was like when you think you were a child once and you say, 'If only I'd known about it I could have played there.' But if someone were to say, 'You can play,' you wouldn't even know how to begin. (*Compagno* p. 211)

However, this awareness is not finally sufficient to alienate Pablo from his new-found political faith. When Gina remarks: 'It's terrible. You came to Rome quite by chance,' he replies: 'It's not that that matters. That's how things do happen. What matters is that you really want whatever it is you are doing.' The meaning we perceive in our actions before or immediately after they are completed is the only one which must concern us. Pablo's final choice is action, not contemplation, for only action will change the course of history.

It is in part this same existential tragedy which grips Corrado in *La casa in collina*. In his preface to the *Dialoghi*, Pavese had confessed: 'We have a horror of everything that is without order, eccentric, accidental and we try – even in a material sense – to set limits for ourselves, to give ourselves a framework, to insist on something fixed', and in *La casa in collina* this 'horror' is present throughout, for it is against the sense of pure hazard that Corrado seeks to defend himself. At the outset he tells us that 'What happened to me can't be blamed on the war; in fact, I'm convinced the war could still save me'. He continues:

> The war merely removed my last scruples about keeping myself to myself, ... about eating up my life in solitude, and suddenly, one day, I realised that my great dog, Belbo, was the only close friend I had left. With the war it became perfectly acceptable to close up inside yourself, to live from day to day ... That sort of dull grudge in which my young life had ended found both a refuge and a horizon with the war. (*Casa* p. 114)

We are here effectively at the same point as that at which Pablo arrives: withdrawal as a means of self-protection from the suffering which, Pavese was convinced, any close relationship must bring in its wake. The novel is full of expressions of fear at the apparent rule of hazard: 'Why salvation should have come my way and spurned Gallo, Tono and Cate, I can't say' (*Casa* p. 213); or 'At any moment the sky could start to roar again and burst into flames and nothing would remain of the school but a deep crater in the ground. Only life, naked life, counted for anything' (p. 127); or again, 'You spend months together, even years, then it happens. You fail to turn up on a particular occasion, you move house, and someone you were used to seeing every day, you don't even know whether he exists any more' (p. 136). These are typical examples.

The war is not what Corrado believed it would be: 'When you think about it beforehand, war is a kind of rest, a sort of peace', he admits; but in practice he finds that because of it

> I've got to the point where being alive by sheer chance, when so many people better than I are dead, is no gratification, is not enough. There are times, when I've been listening to the ridiculous radio and I look out at the deserted vineyards, that I think living by chance isn't really living at all. It's then that I wonder whether I really have escaped. (*Casa* p. 213)

When he says: 'I'm convinced the war could still save me', he is talking about salvation from himself, from that habit of solitude into which he has willingly fallen. Cruelly, ironically, the situation which reawakens him (his meeting with his former fiancée, Cate, and her son, Dino, who he suspects may be his own son) is destroyed by the war, for Cate is taken away by the Germans, and Dino eventually runs away from Corrado to join the partisans. The conviction that emotional attachment means vulnerability and inevitable suffering is reinforced. Stability and peace of mind are not to be found in people – this is the great tragedy of life for Pavese – and it is therefore to the world of nature, with its unchanging rhythms, that Corrado turns again, when he decides to return to his parents' home in the hills of his childhood. But the war 'pursues' him even there: he cannot ignore it, or pretend it does not concern him.

Pavese analyses the gradual disintegration of Corrado's *Weltanschauung*, his 'long illusion', as a direct consequence of the War of Liberation. The novel's perspective is, typically, that of the individual in search of himself; it is not concerned with the heroism of the Resistance, but rather with laying bare the interaction of individual thought, feeling and motivation with the events of history as they occur; with that process, in short, which gradually compelled more and more Italians to face up to the choice which the majority of them had not dared, or wanted, or deemed it necessary to make during the twenty years of Fascist rule. This feature is apparent throughout, but the following incident seems especially relevant:

It was on one of those evenings when we were in the yard waiting for the all-clear that Cate's mother told me what she really thought. I had just finished telling Fonso: 'It'll take bombs to make the Italians take things seriously,' and the old woman said: 'Who are you to come telling working people that? The war's a joyride for anybody with enough to eat who can stay up on the hill. It's people like you who brought the war on us.' She said it quietly, with no hint of rancour, as if I'd been her son.

There and then it didn't bother me. 'If only they were all like him,' said Cate. I didn't speak. 'What are you talking about?' Fonso cut in. 'Everybody looks after his own skin.'

'Even us, mamma,' said Cate, 'We come and sleep up on the hill.'

The old woman was muttering away to herself. I wondered uneasily if she realised how deep she had cut, how right she had been. What the others said in my defence meant nothing; in fact, in a sense, even they humiliated me. (*Casa* p. 169)

Quite apart from the personal reasons for Corrado's flight (about which the old woman presumably knows nothing), she has aroused his sense of guilt by identifying him with those responsible for the war, for he himself has earlier observed how social class has become a prime discriminator in the war situation:

A whole class of people, the fortunate ones, the people who were always at the front of the queue, were going, or had already gone, off to the country or to their villas in the mountains or by the sea. There they went on living normal lives. It was left to the servants, the porters and the poor people to look after their houses and, if fire broke out, to save their things for them. It was up to the porters, the soldiers and the mechanics.... I felt ashamed I didn't belong with them, and I should have liked to meet some of them along the avenues, to have talked to them. Or maybe I just enjoyed the cheap thrill and did nothing to bring about change. I liked being on my own, thinking that nobody was waiting for me. (*Casa* p. 131)

Because Corrado believes that 'there is no love which isn't a form of egotism' (p. 166), he scornfully dismisses the publicly declared opposition to the Regime of his colleague, Castelli, suggesting that 'he thinks he's serving his own ends just like everybody else' (p. 199). Corrado is nevertheless forced towards a new awareness of the war's significance:

Take care, though: it's not the Germans you're fighting against, well, not just them. It's those who were running the show before. It's not just a war of soldiers that can finish even tomorrow; it's the war of the poor and of the hopeless against hunger, misery, prison and all this disgusting mess. (*Casa* p. 188)

The war and the personal circumstances which preceded it, hitherto regarded as entirely separate, are reconnected, the one being seen as an extension of the other. Yet Corrado still has a long way to go before he achieves a meaningful perspective. Immediately following the above-quoted observation, we find:

'The day will come,' I said as I stood up, 'when we shall have the dead in the ditches up here on the hillside.'
    Cate looked at me, a serious look in her eye. 'You know such a lot of things, Corrado, but you do nothing to help us,' she said quietly. 'Send Dino to my house, tomorrow, and I'll teach them to him,' I said, laughing. (*Casa* p. 189)

Laughter or not, this statement suggests something of the conviction that the intellectual's role is that of 'creator of consciousness' and, in some undefined way, that this may absolve him from direct action. The leap from the 'long illusion' of a self-imposed alienation into direct political action is far too great for Corrado; nevertheless, something begins to change. After eight years, Corrado meets up with Cate once again, and because she has named her son Dino,[9] and because of his age, he suspects that the child may be his own. In spite of Cate's denials, he asks her –

albeit reluctantly – to marry him, so that he can be a father to the boy. Cate refuses, recognising that a sense of guilt is no basis for a successful partnership. Nevertheless, something more positive than this has flickered back to life in Corrado:

Menacing though the immediate future was, the past was trembling back to life, and my life was all constructed on that past, on the fear, the malice and the sense of disgust that it aroused in me. Now I was forty years old and there were Cate and Dino. It didn't really matter whose son Dino was; what did matter was that we had found each other that summer after the unkind absurdities of the past, and that Cate knew who she lived for and why. (*Casa* p. 156)

This tenuous reawakening is at times accompanied by the suggestion that people can create more positive feelings than suffering and nausea. Particularly relevant here is the effect the news of the armistice has on Corrado:

The summer's evening, full of hope and suggestion, went to my head. Then we all went down into a paved courtyard, in the shadows, and people came along – workers, fellow-tenants and girls – and there was a man, a young chap, who climbed up on to the balcony of the mezzanine and spoke, with a passion which was anything but naive, about the great events of the past few days and of those to come. It was like dreaming, hearing those things being said in public. 'Neither propaganda nor fear have touched these people,' I thought. 'Man is better than we gave him credit for.' (*Casa* p. 160)

The euphoria is infectious, and it is by no means wholly ephemeral:

On those days when Fonso, Nando and the girls stayed the night in Turin ... [Le Fontane] seemed abandoned, lifeless, a bit of the woods. And it was just like it is in a wood: all you could do was look at it or smell it, you couldn't live there or really possess it. (*Casa* p. 166)

Although Corrado oscillates between hope and fear throughout the novel, the realisation that one's life has no meaning unless it is with and for other people comes in the opening pages. At the end of the novel, he himself comments on the change which has taken place in him:

It seemed to me that I had changed a great deal from the year before, from when I used to wander about the woods, completely alone, with the school waiting for me in Turin, and me patiently waiting for the end of the war. But now Dino had been with me in that yard ... (*Casa* p. 230)

Ironically, the war which brings Dino and Corrado together, and opens up the possibility of salvation for the latter, is also responsible for their separation. Yet even before this, Corrado realises their relationship must fail because the child's values are in conflict with his own. Dino can think and talk of nothing but the war, which for him is normality and adventure, and Corrado is compelled to acknowledge

the tremendous legend that was being created in those days, and how only a boy, who marvels at everything he sees, could live in the midst of it without any sense of wonder. That I wasn't a child like Dino was just a matter of chance; I had been twenty years before, but the things I had marvelled at then were paltry in comparison with the things which gripped him now. (*Casa* p. 191)

Corrado's 'things I had marvelled at then' he clings to now, for they are more real, more lasting than the war: they contain his essential self. He tries to steer Dino towards the unending values of the world of nature, but for the child, despite an initial curiosity, they cannot compete with the more urgent reality of the war. Corrado himself is by no means untouched by events, and, in odd moments, is forced to recognise the futility of his attitude. There is one occasion when he is standing in the orchard, waiting for the imminent air-raid to start, in an atmosphere heavy with foreboding:

I wondered how many hearts stopped beating in that moment, how many leaves quivered, how many dogs flattened themselves down on the ground. Even the earth, the rugged hill itself, must have trembled. All of a sudden, I realised how silly, how useless, my self-indulgent attitude to the woods really was, that conceitedness about the woods that I was always going on about even with Dino. Beneath that summer sky, which was as if turned to stone by the wailing sirens, I realised that I had only ever played at life, like some irresponsible child. What was I for Cate but another child like Dino? What was I for Fonso, for the others, for myself? (*Casa* p. 174)

In this topsy-turvy situation, it is Corrado and the older people who are amazed by the new reality. They take on the role allotted to children in Pavese's earlier writing, whilst the true children, who have known hardly any other reality, are able to accept whatever the war brings as normality. This leads inevitably to observation of the bizarre or of the apparently bizarre, emphasising the nightmarish quality of the 'new' world. Something much more important than the destruction of buildings is taking place: the disintegration of a whole way of life and its moral foundations. This disintegration is symbolised by 'a great rat' which Corrado sees 'in Turin, on top of a pile of rubble, ... tranquil in the sunlight. So tranquil that at my approach it had not turned its head nor even started. It was sitting up on its hind legs, watching me. It was no longer afraid of men' (*Casa* p. 190). The *selvaggio* is re-establishing itself; indeed, as Corrado observes, 'the city had become more savage than my woods'. Continually, statements such as 'it seemed incredible', 'it was strange to see', 'it was as if in a dream', 'it seemed impossible that' are encountered, underlining the unreality of the real.[10] It is with touches such as these that Pavese insists on the tenuous nature of civilisation at any moment in history. Without man's constant vigilance, the *selvaggio* re-emerges from time to time to wreak havoc in his world. War is the *selvaggio*, but, ironically, it seems the only way to end it is to join it. With each day that comes, someone in *La casa in collina* observes that the war must surely end soon, and until such a hope proves to be utterly futile, Corrado (indeed, all the Corrados) will resist a little longer the pressure to enter the conflict. At the very end he tells us: 'I don't think that it can finish', and in any case, one great problem always remains:

Now that I've seen what war is, what civil war is, I know that if one day it finished we would all have to ask ourselves: 'What about those who have fallen? Why are they dead?' I wouldn't know what to answer. Not right now, at any rate. Nor do I think anyone else knows. Perhaps only the dead know, and only for them is the war really over. (*Casa* p. 255)

The problem is clear but unresolved. How is it possible to kill another human being in the name of humanity? The decision to take life in the interests of a better world – no matter whose theory of a better world one is following – poses a dilemma which Corrado–Pavese could resolve only through inaction at the time of the War of Liberation in Piedmont, for to have taken up arms would have represented a conscious capitulation to the *selvaggio*, and a denial of the creative humanism which was Pavese's interpretation of the rational principle.

After the arrest of his friends at Le Fontane, Corrado's life, up to then merely evasion, becomes headlong flight. In a physical sense, he journeys back to his origins, seeking confirmation of what he considers to be the only meaningful reality. With each successive phase of that experience, however, he is compelled to question the adequacy of his attitude, even though he does find that reality intact. He takes refuge for a time in a college which is run by priests, and finds that for a while the place answers his deepest needs:

> The days went by in the cloisters. Chapel, refectory, lessons, refectory, chapel. Divided up in that way, time shut out all thought, it moved on and it lived in my place. I would go into the chapel with the others, listen to the voices, bow my head and raise it, and repeat the prayers. (*Casa* p. 216)

Though not a believer, Corrado is content to subject himself to the rhythm imposed by the religious life, for in it he finds the sense of order and security he needs most. That rhythm, like a poem or a song, has a mesmeric effect, distancing him from the chaotic world outside the college. He converses with Padre Felice, and 'these conversations calmed me, gave me a sense of peace'. He asks about the utility of the breviary ('does it have any point, always reading the same words?'), and experiences a curious sense of elation when Padre Felice explains:

> With prayer, ... novelty doesn't matter. If it did, then we might as well reject the hours of the day. As the year turns we epitomise its life. The countryside is monotonous, the seasons always return. The Catholic liturgy accompanies the year and reflects the work in the fields. (*Casa* pp. 225–6)

The essence is the form and the rhythm, and what Padre Felice does is to make the connection between the soothing life of the college and that of the fields and woods of which Corrado is so deeply aware:

> That ancient world of cult and symbol, of vine and corn, of women who prayed in Latin but only understood dialect, gave a meaning to my days and to my life in hiding. There was no difference really; I saw clearly enough that I had passed over to the sacristy from the woods. (*Casa* p. 226)

Here, a number of important themes in Pavese's narrative come together: the insistence on the recurring event as a symbol of essential reality which, in his poetry, becomes the recurring word; need for a 'framework' which not only contains the reality but provides its most constant and inalienable feature; and an ambivalent attitude towards a clearly defined, yet static situation, such as imprisonment (in this case, Corrado's 'life in hiding') which is both protection and alienation. For Corrado, this all adds up to order in the midst of chaos.

Nevertheless, the college and its life do not constitute another, separate world. They are a small part of the reality of a world at war, and are subject to its regulation. Corrado is forced to flee at a moment's notice: here, chance again intervenes. Eventually, it is safe enough to return to the college, but in the meantime Dino has gone away, so that the former equilibrium is lost:

> to spend my days in that useless waiting seemed, with each day that came, ever more futile. Now that the past was only a small cloud, a grief, a common regret, my stay in the college became as frustrating as if I were in prison ... Indeed, the war could finish only after it had destroyed all memories and all hope. This I had known for some time. So I realised I would have to leave the cloisters, stride over the memories and accumulate another life ... Without fear, it was impossible for me to stay there. I could understand Dino. I could understand Padre Felice. I ought to have been a priest. (*Casa* p. 230)

Here, most succinctly, is Corrado's – and Pavese's – endless emotional turmoil: poised between the world outside and total solitude, unable to find sufficient reason for choosing either. Peace of mind can come only through a rationally ordered way of life, carved out of and imposed upon the mindless rhythms of nature. Corrado rediscovers such a life at his parents' home in the hills. Yet the peace of mind does not come even there, for Corrado has by that time experienced enough of war to know no-one is exempt from its effects, whatever truths they possess. Once again, he finds himself in a 'prison' (or a 'college'), a temporary haven to which he clings, not through fear only, but in the conviction that the war, real though it is, is a denial of all that man aspires to. His indecision is explained in the following:

> This is the thing which deludes me: here in the house I find before me a reality from the past, a life which comes from beyond my years, beyond Elvira, Cate, Dino and the school, beyond what I have hoped for and wanted as a man, and I wonder whether I shall ever be capable of leaving it behind. I realise now that in the whole of this year, and even before, even at the time of my lesser follies – Anna Maria, Gallo and Cate – when we were still young and the war was merely a distant cloud, I realise how I have lived through a long isolation, a useless vacation, like a child playing at hiding who goes into a thicket and likes it there so much, looking at the sky from beneath the leaves, that he forgets to come out ever again. (*Casa* p. 254)

Corrado has perceived and clung to an image of a world which, because not shared by the world at large, has led him to alienation. He has refused to move with history, and in this seems to speak for a conservative, even reactionary element in man's nature. In the years immediately following the war which for so many had been fought in the name of progress, when hopes ran high for a better world, such a position could not but be unpopular, especially with the Italian Communists, the party of progress. At a distance of some thirty years, when so many of those hopes have foundered in a world which (largely because of the industrialisation which spearheaded the forward drive) finds so many of its vital natural resources drying up, its earth and seas being perhaps irremediably polluted, Pavese's view looks more and more like sanity. Would he have felt that Corrado's final question – 'What about those who have fallen? Why are they dead?' – had found a satisfactory answer?

It is worth examining the organic structure which gives this novel such a satisfying sense of wholeness. In chapter 15, for example, the narrative opens by focusing reported speech, specific memories and random thoughts on Castelli, Corrado's colleague who, having refused to compromise himself any further with Fascism, has been denounced and arrested. Though he soon ceases to be a topic of conversation, he frequently comes into Corrado's mind, a symbol of the tensions and uncertainties of the times in which all are living. The narrative then moves on to a reported conversation with Egle about her brother, another who has withdrawn from Fascism. He 'hadn't joined yesterday's enemies, he was too loyal for that', but is working as an engineer, hidden by friends in Milan. Corrado misses the essential significance of these withdrawals; for him, the question they raise is not a moral or political one, but is concerned rather with his own self-preservation: 'If I had to run away ... and hide, where would I go, where would I sleep at nights, where would I find a bite to eat?' (*Casa* p. 204) This leads on to the theme of refuge, particularly in religious institutions, and to the rituals, especially prayer.[11] This, in its turn, reminds Corrado of childhood innocence; and the 'joy' experienced in the thought of entering a church and 'living there a moment of peace, being reborn into a world without bloodshed' (p. 205) derives from the memory, *not* from the ritual, as his subsequent disappointment on translating the thought into action suggests: 'I fixed my eyes on the floor and summoned up my thoughts once more. I wanted to' experience yet again the joy and certainty of that sudden peace; but I didn't manage it' (Ibid.). He concludes that the most beautiful part of the cult and ritual is experienced when one steps out into the fresh air, where one feels free and alive. The church, the convent, the monastery, which protect against the trials and torments of life lived beyond their walls, are no accidental objects of interest for Corrado in this moment of crisis, for they offer a socially acceptable, age-old form to his own propensity for isolation; yet his recognition that life and liberty lie outside them suggests that his habit of solitude is now being seriously questioned.

This movement of his thoughts from the darkness and closedness of the church interior out 'under the sky' is immediately reflected and continued in kind, for 'in the warmth of the dining room, beneath the cone of light' (in the church it had been 'a little red light') he thinks of 'frosts and corpses and flight through the woods' and realises, with something like optimism, that soon the spring will come and that 'the hill would be clothed in green; something new, something delicate, would come to life under the sky. The war would be decided', and this too 'would be like emerging from some place of refuge' (*Casa* p. 205).

Without confessing his own experiment, Corrado tries to discover Cate's attitude towards religious observance. Her work in the hospital, her continuous involvement with suffering, forces her towards the practical rather than the metaphysical, and she even suggests that the serenity of nuns and priests has more to do with their practical involvement with people than with prayer. Out of this discussion comes Corrado's recognition that the idea of the 'moment of peace, the useless pause ... now seemed absurd and irrelevant' (p. 206). Nevertheless, there is no sudden conversion to an acceptance of responsibility for others; on the contrary, he seizes on the idea of the hospital and weaves around it a new version of the myth of a 'sick humanity'[12] which can find its cure only in prayer and faith. This takes Cate completely by surprise, so out of character is it. She counters it with Fonso's belief that 'it's what you do that counts, not what you say'; thus Corrado's evasion of commitment through action is brought sharply into focus, though no comment is offered by either Corrado or Cate. The following evening, walking back up the hill alone, Corrado recalls his conversation with Cate when finding himself thinking about Castelli. Again, no explicit connection is made between these two topics, though it is not hard to find one: 'It's what you do that counts, not what you say', and it is by such juxtaposition that we are continually made aware of Corrado's inner debate.

Then comes a sudden, dramatic heightening of tension with the news of Giulia's arrest, and even here Castelli haunts Corrado's mind, for he (unlike Giulia) will not know that anyone remembers him and his honest self-sacrifice, which will thus have meaning for him alone. There follows one of those typically bizarre Pavesian paragraphs, a seeming *non sequitur* which, in reality, restates neatly, symbolically, the contradictions in Corrado's mind, the philosophical question about the nature of reality which underpins the whole novel:

> Then it was carnival time and, strange to relate, the piazza which I crossed every day to go down to the school filled with marquees, with crowds of worn-out people, with carousels and stalls. I saw acrobats who were frozen to the marrow, and caravans. The bit of noise that was coming from there didn't make me feel uneasy as it had done in the past. It seemed miraculous that there were still people who were willing to travel about, to whiten their faces and parade themselves like that. Half the piazza was in ruins because of the bombing, and one or two Germans who had nothing to do were wandering about having a look around. The gentle February sky was opening up its numbed heart. Up on the hillside, under the sodden leaves, the first flowers were surely about to appear. I promised myself I would go and find them. (*Casa* pp. 208–9)

The carnival, which marks the year's turning, belongs to the cyclic-seasonal order of reality, to 'such permanence as time has' (the Titan in Pavese's ideal schematisation) whereas the war, represented here by 'Half the piazza was in ruins because of the bombing' and by 'one or two Germans ...', represents mere transience, however imposing, however demanding on our emotions – another trick of the Olympians.[13] It is the carnival, 'the gentle February sky' and 'the first flowers' which speak of hope for the world. In the last paragraph of the chapter, although the immediate fears and activities of this newly intensified phase of the war are allowed to reassert themselves, Corrado's 'I promised myself I would go and find them' still echoes in our memory.

The vital, unifying links are made not only by recurrent themes (the warp in Pavese's closely woven texture) but by the weft of key words, phrases and verbal echoes. The verb 'trasalire' (to start, to jump), for example, which conveys immediately the nervous tension characteristic of this moment in the war, is used with reference to the headmaster at Corrado's school ('He would sigh from time to time and jump every time the phone rang' – p. 203); to Corrado himself, at the sudden realisation that prayer could be the cause of one's rebirth 'into a world without bloodshed' (p. 205); and again to Corrado when, after the unnerving discussion about Giulia's arrest, his dog, Belbo, 'made [him] jump' in the dark (p. 208). Other word-myths govern this chapter, such as 'respiro' (breath, breathing-space) and 'rifugio' (refuge); clauses such as 'la certezza dileguava' (the certainty was fading); and even paragraphs in which meaning is not explained but, as it were, put on view – as, for example:

I found them all there, except Fonsò and Giulia. Nando, who was at the door, let me see he was worried. I noticed the suitcases and bundles on the little tables, out in the yard. Everybody was wandering about in the kitchen and Dino was nibbling away at an apple. (*Casa* p. 207)

Here 'suitcases and bundles' and 'wandering about' suggest uncertainty verging on panic.

Many of these features, both verbal and thematic, are echoed right through to the final chapter of the novel: in the first paragraph, for example, we find:

this winter, everyone says, no-one will have the will to fight, it will be hard enough just being in the world expecting to die in spring. If, as they say, there is a lot of snow, including that which didn't come last year, it will wall up doors and windows, and it's to be hoped it will never thaw out again. (*Casa* p. 252)

Here the hopes implicit in the coming of the previous spring – 'the hill would be clothed in green; something new, something delicate would come to life under the sky' and 'Up on the hillside ... the first flowers were surely about to appear' – are now denied absolutely, as is the previous year which 'finished without any snow' (p. 203) for 'there will be a lot of snow, including that which didn't come last year'; ironically, the world and its values have been turned upside down. This bitter, almost cosmic irony is much in evidence in the final chapter; earlier, Corrado has confessed that 'I was ashamed of my peaceful existence' (p. 204), while now, as a fugitive himself, he speaks of 'running bent double across the vineyard, and the wait, the humiliating wait' (p. 252); and yet again, Corrado's grim thought when Belbo had startled him – 'We are the hare and the hound' (p. 208) – is echoed ironically in 'They pursue us like hares from one hiding-place to another' (p. 253). Even the search for 'a moment of peace' has been replaced by the recognition that only if everyone actively involves himself in the war is any sort of peace likely to come.

The symbolic significance of the carnival is echoed in the observation that 'In spite of the times we are living through, here on the farms the husking and the grape harvest have taken place' (p. 253), whilst for the old peasants, like Corrado's parents, 'guerrilla warfare, indeed everything to do with this war, is like children's brawls, like those which used to happen at the festival of their patron saint'

(p. 255), so that the natural, seasonal order of reality is not denied, despite the intensity and persistence of the claims of 'history'; indeed it is constantly reaffirmed: he confesses, 'for me the hillside always remains the world of childhood, of bonfires and adventures and games' (p. 253). These few examples of thematic and verbal repetitions and echoes are far from exhaustive, but are sufficient to illustrate the vital, organising function they have within the novel.

Prior to *La casa in collina*, Pavese had written many 'belle pagine' but never, quite, the complete novel, in which style, structure, tone and subject matter were in consummate harmony one with another. Here, however, Pavese controls his resources so well that one is seldom aware of *tecnica*; indeed, one can open this novel at any page – and this is perhaps the supreme test of the novelist's mastery of his craft – and recognise there all the signs of what has gone before and all that is to follow.

This novel moves forward on two different, though interacting, planes of reality – the collective–historical and the individual–psychological – and tells the story of the contradictions between them and the tensions they create in Corrado. Just as imprisonment and *confino* provide the objective conditions in which Stefano, in *Il carcere*, experiences a heightened awareness of the absurdity and limitations inherent in all of life's occurrences, so too the relentless encroachment of the war, of blind chance, on the 'certainties' afforded by the cycles and rhythms of nature by which he chiefly lives determine in Corrado a fundamental questioning, an imminent revision of his deepest values, a potential remaking of the self. The significant action of the novel takes place within Corrado's consciousness, for it is there rather than in history (which seems almost at a standstill) that a felt change is gradually registered in a process of attrition.

9

Structure and style as myth in *'Il diavolo sulle colline'*

This novel, which is amongst the most polished and satisfying that Pavese wrote, seems to take as its starting-point the Preface to *Dialoghi con Leucò*:

> We have a horror of everything that is without order, eccentric, accidental and we try – even in a material sense – to set limits for ourselves, to give ourselves a framework, to insist on something fixed.

In the early pages, the easy-going routine of the three students, Oreste, Pieretto and the unnamed narrator, is interrupted by their chance meeting with Poli, the son of 'a man who is fabulously wealthy, a *commendatore* from Milan'. This Poli, known to Oreste since childhood, is seeking by every available means – but especially cocaine, alcohol and women – to escape the destiny of boredom and absence of purpose which his upbringing and environment seem to have imposed upon him. Materially, he and his class have access to everything, and might at first sight be thought to represent civilisation at its most refined, but here and in Pavese's next novel, *Tra donne sole* (Among women only), we gradually perceive that behind the façade of gentility is a moral and spiritual wilderness in which countervailing, dehumanising forces are at work. Ironically, Poli's escape routes lead him always, seemingly inevitably, back to his starting-point, for in varying degrees all imply the *selvaggio* (i.e. 'everything that is without order, eccentric, accidental') in that they represent a descent to the level of merely physical sensation, the abandonment of creative rationality. For the duration of the novel Poli sees, or thinks he sees, the promise of salvation in his association with the three students, albeit a salvation through words rather than through any significant action on his part:

> 'There is an innocence,' said Poli, 'a brightness which comes from the depths ... this innocence is what I'm looking for,' he said, babbling stubbornly on, 'the more I become aware of it the more I'm convinced that I'm despicable, that I'm a man. Are you agreed or not that man's condition

is one of weakness? How can you raise yourself up if first you don't fall headlong?'[1]

Awareness of one's failings is one thing; summoning up the moral resources, the courage and strength of will to combat them successfully is quite another, as Poli is destined to discover. The typical Pavesian character, captive of his own myths, Poli can only delude himself for a limited time before the hopelessness of his struggle overwhelms him. Poli's world is refracted, with as much compassion as disgust, through the individual standpoints of his three student companions, the disgust belonging more to the narrator, who is puritanical and unbending, than to the other two, or, for that matter, to the author. All recognise in some measure that Poli is a victim. If there is condemnation on Pavese's part it is of the enormous wastage of human energy, ability, resources, which that particular social milieu seems to foster.

Early in the novel, Pieretto and the narrator spend an evening with Poli and his vapid mistress, Rosalba, and the tone of the narrator's account of it characterises him as much as it does them and their chosen pastime:

A small orchestra started up noisily, softening immediately, and at the centre of the circle of shaded lights appeared a woman, and she sang. This woman was wearing an evening dress and had a flower in her hair. From the tables, couples gradually emerged and danced, holding each other closely in the semi-darkness. The voice of the woman led them, it spoke for them, it sank down and moaned with them. It seemed like a ceremony, a feverish rite acted out between the river and the hills, in which everyone's actions were a response to the woman's cry; because the woman, another Rosalba dressed in olive green, cried out in the song, she rocked to and fro with her hands on her breasts and cried out, invoking something or other.
Now our Rosalba blissfully squeezed Poli's hand and he, quite casual, chatted away with Pieretto. (*Diavolo* p. 107)

Most striking in this narrative is the total absence of adjectives, and even though Pavese has a keen eye for detail, it is through verbs and nouns that it operates here. Adjectives would have suggested interest, might even have been mistaken for approval. The inversions in 'comparve una donna' (appeared a woman) and 'e-mersero coppie' (couples ... emerged), though normal and expected in these constructions, do suggest in the first case magic, in the second the spell of enchantment in which mindless movements are being performed in response to the seductive rhythm and atmosphere which have been manufactured for the precise purpose of inducing that false, wholly gratuitous sense of 'blissfulness' observed in Rosalba.[2] One may argue that insistence on the ritualistic aspect of this scene is too rhetorical, that the symbolism of 'a flower in her hair' and 'olive green' is too obvious, as well as the parody of Oreste's all-important 'cry', but for the sardonic young narrator this capitulation to an artificially induced mindlessness is loathsome, and the negation of the significance of the symbols, including that 'cry', emphasises his puritanical idealism:

> The orchestra started up again, but this time there was no song. Then the other instruments were silent and there was only the piano, which performed some acrobatic variations for a while, touting for applause. You had to listen even if you didn't want to. Then the orchestra rose above the piano and drowned it. During this number the spotlights and reflectors which were illuminating the trees magically changed colour, and we were green, then we were red, then yellow. (*Diavolo* p. 107)

What is so insidious, the narrator reveals, is that 'You had to listen even if you didn't want to', whilst he finds it intolerable that so much ingenuity and *tecnica* should have been expended on this utterly trivial and meaningless distortion:

> I listened to some of the words of the song which was leading the couples. It was telling them to live, live – take, take – but without any spark of passion. However much you disliked it, however bored you were, it was hard to resist the beat of that song. I wondered whether they could hear that voice up on the hillside. (*Diavolo* p. 110)

It is the form of passion without the content, the contradiction between the message in the words and the irrational, self-negating anti-communication of the more powerful medium, which appears so dangerous; it constitutes a resignation of personal responsibility ('pagare di persona') in that 'the voice of the woman led them, it spoke for them'. If this viewpoint were a response to a casual or isolated incident, it could with some justification be dismissed as narrow-minded; but resignation of responsibility is a tendency in this novel and in *Tra donne sole*, perhaps reflecting a social norm, actively encouraged – imposed even – until very recently by Fascism in Italy. In such circumstances, the attraction that the morally austere, supposedly rationalistic Communism of the immediate post-war years held for Pavese is understandable. It is in Pieretto's comment, which closes the chapter, that the extent of Pavese's vigilance in his continuing struggle against the *selvaggio* is felt: 'These modern nights ... they are as old as the world.'[3]

This novel, however, is not merely an indictment of the mores and the morals of the Italian ruling class; to see it as such would be too simplistic, would indeed be to miss the point. If Poli and Rosalba, in their different ways, are guilty of self-delusion, so too is the narrator; indeed, Poli's oft-stated belief in, and search for, 'an innocence... a brightness which comes from the depths' (*Diavolo* p. 114) is paralleled in each of the students by other myths, at least some of which are as questionable as Poli's.[4] The three students present widely differing attitudes to the problems and circumstances which face them as the novel progresses, and it cannot be otherwise, for each one speaks out of, and for, a different kind of formative background. Oreste is the true *campagnuolo*, transplanted briefly to the city, but essentially untouched by it; the narrator, although the son of country people, was born and bred in the city (like Pavese himself), yet clings to a whole mythology of nature and rural virtues (a tendency common enough amongst all types of 'expatriates'); whereas Pieretto is a product not only of modern urban society, but of an essential rootlessness, owing to his father's occupation:

he hadn't been many years in Turin and had lived before that in a number of towns, following his father, an architect who was always on the move, making a home for his family in some place or other, then uprooting them, following his whims. (*Diavolo* pp. 120–1)

It is Pieretto who – to borrow an earlier expression of Pavese's – represents 'the good sense, the measure... of the pavements' (*MV* 10 July 1947) to counter the narrator's 'superstitious' attitude to the countryside.[5] The following sequence underlines the conflict of views and personalities which exists between them:

Those times when I sweated away on the water, my blood seemed to tingle for the rest of the day, reinvigorated by my clash with the river. It was as though the sun and the living force of the current had saturated me with their essence, a blind strength, full of joy yet unconsciously there, like that of a tree trunk or an animal of the forest. Even Pieretto, whenever he came with me, enjoyed the morning. Drifting down to Turin with the current, with our eyes bathed by the sun and the water from our diving, we would lie there drying out, and the banks, the hills, the villas and the blur of trees in the distance would carve themselves out in the air.
'Anybody who lived like this every day would become an animal,' said Pieretto.
'You only have to look at the sand men...'
'No, not them,' he said, 'all they are doing is working. An animal full of health and strength... and egoism,' then he added immediately: 'that mild egoism which is typical of those who grow fat.'
'It's not a sin,' I grumbled.

'Who's accusing you? It's nobody's fault being born. The blame belongs to others. We just go in a boat and smoke our pipes.'

'We're not animal enough.'

Pieretto laughed. 'Who can say what a real animal is,' he said, 'a fish, a blackbird or a lizard ... Even a squirrel ... There are some people who say that inside every animal there's a soul ... a soul in torment. That's purgatory, I suppose ...'

'There's nothing tastes of death,' he went on 'more than the summer sun, more than the great glare, more than teeming nature. You breathe the air and hear the noise of the woods, and you realise that the trees and the animals don't give a damn about you. Everything lives wrapped up in itself. Nature is death ...' (*Diavolo* pp. 119–20)

It is perhaps in this conflict that one perceives the 'two contrary states of [Pavese's] soul', the fundamental contradiction within him between rationality and instinctive belief. However, the novel is not so much 'confessione dell'anima' (self-confession) as the author's attempt to work out, in imaginative terms, a perspective which is right for him. Like the narrator, Pavese is strongly attracted by 'natural magic',[6] yet rebels against it continually, recognising in it something of the *voluttuoso* against which he believed he had been in conflict since his return from Brancaleone in 1936. The narrator here confesses to the attraction for him of the 'blind force' of nature, seeing it entering into him as a strength, as a result of his contest with it ('the clash with the river'). Pieretto, without explicitly condemning his friend's attitude to the experience, attempts to qualify it in negative terms, but the latter is quickly on the defensive, and Pieretto, as frequently happens, assumes the role of devil's advocate, stressing the unbridgeable gulf which divides man from the natural world. The narrator is clearly annoyed by all this questioning of his personal myths:

It was one of his favourite themes. That's what annoyed me about Pieretto. I'm not like Oreste who would shrug his shoulders and just laugh at such things. If anyone says anything about the countryside, it affects me, it gets my blood up. (*Diavolo* p. 120)

He evades the issue by taking refuge in a facile condemnation of Pieretto's supposed failings, which are wholly explicable – in his view – in terms of his friend's past life, especially his relationship with his father: 'To tell the truth,' he confesses, 'I don't like these too liberal ways, and the father seemed to me just like some inept chap of our own age' (*Diavolo* p. 121). This puritanism is perhaps little more than a screen behind which he hides when he feels challenged and threatened. His refusal to question his own values is particularly in evidence with relation to natural phenomena. Having vainly attempted to seduce a girl by the river, he comes to the conclusion that

> In the sun, on the grass, that scent and our bodies were out of place; they are things you should do in a room in the city. A naked body has no beauty in the open air. It bored me and offended the places around us. (*Diavolo* p. 123)

Later, remembering the incident, he recounts it to his friends, slightly embroidered, however, in that he suggests the girl was willing enough, but 'I couldn't do it. It seemed as though we were offending something or someone' (p. 146). There is something artificial in this, something suggestive of a pose consciously struck. It is in this particular conversation that the extent of the 'superstition' inherent in his attitude to the natural world is revealed, for he admits that although he, like his friends, bathes 'in the marsh', he does so 'with bated breath'. Nature is raised to the level of a primitive religion, for he speaks of his 'offence' to it in terms of 'sin'. When the three are reunited at Oreste's house in the country, it is Pieretto who attempts to define 'religion', and his definition could well contain, and explain, the narrator's feeling of awe with regard to nature:

> Religion ... is understanding how things are. Holy water's no use. Talking with people, you need to, to understand them, to know what each one wants. Everybody wants something in life, they want to do something, though they're never sure what. Well, God's in this wanting for everybody. It's enough to understand and to help to understand ... (*Diavolo* p. 155)

According to this definition, the very act of writing was 'religious' for Pavese, for as he had argued earlier, 'a book is made out of all the things the author would like to be and isn't' (*La lett. am.* p. 256); and in this sense, too, there could be for Pavese no contradiction between religion and politics – an attitude which was to mar severely his relations with the Italian Communist Party.

The experience of the three students unfolds in the countryside, though a countryside which is fragmented, divided in such a way as to reflect three different stages in man's relationship with it. There is their encounter with primeval nature, symbolised aptly enough by the marsh 'where no-one has ever set foot, where since the beginning of time the rain and the sun and the seasons have followed their course unbeknown to man' (*Diavolo* p. 142). There is 'Oreste's countryside', intensively cultivated, representing a state of harmony between man and nature from which an overt moral and physical health derives; man is an integral part of it as it is of him, and this 'phase' achieves a kind of apotheosis in the relaxed, Virgilian atmosphere surrounding the lives of Oreste's cousins at Mombello. Finally, there is the hill of Il Greppo, Poli's country estate, with its bizarre, exotic wilderness, set in the midst of intensively farmed lands and contrasting with their order and harmony, but quite separate from them, like an island, ironically the artificial creation (through neglect) of the wealthy, leisured class of city entrepreneurs. It is in this parody of the Garden of Eden that Poli and his bored, disenchanted wife, Gabriella – part Eve, part Circe – try, with the help and continuing presence of the students, to work out a new beginning and a new meaning for themselves.

The marsh is given an extra, Freudian dimension, in that it is 'a stretch of water right in the middle of the coomb which separated our hill from a rough plateau' – and here one recalls the 'breast-hill' of *Paesi tuoi*. 'In it, a trickle of water formed a succession of pools, and one of them was at the bottom of a deep hollow from which only the sky and the bramble hedge were visible' (*Diavolo* p. 133) – so that it is difficult to resist the interpretation of it as a return to the womb of the Earth-Mother. This anthropomorphism is continued in further reflections on the place:

I felt the earth trembling and humming. I thought of that idea of Pieretto's that the scorching countryside beneath the August sun makes you think of death. He wasn't mistaken.

Moreover, it is accompanied by suggestions of metamorphosis from the human to the vegetable or animal:

That thrill we got from being naked there and being conscious of it, from hiding from all eyes, and bathing and going black like tree trunks, had something sinister about it, more animal-like than human. In the high wall of the fissure I saw roots sprouting and filaments like black tentacles: the inner, secret life of the earth. (*Diavolo* pp. 136–7)

The narrator has the sense of being in the presence of a supreme, natural deity, but more than that, of wanting to negate all traces of his humanity, physical and mental, so as to fuse into it, become one with it. Yet, at the same time, he experiences feelings of guilty revulsion in the recognition that 'it had something sinister about it, more animal-like than human'. For the post-*Leucò* Pavese this contradiction is inherent in the dual nature of man himself, instinctive animal and rational god that he is, and if his momentary urge is towards the instinctive, as in this instance, it is arguable (and Pavese, following Jung, certainly believed it) that it is as valid a part of the individuation process as any initiative whose motivation is wholly conscious, indeed that it is the *principium individuationis* itself. Since the eighteenth century at least, the sense of guilt has been something taught us by the civilising mind; but, in Pavese's view, it is symptomatic of the lost harmony between the two aspects of human nature. What is reprehensible is not the urge itself, but the unbalanced world which makes it necessary for a man to seek it *consciously*. It is this imbalance, affecting urban civilisation more than rural, which is at the root of Pavese's insistence on the 'magic' inherent in the most commonplace objects and experiences, a magic which, in general, we fail to perceive because our eye has been educated away from it towards other values. The following is typical of Pavese's continued insistence on this magic:

We were sitting on the dyke under the vine, and looking upwards you could see the tendrils swaying to and fro. Looking at a vine from underneath, rising up towards the sky, makes it seem as though you are outside this world. At your feet you have the limed clumps of earth, the twisted boughs, and in your eyes the green festoons in flight, and the poles, which are all the same height, are touching the sky. You breathe in and you listen. (*Diavolo* p. 143)

With this kind of attention to detail, Pavese seeks to reopen paths which contemporary life obstructs or even closes completely, and in so far as the particular observation lies outside the experience of the great majority, it often appears bizarre.[7]

For the narrator, the time spent with Oreste and Pieretto in the Piedmontese countryside constitutes a pilgrimage to his origins, in more or less conscious search of confirmation of his deepest-held beliefs:

I knew these piled-up little villages in the country. I knew the summer garden at my grandparents' house where they used to send me to the country as a boy, a village down on the plain, between irrigation ditches and lines of trees, with narrow streets and low porticoes and patches of sky so high overhead. Of my childhood nothing remained but the summer. The narrow lanes which opened out into the fields from all sides, during the day and in the evenings, these were the gateways to life and to the world. (*Diavolo* p. 114)

On the evening of his arrival, he goes with his two friends into the piazza in the village, and there, immediately, a deep, personal chord is touched, and in the experience there is a real sense of liberation:

Words and jokes exchanged beneath the stars with people who couldn't see one another's faces clearly, with a woman, with an old man or with one of us, had awakened in me a strange feeling of elation, a gay, irresponsible feeling, which the gusts of warm wind, together with the swaying of the stars and distant lights, extended to embrace the whole future, the whole of life. (*Diavolo* p. 137)

This sense of anticipation, induced by the evident harmony and tranquillity which he finds here, is abundantly realised in the days which follow, and always there is the connection with the earth, the wind, the rain, the natural world in its innumerable manifestations:

The three of us drank under the portico which opened on to the fields. I wasn't sure whether all that sweetness was going from the wine into the air or vice versa. We seemed to be drinking the scent of the hay. (*Diavolo* p. 145)

I watched the older women, Giustina and the others, Oreste's mother, and compared them with the village girls you saw at their work, with solid legs, dark, with dumpy faces and fine blood in their veins. It was the wind, the hills, their thick blood, which made them so hard and robust. At times, when I was drinking or eating – soups, meat, peppers, bread – I wondered what effect that rough, rich food would have on my blood, those juices from the earth which were the same as those borne on the wind. (*Diavolo* pp. 147–8)

Though the view of the narrator is romantic, seemingly superstitious, Pavese nevertheless makes use of it in order to re-establish an awareness of man's place in the natural order of things, of an interdependence between man and the earth. This motif is emphasised in the epithets applied to individuals in the novel. Thus 'Dina was blonde, slight, *a wasp*' and 'Cinta, I thought, must be slim and delicate, *a vine*' – my italics. This metaphorical language, already commented on in relation to the marsh, serves not only to connect the human with the natural, but also to 'humanise' the inanimate: 'A storm came which *lashed* the countryside', and 'I imagined ... the *most jealously guarded fissures of the earth being penetrated, being violated*'; and to 'dehumanise' the work of man: 'a storm which ... *gnawed away* the roads'. It serves to transform violently the handiwork of man, though in essentially human terms: 'the *blinded* skylight'; to animate the inanimate: 'You could hear the mass of water ... *bellowing*', and 'the clouds were *galloping*'; and even to translate one aspect of the natural world into another: 'the sea of hills'. The purpose of this essentially violent linguistic fusion is to mend the breach between man and his world, the alienation which man himself has brought about in his historical development, largely over the past two hundred years. The ultimate purpose for the individual, as for society, is perhaps the realisation of a wholeness which derives from a sense of oneness with all living things, with inorganic matter, with the cosmos itself.

Pieretto brings with him the result of that alienation: the scepticism of the twentieth century. He sneers when Oreste's father compares the land to a woman with her endless ailments. 'There's nothing mysterious about the country', he argues. 'Even a hoe is a scientific instrument.' He distinguishes, however, between 'the marsh' and 'these vines, for example', arguing predictably that 'here man rules, down there it's the toad' (*Diavolo* p. 141), a view wholly in keeping with that expressed earlier:

the hares and snakes are driven underground and are afraid of anyone who passes by. The smell which reigns is that of petrol. Where is the country now that you lot would like? (*Diavolo* pp. 94–5)

This view, however, has by this time been discounted in the marsh, and is to be further called in question on the hill of Il Greppo. The narrator perceives that Pieretto's distinction comes from either ignorance or prejudice, which he hastens to correct:

But the toads and snakes are all over the countryside. As well as crickets ... and moles. And the trees are the same everywhere. Day and night. In a piece of uncultivated ground there are the same roots as there are here. (*Diavolo* p. 141)

The essential oneness of the land with *all* life above it, on it and below it is stressed, and although man may avail himself of it for a time, he may never possess it absolutely. It is Oreste's father who tries to convey something of the endless struggle with the land which he, as a farmer, must maintain at all costs, using whatever means are available to him ('ploughs, chemicals, oil') because 'the fact is that now, if you turn away for an instant, the next day you've got trouble' and 'you see what a hoe's worth when a field gets overgrown. You don't recognise it any more. It's like a desert' (p. 141).

Though the balance between man and nature is hard won, its resulting pattern and orderliness are reflected in the lives of those engaged in the struggle – Oreste's father and his family, and the two cousins at Mombello, Davide and Cinto – so that the sense of harmony and serenity in the midst of abundance is presented as an alternative, which is preferable to the complication and anxiety of modern life as exemplified in the unfortunate Poli. It is Oreste's father who prepares us for the transition to the world of Il Greppo, at the same time seeming to endorse the view that the land and the lives of those on it are each a mirror of the other:

> To see what uncultivated land is really like all you have to do is go to the land belonging to Il Greppo. Good God! I've been thinking about that lad [Poli is meant] all day, and about his father. Some things are clearer now. That was an estate where, when the grandfather was living, all they ever had to buy was oil and salt. It's a wicked shame having land and not living on it. (*Diavolo* pp. 141–2)

If the marsh represents nature in its pristine form, never having been 'violated' or 'possessed' by man, Il Greppo is the land which once was 'possessed' but in which the force of nature is once more asserting itself, returning it to the wilderness whence it originally came. We are reminded that the Titans, as the primitive natural deities, are never finally defeated; they must ultimately be the victors, and in the human sphere it is the myth, the instinctive–irrational which, in Pavese's view, must always, inevitably, have the last word. Something of the violence of this perennial flux – in its downward phase from the civilised (Olympian) to the primeval (Titan) – is conveyed by the narrator's first impressions of the place:

> But what really amazed you was the tangle, the desolation: after a few untended vines, swallowed by the grass, the woodland was made up of fruit trees, fig and cherry all covered in creepers, willows and acacias, plane trees and elder, all tangled together. At the beginning of the slope there was a wood of great hornbeams and dark, almost cold poplars; then, as we came out into the sun the vegetation thinned out, but mixed in with the more recognisable types were unusual trees such as oleanders, magnolias, the occasional cypress, and strange trees that I'd never seen before, in such confusion that they lent an air of exotic seclusion to the occasional clearings. (*Diavolo* p. 156)

It hints at the exotic, the mysterious, at the fascination for chaos which the narrator had already guiltily observed in himself at the marsh. Here, however, in spite of the natural profusion, there is an admixture of something artificial – unnatural, in fact:

> I was struck immediately by the smell in the air, a mixture of scorched, rotting vegetation, earth and sun, and the fleeting burning scent of the asphalt. It was a smell which suggested motor cars, getting away, coast roads and gardens overlooking the sea. (*Diavolo* pp. 156–7)[8]

It is clear, however, from what has gone before that the narrator is predisposed to think ill of anything connected with Poli, and even though he insists with Gabriella, Poli's wife, that 'only by working one's own land does one earn the right to live on it, and everything else is enslavement' (p. 173), he nevertheless comes round to confessing his delight in the very wildness of the place. His admiration for Cinto and Davide – and for that matter, for Oreste and his father – and the order and sheer creativeness they epitomise seems in conflict with this delight:

The hill seemed to be cooking in the August sun; honeysuckle and mint formed a concealing wall all around them, and it was lovely wandering about in there and, on getting to the point of coming out into the wood of hornbeams below, to turn back into the scrub like an insect or a bird. There you seemed as if you had sticky paws, in that scent and that sun. (*Diavolo* p. 172)

Quite apart from the continuance of the unresolved contradiction, there is something apparently decadent about this denial not only of civilisation but of his humanity, for not only does it reduce him to 'an insect or a bird', but he seems to rejoice in the destruction of 'creativeness that is responsibility' (the phrase is Leavis's) in the 'vines suffocated by weeds' and so on, admitting that for him

the contrast was nothing to get upset about, the scrub looked all the more virgin and wild. Our voices among the bushes were not enough to violate it. The idea that in the woods the great summer sun tastes of death was true. (*Diavolo* p. 172)

In short, there is clear recognition that in embracing the wilderness and its denial of mankind he is embracing a kind of death, which, however, is also the equivalent of a state such as exists before the beginning of life. Then, almost simultaneously, we find him acknowledging that

that desolation, that isolation on Il Greppo was a symbol of her [i.e. Gabriella's] mistaken way of life and Poli's. They did nothing for their hill and the hill did nothing for them. The savage waste of so much land and so much life could not bear any fruit other than anxiety and futility. I thought back to the vines at Mombello and the rugged face of Oreste's father. To love a piece of land you had to work it, to sweat over it. (*Diavolo* p. 175)

And so he continues, oscillating between the *voluttuoso* and responsibility, apparently unaware of the contradiction that is in him.

Pieretto, on the other hand, does not lose his sense of proportion, even though, like the others, he derives much pleasure from being there – though it must be said, more from his conversations with Poli (and the others) than from the exuberance of nature around him. Though much of what he says is with tongue in cheek, it has clear, uncompromising values behind it:

I mean it. The countryside in August is indecent. What's the meaning of all these sacks of seeds? There's a stink of coition and death. And the flowers, the animals on heat, and the juices that drip?

He continues,

The wintertime, the winter ... at least the earth is buried then. You can think about the things of the spirit then. (*Diavolo* p. 173)

This suggestion of the orgiastic character of the world of natural phenomena in summer – though not, it should be noted, the apparently puritanical attitude towards it – is reminiscent of the parallel between the earth and woman voiced earlier by Oreste's father (and ridiculed then by Pieretto). The moralistic tone is rejected by Gabriella who, with her 'I like this indecent smell' identifies with the image, and from here on evolves as a kind of Circe figure, who weaves her captivating magic around the innocent Oreste: a goddess of degrading love who 'poisons' her husband and turns all men into animals. Almost simultaneously we discover that Oreste 'was no longer his old self' and that, although recognising the need to escape from this 'island', the narrator too has been 'transformed' – 'and what's more,' he confesses, 'the game appealed to me as well' (p. 180). This attraction of forbidden fruit, contravening his own puritanical standards, receives a partial explanation a little later, ironically from the much-despised Poli; and it is clear from his reaction that the explanation has touched him, has included him.[9] In this question of the attraction of Gabriella, he is less than honest with us and with himself:

I wasn't jealous of Oreste; I didn't think about Gabriella in a serious way; but neither did I wonder whether he thought about it. I enjoyed the game, that was it; it was a bit like another secret like the marsh, just as harmless, and yet I was careful to see that Pieretto didn't get wind of it. It would be just like Pieretto to talk about it at the table. (*Diavolo* p. 181)

But he is mistaken, for 'harmless' it certainly is not, nor can it be described as a 'game', at least, not for Oreste. Gabriella soon tires of him and he suffers humiliation and frustration as a result. Only when the *milanesi* arrive, and the Bacchanalia they create is in full swing, does he realise how corrosive her influence is, and that what he witnesses then, and not the interlude she has been living in the country, is her real life, her true self. In spite of this realisation, he is drawn into the vortex:

'Listen,' I said to her. 'What have you done to Oreste?'
She didn't answer and went on holding my hand. I was conscious of her breathing and her scent. I put my cheek against hers and kissed her.
She pushed me away. She said nothing and pushed me away. I hadn't kissed her mouth. She hadn't responded. And now my heart was thumping – she felt it as well.
'Fool,' she said coldly. 'Don't you see? That's what I've done to Oreste.'
I was humiliated and felt desperate. I listened to her with my head bowed. (*Diavolo* p. 211)

But Gabriella, like Pavese's Circe before her, though fully conscious of what she is and of her inability ever to escape it, has glimpsed something different in another: a purity and honesty in Oreste which she has believed momentarily she is capable of grasping. 'Compared with him we're all shit,' she says, 'he's the only one of us who's honest and sound' (p. 176). Now, however, she has realised that it would be his innocence that would be destroyed, and that for her it is already too late for any significant change. It is, incidentally, this realisation about herself which makes her so sceptical of Poli's insistence that fundamental change is indeed possible in an individual. She implores the narrator to take Oreste away. Her destiny is with Poli, for they are alike. In spite of his talk of a search for a new innocence – paralleling her own search in her relationship with Oreste – he falls yet again, and recognises his persistent folly and its inescapable origin: 'It's incredible,' he said, 'how your deepest self is what you were as a child. It seems to me I've always been a child. It's the oldest habit we've got ...' (p. 212). We know, by this time, what he means, for we have already received a graphic account, through Pieretto, of his debauched and neglected childhood. The lesson is ever the same: 'what has been determines what will be'.

Poli equates the search for innocence, for a new beginning, with the search for our real selves: that in which we are truly in 'God's image':

'You still stick to it,' said Pieretto, 'that we're like the Heavenly Father?'
'What else is there?' Poli said, full of conviction. 'Do the words make you afraid? Call it what you want. I call God absolute freedom and certainty. I don't ask myself whether God exists; it's quite enough being

free, certain and happy, like Him. And to arrive at it, in order to be God, all a man has to do is touch the bottom, know his basic self.' (*Diavolo* pp. 177-8)

Here, in slightly different guise, is the desire of men to be gods which is central to *Dialoghi con Leucò*: a desire which springs from the fond belief that absolute freedom must go hand in hand with absolute certainty.[10] For Poli, the only truth which matters is what we are, and yet 'Simply who you are, nobody can tell you', so that contemplation of self, in monastic isolation such as Il Greppo allows, is preferable by far to the society of men – which, ironically, is tantamount to a recognition and an embracing of the alienation of contemporary man. Pieretto, as might be expected, takes up the 'personal responsibility' argument in opposition to this viewpoint, asserting that 'consciousness is nothing but a sewer; health is out in the open air, among people' (p. 178). However, this argument is not made for social, political or humanitarian reasons; rather because it is only by living amongst people that one can ever discover how one would react 'if the flood came'. The point is that it is our instinctive reactions, not what we would like to think they would be in any given situation, which tell us what we are. However he evaluates his personal search, Poli's emotional needs seem clear enough from the story he tells of childhood neglect, particularly by his mother. These needs have never been adequately fulfilled either by his pet animals or by women – indeed, of the latter he claims:

There was a time when I thought they were sensual [and it is precisely a sense of *physical* warmth and nearness which Poli lacks] ... I believed that they knew at least that much. But it's not so. They're only skin deep. There's no woman worth as much as a fix of dope. (*Diavolo* p. 195)

Gabriella is unfortunately different in that she needs the company of many other people, and it is perhaps she whom Poli has most in mind when he laments, of women in general, 'that they have no inner spiritual life'. Poli's ideal, we realise, is but a 'virtue of necessity', an attempted stoicism: the 'descending into our selves' and its accompanying solitude are merely surrogates for the woman in whom he once hoped to find his personal salvation. Though one need not insist on a total identification between the author and his creation, this was clearly Pavese's own viewpoint for most of his adult life. Poli is doomed, however, whatever his beliefs and intentions, because he is that unique, predetermined blend of experience which is Poli. The tuberculosis which takes him by surprise at the end of the novel is attributed by the narrator to 'the life that he has led', with the further comment: 'it's not enough just to think about health, so as to do a thing or not to do it' (p. 215). This view is endorsed by Poli himself in the already cited 'It's incredible how your deepest self is what you were as a child', etc. (p. 212).

In Pavese's diary we find this note for 7 October 1948:

4 October finished *Diavolo in collina*. It has an air of something big. It's a new language. It adds 'student discussion' to the dialectal and the cultivated styles. For the first time you really have planted symbols. You have salvaged *Spiaggia* by grafting on to it the young people who make discoveries, the world of conversation, mythical reality.

Whilst anyone who had followed Pavese's development up to the publication of *Diavolo* would have had no difficulty in recognising the work as his, it does nevertheless constitute his first wholly mythico-symbolical novel, and because of this it is difficult to understand how much of it might be intelligible to those who were not familiar with his work, including his essays on symbol and myth. Though Pavese built on diverse strands of the European and American literary traditions, by the time he arrived at *Diavolo* he had developed a symbolism and a theory of myth which, if not entirely original (the influence of Jung and Thomas Mann, in particular, are much in evidence), were nevertheless highly personal, and the 'new language' to which he refers makes tremendous demands on the reader.[11] A point which admirably demonstrates this is the reference to 'scarlet geraniums' in the description of Gabriella's 'secret' hideaway, the little loggia to which she disappears each day to lie in the sun, almost certainly (the students conjecture) completely naked:

Stools and towelling bath-robes and a divan were all folded away against the wall. I thought that from the divan, when it was opened out, you must be able to see nothing but the sky and the geraniums. (*Diavolo* p. 180)

This echoes the narrator's description of the marsh, where he 'saw the pale-coloured sky' (p. 136), and subtly hints that for Gabriella this is an equivalent. Moreover, the geraniums too have a significance beyond the merely connotational, but a significance which belongs to Pavesian language, originating in *Il carcere*, where they are associated with Stefano's erotic fantasies surrounding the wild and beautiful Concia. Here, too (where they are mentioned twice in quick succession), they add a similar erotic dimension to what is apparently merely factual description. One must presume the allusion would be lost on anyone unfamiliar with Pavese's writing.

There is an interesting passage in the novel itself which throws some light on this sort of association and which hints at what Pavese is attempting to achieve by it – which is certainly not abstruseness. The passage in question, which immediately follows on from a description of Oreste's house and its village setting, gives us the narrator's impressions and thoughts as he waits for someone to come and open the door:

> Whilst I waited I looked around me: the whitewash patchy in the sunlight, a tuft of grass on the terrace against the sky, the great noonday silence. With the clanking of the cart as it moved away, I thought how for Oreste those were familiar places, that he had been born and had grown up there, and goodness knows what they must say to him. I thought about how many places there are in the world that belong to someone in that way, that someone has in his blood and nobody else knows. (*Diavolo* pp. 128–9)

What he is suggesting is that whatever Oreste is must be inextricably bound up with the scene previously described, and that whilst to anyone else, like himself, coming there as an outsider, it appears commonplace, unworthy even of comment, for Oreste – and presumably his fellow-villagers – it is perhaps the key to their deepest reality. The colours, objects, sounds, smells and typical experiences of that place are those which have determined Oreste's attitudes towards all experience, whether it be there or in any other environment ('You don't lose the Langhe', Pavese told us, years before, in 'I mari del Sud'); and so it is for everyone else, the deep, intimate, unconscious ('in the blood') relationship between a specific environment and a personality. The uniqueness of the total determining experience of the individual points inevitably towards a unique set of symbols and myths, which make his language (as well as his personality) unique. A similar observation was made by Pirandello in *L'uomo dal fiore in bocca* (*The man with the flower in his mouth*) in which the man, in attempting to explain his choice of 'una seggiola di queste sale di medici' (a chair in one of these doctors' waiting rooms) as a composite symbol of a given state of mind, suggests:

> Particular recollections of images, some of them remote, are so specific to each one of us, and are determined by reasons and experiences that are so individual, that we should no longer be able to understand each other if, when we spoke, we didn't stop ourselves making use of them. There's nothing more illogical, often, than these analogies.[12]

If a personality is to be truly known – by the subject himself or by others – this personal language must be penetrated, that is, 'clarified', and this is the enormous task which Pavese set himself in his writing. He aimed at dispelling obscurity, but often, because operating on the very frontiers of consciousness, fell inevitably into that obscurity; the already-mentioned geraniums are perhaps an illustration of this point.

Armanda Guiducci, in her assessment of Pavese's prose style, argues:

With an infinite number of adjectives, always deriving from the psychological effects of one's reading, this property of his mode of writing has been underlined: it has been said that his writing is rugged, concise, essential, rigorous, sharp – or reticent, and so on. He himself defined it as 'sober and essential'.

But we are dealing with something more than conciseness. We are dealing with the abolition of any graduation of effects indicative of where the meaning is to be found.

We are dealing with a kind of neurosis which is, in a way, elegant (if you will allow me the word) and by virtue of which everything is cast, as in the schizophrenic's vision (if you will still permit the expression, for it serves as an example), under a harsh blade of light which never varies in intensity. The page is not merely concise; it is contracted. It is not only sober, it is constrictive. It is bound not only by the speed of the rhythm which creates an effect of lightness and fluency, but by the merciless drive of that rhythm which, as in its movement it destroys all in its path, will brook no delays, and claims to accentuate every word in a significant way.[13]

In so far as the language is often very personalised, allusive in the way just discussed, it does not always make for successful, immediate communication, but there is nothing gratuitous about it; there is 'conciseness' because every word counts in a way that is more typical of poetry than of prose. But more than this, the author's writing proceeds always on two different planes of meaning, the historical and the mythical, because its function is not only to tell a story but to 'clarify his own myths'. The second of these two functions is frankly personal – Pavese never made any secret of it – and the technique has much in common with medieval allegory, except that the symbols are often personally developed rather than belonging to any universal system. Nonetheless, real communication is made, even though the reader may sometimes be perplexed by a paragraph or a conversation because of the apparent leaps in sense from one sentence to the next, and because some words have reference to a significance which originates outside the work he happens to be reading. Let us consider this:

Oreste and Pieretto arrived, with their shirts off, and slapped my back in greeting. They were black and famished and we sat down at the table at once. The father sat at the head, while the women came and went – old aunts and little sisters. I recognised Pieretto's 'victim', the sister-in-law, Giustina, an energetic old girl, at the other end of the table. The children were joking; they pulled her leg, referring to some flowers for the altar that the sacristan had put in the holy water. Then an allusion to Our Lady of August slipped out. I kept an eye on everybody, but Pieretto seemed to know what was what; he ate and kept silent.

Nothing happened. We talked about Oreste's bathing. I said that I'd been on the Po to sunbathe, that the Po was full of people bathing. The children listened attentively. The father let me finish, then said that the sun was everywhere but that in his day only sick folk used to go on the Riviera. 'You don't go for the sun,' said Pieretto 'nor for the water, either.'

'Why do you go then?' said Oreste.

'To see your neighbour naked like yourself.' (*Diavolo* p. 130)

The choice and association of details, coupled with the apparent *non sequiturs* and the rapid pace of the passage, create a sense of the bizarre. Why, of all possible epithets, are 'black' and 'famished' chosen? 'Famished' alone would have caused no stir, but when both are together their difference in kind, the one immediately visual, the other discernible only through observation of behaviour or some verbal comment, does constitute a kind of shorthand which, whilst it is not metaphor, is something akin to it. Over and above this effect, there is the fact that 'black' is also a 'Pavesian' word, which is connected always with the earth and chthonic forces, and in this particular novel its full significance does not become apparent until after the narrator's introduction to the 'marsh', which occurs only *after* this reference. This technique is used again in the same passage in relation to 'some flowers for the altar', which, as it occurs in the flow of the narrative, seems to be without particular significance. Only when Giustina reveals her religious bigotry in the following pages does it fall into place, connecting with 'they pulled her leg'. Obviously this makes great demands on the reader's memory whilst giving to the prose something of the organic nature of poetry, for it is not merely the plot but the verbal themes which the reader must store in his mind as he progresses through the novel. Indeed, to read the post-war Pavese intelligently, profitably, one needs almost to read each chapter a second time before progressing to the next, as well as to refer back continually to earlier moments.

On the face of it, Armanda Guiducci is right; yet one feels that she has 'had the experience, but missed the meaning'. Pavese's style presents many more facets than her comments allow; nor was it static, as her comments imply, but developed continually and variedly from novel to novel. Certainly there are constants, but they are far from being all. Even within this one novel the range is impressive, as we shall see:

> I took a girl on the Po towards the end of July, but there was nothing new or sensational about it. I had known her before; she was an assistant in a bookshop, bony and short-sighted, but she had nicely manicured hands, a languid manner, and as I was looking at the books it was she who asked me where I'd caught so much sun. She promised, happy enough, that she would come that Saturday.
>
> She came wearing a little white bathing costume under her dress, and she took the dress off turning her back on me and laughing. She stretched herself out on the cushions at the end of the boat, complaining about the sun, and she watched me rowing. She was called Teresina – Resina for short. We talked about the heat, the fishermen, the bathing establishments at Moncalieri. She talked more about swimming pools than about the river. She asked me if I went dancing. With her eyes half closed she seemed preoccupied.
>
> I stopped the boat under the trees and I started swimming. She didn't swim because she had covered herself with sun-tan lotion and she smelled like a chemist's shop. When I came out of the water dripping she said I'd been clever and she walked about on the river bank. Her long, reddened legs weren't bad. I don't know why, I felt sorry for her. I brought her some cushions on the shingle and she told me to take her bottle of oil and do her back for her, where she couldn't reach. Then, kneeling down, I rubbed her back with my fingers and she was laughing and she told me to be good, she was laughing with her neck against my mouth. Twisting herself round, she kissed me on the mouth. No mistake, she knew what she was up to. I said to her: 'Why have you put that oil on?'
>
> And Resina, touching my nose with her own, said: 'What do you want to do, filthy beast? It's not allowed.'
>
> She went on laughing, with those little eyes of hers, and asked me why I didn't use any oil. Then I squeezed her body against mine. She broke away and said, 'No, no. Put some oil on.'
>
> She didn't do anything more than kiss me, even though she did agree to come into the bushes. After the initial feeling of annoyance, it didn't displease me that the thing finished there. In the sun, on the grass, that scent and our bodies were out of place; they are things you should do in a room in the city. A naked body has no beauty in the open air. It bored me and offended the places around us. I said I would take her to the pool at one of the establishments, where Resina peered contentedly at the other bathers and drank fizzy lemonade with a straw. (*Diavolo* pp. 122–3)

Here we have the narration of a series of events which have taken place earlier in the year. In terms of the information it affords it is 'essential', and yet it is devoid of the apparent leaps in sense of which Guiducci complains. Clearly, this is prose, and equally clearly it is typically Pavesian. What makes it so – quite apart from its subject – are certain stylistic peculiarities which, nevertheless, do not detract from the flow of the narrative: 'Una ragazza *la* portai', (I took a girl) 'ma non fu niente *di stupendo o di nuovo*' (but there was nothing new or sensational about it), 'era commessa di libereria, *ossuta e miope*' (she was an assistant in a bookshop, bony and short-sighted), 'mentre guardavo i libri *fu lei* a chiedermi' (as I was looking at the books it was she who asked me), 'un costumino bianco sotto *la gonna, e la gonna* se la tolse' (a little white bathing costume under her dress, and she took the dress off) – all of which are taken from the first paragraph. No attempt is made to 'accentuate every word in a significant way', rather to create a total significance through the concatenation of essential details: normal, economical prose, in other words. The tone in this particular passage is ironical, hinging on Resina's seeming enthusiasm for the sun – 'it was she who asked me where I'd caught so much sun' – and her behaviour when really confronted with the possibility of becoming sunburnt: 'complaining about the sun' almost as soon as she is exposed to it! The irony goes further, being levelled at the banality and predictability of the girl and the quality of the experience the narrator shares with her. Resina belongs to the city in the sense that she is wholly possessed by its values, as her attitudes and actions display; she has lost the capacity for establishing even a temporary harmonious relationship with the natural world. She finds her true milieu when she finally persuades the narrator to take her to the swimming pool, which is expressive, perhaps, of a preference for the artificial and synthetic, inculcated by the society of which she is so much a part. It is perhaps the narrowness of her vision (and here Pavese's use of 'short-sighted' is double-edged), which occasions the comment 'I felt sorry for her'; and yet there is real scorn in the observation 'Resina peered contentedly at the other bathers and drank fizzy lemonade with a straw', not least because that 'Resina felice' echoes 'promise, felice' (she promised, happy enough) – which had been her mood at the outset of their brief relationship, suggesting a stock response to all experience, real and artificial alike. Like Poli (though the symptoms are different) she too is seen as a victim of modern, urban values.

From this piece of narrative we move on to description:

It was a stretch of water right in the middle of the coomb which separated our hill from a rough plateau, and you went down from the vineyards, among fields of millet, as far as a steep-sided fissure which was full of acacias and alders. In it, a trickle of water formed a succession of pools, and one of them was at the bottom of a deep hollow from which only the sky and the bramble hedge were visible. During the hottest hours of the day the sun beat down into it from directly overhead. (*Diavolo* p. 133)

Again this is typical of Pavese, and what makes it so more than any other single feature is the association of certain nouns: 'coomb', 'hill', 'vineyards', 'fields of millet', 'fissure', 'pools', 'hollow', 'sky' and 'the hottest hours'; yet their significance is simply connotational, their meaning is all on the page.

Another frequently recurring feature is the passage which describes not only a scene but also its effects on the observer, so that the world of objects acts like a mirror reflecting his inner self:

Oreste and Pieretto called me from up above. They were under a tree and jumping up at it. 'Off you go and eat some plums,' he [Oreste's father] said. 'That's if the birds have left any.'

I went across the scorched stubble and joined them on top of the hill. It was like being up in the sky. At our feet, very much smaller, was the village piazza and a jungle of rooftops, steps and straw-ricks. I suddenly felt the desire to leap from hilltop to hilltop, to embrace everything at a glance. I looked over to where we'd been in the morning, where the plateau ended and looked for the tops of the pine trees there. The blinding light flooded down into the space between the slopes and the horizon shimmered. I had to close my eyes almost and could see nothing but spots of light. (*Diavolo* p. 140)

This is more subjective than either of the passages previously examined. Its language tends much more towards the figurative, the quality of the thought expressed by it towards the fantastic. The principle underlying the effect is a rearrangement, in the mind, of the phenomena observed, according not to how they are known to be in reality but to how they register on the eye of the observer. If one were to believe the truth of the eye without interference from the mind – that is, if one were to approach reality as does the child or the untutored savage – then the village 'at our feet' and 'leap from hilltop to hilltop' would be expressions no longer of fantasy, but of what was believed in as real possibility. This constitutes an attempt to see the world in a historically earlier light, to achieve what Pavese, in his degree thesis on Whitman, had termed the view of the 'virgin eye', not merely as stylistic novelty but, more importantly, as a way of re-establishing a connection with what he believed to be the essential, revitalising power of his natural, primitive origins. And yet, for all this, though we are struck forcibly by its effects, there is nothing abstruse in it, nor any 'abolition of the graduation of effects'.

Finally, because Pavese himself mentioned it as an important innovation in his stylistic repertoire with regard to this novel, let us examine a couple of passages of 'student conversation'. The first one occurs whilst the three students are returning from their visit to Oreste's cousins at Mombello:

Then they winked and said: 'You who don't want to drink or make love in the country ... what do you say?'

I brushed the question aside as you do a fly. 'I like those two,' I said into the slipstream.

Then we talked about Davide and Cinto, about the wines, about the grapes in the bucket and about how fine the genuine, natural life is.

'The great thing,' said Pieretto, 'is the way they keep their women. Us outside, drinking and telling the tale, and them and their brats in the kitchen so they don't pester.'

The sun was just shaving the tops of the vines, distilling a red glow, a rich shadow, from the clumps of grass and from all the trees.

'And the fact is they work,' I said, 'they make this land theirs.'

'You are mad, Oreste,' said Pieretto. 'What do you want with Turin? With the anatomy theatre? You should marry what's-her-name and work your land in peace ...'

Oreste, with his eyes fixed on the horse's neck, following the curve of the road with his chin, said calmly: 'Whoever said that I didn't want that? ... Just give me time.'

'What a queer pair you are ...,' I remarked. 'You have fathers who want one of you to be a friar and the other an agronomist, and you don't want to know about it, you'll drive them crazy; and you'll end up, Pieretto, as an atheistic friar, and you, Oreste, as a country doctor.'

Pieretto smiled contentedly. 'You should always help your father,' he said. 'You need to teach him how difficult life is. If afterwards – as is only right – you get where he wanted, you have to convince him he was wrong and that you did it for his good.'

'Will you really marry the girl?' I asked Oreste.

'He's not saying anything, he won't talk,' said Pieretto. 'He has the excuse that we're drunk.' (*Diavolo* pp. 152–3)

The conversation develops naturally and the thread is never lost, despite the pace, vivacity and badinage which, at times, turn it almost into repartee. It serves several purposes. It of course furthers the story in that it evaluates the experiences just lived through; it presents the character and attitudes of the students in statements which are typical of each of them, in terms not just of content, but of tone and style; it adds an element of humour, which is largely absent from the narrative passages, reminding us that, in spite of the underlying seriousness of the author's intentions, these central characters are young, exuberant, even wayward students, who are venturing for the first time into the web of complications that adult life appeared to be for their creator, and which it certainly is for Poli.

The second example is taken from the scene, already partially examined (see pp. 181–2), in which the narrator and Pieretto are rowing and swimming in the river in summer. This presentation of the quintessential in the form of a paradigmatic episode was a typical feature of Pavese's prose which derived, in all probability, from his theory of the recurring nature of essential experience. In this particular example we are given special insight into the way in which Pieretto's mind works; we witness the confidence with which he makes his assertions, the rationality of his arguments, his insistence on precision of thought and expression of thought. For him, the example of the 'sand men', provided by the only partially comprehending narrator, is inadequate, for the distinction he is seeking to make is that between incidental immersion and voluptuous self-abandonment (or addiction) in the world of natural phenomena, the second of which, he hints, is socially disintegrative. His conversation is an almost continuous attempt to define and evaluate experience, a process of 'clarification'. The narrator, typically, is immediately on the defensive, presuming a moral censure in his friend's comments which, in truth, is not there. He becomes sullen in his own defence, totally ignoring – because not noticing, presumably – Pieretto's all-important condition of 'every day'. Pieretto, however, is not interested in trying to prove the superiority of one view over another and indeed, a little later, is himself guilty of the kind of self-indulgence he remarks on here when at the marsh – though it never reaches the proportions of addiction.

It is at this point that we encounter that kind of conciseness of expression which infringes the accepted conventions of prose discourse: 'It's nobody's fault being born.' Clearly there is a sense leap here (such as occurs frequently in conversations between people who are on intimate terms with each other), and for anyone unfamiliar with Pieretto's views (or his style), apprehension of meaning ceases to keep pace with the flow of speech – which is a calculated effect on Pavese's part. The gap between the 'animal full ... of egoism' and 'It's nobody's fault ...' must be filled by the reader. He must pause for thought and *create* the meaning for himself, as happens in poetry; but the key is there in the word 'fault' which occurs three times in as many lines. The realisation that Pieretto is arguing that no-one should be blamed for what he is now makes interpretation of 'the blame [which] belongs to others ...' quite possible, and with the 'we just go in a boat ...' the narrator and the reader realise that Pieretto is including himself – further proof that he is not accusing, merely observing. The narrator then makes the assertion that 'We're not animal enough', but Pieretto, without accepting or rejecting its truth, immediately goes beyond it and questions the premises on which it is founded, which the narrator has not done. For Pieretto, discussion is primarily a means of discovery through a continuous extension of consciousness to take in every possibility. From 'a fish, a blackbird ...' to 'That's purgatory, I suppose ...' is not a premeditated conviction or intention to convince, it is just such an extension of consciousness through thinking aloud. On the other hand, the statement which follows – 'There's nothing tastes of death ...' – is a view which is already well established before it is uttered; nevertheless, he illustrates its truth before reiterating the assertion in his 'Nature is death'. And here we have arrived at that kind of aphorism that Pavese was so fond of. 'Nature is death' needs much careful thought before the multifaceted truth it contains can be grasped: if animals are a part of that death, which is nothingness, the absence of all meaning for mankind, then the only way in which they can have meaning is to be in a state of life-in-death, which, by an erudite analogy which has the whole of Catholic civilisation behind it, must – he concludes – be purgatory. Yet once again, Pieretto, far from expressing a conviction, is simply carrying a line of thought to its logical conclusion without regard for truth or untruth. In the process there is partly the sheer pleasure in thought and in argument, partly the desire to explore all possibilities within his reach. His mind is open and continually questioning – unlike that of the narrator, who frequently argues from prejudice, superstition and fear of change. Pavese avoids rhetoric and didacticism precisely by the technique just analysed, and for the reason that he rarely has sufficient certainty to be categorical.

Armanda Guiducci – and she is not alone in this – has seized on those features which stand out and characterised Pavese's style wholly by them, quite forgetting that they must stand out from something, and that that 'something' is equally significant in creating the total stylistic effect. Her analysis of his style is thus as partial as an appreciation of a landscape by a man who is colour-blind in greens.

At a time when entrenched positions had already been taken up – I refer of course to the 'cold-war' period – Pavese, because tormented by doubts, continued to debate within himself the larger effects and causes in the movement of modern history, the total condition of contemporary western civilisation. This novel, like his others, is a debate, and as such is a confession of ignorance, hesitation and, perhaps above all else, of humility – a quality long out of fashion.

10

Being and seeming in 'Tra donne sole'

The debate about moral values in contemporary society continues in Pavese's next novel, *Tra donne sole* (Among women only), where he presents a particular social class consistently living its life at the level of 'seeming' rather than of 'being'. His analysis of its mores suggests links between indolence, materialism and the *selvaggio* in a powerful indictment of the Italian ruling class in the years immediately following the Second World War.

Clelia, who is both narrator and a leading protagonist in the story, returns to the city of Turin, her birthplace, after twenty years. Her specific purpose in coming is to set up a branch of the Roman fashion house which employs her, but her experiences there force her to question the meaning of her own life, her supposed success and the real significance of her much-vaunted self-sufficiency.

Immediately, we see her discovering and remembering the city in her first impressions:

> I arrived in Turin with the last of the January snow, as happens with the acrobats and nougat vendors. Seeing the stalls and the glowing acetylene lamps under the *portici* I remembered it was carnival, and as it was not yet dark I walked from the station to the hotel, peering out from under the *portici* over the heads of the people. The raw air stung my legs, yet, tired as I was, I lingered in front of the shop windows, not minding if people jostled me, looking around me and huddling into my fur coat. I thought that by this time the days were getting longer and that soon a bit of sun would be melting that slush and ushering in the spring.[1]

Yet this is something more than a description of a series of actions, for those actions are in themselves an expression of her character, whilst certain verbal motifs in the passage have already been encountered in other of Pavese's writings, and therefore have a particular suggestiveness in the light of subsequent developments in the novel. Clelia seems to identify unconsciously with other outsiders who have also come for a specific though temporary purpose ('acrobats and nougat vendors'); their purpose, however – 'carnival' – becomes, ironically, the epithet which best describes the lives and attitudes of the people with whom Clelia associates whilst in the city, and in this sense, the 'carnival' is seen to be anything but 'temporary'. The 'glowing acetylene lamps', another manifestation of light, reminding us of the 'faro lontano di Torino' (far-off beacon of Turin) of 'I mari del Sud', illuminate a scene which 'was not yet dark', for, in the metaphorical sense, Clelia had not yet begun to make her descent into the dark, tormented world of the Torinese upper classes; the 'shop windows' are also mirrors, especially apt in Clelia's case, because they reflect so much of what she is; whilst the act of 'huddling into my fur coat' is as much an expression of refuge from 'people [who might] jostle me' as it is from the cold; and finally, there is powerful irony in the thought – if interpreted in a figural sense – that 'soon a bit of sun would be melting that slush and ushering in the spring', for of course the 'spring' or 'new beginning' in this novel is all 'slush'.

Once she has reached her hotel, Clelia wants to be alone for a while, for she needs time to reorientate herself gradually. She has told no-one of her intended visit to the city, but even so her solitude is to be shortlived, for a garrulous chamber-maid, an insistent caller, a constantly ringing telephone, followed by the sensational events (an attempted suicide) in the room across the corridor, serve to draw her out of herself and her memories into the life of the city and the present. Solitude, she soon finds, is difficult to attain in the social milieu in which she becomes embroiled, for although it is never explicitly stated, it is a condition which is equated with *noia*, itself a product of an inner moral and spiritual chaos. Indeed, attitudes to solitude are of capital importance in this novel, for just as in the individual 'maturity' is recognised by Pavese as 'solitude which is self-sufficiency', so it is with regard to an entire society or a class; and here the upper classes, both collectively and individually, fall far short of the required ideal.

As a girl, Clelia left Turin with Guido, her lover, poor and without any apparent means of improving her lot in life; but she worked hard, driven on by her ambition to lift herself out of the poverty she was heir to, so that now, on her return, she moves in far grander social circles than those she had known as a child. Clelia, by her own efforts, has succeeded in life; she has returned full of self-respect, with more than a hint of self-congratulation. Certainly it has not been easy. She has made enormous sacrifices; yet, triumphantly, she has finally arrived. But there is a dark side to her success, and her experiences in Turin make her fully aware of it, and in so doing make her question the meaning of her success, her attitudes and herself as she had never done before, so that the novel's *terminus ad quem* is a sense of remorse and of failure in human terms.

In pursuit of her goal, Clelia has been ruthless with herself but also for herself. People have become a secondary consideration – not necessarily consciously so, but certainly so in practice. She has perforce cut herself adrift from the people and places which had been her origins, so that now, whilst she can still remember poverty and squalor, she can no longer identify with them. Nevertheless, though she has achieved the outward manifestations of a place amongst the 'haves' in society – material wealth and security and the respect of her employers and her clients – she cannot identify with them spiritually or morally. They know nothing *from experience* of the means by which she has arrived, nor what it means for her – a point which is made crystal clear in the conversations which she has about her work with Rosetta, Momina, Mariella and others of the social set to which she is temporarily attached. She is thus divided in herself, belonging yet not belonging, and Turin makes her fully aware that in truth she is classless and quite alone. Her expressions of doubt, even regret, permeate the novel; the following is typical enough:

I wondered whether it was worth toiling away to get where I had got, just to be nothing any more, to be worse than Momina who at least lived among her own people. Other times when I felt like this I had taken comfort from the thought that my life was valid not for the things I had obtained or for the place I had made for myself, but because I had made it, because I had obtained them. 'This is a destiny just like any other,' I would say, 'and it's me who's created it.' But my hands were trembling and I couldn't get control of myself. (*Donne* p. 291)

A fundamental shift has begun to take place in her assessment of her own life's worth. 'Other times' she knew how to stave off doubt by convincing herself that what really mattered to her was not the prize but the successful struggle, whereas now 'I couldn't get control of myself'. It is the realisation of '[being] nothing any more' (because totally isolated) which is recognised as the necessary, tragic prerequisite of her hitherto cherished 'solitude which is self-sufficiency'; like Stefano long before her she has 'made a home of a prison cell' out of necessity. In such moments of awareness as these, she too becomes a victim of that *inquietudine* which grips the great majority of Pavese's protagonists once they have left childhood behind them. Thinking back over her life she realises what it is that she has lost:

I saw those ambitious faces, those pale, lined, twitching faces – was there ever any one of them that had been able to relax in a moment of peace? Not even when they were dying did that passion let up. I had the impression that I had never let myself go for a moment. Maybe twenty years before, when I was still a little girl, when I used to play in the streets waiting with pounding heart for the season of confetti, booths and masks, maybe then I had been able to let myself go. But in those times carnival meant for me simply carousels, nougat and false noses. Later, there was the frenzy of going out, of seeing things, of running about all over Turin, with my first adventures in the alley-ways together with Carlotta and the others, heart beating at knowing we were being pursued for the first time – even this innocence came to an end. (*Donne* p. 222)

It is that 'Not even when they were dying did that passion let up' which gives the clue: ambition becomes a way of life, an instinct, and so too do its attendant preoccupations, which are corrosive of one's humanity. The constant vigilance, suspicion and fear destroy even the possibility of 'a moment of peace', of forgetfulness of self. It is principally this condition of 'self-abandonment' which constitutes the childhood 'innocence', the ability, that is, to be absorbed in and by whatever experience offers itself to us, without any sense of priorities or urgency. The very structure of the paragraph from which this passage is taken reflects that sense of contraction which it describes: it begins with what is not (grammatically speaking) a fully expressed thought – 'Un bagno e una sigaretta' (A bath and a cigarette) – suggesting something hurried, snatched, and ends abruptly with the equally terse, though much more assertive 'Squillò il telefono' (The telephone rang), which, like the cockcrow in *Hamlet*, ushers in tragic, significant change. Indeed, the novel's *terminus a quo* is the rupture of Clelia's cosy, contemplative, self-indulgent solitude in a long series of interruptions which prove to be the norm in that particular milieu. The intrusions, however, frustrating though they are, are the beginnings of that questioning process which leads to Clelia's 'new awareness'. In this sense, Clelia's experience in Turin has a function equivalent to that of the war for Corrado, in *La casa in collina*. In themselves, the intrusions on her privacy by the effete, morally corrupt or insensitive members of the circle are a continual source of irritation and are treated with irony and contempt in the telling, for Clelia never suffers fools gladly. She is intolerant of insincerity, pretentiousness or hypocrisy, and it must be admitted that she finds little else among this human dross. Naturally enough, considering the route her own life has taken, she is most scathing of those whose 'business' – whatever it may be – is not taken seriously, is in effect 'a game', a reflection of the fact that the very 'business of living' is itself treated as 'carnival'. It is thus one of the ironies of this novel that Clelia's own, much-vaunted dedication to hard work is wholly in the service of this class of people whom she despises, in the perpetuation of another form of seeming, that of fashion, the ephemeral, the whimsical. She is their 'possession' socially, but even her innermost being has been moulded in part by their demands, and it is growing awareness of this which forms the substance of her 'new awareness' as we progress through the novel.

The world of the arts – or, more correctly, of seeming or pseudo-art – is continually the focus of her caustic irony; the following passage is typical:

The violinist played well, as they always do on these occasions. He was a fat little man, with white hair, who kissed everybody's hand. You couldn't tell whether he was being paid or whether he'd come as a friend. He laughed with tongue in cheek and looked at our legs. A pale, flabby woman, with glasses and a red rose on her shoulder, accompanied him on the piano. The ladies all shouted 'Bravo!' All in all, I was bored stiff. (*Donne* p. 281)

She recognises immediately that the violinist has done his job well, but it is the heavy pretence, the public seeming, of which she is intolerant, and it is clear that she regards the whole scene as a sham. However, her contempt goes much deeper than this, for it is linked with her own ideals of personal and moral responsibility; and in this respect, it is the painter, Loris, who becomes the focal point of her scorn:

All painters' studios are alike. There's the same lack of order in them that you find in certain shops, but it's like that on purpose, arranged. It's never clear just when they get any work done, they always seem to be complaining about the light. We found Loris lying on the unmade bed – but without his pussy-bow this time ... (*Donne* p. 246)

The sentiments are exaggerated in expression, but that is Clelia's character; her measure is always the job well done and a passion for orderliness, and in Loris's case, it seems, she finds neither. She is no connoisseur where art is concerned, but she judges according to attitude, atmosphere and output, and she instinctively rejects the scene which she finds on entering Loris's studio. It seems that Pavese, in bringing together 'art' and some other kind of 'business' in this contrastive way, was seeking some sort of common denominator, probably in the idea that any job or occupation of any kind is creative – or should be – not only of an object or situation, but also of a 'form' which establishes order (the 'something fixed') in an area which was previously empty or formless, in an assertion of one's humanity over the inanimate. Though Clelia never reasons it out in this way, her reactions point towards her instinctive acceptance of just such a position.

Yet, even if the execution was inadequate or even non-existent, the *philosophy* of the artist could – at least in theory – suggest a purpose in art which would be creative in the way outlined above. In such a case, the failure of the artist would be one either of temperament or of technique, and whilst he would still merit – and no doubt receive – Clelia's disapproval as an artist, he might still be exonerated as a man. In Loris's case this condition does not apply, for his *philosophy* is found lamentably wanting in human terms, as the discussion about the staging of the play serves to illustrate. Having listened to the objections to going ahead with the play – mainly owing to its topicality in that it contains a suicide and might therefore be thought to be in bad taste in the light of Rosetta's recent attempt on her own life – Loris offers his own opinion:

But we're dealing with the Martellis, with people who pay well. I don't know what it is Rosetta has done ... in fact, I rather like this illusion of reality, where artistic situations lose some of their equilibrium and become life. Just where personal matters come into it doesn't interest me ... Still, it would have been superb if Rosetta really had been prompted by ... Anyhow, the Martellis won't stand for it. (*Donne* p. 247)

There is real confusion here between being and seeming in the classical Pirandellian sense, where *arte* and *vita* are no longer distinguishable one from the other. It is but a short step from aesthetic delight in the possibility that a play might have led a friend – 'by suggestion' – to suicide and a similar delight in lampshades made from tattooed human skin. And should this seem too severe, too rhetorical, we should not fail to notice Loris's 'Just where personal matters come into it doesn't interest me ...'. The examples in European history were too near Pavese's own time for him not to be aware of them, and of the process of systematised dehumanisation in the thirties and forties which had made such distorted expression of the human spirit possible. And connected with this attitude, if not directly responsible for it, is the argument that 'we're dealing with people who pay, and who pay well'. But Loris is not alone in his belief, as we learn from the following:

'Nene leapt up, vivacious. "If Rosetta really had died, we could have done it. *Un hommage à Rosette*...".' Clelia's reaction is one of amazed disbelief:

> In the shop, I'm used to hearing scandal and tittle-tattle from all over Rome, but this squabbling between friends just because another of them hadn't succeeded in killing herself, this really struck me. I had the impression, almost, that the play had begun and that everything was unfolding as make-believe, as in a theatre, just as Loris wanted. Arriving in Turin, I had stepped into the scene, and now I was acting as well. 'It's carnival,' I thought. 'Just you see, they get up to these tricks every year in Turin.' (*Donne* p. 248)

At this juncture we are prompted by the key word 'carnival' to recall that Clelia herself has lived through a parallel situation as a child:

> On the evening of Carnival Thursday, when my dad had got worse, and was to die a bit later, I wept with rage and hated him, thinking about the party I was going to miss. Only my mother understood me that evening, and she made fun of me, telling me to get from under her feet and go and cry in Carlotta's yard. But I was crying because the fact that my dad was probably going to die frightened me and wouldn't let me go off and enjoy the carnival. (*Donne* p. 222)

Once the first childish reaction was past ('I ... hated him, thinking about the party I was going to miss'), her tears were recognised by her *even as a child* as being an expression of fear and of identification with the one whose dying would change 'carnival' into 'reality', childhood into maturity. Instinctively she had felt a sense of responsibility and identification: her humanity, then at least, had been intact. Here we recall the words of one of the two unidentified speakers in the dialogue *Gli dèi*: 'Who we are and what we believe comes out when we're faced with difficulties, when we have to take risks.' In the example quoted – always assuming the truth of Pavese's dictum – Clelia, in human terms, is of a very different calibre from Loris and Nene.

It is hardly surprising that in a society which asks only to be 'distracted from distraction by distraction' sexual love, like art, should be treated as a diversion. When the *festa* is flagging and la Nene, the hostess, is becoming desperate,

> One or two of them were talking about going off with a bottle and sitting on the steps of the Monument to the Artilleryman. 'Let's go in a boat,' somebody else said. 'Let's go after some women,' said the foolish voice of a boy ... (*Donne* p. 329)

And away they all go to via Calandra, the street of brothels. But the incident is by no means isolated in the novel. There is the empty, meaningless self-gratification of the feckless Febo with Clelia, the hinted lesbian phase in the relationship between Rosetta and Momina, the discussion about which of the women would make the best prostitute, and so on: in Pavese's view, all examples of the debasement, the – to use an apt Marxian epithet – reification of sexual love. Indeed, the only positive experience of this kind in the whole novel is that between Clelia and Becuccio, for between them there exists a mutual respect, and the love-making grows naturally out of the evening they spend together, despite the many reservations registered by Clelia herself in the narration.

The degradation of art and of sex are brought together in a sequence involving Clelia, Rosetta and Momina towards the end of the novel, where they appear significantly as kinds of 'prostitution':

Momina said that exhibitions, concerts, the theatre are nice only because a lot of people go there. 'Just imagine,' she was saying, 'being on your own in a theatre, or in a gallery ...'
'But it's the people who are so boring.'
'Sure enough,' said Momina. 'You don't always like concerts or being with people or the ballet. You go only when you want to see them and to talk. It's like calling on somebody ...'
'No, not music,' Rosetta said. 'With music you have to be alone. When they used to put on decent concerts in Turin ...'...
I asked Rosetta: 'Do you really like music?'
'I don't exactly like it but it just is,' she said. 'It's something. Maybe it's just suffering.'
'It must be like painting,' Momina said.
'Oh no,' said Rosetta, 'painting is an ambition. Listening to music, on the other hand, you just give yourself up to it ...'
I just managed a secret smile. With all the many things there are in this world, with all the things that the two of them knew and possessed, they were talking about music as if it were cocaine or their very first cigarette. 'I think that artists don't suffer at all. It's anybody who listens to them they make suffer, if they take them seriously.'
'It's others who suffer and enjoy things,' said Rosetta. 'Always the others.'
'Those who make the wine never get drunk,' I said. 'Is that what you mean?'
'Prostitutes never enjoy what they do,' said Momina. Even Rosetta winced at this.
'Is there anybody more of a prostitute than Nene?' Momina went on. 'She's intelligent, she has her craft at her fingertips, and all the temperament a sculptress could have. Why doesn't she settle for that? Oh dear, no.

She has to dress like a little girl, fall in love, get herself pissed. One of these days she'll end up with a kid. She's got the face for it ... She thinks nobody sees through her.'

'You're wicked,' said Rosetta.

'Momina's right,' I mumbled. 'What counts is the work, not the show.'

'I don't know what counts,' said Momina. She looked at us almost as if she were surprised, naively. 'I'm rather afraid that nothing counts. That we're all prostitutes.' (*Donne* pp. 318–19)

Quite apart from the fact that in Momina's view 'public' art is merely a social focal point, a meeting place, and has apparently no specific merit or value in itself, what is so disturbing to Clelia is the inability to distinguish qualitatively between experiences, in spite of the clear educational and social advantages enjoyed by Momina and Rosetta. The reduction of all experience to the same banal level is symptomatic of the moral and spiritual disintegration which Pavese feared in a society dominated by materialistic goals, and which he, like many other intellectuals in the period 1945–56, felt could most effectively be opposed from within the Communist Party. The *snobismo* which always attaches itself to 'art' in such social circles, already indicated in the 'ladies [who] all shouted "Bravo"'on listening to the Roumanian violinist, is suggested again in Rosetta's 'When they used to put on decent concerts in Turin ...', and contrasts clearly with her inability to make any intelligent assessment of her own reaction to music, it being reduced to 'sofferenza', that is, to a reflection of her own state of mind. Typically, even Momina's confession of ignorance is expressed assertively, as though it were its opposite ('It must be like painting'), whilst Rosetta's evaluation of 'painting' as 'an ambition' reveals that she has seen no further than the desire for public acclaim as possible motivation in painting. Music, for her, is simply escape from self ('Listening to music ... you just give yourself up to it') and from responsibility for self and others. Momina, on the other hand, sees music (and presumably other art forms) as a confidence trick, whereas Rosetta seems to see it as a product which is consciously designed to have a given effect but which is none the less quite detached from the emotions of the producer. It is at this point that the leap from art to prostitution is made, and even Rosetta is taken aback by it. It is presented by Momina as a straightforward analogy: that is, if artists don't enjoy their 'business' they must be like prostitutes who also do not enjoy theirs. Logically, the argument is false, and is intended presumably as further insight into the quality of Momina's mind; and even though her scurrilous comments on her friend Nene are apparently sufficient justification for the 'leap' in her eyes, the statement remains a *non sequitur*. Relentlessly she moves from iconoclasm to nihilism with her comment 'I'm rather afraid that nothing counts. That we're all prostitutes.' Both parts of the statement are important: the first because it does indeed express an emptiness at the centre of the particular individual life, which is itself a reflection of the emptiness at the centre of the society; the second because it forces us back to the 'prostitution' idea, extending it beyond 'artists' to 'all'. It is more than an expression of self-disgust or disillusionment, though it is that too, for of course it calls in question the nature of the relationship of every individual with the society of which she is a part. Certainly Pavese had used the figure of the prostitute on many occasions before, perhaps because he did indeed believe himself to be 'bought and sold', particularly in the post-war Communist period in his life, when he had achieved a degree of public acclaim – that is, when his work was bought by the Italian reading public, which meant the bourgeoisie. It can be argued that, in any society in which the hegemonic class is characterised by cultural banality (even vacuity), viciousness and hypocrisy in its relationships, and gross materialism as its sole *raison d'être*, everyone, whatever his occupation, is in some measure guilty of 'prostitution'. Certainly this appears to be a part of Pavese's message in this novel, even though Momina seems not to perceive the full significance of the observation she has made. Clelia's own position vis-à-vis this class of people, whom she despises, has already been discussed.

Though Clelia is not an attractive character, she is honest in the sense of being true to herself to the degree in which she is aware of that self: the Marxist would presumably argue that she is guilty of false-consciousness. She reveals a real capacity for sympathy with others, though it is often marred by a failure in sensitivity, so that, whilst one may choose to argue about the contradictions inherent in her social position, at the level of person-to-person relationships she is far more sincere in her caring than the other characters with whom she associates. The callousness with which Rosetta's 'cry for help' is treated appals her, as well as the fact that the worst offender is her closest friend, Momina. This lack of 'caring' for one of their number is magnified when it comes to others who are not known or who are the victims of some misfortune; Clelia's description of the collection for the blind, taken at the first masked ball she attends with Morelli, is example enough:

Then there was a collection for the poor blind people. A gentleman in evening dress, wearing a red paper hat, made a speech which was full of jokes about the blind and the deaf, whilst a couple of ladies charged blindfolded around the room catching the men, who paid a certain amount of money to be able to kiss them. (*Donne* p. 231)

Caritas is reduced to 'charity' as is common under the Capitalist system, so that there is only the appearance of *caritas* – another seeming. Much worse, it is turned into an entertainment in which, in human terms, the 'poor blind people' (the irony is heavy here) are actually exploited. Human misfortune becomes a game, whilst at the same time the kiss, symbol of love or affection, is sold, presumably as inducement. Pavese, in this novel more than in any other, makes use of the technique in which adverse criticism is implicit in the description rather than overtly made, a method which enables him to present the sardonic–ironic aspect of Clelia's *stile* without intrusive comment from the writer himself. Clelia, whose point of view is determined by the character of her own experience in life, connects this lack of caring – and indeed the general moral degeneracy – with the inactivity of these people, with their lack of a social function, with their non-productivity. And in case we are tempted to recognise in this viewpoint merely a deferential bow on Pavese's part towards Communist ideals, we should not forget the closing lines of 'Il dio-caprone' (The goat-god) of 1933:

> Perché, quando una bestia non sa lavorare
> e si tiene soltanto da monta, gli piace distruggere.

(Because when an animal doesn't know how to work and is kept only for mating, it likes to destroy things.)

The sentiment there expressed is precisely the same.

Clelia is unable to resist the temptation of returning to the scenes of her childhood:

One of those days – it was drizzling at the time – I had to come back from the Consolata district before the evening. I was looking for an electrician and it had an odd effect on me seeing those old bottles again, those great doorways in the narrow streets, and reading the names – Le Orfane, Corte d'Appello, Tre Galline – recognising the signs. Not even the cobblestones in the streets had been changed. I hadn't brought my umbrella, and beneath those narrow strips of sky between the rooftops I discovered that smell the walls had, all over again. 'Nobody knows that you're that self-same Clelia,' I was telling myself. I didn't dare stop and peer into those old shop windows.

But when I was on the point of going back, I couldn't resist. I was in via Santa Chiara and I recognised the corner, the barred windows, the dirty, opaque glass. My mind made up, I crossed the little threshold and the bell tinkled, as it always used to, and passing my hand over my fur coat I felt that it was wet. In the musty air the little shelves with their displays of buttons, the little counter, that smell of linen, they were all the same.

The only new thing was a green light that illuminated the cash register. At the last moment I hoped that the shop had been sold, but the thin woman, with the bony, careworn face, who stood up behind the counter, really was Gisella. I think I changed colour, realising that I, too, had aged like that. (*Donne* pp. 257–8)

Unbelievably, what has remained in her memory for twenty years suddenly takes on concrete form before her eyes. Time is seemingly cancelled by this discovery of a whole series of objects, places, even smells which had been there at the centre of her childhood. It is this discovery of the 'minute particular' which, for just one brief moment, deludes her into thinking – or rather, feeling – that she can step back through time to be again what she was then and meet the people she knew then on exactly the same terms. Clearly, she has made the decision not to go back ('I didn't dare stop', 'I couldn't resist') knowing full well that the experience can only be a sad one, and yet it is like being drawn into the centre of a whirlpool; nevertheless, having taken the decisive step over the threshold into that other time, she panics, perhaps realising that the objects she recognises around her are only the husk of meaning, the 'empty formal appearances' of experience, the semblance, not the essence, of reality: for so they are. Even then, the 'green light' hints at hope that the experience will not prove negative, even as the ghost rises from this tomb of Clelia's past. This Gisella, who cancels out the Gisella of Clelia's memories once and for all, is a mirror in which Clelia is forced to see herself, so that the journey into her past paradoxically makes her more aware of the present. The seeming – whether invention, illusion or evasion – cannot survive this sort of experience, and Clelia's reaction, on looking into this mirror, is – in accordance with Pirandello's formula – one of terror and confusion:

I wished I could go away. That was all my past, unbearable and yet so different, so dead. I had told myself so many times in those years, and then again later on, whenever I thought about it, that my aim in life was really to succeed, to become somebody, so that I could go back one day to those narrow streets where I had been a little girl and exult in the warmth, the amazement and the admiration of those familiar faces, of those ordinary people. Well, I had succeeded and I'd come back, but the faces and the ordinary people had all disappeared. Carlotta had gone, and Lungo, Giulio, Pia and all the old women. Even Guido had gone. Those who remained, like Gisella, did not give a damn about us, or about the old times. Maurizio always maintains that we get things, but when they're no longer of any use to us. (*Donne* p. 260)

The result of the return is a kind of implosion, a black hole within consciousness; chaos returns – the totally incomprehensible.

Though outwardly so self-assured, Clelia is increasingly forced to question the rightness of her attitudes and actions. Gradually she comes to suspect the significance of her own self-possession, for if at the outset she believes that 'You can't love another more than yourself. If you don't save yourself, nobody will save you', as though it were a deliberate choice on her part, that is hardly the case at the end of the novel. One of the most difficult moments for Clelia is that in which Momina, without any warning, asks her: 'but if you were to marry, would you want to have children?' It is not the question itself so much as its implications for her which touch her so deeply, for Momina, dogmatic as ever, maintains that 'Anyone who has children ... accepts life', adding quizzically: 'Do you accept life?' (*Donne* p. 256). Clelia tries to wriggle out of the trap, and whilst she succeeds in doing so at the level of the discussion, she remains troubled inside. Momina has insisted that 'to have a child you would have to carry it inside you, become like a bitch, bleed and die – you'd have to say yes to a lot of things', and it is this that she means by 'accepts life'. The connection is a new and disturbing one, as Clelia admits:

I'd never thought in that way about the things Momina had said, they were just words, and I already knew 'we are here to enjoy ourselves', but there was no getting away from it, it was true that not having children means being afraid of living. (*Donne* p. 257)

This, too, is a question of responsibility, she recognises, of 'pagare di persona': the acceptance of total responsibility for another human being for many years, a different kind of responsibility from that which she has in her work, for that can be rejected even at a moment's notice. She is hyper-critical of her new acquaintances in their rejection of responsibility for those around them, particularly so far as Rosetta is concerned; but here she comes close to the realisation that there is not very much difference between ignoring one's existing responsibilities and refusing a situation in which such responsibilities will be created. If the one refusal represents a selfish egotism, the other is no less selfish, and perhaps even cowardly. In this classically Pavesian 'urtarsi di due modi di vita' (clash of two different ways of life) Clelia is continually revealed to herself, and the lesson is that she is nearer in practice to those whom she despises than she has ever believed possible.

It is her growing sense of repugnance and frustration which causes her to seek out Becuccio, the working-class foreman–joiner at the shop, perhaps in the hope of being able to find some semblance of equilibrium through his down-to-earth, common-sense view of things, even perhaps to touch again the roots she has long ago rejected. The evening she spends with him is as much a return to her origins as was her visit to Gisella and the *quartiere*. Almost at once, however, she realises that there is far too much that she has outgrown for this association ever to be anything more than a game: all time is unredeemable, she learns. Nevertheless, the evening serves its immediate purpose:

Inside me my mind was made up. I wasn't drunk but the bad mood, the feeling of tiredness and the spitefulness I had felt earlier had passed, and I danced and chatted contentedly, feeling warm inside. (*Donne* p. 313)

Even on the following day the sense of well-being remains with her:

I went back to the hotel, alone. I wasn't tired, I was calm and contented. Becuccio had understood me and hadn't insisted on coming with me. I was so satisfied that I was on the point of telling myself: 'Up to Sunday you can see him whenever you want.' But I knew I mustn't do that; already that gesture of Becuccio's of catching hold of my chin and looking into my eyes had sickened me. (*Donne* p. 315)

Once again, Clelia rejects involvement – ostensibly, it would seem, to avoid being the possession of, and therefore being dependent on, another person. This withdrawal – despite her instinct to the contrary ('I was on the point of telling myself...') – has its ironical corollary, for somewhat later, when Clelia refuses an invitation 'to take tea', staying behind at the shop expressly 'per provare Becuccio' (to put Becuccio to the test), she is relieved – or is it disappointed? – to find that not only does he once again address her using the 'Lei' form, but, after offering her a *vermut*, goes off home leaving her to her own devices. Her suspicions (or is it hopes?) have proved groundless; it is she who has been rejected. The question for Clelia is not, in reality, which people to relate to – as she tries to convince herself – but rather whether or not she is capable of any deep, meaningful 'passage to other men', should the right sort of relationship come her way. She has reached an extreme point in her self-imposed alienation and then has not known how to find a way back. She, too, has thereby suffered a measure of dehumanisation. Clelia's own evaluation of dependence in a relationship is made in the following terms:

'All in all, being on the game means nothing more than putting up with somebody's company and going to bed with him even if you don't feel like it. Having money means being able to shut yourself off. So why is it [she wonders as an afterthought] that all these layabouts who have money are always on the lookout for company and a constant noise?' (*Donne* p. 295)

Continuous compromise, which any lasting relationship demands, and which is also 'responsibility', represents something like a prostitution of the will in Clelia's view; it is interesting, too, that although she has probably correctly diagnosed the reason for Rosetta's attempted suicide ('She wanted to be alone, she wanted to shut herself off from all that noise; and you can't be alone in that society, you can't ever do anything on your own except by getting out of it' – p. 295) she has done so, in all probability, in terms of her own experience and idiosyncracies, projecting herself into the girl's situation. It is specifically a failure of humanity which revolts Rosetta, as her reaction to the story of the 'negri di Tombolo' confirms. It is told expressly to shock – and entertain – the audience with its atrocities and obscenities, but Rosetta appears unmoved: '"Are you shocked?" Rosetta said to him. "Have they done anything different from what we do? ... They do exactly the same in Turin. Where's the greater evil?"' (p. 328). And for Pavese it is the final question which must receive an answer. Physical brutality is not the only form of violence. This view had been constantly present in Pavese's thinking from 'I mari del Sud' ('La città mi ha insegnato infinite paure:/una folla, una strada mi han fatto tremare,/un pensiero talvolta, spiato su un viso') through to the *Dialoghi con Leucò*.[2] The suspicion, and fear, is always that it is those societies which achieve the highest degree of civilisation which develop the most sophisticated forms of cruelty. Pavese and his contemporaries had experienced this syndrome in the Europe of the nineteen-thirties and forties.

Momina especially, with her continuous expressions of disgust with life, is an instrument of that insidious violence through her undoubted prolonged influence over the young, impressionable Rosetta: 'Living is so ridiculous that we cling on to it, even to the foolishness of being born ...', she affirms (*Donne* p. 253). She is the *selvaggio* at its most brutal, and as such is probably the most corrosive single factor in Rosetta's own failure.

It is Momina who, more than any of the others, insists on the need for continuous change, novelty in diversion, and yet at the same time proclaims the utter boredom of existence. Rosetta, we learn, has previously wanted to enter a convent because, accepting this mistaken perspective that the beauty of experience consists *only* in its freshness and novelty, she felt that the forced abstention which the convent represented would preserve that beauty by withholding it: 'It's so beautiful up here,' she remarks, 'but tomorrow it'll already be less beautiful. If you want to preserve your respect for the world and the people in it, you have to do without everything ... the convent does that for you' (*Donne* pp. 299–300). She has experienced too much too soon – that is, before she has sufficient maturity to realise that familiarity brings depth. Now, in the Pavesian view, depth brings satisfaction and real meaning, for life is not a search for 'experience' but 'for our selves'. 'The surest and swiftest way of astonishing ourselves is to fix our eyes remorselessly always on the same object. All of a sudden, miraculously, it will seem as if we have never seen this object before' (Preface to *Dialoghi con Leucò*). 'A virgin subject so far as names and places and voyages of adventure are concerned': that which Momina and her circle, including (perforce) Rosetta, seek as a way of life was for Pavese a search for illusion, a manifestation of the *voluttuoso*, seeming rather than being. The convent, as Corrado discovers in *La casa in collina*, not only symbolises 'deprivation' but, in the rhythms and repetition of its liturgy and its way of life, represents and continuously celebrates the essential rhythms of all natural life. Rosetta needs authority she can trust and respect: 'To have someone to tell you what to do and what not to do ... That is salvation,' she affirms (*Donne* p. 286). She needs solitude, which is also protection; she needs to be taught the relative values of experiences and objects; and above all else, she needs a clearly defined purpose – all of which she might have found in a convent. Unfortunately – and there is immense irony in this – the sin she is seeking to escape precludes her access to the remedy, for 'you have to be a virgin to become a nun'. The convent, like the game of chess in *Le streghe*, is pure *stile*, where form and meaning are indistinguishable; it represents 'something fixed', but also 'un modo d'intendere la vita che sia una nuova conoscenza' (a way of understanding life so that it becomes a new awareness). For Pavese, the only change which is of significance for the human being is one of awareness, and changes in external circumstances seldom create the conditions for this.

In a letter written to Augusto Monti, who had been highly

critical of his insistence on the theme of suicide, Pavese tried to explain and justify the very positive moral and artistic purpose which was in his mind when using it in *Tra donne sole:*

> Here we have the bitter experience of someone who works, who is self-made, self-sufficient, who comes into contact with what? with the usual futile world of those who believe in nothing or in trivialities – above all because they are drones – and she observes this world as it putrefies and destroys itself. But even in this world you try and save what you can. *The suicide is a victim* who is basically naive, the most innocent of them all, and if she dies it's really because, of all of them, *she's the only one who is still capable of feeling what it is she is lacking* ... [my italics][3]

Rosetta is not only a victim; she is also – in artistic terms – a symbol of the urge towards self-destruction which is inherent in the 'moral indifference' of any society. Her first attempt at suicide has no purpose that she can define, just as remaining in life has no purpose ('not even she knew why she had gone into the hotel that morning') so that death, far from being a positive choice, is sought in the same spirit as any other distraction. In this, it seems, Pavese wanted to show that the urge to self-destruction (and presumably violence of any kind) is the natural complement of any way of life which lacks order, definition and purpose, which is, in effect, a microcosm of chaos. The question for Pavese is clearly a moral one; and only in so far as it can create the conditions for a new moral order is politics, or indeed any political party, of interest to him. Clelia's expression of remorse when Rosetta is finally dead, though bearing with it some element of self-justification and exoneration, is also a confirmation of the inevitability of the deed and of the spirit in which it has been carried out; it could not have been otherwise given the total context in which it occurred – 'what has been determines what will be':

> It seemed as if I had been deaf and blind; Rosetta's words came back into my mind, her wry faces, her glances, and I knew that I had known, had always known, and had taken no notice. But then I asked myself: 'Could she have been stopped?' and then I thought: 'Let's hope she's gone off somewhere like you did with Becuccio' – but then the faces and the words and the glances came back again. (*Donne* p. 336)

Even here, Clelia not only fails to accept responsibility, but also finally fails to understand the logic – the superb logic – in the manner of Rosetta's death, showing yet again that her understanding goes only as far as it confirms her own experience, attitudes and so on:

> The odd thing had been the idea of renting an artist's studio, having them fetch in nothing else but an armchair, and dying like that in front of the window which looked out on to Superga. (*Donne* p. 337)

The death here – as in the final conflagration in *La luna e i falò* – is clearly symbolic, the empty room being the nothingness of her life, the 'artist's studio' the most characteristic representative of the continuous seeming her life has been, 'the window' the barrier/communication with the ideal of life she felt must exist but which she could never grasp, and 'Superga', as the seat of the shrine to the Virgin, representing that ideal of purity and innocence she felt existed in the convent, but from which she was eternally excluded: 'you have to be a virgin to become a nun'. And most logically and ironically of all, this carefully constructed death is itself but another *mise-en-scène*.

Pavese's call is for compassion, for a more active, practical demonstration of caring for others. This is obvious enough; but it is also for a new and different perspective in the life of all societies, and especially amongst the hegemonic classes in Italy, for this latter group as it appears in this novel is an absolute denial of that Humanistic–Enlightenment ideal of civic society which Italy gave to the world: indeed, it is the epitome of chaos, where the *selvaggio brutale* reigns unopposed. In such societies, the moral tone is set by the hegemonic class, so that relatively healthy personal moralities, such as Clelia's, are insidiously blighted. Clelia, at the outset, makes a virtue of her self-sufficiency, but the novel shows it to be alienation, for even though *solitudine* has been Clelia's conscious choice, Pavese – who never made a virtue of *solitudine* – suggests that it is predetermined by the values of the society as a whole, which, in Gramscian terms, means that it can be traced back to the moral and cultural choices of the hegemonic class. The Pavesian character who seeks 'isolation which is self-sufficiency' does so as a last resort, having failed in the desperate search for 'a passage to other men'. In this sense, Clelia is as much a victim as is Rosetta, but is far less conscious of being so. Hers has been truly a 'private enterprise'; but success, in the conditions which this particular society provides, is only ever a seeming success, for whilst it gives material rewards it takes away or prevents the development of man's humanity. There is a morbid fascination amongst the characters in this novel for low life in all its forms, a kind of voyeurism, and Rosetta, explaining why she personally has indulged in it with Loris, says: 'They are things you do to see what it's like ... It's a way of life, a poverty which eludes us.' It is precisely the position of the gods in *Dialoghi con Leucò*: the misery of mankind as amusement – 'they kill us for their sport'. It is the position of seeing or watching, that of spectator rather than of participant, which characterises the exclusion of the gods and of the Rosettas, Mominas and the like from creative life. As Clelia argues, 'Le cose non basta vederle' (It's not enough just to see things): thus it is no accident that Rosetta is made to die 'in front of the window which looked out on to Superga'. Only commitment which is total – and that means commitment to others – can create the conditions for a morally healthier society, for, in Pavese's view, continuous identification with an action or purpose which causes us an effort or even discomfort (that is, some measure of *self-sacrifice*), creates its own order, structure and rhythms, which become our 'framework'. In short, it creates our *stile*, our 'way of understanding life so that it becomes a new awareness', in a continuous process of humanisation in which magnanimity and empathy become the sure bulwarks against the *selvaggio brutale* and the ever-threatening chaos.

11

History, symbol and myth in 'La luna e i falò'

There is a particular passage in Eliot's 'Little Gidding' which is oddly reminiscent of *La luna e i falò*:

> And what you thought you came for
> Is only a shell, a husk of meaning
> From which the purpose breaks only when it is fulfilled
> If at all. Either you had no purpose
> Or the purpose is beyond the end you figured
> And is altered in fulfilment.
>
> (ll. 30–5)

This is not to suggest any influence of the one author upon the other, nor any sort of connection between the two works other than a rather tenuous *Zeitgeist*. Yet the flavour is unmistakably that of Pavese, of the progressive experience of his whole work over a period of twenty years. At the very beginning, in 'I mari del Sud', is the motif of the man who sets out from the Langhe to spend twenty years of his life wandering all over the globe, believing that life at its fullest is to be found anywhere but where he started from – a belief which, in his youth, the narrator of Pavese's last novel evidently shared, judging by his own 'escape' from the Langhe and subsequent emigration to America. This is the Ulysses of the Dantesque tradition for whom

> né dolcezza di figlio, né la pièta
> del vecchio padre, né 'l debito amore
> lo qual dovea Penelopè far lieta,
> vincer potero dentro a me l'ardore
> ch'i ebbi a divenir del mondo esperto
> e delli vizi umani e del valore.
>
> (*Inferno* XXVI, ll. 94–9)

(not fondness for a son, nor duty to an aged father, nor the love I owed Penelope which should have gladdened her, could conquer within me the passion I had to gain experience of the world and of the vices and the worth of men.)[1]

Yet even this earliest of Pavese's published poems is ultimately a negation of the exotic for its own sake, an outright rejection of 'a virgin subject so far as names and places and voyages of adventure are concerned' – as is, for that matter, *La luna e i falò*. What matters is not the external drama but the way in which it is absorbed and evaluated, and whilst all experience undoubtedly has some validity, in Pavese's final view what is most valid is that which reflects our deepest – which is to say our earliest – selves. The Ulysses theme continues in Pavese's writing, but in a different key, featuring the child's discovery of the world about him and the adult's rediscovery of that same world of his infancy reflected in his present life. In metaphorical terms the child 'goes forth' into the world of 'not self' and creates 'self' largely from his contact with it, whereas the adult 'descends' (as does Pavese's Orpheus) into that 'self' and knows it 'for the first time'. While engaged in writing *La luna e i falò*, Pavese noted in his diary that

> In art, you shouldn't start from complexity, rather should you arrive at it. Don't start from the symbolic folktale of Ulysses to induce a sense of wonder, but start from the humble, common man and gradually give him the significance of a Ulysses. (*MV* 23 August 1949)

Something like this *capovolgimento* is at the root of the gradual change of purpose that Anguilla, narrator–protagonist of *La luna e i falò*, experiences and which makes Eliot's statement such an appropriate expression of it.

Anguilla has returned to the Langhe after an absence of some twenty years, and begins the story of his return in a forthright enough manner, dealing instantly in specific detail:

> There's a reason why I came back to this village, here rather than Canelli or Barbaresco or Alba.

But the promise implicit in those opening words is not fulfilled until the end of the paragraph, and even then obliquely, inadequately almost:

> I've travelled about the world enough to know that every race is as good as any other. But that's why you get fed up and try to put down roots, to have your own bit of land and your own village so that what you are will be worth a bit more, and will last a bit longer, than a mere cycle of the seasons.

There is something hesitant, even reticent about this, as though the speaker does not wish to acknowledge the purpose hinted at as his own, recoiling from it at the last moment, transposing it, as he does, to the level of the general 'you'. He then plunges into a series of reminiscences of his remoter, then his more recent, years, coming back only at the end of the chapter to the question of his purpose in returning. But it is with the same hesitancy, even detachment, as before:

You need a village, if only for the pleasure of going away from it. A village means not being alone, knowing that in the people, in the vegetation and in the earth there is something that's yours which, even when you're not there, is there waiting for you. But it's not easy being there without getting restless.[2]

In the meantime, however, we have learned that the idea of return and the reality of it have proved to be disconcertingly different: a small, almost trivial episode, the discovery that a particular clump of hazel trees, which has some deep, unstated – perhaps because not wholly conscious – significance for him, is no longer there, forces him to admit that 'it meant that everything was finished' (*Luna* p. 11). It is perhaps this discovery which discourages him so much that the projected return is never completely made; for he returns only as far as Genoa – his gateway to the world *and* to the Langhe, something like Eliot's 'point of intersection of the timeless with time' – almost as though losing his nerve, profoundly shocked by what he has found:

I've had my eye on it for a year now and whenever I can I get away from Genoa and go there; but I still can't fathom it. (*Luna* p. 13)

The purpose which had been clear enough in his own mind before he arrived back is not explicitly stated in the whole of the chapter, for his first experiences of the place have significantly altered that purpose through the doubts they have raised in him. His bewilderment is clearly expressed in that 'I still can't fathom it' and so is ours, for the very digressiveness of the novel, its fits and starts, make it difficult to pin down and hold the meaning long enough for us to be sure where it is leading. This is not intended as an adverse judgement, for the very structure of the novel is a function of the search whose object is never fully known to the narrator or to the reader until the end is reached, and even then it is too complex to be expressed conclusively in the language of prose. What we are left with is a series of impressions, images, symbols; but there is no doubt that they lie 'beyond the end' which Anguilla 'figured' at the outset.

There is one significant detail in which the hero of 'I mari del Sud' differs from the narrator in *La luna e i falò*. Whilst the former makes mistakes during his period of readjustment to life in the Langhe, he holds to his opinion that 'You don't lose the Langhe', and we are left with the impression that he has been reabsorbed by his once-rejected *paesi*, almost as though he had never been away. Not so his later counterpart, who gradually realises that he can never return to his childhood environment precisely because he has been away from it for so long and has become used to a wholly different way of life, one which has created in him attitudes, expectations, habits which life in the Langhe would be incapable of fulfilling. Anguilla now belongs to the city, and knows it well enough, and yet there is in him a wistfulness that will not allow him to relinquish his hold on the Langhe, for the Langhe is the symbol of his formative years, of a rounded, complete experience which is within him, even though he can express it only as detail, at the level always of the 'minute particular':

I don't know whether I will buy a bit of land, or start courting the daughter at La Cola – I don't think so; my day is now made up of phonecalls, packages and city streets – but even before I came back, often when I was coming out of a bar or getting on a train or coming home in the evening it happened that the scent in the air would remind me what time of year it was: that it was time for pruning, for reaping, for spraying the sulphur, for washing out the vats or stripping the reeds. (*Luna* p. 83)

It is in this interiorised sense, Anguilla's experience shows us, that 'You don't lose the Langhe'; but in itself the experience is no guarantee that a man may return and take up his life there where he left off years before. The 'altered' purpose of Anguilla's return is not merely another 'recherche du temps perdu', nor merely to 'inform curiosity', but rather the desire to understand why, after so many years of absence, that country can still have a mirage-like effect on him. In order to arrive at such an understanding he must piece together the historical process of change which, in twenty short years, has depopulated *his* Langhe and repopulated it with strangers. Yet Anguilla's initial reaction to what he finds – or more precisely, does not find – amounts to panic, and there is an interesting aside on this aspect of the novel in one of Pavese's diary entries at the beginning of 1949, the year in which the novel was written. In it he discusses the motif of *gloria*, which had a place in Anguilla's calculations in returning: the desire to show that the boy who had started out in the world with nothing had eventually done well for himself, a theme already developed in *Tra donne sole*:

For one's glory to be enjoyed to the full, the dead would have to come back to life, the old become young again, and those who were far away would have to return. We dreamed about it in a small community, among familiar faces which for us, at one time, were the *world*, and now we are grown up we would like to see the effect of our adventures and our words on that environment reflected on those faces. They have vanished, they are gone, they are dead. They will never come back again. And so we look around in desperation, trying to recreate that environment, that little world which didn't know us though it loved us and should have been amazed at what we had done. But it no longer exists. (*MV* 8 February 1949)

These statements are absorbed almost verbatim into the opening paragraph of the fourteenth chapter of the novel. However, though it touches him deeply, this aspect of Anguilla's discovery does not paralyse him; rather does it serve to take him on to more significant discovery, as we see, for example, in the following observation:

It was strange how everything was changed and yet the same. Not a single one of the old vines remained, not one of the animals. Now the meadows were stubble and the stubble was rows of vines. The people had moved on, or had grown up, or were dead. Roots had slid down into the Belbo and been swept away – and yet, looking around you, the great slope of Gaminella, the far off, narrow lanes on the hills of Il Salto, the farmyards, the wells, the voices, the hoes, everything was the same as it always was, everything had the same smell, the same taste, the same colour as it had then. (*Luna* p. 37)

The movement of his thought from the particular and individual to the typical involves also a shift from historical time to cyclic or mythical time, that which in its sights, sounds, smells and actions creates the illusion that 'time doesn't pass on the hills'. It is this sameness in difference which allows Anguilla the possibility of rediscovering his 'first world' and with it something more of himself, the roots of his very being. Again, reference to Pavese's diary gives us some insight into the author's intention in this journey which begins in time but which brings us continually face to face with 'the point of intersection of the timeless with time' (which Pavese himself referred to elsewhere as the 'istante– eternità'), the absoluteness of what is already past, yet strangely present, as if in some contemporary *Divina commedia*:

Strange moment when (at twelve or thirteen years of age) you broke away from the village, caught a glimpse of the world and left in your imagination (adventures, cities, names, decisive rhythms, the unknown) and you didn't realise that you were beginning a long journey which, by way of cities, adventures, names, flights of fancy, worlds unknown, would lead you back to the discovery, on looking back, of *how very full of all that future* was precisely that moment in which you broke away – a moment in which you had much more of the village in you than of the world. And because now you have the world and all that future inside you as the past, as experience, as technique, the fertile, perennial mystery turns out to be that very childhood self which you were too late to understand.

Everything is in childhood, even the fascination which will be our future, for it is only then that we feel it as a wonderful incentive. (*MV* 13 February 1949)

This personal note is artistically transformed in the novel into the following:

I realised that as a child, even when I was chasing the goat, when I was angrily breaking the firewood in winter by stamping on it, or when I was playing and shut my eyes to see whether, when I opened them again, the hill would have disappeared – even then I was preparing myself for my destiny, for living without a home, for hoping that beyond the hills there would be a country which was richer and more beautiful. This room at the Angelo – at that time I'd never even been here – I felt as if I'd always known that a gentleman, a man with his pockets stuffed full of money, who owned farms, whenever he set off in his cart to see the world, would find himself one fine morning in a room like this, would wash his hands in the white bowl, would write a letter on the old, shiny table, a letter that was going to the city, was going far away, and which would be read by hunters and mayors and ladies with parasols. And here it was happening now. In the mornings I would have some coffee and write some letters to Genoa, to America; I had money to think about and people dependent on me for a living. In a month's time perhaps I should once again be at sea, following after my letters. (*Luna* p. 46)

What is so simple in Pavese's expression of experience, and yet at the same time so beautiful and profound, is his insistence on the indissoluble link between the single moment, the single experience, the single object, and the totality of personality, Destiny or history. It is the close attention to the 'minute particular', all of it significant, which gives his poetry its highly individual colour. In the piece just quoted, what is recalled is a series of historically disconnected moments of experience, yet they are recalled because they were recurring or even cyclic experiences in the childhood of the narrator. It was their repetitive nature which made them contribute significantly to the rhythm of his young life and which caused them to leave as a residue in him something perhaps indefinable but which is something more than mere memory, something which is 'in the blood' (to use a favourite phrase of Pavese's). It is worth pausing over these single manifestations and noting the fullness that each one contains, but more than that, the curiosity that so many of them arouse in us about the world of 'then'; they are powerful in their suggestiveness, totally credible. Why was Anguilla angry when chopping firewood? And why does he tell us precisely how he did it? And why did he chase the goat? Why, of all possible details that could have been selected, does he speak of the gentleman washing his hands 'in the white bowl'? Why are we told so much about the letter? Where it was written ('on the old, shiny table'), where it was destined for ('was going to the city, was going far away'), who might read it ('hunters and mayors and ladies with parasols'). Why are these individuals singled out in what is, in any case, an extended 'suppose', pure conjecture? Each one of these single items had its own symbolic significance in the life of the child Anguilla in that it served to tell him who he was and who he was not, what he was worth and what was beyond his reach, and so forth. The 'ladies with parasols' were not only *la signora* Elvira, Irene, Silvia, but all of those ladies who belonged to the employing class; the mayors were the most important civic dignitaries in Anguilla's world; whilst the hunters represented adventure, open possibility ('they came from far off, from the hilltops and the bandsmen, the hunters and the mayors would come' he tells us: they were people who represented spatially and socially the horizons of his world, and the imagined paradise which lay beyond). They, like 'the farmyards, the wells, the voices, the hoes', not only belong to the rhythm of the world of Anguilla's childhood but, as 'the things which never end', define the landscape of his personality in the making. Each one is a nucleus of compressed emotions and reflections, and as such is charged with the high tension from which the poetry of the novel is derived. Pavese makes many attempts in his diary and essays to explain what he means; the following is typical and enlightening:

The memory of an emotional high spot (a moment of ecstasy) touched in the past – the field of marguerites, which was the whole of nature for your childhood – moves you so profoundly now because it has become a symbol of a great experience, of all that infinite number of possible experiences which presented themselves in that high point of that time. Remembering it now, you delight in a symbol of all those possible experiences, and you breathe the atmosphere of the emotional high spot, and you do it with no difficulty, given the comprehensibility, the accessibility of this little memory. Symbol means just this. To objectify yourself in the same way as you would an enormous landscape through the wrong end of a telescope, and deal with it as a thing you possessed completely and which had implicit within it suggestions of endless possibilities. (*MV* 26 June 1948)

Time and again these symbols recur in the novel, and at one point Anguilla comments on the way they are reawakened, and from what he says it becomes obvious that they belong to a particular place and are both personal and communal within that place, but exclude and differentiate in their operation:

What would this valley be for a family which came from the sea, which knew nothing about the moon and the bonfires? You need to have had your bones made here, to have it in your bones like the wine and the polenta; then you know it without even talking about it, and all that that you've carried around inside yourself for years and years without knowing it awakens now at the jingling of a cart, at the swish of an ox's tail, at the taste of broth, at the sound of a voice heard in the piazza at night. (*Luna* p. 57)

The Pavesian Ulysses thus sails inwards towards his own past, towards the most familiar yet generally least understood (because least questioned) part of his own life's experience, in order to attain something like that Dantesque 'divenir del mondo esperto'; and it is there, not in some strange, foreign land, that he is genuinely amazed by what he finds. Anguilla felt continual shock, but not this childlike amazement (*stupore*), in America, whilst his earlier counterpart, the cousin of 'I mari del Sud', 'doesn't talk about the voyages he made', so little lasting impression have they made upon him – on his essential self, that is. What each one seeks is to identify and to rationalise, in so far as it is possible to do so, the informing myths of his childhood, because with that rationalisation will come a measure of freedom, 'that is freedom to choose one's actions rather than merely perform them mechanically because they are predetermined precisely by the *selvaggio*, the irrational within us' (*MV* 17 January 1950). Pavese has been accused of persistent evasion of reality in his obsession with myth, which is seen, especially by some Marxist critics, as synonymous with mysticism; but he leaves us in no doubt at all that he is well aware of the pitfalls inherent in the 'mythical' view of history, as the following note in his diary makes clear:

The superstitious man is one who still *believes* in a myth which has already been overtaken by history – that is, in a myth for which the means of dissolution already exist ... Anybody who makes a show of a myth that he no longer believes in is a hypocrite, a reactionary. (*MV* 30 January 1950)

This notwithstanding, Pavese, like Leopardi before him, regretted the destruction of 'illusion', the reduction of the 'open possibility' it afforded in childhood to the *noia* of rationalised certainty, the bane of his gods in *Dialoghi con Leucò*. Towards the end of his life, he often expressed the fear that his own store of 'personal myths' might one day be 'clarified', so that his writing would be bereft of its prime function, which he had long claimed to be precisely that of 'clarifying his own myths'. This fear may well have led to a degree of prevarication on his part with regard to his 'myths', though I see very little evidence of this in his later works, certainly none that cannot be disputed. Even as he was writing *La luna e i falò*, he noted in his diary:

You no longer have any private self. Or rather, your private self is objectified, is, in fact, the work you do (drafts, letters, chapters, meetings). That's dreadful. You no longer experience any hesitation or fear or amazement in your day-to-day existence. You're drying up.

Where are the anguish, the howls and the loves of your twenties? Everything you use was accumulated then. So what will you do now? (*MV* 30 September 1949)

This, coupled with his view of the historical significance of that novel within his own canon – that with it he had 'completed the historical cycle of his own times' (*MV* 17 November 1949) – makes it difficult not to see the epigraph, 'Ripeness is all', as a confession that he had nothing left to say, perhaps nothing left to discover. The letter he wrote to Aldo Camerino at the end of May 1950 seems to corroborate such a view:

In reality, *La luna* is the book that I have been carrying around inside me for a very long time and the one I have most enjoyed writing – so much so that I don't think I shall write anything else for a while – perhaps never again. It wouldn't do to tempt the gods too much. (*Lett. II*, p. 532)

As a writer, Pavese was conscious of having 'arrived' during the last few years of his life: 'The fact is', he wrote, 'you've become that strange animal, the man who's made it, a name to be reckoned with, a big shot' (*MV* 15 December 1940); but along with the obvious satisfactions (and here we should not forget Clelia's experience in *Tra donne sole*) came the fear that he would – indeed, possibly had already – become an institution, crystallised, defined, like his own Olympians. If the answer to his persistent question 'So what will you do now?' was a silence emanating from his presumed emptiness, it is not too fanciful to suppose that this frame of mind, this sense of impasse, contributed to his suicide.

In Pavese's 'mythical' view of history, the search for an individual past and identification of its essential, informing myths is necessarily bound up with the history and myths of the whole community in which that process of individuation took place. As 'myth' means 'that which returns', the past, whether collective or individual, will have innumerable echoes in the present in the shape of customs, occupations, natural and topographical features, and so on, and it is through identification with these 'objective correlatives' and the memories they evoke that a past is penetrated and its mysteries are unravelled by the analysing mind. Effectively, Pavese argues that the form of reality remains ever intact, whilst its content of specific individuals, details and experiences is in a perpetual state of flux; and this is the substance of Anguilla's discovery when he returns to the scenes of his childhood. It is this element of repeatability, inherent in the form, which explains the persistence in the novel of the regional 'type' and which accounts for the many parallels (not all involving people) in each of the three interweaving time levels of 'then' (his childhood in the Langhe), 'since' (his twenty years of absence) and 'now' (the time of his return) which are the key element in the structure of the novel. In a carefully argued essay, Bruce Merry has suggested that

> Pavese's ideal reader should turn to the Russian Formalist school, where he will find a powerful key to *La luna* in Sklovskij's axiom: 'The content (and therefore the "spirit") of a work of literature is the sum total of the stylistic devices employed in it.' The structure of the novel and the apparent repetitions and matching groups of characters in *La luna* come into better focus when viewed in the light of two principles formulated by Vladimir Propp in his *Morphology of the folktale:* (1) 'transferability' of characters – 'the principle whereby one character in a story can quite easily be replaced by another', and (2) identity of action – 'the story often ascribes the same action to several characters'.[3]

There can be no doubt that Propp was in Pavese's mind certainly at the beginning of 1949, the year in which *La luna e i falò* was written, for he wrote to Giuseppe Cocchiara informing him that 'In a little while I shall have the first draft of Propp on the Folktale and I'll send it to you so you can correct it' (*Lett. II*, p. 346) and the work in question was mentioned in subsequent correspondence between the two. However, it would be a mistake to suggest – and Merry's essay runs the risk of doing so – that Pavese wrote his last novel wholly under the influence of his reading of Propp; he was attracted to the theories of the Russian precisely because they seemed, in large measure, to corroborate his own, and at the same time offered possible solutions to a number of stylistic and structural problems raised by his own 'mythical' material. In the main, Propp's theories were a confirmation, at the level of *tecnica*, of Pavese's own views on the nature of history, and as such possibly played some part in his literary transformation of 'myth ... into history' in *La luna e i falò*. There was nothing either formative (so far as his *Weltanschauung* was concerned) or arbitrary in Pavese's interest in Propp and Formalism.

La luna e i falò posits two different orders of time: the cyclic, that is, mythical time of the natural world, and the linear time of history, arbitrarily superimposed by man, having no root in the essential, enduring reality of the earth.[4]

What happens to the *selvaggio* is that it becomes transformed into a place which is known and civilised. The *selvaggio* as such has basically no reality. It is what things *were* in as much as they were inhuman. But things are of interest precisely in the degree in which they are human. (*MV* 10 July 1947)

Though submerged for a time by history, the *selvaggio* reasserts itself sooner or later, as Anguilla realises after the destruction of the house at Gaminella:

We went up the path. It was a skeleton of blackened, empty walls, and now over the top of the vines you could see the walnut tree, which was enormous. 'All that's left is the trees,' I said. 'Was all that cutting back that Valino did worth it? ... The hillside has won.' (*Luna* p. 108)

Here, mindful of the close parallels between the Eliot of *Four Quartets* and Pavese, particularly in *La luna e i falò*, we recall the former's

> The parched eviscerate soil
> Gapes at the vanity of toil,
> Laughs without mirth.
> This is the death of earth.
> ('Little Gidding' ll. 66–9)

Pavese is committed to human reality, but has too much integrity, too much humility, to pretend that that is all:

You long for the countryside, the Titan – the *selvaggio* – but you appreciate the good sense, the measure, the intelligence ... of the [city] pavements. The *selvaggio* interests you as mystery, not as historical brutality ... *selvaggio* means mystery, open possibility ... You exalt order by describing chaos. (*MV* 10 July 1947)

Pavese's seemingly ambivalent attitude towards myth (which is reflected in Anguilla's attitude towards the Langhe) is rooted in the circumstances indicated here, and in *La luna e i falò* he is concerned to show how mythical time, that of the seasons, is the prime mover in the life of the community to which Anguilla returns, in spite of the recent incursions of history and modern 'civilisation' (notably the civil war in Italy between September 1943 and April 1945) upon the apparent timelessness of the countryside. The following is typical:

The lovely thing about those times was that everything had its season and each season had its customs and its games, which depended on what work was to be done and what the crops were, on whether it was rainy or fine weather. In winter you went back into the kitchen with your clogs heavy with earth, with your hands skinned and back aching from ploughing, but then, once the stubble had been ploughed in, everything was finished and the snow would fall. We spent hours and hours eating chestnuts, staying up late, wandering about the stalls, so that every day was like Sunday. I remember the last job of winter and the first after the blackbird came – those black, rain-soaked heaps of leaves and millet stalks which we set alight and which smoked away in the fields, already suggestive of long winter evenings and staying up late, or promising fine weather for the following day. (*Luna* p. 108)

Pavese's intended 'transformation of Destiny into freedom (and nature into causality)' (*MV* 17 January 1950) meant also the transformation of myth into history. However, Pavese realised that the transformation process works both ways, so that history passes as readily into myth, and furthermore that historical 'fact' is more fragile, more vulnerable and therefore more susceptible to transformation than is myth. The resulting state of flux is illustrated in two episodes which follow each other in the novel. Firstly:

Cinto listened open-mounted, with his scab below his eye, sitting against the bank.

'I was a boy just like you,' I told him, 'and I lived here with my foster-father, and we had a goat. I used to take her out to graze. In winter-time, when the hunters were no longer to be seen, it was unpleasant, because you couldn't even go up the hillside, with all the water and ice that there was, and one time – now there aren't any more – the wolves came down from Gaminella because they couldn't find anything else to eat in the woods, and in the mornings we would see their tracks in the snow. They're like a dog's only deeper. I used to sleep in the room at the back there with the girls and at night we would hear a wolf howling because he was cold up on the hillside ...' (*Luna* p. 38)

Secondly:

'Up the hillside there was somebody dead the other year,' said Cinto. I stopped and asked him who it was.

'A German,' he told me, 'that the partisans had buried on Gaminella. He was all flayed ...'

'So near to the road?' I said.

'No, he came from up yonder, right up the hill. The water had carried him down and Pa found him under the mud and stones ...' (*Luna* p. 39)

Here the factual events of a remoter past (Anguilla's) are recounted in such a way ('you couldn't even go up the hillside, with all the water and ice that there was'; 'and one time – now there aren't any more'; 'the wolves came down'; 'at night we would hear a wolf howling because he was cold up on the hillside') as to create a sense of wonder in the listener, demanding from him a necessary 'suspension of disbelief' as if he were listening to a fable. This fabulising aspect of Pavese's style permeates the whole novel and accounts for much of its suggestiveness; words and phrases abound which point evocatively to an emotionally charged area of the past, frequently accompanied by the imperfect tense, hinting always at the 'normal' or the 'habitual' character of the events described: 'allora' (then, at that time), 'c'era stato un tempo' (at one time there had been), 'Fu una di quelle notti' (It was on one of those nights ...), 'ai tempi di' (in the days of ..., in those times), 'Il bello di quei tempi era' (The lovely thing about those times was), and so on. However, this myth-making process is interrupted by the intrusive memory of an event which is less remote in time, the discovery of the corpse on the hillside. The event is recounted by Cinto directly, with no thought of creating that sense of wonder in the manner of the telling which is more or less consciously there in Anguilla's story. It is the event itself which is the cause of wonder, not the way in which it is presented. The layer of experience which is remoter in time is well on the way towards becoming a myth. For Anguilla it undoubtedly already is, otherwise he would not feel the need to recount it as such; whilst the more recent event remains, as yet, more history than myth. The meeting point of the two experiences is the hillside, representative of the *selvaggio* in its characteristic brutality into which all history eventually inevitably subsides, for the time of history is subsumed in the time of the *selvaggio*. This latter point is accentuated by the way in which the hillside has reclaimed the man who died in historical time (the war), and later reclaims Gaminella.

The mythical event, in the Pavesian sense, is one which contains within itself the seed of its own continual regeneration, and in *La luna e i falò* even the discovery of the remains of soldiers or partisans has something of that quality about it. With the disintegration of the human form and features, which begins the translation from historical to cyclic time, comes also the transmogrification of their significance and the significance of the anti-Fascist partisans, the soldiers of the republic of Salò, and even of the war itself, in 'a new and shocking/Valuation' (to remind us of Eliot once more):

> According to what the women and the shop-keepers said now in the village, blood had run like wine in the presses in those hills. Everybody had been robbed and had their property set on fire and all the women had been made pregnant. Then up gets the Fascist ex-mayor – right there amongst the tables at the Angelo – and says quite openly that such things had never happened in Fascist times. (*Luna* p. 72)

This denial of history is made in the name of the values of humanity and Christianity, initially by members of the old hegemonic class (the local 'notables') who, despite the immediate strength of the progressive parties of the Left, are seen in the novel to be reasserting themselves during the 'cold-war' period in what amounts to a human parody of the cyclic or seasonal movement of nature. It is not clear whether Pavese sees a specific connection between the natural and the historical in these events, or what that connection may be if it exists, but the continuous revelation that 'Everything had its season, and each season had its customs and its games, which depended on what work was to be done and what the crops were, on whether it was rainy or fine weather' suggests a pattern which is fundamental to the lives and attitudes of the people of the Langhe, and with whose apparent stasis sociopolitical conservatism would be wholly commensurate.

In a more general sense, even Anguilla himself has been mythologised, as Nuto reveals early on in the novel:

> When I told him where I had been, he said that he had already known something about it from people from Genoa, and that by that time people in the village were saying that before I went away I'd found a crock of gold under the bridge. (*Luna* pp. 15–16)

The propensity for mythologising, in the sense of encapsulating the particular significance of an event once and for all, within either a fable or a piece of popular wisdom or a cyclic event (notably the *festa*) is most marked in the novel.

There are many passages which underline a 'sameness in difference' between the countryside and the life there as they are in the present and as Anguilla knew them more than twenty years before. The following is typical:

> I had come for a fortnight's break and it just happened to be Our Lady in August. So much the better, because the continuous coming and going of strangers, the chaos and din in the piazza, were such that even a negro would have gone unnoticed. I heard them singing and shouting and playing football; then when it got dark, there were the fires and the crackers. They drank and roared with laughter, and there was the procession. All night long, for three nights, there was dancing in the piazza, and you could hear cars and cornets and the crack of air rifles. The same sounds, the same wine, the same faces as I remembered. The big lads chasing round people's legs were the same; the neck bands, the pairs of oxen, the scent, the sweat, the women's stockings on their dark legs, they were the same. And the gaiety, the tragedies and the promises on the banks of the Belbo. (*Luna* p. 14)

In the very first sentence we have a repetition, in this particular example of 'return', of the theme with which our discussion of this novel began, namely, that of 'intention thwarted' as a direct consequence of the narrator no longer being a part of the continuing rhythm of life in the village and its surrounding region. That rhythm, almost hypnotic in its effect on the reader, is emphasised by the carefully modulated flow of the narrative, which proceeds, for the most part, in phrases which comprise three elements which generally contain within themselves at least one repeated unit of sound, thus: 'cant*are*, url*are*, gioc*are*','*le* mac*chi*ne, *le* cor*ne*tte, *gli* schi*anti*', '*stessi* rumori, *stesso* vino, *stesse* facce', '*le* allegrie, *le* tragedie, *le* promesse'; while the penultimate sentence, divided by the semi-colon, is balanced by the assertion, in the same position in both halves, that the examples given 'were the same', and as this assertion is further implied by that 'And' with which the final sentence begins, the two sentences taken together hint at yet another triad. However, before the tripartite phrasing gets properly under way, Pavese uses pairs of elements which are joined paratactically, e.g. 'coming and going', 'the chaos and din', 'the fires and the crackers', which merge into, and give way to, the triads, so that throughout this passage a sense of order, measure, rhythm and control is maintained. The use of the threefold unit is no accident; indeed, it is signalled semantically by that 'all night long for three nights', which suggests the unifying rhythm of repeated actions not only over three nights, but, by extension, perhaps even throughout the three time levels of 'then', 'since' and 'now' which together embrace the whole action of the novel. The *message* conveyed through this *medium* is that the actions (content) which together compose this event, the 'Festa della Madonna d'agosto' (the form), reflect the larger rhythmic cycle of the seasons (the form) in which this *festa*, as one of several, is in its turn merely a part of the total content, so that ultimately we become aware that in Pavese's mind the 'form' and 'content' of reality (*il vero* – Eliot's 'time not our time, rung by the unhurried / Ground swell') are one and the same, 'the enchainment of past and future' in the rhythm, 'which is always present'. Only the participants and the moment (according, that is, to 'the time of chronometers') are different.

This unity across time is emphasised again much later, when Anguilla has begun to realise a significance which is perhaps the key to all reality – human and non-human – in this seemingly endless pattern:

One thing I always think is how many people there must be, living in this valley and in the world at large, who have the same things happening to them now as we did then, and they don't know it, they don't even give it a thought. Who knows? there may even be a house, some girls, some parents, a little girl – and a Nuto, a Canelli, a station, there may even be someone like me who wants to go away and seek his fortune – and in the summer they'll thresh the corn and pick the grapes, in the winter they'll go hunting, and there'll be a terrace – everything just like it was with us. It's got to be like that. Boys, women, the world, they're not changed at all. They don't carry parasols any more, and on Sundays they go to the cinema instead of to parties, they send their corn to the grain pool, the girls smoke; but for all that life is the same, but they don't realise that one day they'll look about them and for them too it will all be over. (*Luna* p. 140)

Here the sense of inevitability, of a pattern imposed through the blood, the human sap as it were, is most emphatic. But in this second passage there is confirmation, in the suggestion that comes with 'a Nuto, a Canelli', that individual people, places and actions are all merely paradigms of, and variations on, the pattern which is itself reality. From place to place the details of the pattern may be different, but the principle remains ever the same; and what is true in a spatial sense is true also from one period of time to another, so that what Anguilla gradually pieces together is a whole series of parallels across time, the connecting tissue between the different time levels of the novel.

Anguilla, in childhood, found a friend, teacher and protector in Nuto; and Cinto has apparently a similar relationship with a boy named Piola ('Piola was his Nuto'). Padrino, the one-time owner of

Gaminella, lived a life of poverty and misery and eventually died 'on a road, where his daughters' husbands had dumped him', whilst old Valino, the present tenant, is driven to murder and suicide as a result of the oppressive poverty and degradation of his life. Anguilla had bought himself a clasp-knife with his very first wages as a child and now buys a similar one for Cinto. Anguilla once drove Irene and Silvia to the *festa* at Buon Consiglio, and some years later, Nuto drove their younger half-sister, Santa, to the fair at Bubbio, and whilst nothing is explicitly stated in either case, Nuto's feelings for Santa appear to have been very similar to Anguilla's for Silvia. All three of the sisters, as well as Anguilla's two foster-sisters, have died violent deaths. Anguilla consciously recognises the parallel between his young self and the child Cinto: 'Seeing him there in the yard was like seeing myself.' Sor Matteo 'was mad about women ... just as his grandfather and his father had been mad about property ... That's how they were, made of land and big ideas. They liked abundance: for some it was wine, corn and meat, for others women and money'. Nuto and Anguilla have both done their military service in Genoa. Some time prior to Anguilla's return, Valino found the decaying corpse of a German soldier who had been killed in the war, and whilst he is actually revisiting the Langhe, two more corpses are found in similar circumstances and in a similar condition. Anguilla as a child tore the legs off grasshoppers and Nuto chided him for it, while Nuto now prevents some children from doing harm to a lizard they have caught.

We began this chapter with an extended reference to Eliot's *Four Quartets*, and here again we recall that second movement of 'Little Gidding', in which the 'deaths' of 'air', 'earth', 'water and fire' are revealed by the poet, reminding us that all individuality eventually passes back into the earth, dissolved by one or more of these primary elements:

>   Water and fire succeed
>   The town, the pasture and the weed.
>   Water and fire deride
>   The sacrifice that we denied.
>   Water and fire shall rot
>   The marred foundations we forgot,
>   Of sanctuary and choir.
>   This is the death of water and fire.
>   ('Little Gidding' ll. 70–7)

This endless process is at work in *La luna e i falò* also: we see it in the already mentioned physical disintegration of the corpses of victims of the civil war, brought about – as Cinto informs Anguilla – by 'water ... mud and stones' (see p. 235), in the conflagration which destroys Gaminella, in the bonfire which burns away Santa's body. Yet neither for Pavese nor for Eliot is that an end of it, for, as the latter reminds us:

> See, now they vanish,
> The faces and places, with the self which, as it could, loved them,
> To become renewed, transfigured, in another pattern.
> (Ibid. ll. 163–5)

For Pavese, fire, in particular, seems to have a regenerative function in *La luna e i falò*, its paradigm being precisely those propitiatory bonfires lit by the peasants of the Langhe each year to ensure that the land will renew itself and provide a rich harvest in the following year. It destroys Gaminella, but in doing so liberates the young Cinto from a destiny of poverty, ignorance and social degradation with Valino, while in the case of Santa it perhaps has a symbolic function, in that it signals the destruction of the old Italy – both Fascist and pre-Fascist – from the ashes of which will rise the new, more equitable society for which so many of the partisans fought and died.

Only in so far as human reality is able to imitate the cycles of natural time can it defeat time, with the result that in *La luna e i falò* the significance of the individual is reduced to that of 'names and types, nothing more', in what effectively constitutes a repudiation of the Renaissance–Humanistic cult of the individual – a point of view at which Eliot had arrived, albeit by a very different route, by the time he composed *Four Quartets*.[5] However, after twenty years of Fascist regimentation, wherein the individual interest was always subordinate to that of the State,[6] one of the fundamental principles of the Italian Resistance had been the restoration of the freedoms of the individual, so that in the immediate post-war years it is hardly surprising that Pavese should have encountered hostility to a theory of the novel in which 'The characters ... are on the same level as a tree, a house, a storm or an air-raid' (*La lett. am.* pp. 294–5). Pavese, not unnaturally, was misunderstood in his 'sacrifice' of the individual to the 'impersonal' rhythms of nature, for in reality it no more represents a denial of the rights of the individual than did Leopardi's:

Non ha natura al seme
Dell'uom più stima o cura
Che alla formica
(Nature no more cares for or values the seed of man than she does that of the ant. 'La ginestra', ll. 231-3)

and with much the same purpose in mind, the restoration of a right perspective. Not, then, anything like the Fascist arrogance, but in its way Pavese's own affirmation of the truth which both Leopardi and Eliot had earlier arrived at:

> The only wisdom we can hope to acquire
> Is the wisdom of humility.
> ('East Coker' ll. 97-8)

Anguilla, like so many Italians who left their homeland, whether for economic or for political reasons, discovers that the real America bears little resemblance to the dream, so that he, too, after twenty years of drifting, humiliation and continuous living from hand to mouth, comes to something like that 'wisdom of humility'. What he gradually comes to realise is that America is synonymous with rootlessness and alienation, and that even the native Americans themselves are as much victims of a deep-seated restlessness as were the immigrants, of whatever origin. 'As I saw it,' he confesses, 'they were a nation of bastards' (*Luna* p. 115), and just what he intends by this becomes clear when he explains:

It's a fact that there were countless families, especially up in the hills, in their new houses, in front of their smallholdings and fruit factories, and on summer evenings there was a constant din and the smell of vines and figs in the air, and gangs of lads and little lasses running around the narrow lanes and under the avenues of trees; but they were Armenians, Mexicans, Italians, and they always seemed to have just arrived, and they worked the land in the same way as the roadsweeps cleaned the sidewalks in the cities, and they slept and found their amusements in the cities. Where they came from, who their father was or their grandfather, there seemed no point in asking. There weren't any real country girls; even those from well up the valleys had no idea what a goat was, or a hillside. They went off to work in cars, on bicycles, on trains, just like the office girls. They did everything in gangs in the cities, even to making the carnival floats for the Grape Festival. (*Luna* p. 115)

There is a suggestion here of something which lies very deep within the Italian literary tradition: not just the connection – manifested as a special kind of pride, or *campanilismo* between the individual, his plot of land and his immediate environment (though that also), but the suspicion that rootlessness, being essentially outside a tradition ('molti paesi vuol dire nessuno' – if you live all over the place it means you are nobody; *Luna* p. 63) is synonymous with chaos, both social and spiritual. The most obvious 'example', and one which Pavese may well have had in mind when we remember the nightmarish, indeed hellish quality of what Anguilla had found 'at the very centre of America', is Dante's description of the opportunists, 'la setta dei cattivi / a Dio spiacenti ed a nemici sui' (the worthless crew that was hateful to God and to his enemies), where that spiritual rootlessness (being essentially outside the systems of salvation and damnation) is imaged precisely as aimless movement:

> vidi una insegna
> che girando correva tanto ratta,
> che d'ogni posa mi parea indegna;
> e dietro le venía sí lunga tratta
> di gente, ch'io non averei creduto
> che morte tanta n'avesse disfatta.
> (*Inferno* III, ll. 52–7)

(I saw a whirling banner which ran so fast that it seemed as if it could never make a stand, and behind it came so long a train of people that I should never have believed death had undone so many.)[7]

The rejection of America is thus the rejection of alienation and rootlessness (and here we touch once more on the reason for Anguilla's return to the Langhe), and in this America is but a function of the novel, a fact which seems to be confirmed by Anguilla himself when he tells Nuto

> that Cinto was a bright lad and what he needed was a farm such as La Mora had been for us. 'La Mora was like the world,' I said. 'It was an America, a sea port, with its comings and goings, and its work and its talk...' (*Luna* p. 30)

America as a symbol of chaos – its own and Anguilla's moral and spiritual chaos – is allegorised in terms which are reminiscent of Dante, Coleridge and Eliot. The desert in which Anguilla (another Ulysses) founders ('that night my truck broke down'), putting too much trust in a machine – the symbol *par excellence* of America's restless search for identity, which is eventually metamorphosed into the great inhuman monster, the train, 'sucking in the air and clattering' across the empty plain, filling it 'with an unearthly din, throwing out sparks', with every living thing fleeing in its path – this desert, rhetorical though the image may be, is the wasteland at the heart of that chaos. Before the train came, Anguilla has been terrified by the many inhuman (though natural) voices of the darkness, by the intense cold, by the gaping emptiness of the landscape; but the train's headlight, shafting through this darkness and desolation, does not fulfil its apparent promise or the hope which Anguilla has invested in it. It comes as the ultimate negation of his humanity, its light illuminating only momentarily, spreading fear, something false, ephemeral, vulgar in the extreme, quite unlike the constant, civilising light of the 'faro lontano di Torino' (far-off beacon of Turin) in 'I mari del Sud'. It is a moment of deep, spiritual truth for Anguilla:

> I had waited for it for so long, but when it was dark again, and I could hear the sand crackling once more, I thought that not even in a desert would these people leave you in peace. If tomorrow I had to run away and hide, so as not to be interned, it was as if I could already feel the policeman's hand on my shoulder like the impact of that train. This was America. (*Luna* p. 66)

It is this realisation which brings him to the brink of choice between two fundamentally different attitudes to life, between, that is, a mechanistic, essentially dehumanised world of 'having' (America) and one of wholly human and natural dimensions in which, in spite of material poverty, one's identity, one's 'being' were never in doubt (Mexico):

> Now it was going through my mind that, for all the Californians were clever, those four ragged Mexicans were doing something that none of them would have been able to do, to camp out and sleep in that desert – women and children as well – in that desert which was their home, where maybe they had some kind of understanding with the snakes. Maybe I should go off to Mexico, I thought, I bet that's the country for me. (*Luna* p. 66)

Mexico, in this sense, stands for the Langhe also. This choice is wholly commensurate with that made in *Dialoghi con Leucò*, in which Pavese had sensed that a world organised by excess of reason only, a world, that is, of something like 'Single vision and Newton's sleep', would represent a kind of 'death in life', in which all was sounded, measured and charted and the Ulysses within each one of us would finally be subdued. In *La luna e i falò*, Pavese rejects a way of life which is organised around a single principle, the unremitting pursuit of wealth, for he seems to have perceived (and here we should recall in particular his earlier essays on Sherwood Anderson and Sinclair Lewis) that an all-pervading materialism must lead inevitably to a dehumanisation of society, comparable in its effects on the quality of life with that which had been enshrined in the institutions of Fascism. For Pavese, there was perhaps little to choose between the regimentation into *squadre*, *balille*, *corporazioni*[8] and so on, which had characterised life in Fascist Italy, and the regimentation demanded by the production line of modern industrialism and 'truck' farming. Anguilla returns in search of the natural dimension, the countryside, for in it he hopes to find his place and his self; but 'countryside' and 'self', it turns out, are not quite compatible, for that 'self', he discovers, by this time needs 'the [city] pavements' as much as the 'campagne' of his origins. Genoa, the gateway to the Langhe (and to the outside world), allows him something like Pavese's own confessed 'pleasurable contemplation' of the countryside, as well as his 'appreciation' of the 'good sense ... of the [city] pavements'. Anguilla's search, then, is for a balance, a wholeness, which in twenty years America has been unable to give him but which, in childhood, the Langhe was likewise unable to provide and even now, he learns, as such and alone cannot give him. And yet, paradoxically, that wholeness contains America, contains the Langhe, is 'an easy commerce of the old and new', though not of any place or places as they are or were as he lived them, but rather of what they become as he absorbs them: 'To become renowned, transfigured, in another pattern.' This, quite simply, is what Pavese means by his 'sono io il mio paese' (I myself am my country). However, for Anguilla the key to that wholeness is nevertheless his Langhe of 'then', for that was his 'first world', and it is as true for him as it had been for the cousin of 'I mari del Sud' that (as Eliot puts it)

> the end of all our exploring
> Will be to arrive where we started
> And know the place for the first time.
> ('Little Gidding' ll. 240–2)

Pavese knew, as Eliot knew, that it was entirely possible, indeed normal, to have the experience and to miss the meaning ('that child self that you didn't manage to catch in time'). And here the two poets come very close in their thinking about the relationship of the individual to his own past life, for it is a tenet of which Pavese could not but have approved, given the whole experience of *La luna e i falò*, that

> approach to the meaning restores the experience
> In a different form
> ('Dry Salvages' ll. 94–5)

and, furthermore, that

> the past experience revived in the meaning
> Is not the experience of one life only
> But of many generations
> (Ibid. ll. 97–9)

La luna e i falò surely confirms this all-important link in the depth of its structure and its historical perspective, as well as pointing (still in the shadow of *Dialoghi con Leucò*) in the direction of

> The backward look behind the assurance
> Of recorded history, the backward half-look
> Over the shoulder, towards the primitive terror.
> (Ibid. ll. 101–3)

History, for both poets, is the specific event in the flow of time, which always inevitably confirms the myth, the timeless, and in this sense 'history is a pattern / Of timeless moments'.

This redefinition of the individual's life-span in a particular society raises an important question in Pavese's mind in view of his attitude towards the relationship between history, myth and individual destiny:

Destiny is that which is made up entirely of the mythical, a drama. It's what happens and you don't yet know that it has happened; that which seems like freedom but which later turns out to be paradigmatic, an iron law, predetermined. Destiny is history before it is understood in its relationships and its necessity–freedom. When it deals with men, poetry is always concerned with destinies: it moves over these destinies and may even understand them, clarify them, turn them into history. (*MV* 10 January 1950)

Can there be any liberation from that destiny? Does rejection of a place and an experience constitute such a liberation? The problem is, in essence, one which, in a slightly different guise, troubled the medieval intellect: the apparent conflict between foreknowledge and free will. As Pavese sees it,

A man who fulfils in himself an authentic myth in which he believes is governed by Destiny. Such a man is not free.

It is impossible to create a character who is completely free. The rhythms of his life (which cannot be eliminated) will be his destiny.

Will it be possible to go further one day and consider even freedom to be a myth? That is, to see it from a point at which it too will be revealed as Destiny? (*MV* 30 January 1950)

Anguilla twice radically changes the environment of his life and its circumstances. By his own efforts he breaks through the barriers of poverty and privilege. The twenty years which separate the one change from the other create in him needs and tastes which make the Langhe wholly inadequate for him. Nevertheless, its rhythm of life, its *cadenze*, he readily recognises, for it is in him, it reflects an important part of him. It had even instilled in him the desire and determination to break its stranglehold over him. Here is a character who is admittedly not 'completely free', yet there is no denying that some measure of freedom has been attained by him. If this does indeed constitute a partial freedom (that is, if liberty does not also turn out to be Destiny – and for Pavese the doubt remains like a dark cloud) then Cinto too seems to be on the point of achieving it at the end of the novel. This freedom depends wholly on consciousness and the will to change – not necessarily the will and consciousness of the individual whose life is to be changed, as we see in the case of Cinto. Nevertheless, there is far more of which one remains unaware than of which one ever becomes conscious, so that the rhythms created by those dark areas will still continue to exert their peculiar determining influence upon the life of the individual, and he will remain a prisoner of them. It is perhaps for this reason that Anguilla 'came back to this village, here rather than Canelli, Barbaresco or Alba'.

If the possibilities of liberation from Destiny (significant change) are in doubt at the individual level, how much more true is this at the level of a whole community or society. Consciousness of a total situation, even if achieved – and at best only the hegemonic class can achieve it, never the whole society or community – does not, as we see from this novel, necessarily carry with it the desire for change, but may clearly embrace the desire to preserve at all costs. In *La luna e i falò* it is the forces of reaction which have the upper hand, despite the apparent victory and strength of the progressive forces in the War of Liberation. In chapters 12 and 13 it is made clear that these reactionary or conservative forces, championed by the local priest, are greatly assisted by the widespread ignorance in the community:

'The terrible thing,' Nuto said, 'is that we're ignorant. The village is entirely in the hands of that priest.' (*Luna* p. 73)

It is through the rite, the procession, the time-honoured words of the mass and the liturgy, the ceremonial robes and the 'parola in latino' – in other words the age-old rhythm of the Church's mythology – that the manipulation of the community is effected.

The antidote Anguilla intuits from his own experience:

> You have to get out of the village ... hear other people's bells, let in some air. In Canelli it's different ... If you want to do something ... you've got to keep in touch with the world. (*Luna* p. 74)

Consciousness of the need for change and of other possibilities in other places is only a starting-point, and both Anguilla and Nuto are aware of this; the latter argues:

> We're too ignorant in this village. You can't be a Communist just because you feel like it ... What we need is some Communists who aren't ignorant. (*Luna* p. 27)

Anguilla suggests that the kind of social change that is required in the Langhe can only come through organised and educated political action:

> Talk. Find yourselves. That's what they do in America. The strength of the parties depends on many many little villages like this one. The priests don't work in isolation ever; behind them they have a whole league of other priests. (*Luna* p. 74)

The principle of repetition, of rhythm, holds good also in the sphere of political action. Change will come about, Anguilla implies, only when the counter-rhythm is strong enough, which means single-minded enough, to displace what is already in existence. Nuto affirms that the counter-rhythm was created in the War of Liberation:

> in the year of the war the world had come to waken them up. There had been people from all over, Southerners, Tuscans, people from the towns, students, evacuees, workers – even the Germans, even the Fascists had counted for something, for they had opened the eyes of even the most stupid people. (*Luna* p. 74)

But it had not been strong enough, for it had offered too many alternatives, having a fragmenting and thus weakening effect on the movement seeking change, and in those circumstances 'i prepotenti di prima ... – passata la grandine – sbucavano fuori dalle cantine, dalle ville, dalle parrocchie, dai conventi' (the ones who had the power before ... – once the storm was over – out they came from their cellars and their villas, from the priests' houses and the convents) – and re-established themselves in positions of local influence and power.

In this analysis of the post-war political situation, Pavese is nowhere denying the possibility of change, nor its desirability, but rather seeks to emphasise the complexities and difficulties which confront those trying to bring it about:

The will is brought to bear on myths and transforms them into history. Destinies which become freedom. (*MV* 1 February 1950)

However, the process whereby this transformation may be achieved is itself a *mimesis* of the mythical chemistry of Destiny ('Destiny is that which exists entirely through the mythical') as Pavese argues:

One conquers nature (the mechanical) by imitating it *in a mythical fashion* (rhythms, returns, destinies). But each generation must take into account however much it knows about the workings of nature, and overcome it with irreducible mythical systems from this knowledge. (*MV* 17 January 1950)

Rhythm – in the Pavesian sense of the word, even the *need* for rhythm – for whatever else it may be it is also certainty, security, 'a framework' – Pavese identifies as the basic motor factor in the human makeup. It operates, for the most part, at the instinctual and the visceral levels, as it does in the animal and vegetable worlds, but because man does have within him the power to reason, and through this, power to change – always within the limits of his own consciousness – he can modify the destiny that his own unconscious assimilation of a whole range of specific rhythms has imposed upon him. However, it follows that liberation from that destiny can never be total, and it is this fact, projected with greatly increased complexity at the communal level, which explains for Pavese the slowness of significant historical change, the impossibility of revolution, and which gives to *La luna e i falò* its atmosphere of 'slow rotation suggesting permanence'.

12

The celebration of a rite: Last poems, 1945–1950

It would indeed have seemed strange had the two groups of poems composed in 1945 and 1950, in the wake of *Feria d'agosto* and *Dialoghi con Leucò, not* revealed a preoccupation with the question of form. In that period, Pavese's conscious search for a 'framework', 'something fixed', came to dominate his writing and his life, for it was through giving form – the rationalistic stamp of his humanity – that order was created out of the absolute, mythico-elemental chaos of the *selvaggio* through the transposition of experience from the aimless flow of time into consciousness. These poems, in which Pavese's search for a style as 'a way of understanding life so that it becomes a new awareness' coincides with obvious attempts at 'clarifying his own myths', are his purest expression of the practical, individuating function of poetry which was always, in some measure, his aim in writing. And it is precisely the personal character of these poems – personal in the double sense of having a narrowly autobiographical *raison d'être* and of employing a highly individual, though precise, series of symbols as a means of expression – which has constantly elicited adverse judgements on the poems and led to their wholesale rejection by Italian critics. Stylistically, they represent (as Giorgio Bàrberi-Squarotti, following Luciano Anceschi, has pointed out) 'Pavese's late contact with Hermeticism, which took place when its creative, innovatory phase had already passed its peak, and it was beginning to seek new effects elsewhere'.[1] In a retrogressive sense they were indeed out of phase with the prevalent historico-poetical needs of their time – unlike the Solaria *Lavorare stanca* which, though equally out of phase, was so in a progressive sense, and later came to be regarded as highly innovatory, formative of a view of poetry which became fashionable in the post-war period. However, poetic taste – which is always inseparable from a total social context – also has its seasons, and whilst these particular poems are very far from seeing 'salvation absolutely and only in a close, jealous, passionate adherence to the object', they nevertheless represent a valid application of poetry – albeit in a minor key – admittedly very different from, but certainly not inferior to, that of the first *Lavorare stanca*. Indeed, in a technical sense, they are far superior to the majority of those earlier poems; and in any case, their language and symbols are but a further development of the direction taken by Pavese's verse between 1936 and 1940,[2] and which was already manifest in a substantial number of poems which appeared in the 1943 (Einaudi) edition of *Lavorare stanca*.

The two main groups of poems – *La terra e la morte* (Earth and death)[3] and *Verrà la morte e avrà i tuoi occhi* (When death comes its eyes will be yours)[4] – though similar in inspiration, intention and form, do have some differences in tone and atmosphere, which stem chiefly from the fact that the second group is also a chronicle of the varying states of mind, the *inquietudine*, of the poet during the time in which these poems were being written. Both, however, are the 'celebration of a rite' in the special Pavesian sense of recording the mythical roots and the cyclic (and therefore predictable) character of a specific type of experience – his relationships with individual women – by raising them to the level of a law, an absolute, a 'framework'. The poem is itself a symbolic 'possession' of an area of experience in that it identifies and encapsulates it without actually fathoming its mystery, as one would capture some ferocious, wild animal. The problem of 'taming' – or understanding – is the occupation of the intellect and is consequent upon, but wholly outside, the scope of the poem. In Pavese's view, therefore, the poem, which is itself a part of the process of 'clarifying his own myths', is the first vital step in the intended liberation from – or exorcism of – those myths. The more mathematical (cerebral) in character the form which manipulates and organises the mythical experience, the better the intention of a symbolic possession of the *selvaggio* is served. The poem is thus a *mimesis* of man's continuing struggle to overcome the natural forces which are the objective and subjective condition of his life, and turn them to his own purposes.

In general, the poems of the latter group do not have quite the emotional detachment which characterises all but one ('Sempre vieni dal mare' – Always you come from the sea) of the love poems of the former. The intrusion of the self, even if it is expressed through the first person plural (a device which, in any case, seems rhetorical, even pompous, in this context), works to some extent against the mythologising and universalising intention of the poet, in that it emphasises the individual character of the failure to communicate with the perennial mystery which woman, 'any woman', represents. The poems 'I mattini passano chiari' (The mornings go by clear and empty) and 'Hai un sangue, un respiro' (You have blood, you have breath) illustrate this contradiction. It is there again in 'Verrà la morte', but its effects are largely offset on the one hand by the change in viewpoint (the identification of death with the woman instead of a description of the woman's mystery and its effect on the 'noi') and, on the other, by the clear-cut, well-sculptured lines which make no concessions to sentimentalism – indeed, here the matter-of-fact tone creates a balance, a tension, which make the poem arguably the finest of the later group.

The first poem of the 1945 group. 'Terra rossa terra nera' (Red earth black earth), which is quoted here in full, well illustrates this *mimesis* of the struggle to discipline the 'formless'. Whilst clearly there are differences in style and structure among these poems, they do not add up to a difference in purpose, so that this detailed example is a fair illustration of the relationship between purpose and means of execution in the whole group.

> Terra rossa terra nera,
> tu vieni dal mare,
> dal verde riarso,
> dove sono parole
> antiche e fatica sanguigna
> e gerani tra i sassi –
> non sai quanto porti
> di mare parole e fatica,
> tu ricca come un ricordo,
> come la brulla campagna,
> tu dura e dolcissima
> parola, antica per sangue
> raccolto per gli occhi;
> giovane, come un frutto
> che è ricordo e stagione –
> il tuo fiato riposa
> sotto il cielo d'agosto,
> le olive del tuo sguardo
> addolciscono il mare,
> e tu vivi rivivi
> senza stupire, certa
> come la terra, buia
> come la terra, frantoio
> di stagioni e di sogni
> che alla luna si scopre
> antichissimo, come

le mani di tua madre,
le conca del braciere.

(Red earth black earth, you come from the sea, from the parched green wherein lie ancient words and bloody toil and geraniums among the rocks – you do not know how much you bear with you of sea, words and toil, you who are rich as a memory, as the bare countryside, a word which is harsh yet most gentle, ancient through blood stored up in your eyes; youthful, like some fruit which is both memory and season – your breath is stilled beneath the August sky, the olives in your glance make the sea gentle, and you live, you live again without wonder, certain as the earth, dark as the earth, olive-press of seasons and of dreams which in the moonlight is revealed in its extreme antiquity, just like your mother's hands, the white-hot centre of the furnace.)

The first thirteen lines vary between five and nine syllables in length, and the greatest variation is found in the first five lines, which are all different. One of the structural features most obviously affected by this variation is rhythm. The first line promises a very regular, swift-moving beat, with the tonic stress falling on the first, third, fifth and seventh syllables; but this is immediately interrupted in the second line where the stress is on the second and (again) on the fifth syllables, a model which is repeated in the third line, but which again proves shortlived, for the fourth line breaks away completely from the hitherto tenuous unity maintained by the fifth-syllable stress by stressing the third and sixth syllables. However, from the fifth line onwards the second- and fifth-syllable stress gradually gains the upper hand, so that in all, eight of those first thirteen lines are made up of tonic stress combinations which contain those two elements.

A third notable feature in the structure of these first thirteen lines is the question of whether or not the individual line is end-stopped, for this indicates how much or how little the rhythmic structure is working in harmony with, or in opposition to, the syntactical structure. It also, of course, in part determines the pace of the verse, as well as having an effect on the comparative strength of the bonds of form. In fact, eight of those lines are end-stopped, but according to an almost regular pattern: the first three end in commas, the fourth and fifth are free, the sixth ends in a dash, the seventh is free, the eighth, ninth and tenth end in commas, the eleventh and twelfth are free, whilst the thirteenth ends the sequence with a semi-colon. The first of each of the 'free' lines always corresponds with a definite break in the rhythm, but, almost as if to compensate for this, each of the three 'free' sequences contains an element of counter-rhythm in self-contained, paratactically joined pairs ('parole / antiche e fatica sanguigna'; 'parole e fatica'; 'dura e dolcissima'; 'di stagioni e di sogni'). The overall effect, to the end of the seventh line, is of substantial variations in pace and rhythm, which gives the impression that the material is difficult to control; however, by the time the thirteenth line has been reached a definite pattern has begun to emerge, and there is an increasing sense of control.

From the fourteenth to the twenty-eighth (and last) line the impression of ever-increasing control is strengthened because all the lines are seven syllables long which ensures that tonic stress can only fall on two syllables in any one line. With the exception of only two lines, the second of those two stressed syllables is always the sixth, whilst the first stress is on the third syllable in seven cases, on the second in three cases, and on the first syllable in only one case.

Moving away now from the purely phonological,[5] we come to two semantic features which have a significant structural function in this symbolic 'possessing' of experience. Firstly, the repetition of individual words or their derivatives contributes (in part phonologically) to the organic nature of the poem (a feature already discussed with regard to *Lavorare stanca*) by continually bringing the reader's attention back to the key words and phrases – in all but a few cases, mythical correlatives of the 'tu' who is addressed – which are at the centre of the poem: the word 'terra' occurs four times, 'mare', 'parola' and 'antico' three times, whilst 'stagione', 'ricordo', 'sangue' and 'fatica' each occur twice.

The second of the two semantic features mentioned concerns possession by association (the creation of a relationship), and is dependent on the use of 'e', 'di' (or *di-articolata*) and 'come'. In the first case, that of the paratactical 'e', diverse elements are linked together and traced back to a specific source which possesses them amongst its characteristics: for example, 'parole / antiche e fatica sanguigna / e gerani tra i sassi' are the 'possessions' of 'mare' (lines 2–6); then 'parole e fatica' (and 'mare', though not joined paratactically here) relate similarly to 'tu' (lines 11–12) as – ultimately – do 'ricordo e stagione' (line 15). It should not go unremarked that several of the items which occur in this particular structure are amongst those already noted amongst the repetitions as mythical correlatives of the 'tu'.

In the second of these associative cases, the use of 'di', the linking takes the form of the subordination of one element to another, the possessing element, which is qualified (that is, more precisely individuated) as a result of the association: 'cielo d'agosto'; 'le olive del tuo sguardo'; 'frantoio di stagioni e di sogni'; 'le mani di tua madre' and 'la conca del braciere'. All five of these examples occur in the 'controlled' part of the poem, and each one refers, either directly or obliquely, to the 'tu', which is itself more closely outlined through the relationships.

Finally, in the case of 'come', the association is, of course, the observation of a certain similarity between two elements. The first example is particularly rich because it presents two such similarities, implying – almost metaphorically – an already established relationship between the two elements which are the non-constants in each of the two similes (i.e. 'un ricordo' and 'la brulla campagna'):

> tu ricca come un ricordo,
> [tu ricca] come la brulla campagna...

The second example is of a slightly different character in that it is reinforced by the repetition of a phrase, as well as by the shared stress pattern:

> e tu *vivi rivivi*
> *senza stupire*, certa
> come la terra, buia
> come la terra ...

In the final example, though it passes through a series of transformations *en route*, the ultimate referent is yet again the 'tu' to whom the poem is addressed:

> e tu
> ...
>   frantoio
> di stagioni e di sogni
> che alla luna si scopre
> antichissimo, come
> le mani di tua madre ...

It is difficult to say just how conscious Pavese was of using these various devices to 'possess', by containment, the mystery which the 'tu' – *a* woman but also *any* woman – represented for him; however, it is such features as these which determine the sheer economy and intensity of the best of these later poems.

The whole of this poem – like the others in this earlier group – presents a complex series of symbols and images, many of which

The celebration of a rite: last poems, 1945–1950

must be well-nigh incomprehensible to anyone who has not closely followed Pavese's poetical evolution up to the point at which *La terra e la morte* was composed. If the first few lines of 'Terra rossa terra nera' reflect the problems of 'possession' in their structure, this is no less true at the semantic level, for it is *not* immediately obvious that 'Terra rossa terra nera', which is evidently synonymous with 'tu', refers to a woman, and several of the symbols used have more than one possible meaning, for they belong both to a conventional, more or less universal system of symbols and to the Pavesian 'mythical' system. Once it has been established that the 'tu' is indeed a woman, the line 'tu vieni dal mare' seems to be an allusion to the birth of Aphrodite, and so it is, except that 'mare', in the Pavesian canon, is a symbol of the 'caos titanico' (the original and the ultimate realities) which is endlessly reclaiming what civilisation believes it has won once and for all, and endlessly regurgitating experience – that which 'has been lost / And found and lost again and again' ensuring that 'the pattern is new in every moment', as Eliot suggests. 'The sea' is the great recycler, similar in function, though not in effect, to Shakespeare's notion of the 'sea-change'. The difficulties continue in that 'il verde riarso' could – through 'verde' – be synonymous with 'mare', though, following the normal collocates of 'riarso', it ought to refer to 'terra'; the problem is further complicated in that according to conventional symbolism 'verde' represents 'hope' or 'new life or beginning', but here its significance in this direction is severely curtailed by 'riarso', not only in its meaning of 'parched' (the salt of the sea is presumably referred to) but also in its suggestion ('riarso') of 'burning again (and again)'. However, a full exposition of the poem's possible meanings – certainly of much of its detail – would run to many pages, and the chief concern of this section is not a line-by-line analysis of the poems' meanings but rather to relate the function and construction of the poems to Pavese's overriding ideal of creating order out of chaos.

In the majority of the poems in the first group the 'tu' is described in terms of 'buio' (darkness) and 'silenzio' (silence); she is frequently 'il mare' (sea), 'le voci della terra' (the voices of the earth); she is 'segreta' (secret), 'nascosta' (hidden), 'chiusa' (closed); ultimately, she is 'la morte' (death); she is the *selvaggio* which no words can ever finally possess. Occasionally, as in the poem beginning 'Tu sei come una terra' (You are like a land), a more optimistic note is sounded, a hint that perhaps, after all, her past mystery will fall away:

> C'è un vento che ti giunge.
> Cose secche e rimorte
> t'ingombrano e vanno nel vento.
> Membra e parole antiche.
> Tu tremi nell'estate.

(There is a wind which comes to you. Dried-up, dead things litter your path and blow away in the wind. Limbs and words which are ages old. You tremble in the summer.)

Yet the seeming promise remains suspended there; it is only for a moment, for in the next poem in the sequence she becomes once again 'la terra e le vigne' (the earth and the vines). In 'Sempre vieni dal mare', where the individual woman is all women, the love relationship is described in terms of perpetual conflict: it is 'uno strappo' (a tearing), 'la morte' (death), for:

> Chi si risolve all'urto
> ha gustato la morte
> e la porta nel sangue.

(Whoever decides on the clash has tasted death and bears it with him in his blood.)

The object of the love conflict is described as 'il sonno della morte affiancati' (the sleep of death side by side) – an eternally shared 'pace' (peace) – yet it is a conflict which, paradoxically, neither must win, for victory would be tantamount to a partial or total destruction of whatever was loved in the other:

> Se tu od io cede all'urto,
> segue una notte lunga
> che non è pace o tregua
> e non è morte vera.
> Tu non sei più. Le braccia
> si dibattono invano.

(If you or I yield in the clash, there follows a long night which is neither peace nor truce nor yet true death. You exist no longer. Your arms struggle in vain.)

Thematically speaking, two of the poems – 'Tu non sai le colline' (You do not know the hills) and 'E allora noi vili' (And then we cowards) – belong only marginally with the other seven in the earlier group, in that they retain, as Lorenzo Mondo has observed, 'something of the narrative about them', as well as being expressions of remorse, which, presumably, has its origin in Pavese's inability to take sides in the war and thus, by entering the conflict, find a measure of human solidarity – a 'passage to other men' – which had proved unattainable in peacetime. In the first poem we learn that

> Uno solo di noi
> si fermò a pugno chiuso,
> vide il cielo vuoto,
> chinò il capo e morí
> sotto il muro, tacendo.

(Only one of us stopped with his fists clenched, saw the empty sky, bowed his head and died beneath the wall, in silence.)

In the second,

> noi strappammo le mani
> dalla viva catena
> e tacemmo, ma il cuore
> ci sussultò di sangue,
> e non fu più dolcezza,
> non fu più abbandonarsi
> al sentiero sul fiume –
> non più servi, sapemmo
> di essere soli e vivi.

(We wrenched our hands free from the living chain and fell silent, but our heart pounded with our blood, and there was no longer any sweetness, no longer the self-abandonment along the footpath by the river – no longer servile, we knew we were alone and alive.)

What does link these two poems with the others is a heightened sense of *inquietudine* in the poet's life with the advent of love or war, for both disturb, and thus emphasise, the *solitudine* at the centre of his life which he is normally able to bear. This notion returns forcefully in the poem 'You, wind of March',[6] which is the fifth one in the 1950 group, *Verrà la morte e avrà i tuoi occhi*. Here the new 'tu', Constance Dowling, is told:

> Il tuo passo leggero
> ha riaperto il dolore.
> Era fredda la terra
> sotto povero cielo,
> era immobile e chiusa
> in un torpido sogno,
> come chi più non soffre.
> Anche il gelo era dolce
> dentro il cuore profondo.
> Tra la vita e la morte
> la speranza taceva.

(Your footstep, though light, has reawakened my sorrow. The earth lay cold beneath a colourless sky, closed and unmoving in an idle dream, like a man who suffers no longer; even the ice in the depths of my heart seemed sweetness, as between life and death hope lay silent.)

Here, and in the other poems in the group, what is described is not so much her absolute mythical significance (though that too) as the alternating moods of hope and despair which possess him as he waits for her return. The emotional equilibrium achieved in the first group is swept away, and with its disappearance comes a new, more intense awareness of solitude. 'Sono cerchi sull'acqua' (They are circles on the water) as Pavese had put it in 'Sei la terra e la morte' (You are earth and you are death), the last poem in the earlier group; merely a further confirmation of solitude, the inescapable condition; 'ripeness is all'. Despite moments of brightness – 'Sei la luce e il mattino' (You are the light and the morning), 'Sarà un cielo chiaro' (The sky will be bright) – there is the gradual realisation that the source of this brightness ('Dove sei tu, luce, è il mattino' – Where you are, light, is the morning) is, as 'she' always has been, the unfathomable depths, the impenetrable earth-darkness. She is

>   una nube, che sgorga
>   come polla dal fondo

(a cloud, which appears like a spring from the depths of the earth)

and

>   Come
>   erba viva nell'aria
>   rabbrividisci e ridi,
>   ma tu, tu sei terra.
>   Sei radice feroce.
>   Sei la terra che aspetta.

(Like living grass in the open you ripple in laughter, yet you are the earth, you are the cruel root, the earth which is waiting.)

A note of resignation, which was there even in 'To C from C',[7] the very first poem of the sequence ('tomorrow is frozen down on the plain'), eventually begins to take over. It is there in 'Verrà la morte e avrà i tuoi occhi':

>   I tuoi occhi
>   saranno una vana parola,
>   un grido taciuto, un silenzio.

(Your eyes will be a word in vain, a cry that is stopped, a silence.)

It makes its appearance in 'The cats will know':

> Soffriremo nell'alba,
> viso di primavera.

(We shall suffer at the dawning, face of springtime.)

However, it is a resignation which points towards death, which is perhaps, after all, the only peace he will ever know – a final embracing of the *selvaggio*:

> Per tutti la morte ha uno sguardo.
> Verrà la morte e avrà i tuoi occhi.
> Sarà come smettere un vizio,
> come vedere nello specchio
> riemergere un viso morto,
> come ascoltare un labbro chiuso.
> Scenderemo nel gorgo muti.

(Death has a particular look for everyone. Death will come and its eyes will be yours. It will be like ending some bad habit, like seeing a dead face appear again in the mirror, like listening to sealed lips. We shall sink into the vortex in silence.)

These twenty or so poems are a microcosm of Pavese's continuous struggle, in poetry and in life, to become 'master of himself'; to achieve that classic harmony between feeling and rationality which he believed to be the source of all happiness and contentment. His own final assessment of his achievement, in art and in life, was not very wide of the mark in either case:

> In my work, then, I am king. I've done it all in ten years. Just think of the hesitations I experienced then.
> In my life I am more desperate and lost than ever I was then. What have I constructed? Nothing. For several years I have ignored my defects and have lived as though they didn't exist. I have been stoical. Was it heroism? No, it cost me nothing. Then at the first assault of the 'restless anxiety'[8] I have fallen back into quicksand. Since March I've been floundering in it. Names don't matter. Are they anything other than names turned up by chance, accidental names – if not those, wouldn't there have been others? It happens that now I know which is my greatest triumph – and this triumph lacks flesh, lacks blood, is lifeless.
> There is nothing more I want on this earth, except that which fifteen years of failure have put beyond my reach. (*MV* 17 August 1950)

These twenty poems present twenty different attempts to possess the myth, but it remains ever the unfathomable silence, darkness, the impenetrable earth. It is, as Biasin rightly observes (speaking particularly of the poem 'Verrà la morte'), 'the poetic counterpoint of Endymion's tale' in *Dialoghi con Leucò*. If other myths had been 'clarified', this one remained unyielding, although it was the one in which all hope of salvation from *noia*, from emptiness, was invested: 'what fifteen years of failure have put beyond my reach'. The convergence of woman with the *selvaggio* in the first group points to the further convergence of woman with death in the second, in that silence and darkness are characteristics shared by all three. In the 'trionfo della morte', the procession into death of all the female characters in *La luna e i falò*, the *selvaggio* returns to the *selvaggio* and carries with her always the elusive secret and meaning of life. Thus only in death, if at all, can that secret be revealed, and love points always towards that nothingness; it is in this sense that death, but also life, are found in her eyes: 'Sei la vita e la morte.'

13

'To bring order and design where there is chaos'

Any attempt to schematise Pavese's work thematically in a progressive sense would be indicative of a gross misunderstanding of the nature of his development. Solitude, violence, love, childhood, politics, city, country and so on were all present in the poems which he composed between 1930 and 1937 at the latest – and he himself drew attention to this fact in 1946 when he suggested: 'all you have to do is reread the first *Lavorare stanca*, to find in terms of problems and sometimes even of images the substance of what I write now'.[1] His subsequent writing became an elaboration, an *approfondimento*, of those themes which were the historical parameters of Pavese's lived and poetical world; they are still there in his last novel, the lymph and sinew of the world which Anguilla returns to find, in which he comes to realise that 'all is always now'. Thematic progression would imply a discarding and an acquiring and would constitute a denial of the mythical interpretation of history – both personal and social – which was always implicit in his writing, even before the theory of it had been worked out. Referring to *Lavorare stanca*, he claimed:

I am convinced that there is a fundamental and lasting unity in everything I have ever written or shall write, and I'm not talking about a unity which is autobiographical or has anything to do with taste, which are trivialities – rather a unity of themes, of vital interests, the monotonous obstinacy of someone who is certain that he touched the real world, the eternal world, on the very first day, and can do nothing more than go round and round this huge monolith and pull bits of it off and fashion them and consider them from all possible points of view.[2]

The real progression in Pavese's writing concerns *Weltanschauung*, implied in that 'from all possible points of view', and the evolution of a style to contain and express it. After 1934–5 his poetry increasingly displays that sense of *inquietudine* whose causes and whose resolution became the central preoccupation in all his subsequent writing. This *inquietudine* emerged initially out of a sense of loss of an inner freedom and oneness which accompanied and motivated the child in his day-to-day encounters with, and assimilation of, experience. That freedom was lost in the social sense when work and its attendant responsibilities entered his life, and in the psychological sense when the libido changed the pattern of his needs, making him dependent upon another without guaranteeing that such dependence would be answered. The resulting spiritual condition is one of alienation and constant frustration of the individual will, for limitations are imposed which are beyond his control, so that the equilibrium and wholeness of the childhood self are lost. From that point on Pavese was seeking ways of coming to terms with this condition through acceptance, or, alternatively, a formula whereby that wholeness might be regained. In these circumstances his writing became a personal *Divina commedia* in the desired resolution of *inquietudine* in peace, the remaking of the self: 'The work is a symbol', he wrote in December 1939, 'in which the characters as much as the environment are the means to the telling of a little parable, which is the tap root of inspiration and interest: the "journey of the soul" of my Divine Comedy' (*MV* 4 December 1939).

Running through the whole of Pavese's work is the concept of antithesis which, although it changes its character and articulation, nevertheless remains central as the symbolic representation of the divided self. It surfaces as the *città–campagna* contradiction in *Lavorare stanca*, where the emphasis is continually on the individual as victim of social and historical forces: a point of view which Pavese derived in part from the American writers to whom he felt most attracted in the early nineteen-thirties (particularly Sherwood Anderson) and partly from the contemporary process of industrialisation and modernisation which was taking place in and around Turin, as well as elsewhere in northern Italy. At this point, Pavese made no distinction between his own *inquietudine* and that of the protagonists of his poems, who represented a broad cross-section of the peasantry, urban working class and *sottoproletariato* of Turin and the Langhe: an *inquietudine* which, he suspected, might find its resolution in some more equitable socio-economic formula. Without arriving at any precise political commitment, Pavese located the origin of the problem partly in the social sphere and partly within an as yet merely intuited 'human condition'. In his first novel, *Il carcere* (which is an imaginative reworking of his own Brancaleone experience), the antithetical element takes the form of opposition between the objective conditions of life in the 'mezzogiorno'/'campagna' (South/countryside) and the consciousness of the northern city-dweller. Yet, even as late as this, the primary cause of the *inquietudine* remains essentially a social one, symbolised by that 'foglio di carta' (scrap of paper), a Kafkaesque image of remote social, ultimately political control. As for the 'natural' element, Stefano's sexual needs, it is actually overcome by the rational will (his vaunted abstention).

At this stage, Pavese identified the formula for attainment of peace in the attuning of will and the 'verità effettuale della cosa' (the way things are in reality – to borrow the Machiavellian phrase) through the application of an ascetic self-discipline on the basis of a rationally worked-out programme: 'a defence against things is waiting in silence, tensed for the spring, but you have to choose it for yourself, it mustn't be imposed from outside. Perhaps choosing the unpleasant thing ourselves is the only defence against it. This is what the acceptance of suffering means; it's not resignation, but rather a kind of coiled spring' (*MV* 10 November 1938). In *Il carcere*, this seemingly paradoxical formula was applied in an attempt to put into practice the famous decision of 20 April 1936: 'costruire in arte e costruire nella vita, bandire il voluttuoso dall'arte come dalla vita, essere tragicamente' (construct in art as in life; expel gratuitous emotion from art as from life; exist tragically), for this is the effective starting-point of his eventual identification of *stile* with 'a way of understanding life so that it becomes a new awareness', that is 'un nuovo modo di vedere e quindi una nuova realtà' (a new way of seeing and so a new reality – *MV* 24 October 1938). Self-discipline was plainly seen as the key to the construction of a new self and a new view of the world, and for Pavese the processes for life and for art were one and the same: 'it's obvious that our style must be understood as something real, something which goes beyond the written page. Otherwise, what seriousness would that discovery of ours have?' (*MV* 24 October 1938). This was a conviction which Pavese had held at least since he began writing his diary, for immediately after his return from Brancaleone, in the midst of his 'terrible collapse', he expressed his faith in the practical value of poetry to him: 'If poetry has taught me anything, it is self-control, concentration, clear-sightedness; poetry *has restored me*, in the most practical sense' (*MV* 20 October 1938).

Reflecting on the period in which he had been writing *Il carcere*, Pavese noted in his diary:

I noticed that in the autumn of 1938 I hit upon a style and a seam of centripetal thoughts. I have also noticed that for the first time in my life I instruct myself on my attitudes, that is, I have theoretically determined my will. And immediately I have been able to write a novel which is the experience of this frame of mind. (*MV* 29 April 1939)

It is the last sentence which is of capital importance, for Stefano 'constructs' his life in the same way as the writer, Pavese, 'constructs' his novel; and with the same degree of emotional detachment from the people and circumstances which are its context. What Pavese had perceived was that forms of experience and forms of expression of experience (i.e. style) were interchangeable, and that a mode of writing which was of practical value without being merely 'self-confession' was indeed perfectly possible. From the very outset of his writing career, Pavese always moved in the direction of an almost consciously desired fusion of his 'medium' and his 'message'. In *Il carcere*, imprisonment – the cause of *inquietudine* – is reduced to a frame of mind in which specific limitations, whether prison walls, the 'invisible' walls surrounding the *confinato*, or even other people, are different facets of the same basic condition; and the logical extension of this view is that life itself is the ultimate limitation, wherever and whenever it impedes the will of the individual. The struggle to assert the will is always accompanied by *inquietudine* because each momentary triumph leads only to further struggle, whilst the peace attained is tenuous and shortlived. For a time, the rejection of the struggle in favour of adjustment of the will in acceptance was seen as a more likely source of a durable inner peace, even though in Stefano's case its precariousness is continually emphasised. Pavese argued – from his own post-Brancaleone experience – that 'l'unico modo di sfuggire all'abisso è di guardarlo e misurarlo e sondarlo e discendervi' (the only way to escape from the abyss is to look at it, get the measure of it, sound it and go down into it – *MV* 24 April 1936).

Yet, even before *Il carcere*, Pavese had begun to take seriously the view that his own *inquietudine* was possibly merely a personal manifestation of a general human condition whose diseased roots lay deep within each individual childhood; he wrote that

All men have a cancer which gnaws away at them, an everyday excrement, an ongoing evil: their dissatisfaction; the point of collision between the real framework of their being and the endless complexity of life. And all, sooner or later, become aware of it. In each one you have to investigate, to imagine their slow perception or lightning intuition of it. Almost all – it seems – trace the signs of the horror of their adult lives back to their childhood. Investigate this breeding-ground of retrospective discoveries, fears, this their anguished discovery of themselves prefigured in the actions and words of their childhood, which can never be altered. The Little Flowers of the Devil. Contemplate this horror unceasingly: what has been determines what will be. (*MV* 26 November 1937)

Here we find the first hints of what was eventually to develop into the Pavesian theory of myth, firstly in the implied determinism of 'what has been determines what will be' – to which we shall return shortly – and then in the sense of 'understanding life' through a patient dismantling of self down to those 'actions and words of their childhood, which can never be altered'. If it was to be of any value in artistic terms, this practical analysis of self – the stripping away of experience in order to arrive at essence – required a formula which would show the process in reverse: that is, a process of synthesis, of *construction*, in which the childhood essence would be shown to be the framework (or *stile*) which encompassed and determined the nature of the experience of the adult.

The determinism of 'what has been determines what will be' rests on the principle of repetition – of the 'actions and words of their childhood' – and it was this which was to be of crucial importance in the gradual convergence of *stile* and *mito* in Pavese's writing. There is a series of diary entries, spanning the period December 1938 – December 1939, which, when taken together, make the convergence abundantly clear. The first of them repeats an idea which Pavese had arrived at in relation to the *immagine–racconto* in *Lavorare stanca*:

To suggest, with a repeated action or a name or any other means of recall, that a character or an object or a situation has a fantastic link with another in the story is to take away materiality from each of the two subjects and to create the story of this link, of this image, in place of that of the separate materiality of each of them. (*MV* 4 December 1938)

What is of capital importance here is the presumed connection between repetition and the 'taking away of materiality' in the fusing of two 'material' elements into a third ('non-material') element which is both and neither, in which that third element becomes not only a symbol of a nucleus of a-relationship-of-things but is, effectively, a 'new awareness'.

In his explanation of *stile*, already cited, Pavese had defined *materialità* as 'la vita (il tempo nel suo fluire)' (life – time as it flows on). Here, this reduction of *materialità* – of historical experience, that is – to a symbol provides the model for the later theory of myth.

The whole idea gathers momentum when repetition is connected with the creation of a particular past, whether of a society or an individual, as the source of its unique character, its specific *stile:*

Creative vitality is made of a store of past events. You become a creator – we also – when you have a past. The early years of a people mean a rich period of maturity (*genius is wisdom and youth*) [In English in original].

Creation is born of the endless repetitions of an act, which on account of the *routine* [in English in original] becomes tedious. There then follows a period when it is lost for a time and goes unheeded. Then the act, forgotten because of its banality, rises again as though it were a miracle, a revelation, and this is the creative impulse (cf. 3 May – last paragraph). (*MV* 12 June 1939)

Here, the idea of the assimilation–submersion–miraculous-resurgence process being the same, essentially, for the individual and the society as a whole should not go unnoticed; but it is the effect of the 'submersion' period (e.g. Anguilla's twenty years away from the Langhe) which is of most interest in the 'creative' sense, for in it 'tedium' becomes 'miracle' by some as yet undisclosed alchemy, and it is this which is described as 'the creative inpulse'. Pavese's writing was essentially *mimesis* – of 'processes' rather than of 'character' or 'things' (the 'how', not the 'who' or the 'what'), and in this the concepts of repetition and rhythm were vital components as he moved towards the theory of myth with the slow composition of *Feria d'agosto* between 1941 and 1944. The diary entry cited above points us to yet another relevant entry, and although Pavese himself suggests relevance only in the 'last paragraph', the whole piece has value for our thesis:

The part of us which suffers is always the inferior part – as is, for that matter, the part which enjoys. Only the part which is serene is superior.

Suffering, like enjoying, is giving in to emotion. To 17 June 1938 add that the same thing happens when we are enjoying something. The only difference is that enjoyment resembles serenity and thus betrays us and makes us waste our time, while suffering compels us immediately to harden ourselves and take a hold upon ourselves.

In effect, in order to transform pleasure into serenity it has to become tedium. And in any case we always reach serenity by means of boredom. Even grief, to become creative, must first become tedium.

This is the reason why we need the leisure for imagination in order to create. In it boredom coagulates into ideas. (*MV* 3 May 1939)

Both 'pleasure' and 'grief' (particularly the latter) are effectively forms of *inquietudine*, for both disturb the equilibrium of the spirit, that desired condition which Pavese here refers to as 'serenity', elsewhere as 'peace'. Pavese's desired ideal, the object of his 'journey of the soul', is close indeed to Dante's, and his later pronouncement that 'All art is a problem of balance between two opposites' echoes that medieval idea of harmony which was as valid as a guiding principle in life as it was in art. Continuing his assumed coincidence of 'tedium' and 'creativity', Pavese suggests that 'the most banal thing' – by which he means any nucleus of experience which lies dormant within us for some indefinite period because, at some previous stage, familarity with it has bred something like contempt – 'becomes extremely interesting' once 'revealed', for then 'it is no longer something banal and abstract, but a hitherto unknown mixture of reality and of our essence'. Although he does not elaborate on the causes or nature of the correlation between this 'banal thing' and creativity, it is clear that what he has in mind – at least, so far as its effects are concerned – is something akin to the Wordsworthian 'emotion recollected in tranquillity'; that is, the reliving through memory of the white-hot moment of experience which, because distanced by time and divorced from its total (including its emotional) context, is also a discovery, a new perspective, indeed 'a new awareness'. At this point, Pavese's hypothesis moves a step further in the direction of the theory of myth when he concludes that

If the only real internal progress abides in that consciousness which coincides with things we already know, *then it is only the unconscious which counts for us and in this resides our true nature, what we are.* (*MV* 2 February 1939; my italics)

The diary entry from which this is taken continues with the thought that if it is indeed true, then

What *one learns* in life, that which *one can teach*, is the technique of the passage into consciousness – which thus becomes the simple *form* of our nature.

The assimilation process (i.e. living life) and the teaching process (i.e. writing) coincide in that both are concerned with the means (*stile*) of bringing the dormant nuclei – which constitute 'our true nature, what we are' – into consciousness (individual and sociohistorical), in what constitutes nothing less than 'self' possession (whether for an individual or a whole society). Having come this far, Pavese was on the threshold of his later formula of 'clarifying his own myths'.

In Pavese's writing the 'new awareness', which, he hopes, is always a step nearer the idealised 'serenity', is achieved either through 'the reflowering of a past' or through 'the clash of two different ways of life'. In his first four novels it was the latter formula which predominated, whilst after *Feria d'agosto*, which signalled the birth of the myth theory, it was the former; however, the two are never entirely divorced from each other, and this is particularly true in Pavese's later, more lyrical prose, for what is the *immagine–racconto* if not a symbolic 'clash of two different ways of life', that is, of two different nuclei of experience?

Pavese himself acknowledged that *Il carcere* and *Paesi tuoi* belonged in the same broad category when he observed that

> Your poetic cannot help but be dramatic because its message is the meeting of two people – the mystery and fascination and adventure of these meetings – not the confession of your soul.
>
> So far you have preferred the contrast between environments (North against South; city against country) because they take on in an obvious manner the differences between the two characters. (*MV* 21 June 1940)

Yet, with slight modifications, the formula holds good for *La bella estate* and *La spiaggia*, his third and fourth novels. In the former the 'contrast' is between the harsh reality of the adult world and Ginia's youthful idealism, whilst in the latter, the Clelia–Doro relationship is constructed on a 'contrast', that of their different origins: in reality, an extension of the city–country antithesis. In the case of Berti, as has already been noted in chapter 5, the 'contrast' is similar to that for Ginia in *La bella estate*: the tensions between youth and maturity. Only with reference to the last of these four novels did Pavese later speak of 'una franca ricerca di stile' (frank search for a style), though he had earlier argued that the first two had demonstrated 'that I know how to desire a style and maintain it' (*MV* 1 January 1940). By 'style' Pavese means a linguistic framework within which to organise and possess a given area of experience. In his first four novels, there was no clear idea of a 'standard' process for the creation of human reality whether at the individual or the collective level, so that 'style' was thought of as the 'self-realisation' of a given experience, each experience largely determining its own form under the overall control of the author. In practice, however, given that Pavese was – as has been shown – gradually moving towards his later mythical view, the organising framework which stemmed from the developing *Weltanschauung* already contained several of the characteristics which were later to be consciously applied in the construction of his novels. The most obvious of them is that each story, with the exception of *La spiaggia*, centres on a specific individual (and whether it is the narrator or not is here irrelevant) who has been placed in a set of circumstances which are unfamiliar to him/her, and who in coming to terms with the new situation learns something significant about himself/herself. It was precisely the developing formula for the acquisition of self-knowledge (and mastery of self) which increasingly provided the unifying elements in Pavese's *stile*.

It is not my intention here to rehearse the whole theory of myth a second time, only to connect it with Pavese's search for a style which might act as a catalyst in his quest for spiritual wholeness and its concomitant 'serenity'. A key statement, in this respect, is the following:

The way everyone goes back and forth along his own tramlines, you realise only today, worried you for a certain period of time (4 April '41, II, and then (12 April '41) it look on the appearance of a joyful reward for vital effort and, in fact, since then you've never complained about it, but ('42, '43) you have investigated with relish how these tramlines are laid down in childhood. Even before reading Thomas Mann's *Jacob* (December '42), you ended (September '43) with the discovery of the myth-in-its-uniqueness, which thus fuses together all your old psychological ravings and your most vital mythico-creative interests.

It is proven that *the need for construction* is born for you out of this law of the return. Well done.

It is also proven at the same time that the meaning of your life can only be construction.

How is it then, that without being aware of it, you have directed everything towards one central point? Internal logic? Providence? or vital instinct?

Everything is repetition, going back and forth, return. In fact, even the first time is a 'second time'. (26 September '42, II) (*MV* 6 November 1943)

Clearly, it was not possible to possess (repossess?) one's past experience in its entirety – two lifetimes would be necessary for that – but what the myth theory did was to reduce that experience, for each individual, to a series of symbols or images, similar in character and formation to Jung's archetypes of the collective unconscious. 'This image is mythical', affirms Pavese, 'in as much as the writer goes back to it as to something which is unique, which symbolises the whole of his experience' (*MV* 15 September 1943). Once these symbols had been identified, the character (or *stile*) of the individual was defined as precisely as it ever could be, and the self was then possessed. Only then could the individual be wholly true to himself, and the *inquietudine* which was the result of the divided, alienated self would disappear. Pavese's writing, after late 1943, consciously became a function of the identification of his personal symbols or myths – a 'clarification of his own myths'.

However, the myth theory brought new and unexpected difficulties in its wake and did not, ultimately, provide that longed-for 'serenity'. Pavese had believed that it would lead him to an 'absolute' wholeness of self, but unfortunately the *inquietudine* became increasingly identified with the *selvaggio* – the 'incomposto, eteroclito, accidentale' (without order, eccentric, accidental) – which he now saw as the eternal condition of all life (*il vero*), and which was continually reasserting its dominance in the life of the individual, the community, the whole of society, throughout the whole of history. *Inquietudine*, in these 'new' circumstances, was the norm, the absolute, whilst 'serenity' was at best merely momentary respite. What had begun in Pavese's mind as the construction of a confident, rational programme for the mastery of self turned into something closely resembling Leopardi's recognition of 'il mal che ci fu dato in sorte / E il basso stato e frale' (the evil that was given to us as our lot, our frail and lowly state), so that his attempt 'to set limits for ourselves, to give ourselves a framework, to insist on something fixed' became a desperate, ceaseless, back-to-the-wall struggle to preserve at least something that was human for a little while longer. It is obvious that Pavese was sometimes seduced away from his rational purpose by the purely aesthetic effects of his theory of myth. He became fascinated by the *selvaggio* and its *mistero*, which, despite its absolute denial – particularly in its *brutalità* – of the human, was also the vibrant substance of all the richness and variety of civilisation. In so far as the *selvaggio* had this hold over him, his rational purpose was weakened, but it was never abandoned in his writing. He had experienced the 'terrible collapse' of his moral and spiritual self during the years 1935–7, and he had lived through a period of history which was characterised by moral and spiritual disintegration, in which the finer values and achievements of the human mind and sensibility had been generally scorned and abandoned in an exaltation of the physical and the instinctive, and the result had been another 'terrible collapse' of much vaster proportions. In such circumstances, despite his own weaknesses – his natural inclination towards the *voluttuoso* – Pavese continued to defend and proclaim the supremacy of human rationality, true to his long-standing ideal of 'bringing order and design where there is chaos'.[3]

Notes

1. The world of Cesare Pavese (1908–1950)

1 See, in particular, the letters of 1925, 1926 and 1927, written to Mario Sturani, now in *Lettere 1924–1944* 'Einaudi, Turin, 1966). Hereafter *Lett. I*.
2 Davide Lajolo, *Il vizio assurdo*, 4th edn (Milan, 1961), p. 105.
3 There is some doubt as to whether Pavese ever took the Fascist Party card, but if he did it was not out of any ideological conviction, rather as a 'meal ticket'.
4 'Working is tiresome': *Lavorare stanca* (*Poesie 1931–5*) (Solaria, Florence, 1936).
5 During the Fascist period, political opponents (or suspected opponents) of the Regime were often condemned to a period of *confino* (detention), usually in some remote part of the Italian South or the islands. The detainee was free to move about within certain specified limits and had to report to the police twice a day, as well as being subject to a strict curfew.
6 *Il mestiere di vivere* (This business of living) (Einaudi, Turin, 1952). Hereafter *MV*.

2. 'Lavorare stanca' and the evolution of Pavese's verse

1 Edited by Italo Calvino. Hereafter *Poesie*.
2 Florence, January 1936.
3 For much fuller treatment of the poetry of the *ermetici*, the reader is referred to the following works: M. Petrucciani, *La poetica dell'ermetismo italiano* (Turin, 1955); G. Pozzi, *La poesia italiana nel novecento – Da Gozzano agli ermetici* (Turin, 1965); G. Manacorda, *Storia della letteratura italiana contemporanea (1940–1965)* (Rome, 1967); S. Ramat, *L'ermetismo* (Florence, 1969); F. J. Jones, *La poesia italiana contemporanea (da Gozzano a Quasimodo)* (Messina–Florence, 1975).
4 Pavese's thesis, written and presented for the degree of Dottore in Lettere at the University of Turin, in 1930, was entitled 'Interpretazione della poesia di Walt Whitman' (hereafter 'Thesis'). A copy of the thesis is to be found in the archives of the Biblioteca Nazionale Universitaria in Turin. The thesis, which is typed (on one side only) on quarto size paper, is 298 folios in length and is divided into seven chapters. The binding is of thin yellow cardboard and bears only the name 'Pavese', written in red wax crayon on the front cover. There is no inscription on the spine of the thesis and no catalogue number. This latter fact may explain why it had been misfiled and why, until March 1963, it was believed to have been lost in the damage done to the Biblioteca Nazionale by allied bombing during the Second World War.
5 The title of the first chapter of Pavese's thesis was 'Il mito della scoperta' (The myth of discovery).
6 In his thesis (fol. 107) he argues: 'In innumerable ways we see W. W. over and over again presenting us with the same myth: that of the man who discovers and proclaims the meanings of life in a world which is seen through "virgin eyes".'

7 See L. Mondo, *Cesare Pavese* (Milan, 1961), p. 17.
8 See, for example, 'Fumatori di carta' (Smokers of cheap cigarettes), 'Estate di San Martino' (Indian summer) and 'Paesaggio I' (Landscape I).
9 In his thesis, Pavese notes: 'There is a passage, in Whitman's biography, that everyone has pointed to, though without ever drawing the obvious conclusion so far as his art is concerned. I am referring to the great pleasure Whitman took in walking about the streets of New York, mingling with the crowds, in stopping every now and again, or on the ferry-boat or on the banks of the Hudson, standing for hours on end looking at the view, drinking in its majesty' (fol. 242).

Although never concerned with the 'majesty' of the view, Pavese's own characters in his poems, short stories and novels are much given to walking the streets, usually in the suburbs, often in the early hours of the morning. And here, one thinks of Pablo in *Il compagno*, of the three students at the beginning of *Il diavolo sulle colline*, of Clelia in the opening sequence of *Tra donne sole*; but the motif is there as early as 'Ozio' (Idleness) and 'Canzone di strada' (Street song) of 1932 and 1933 respectively. It had figured also in Pavese's 'poesie liceali' (juvenilia).
10 L. Mondo, *Cesare Pavese*, p. 15.
11 See his 'Saggio introduttivo' (introductory essay) to Gozzano, *Le poesie* (Milan, 1971), p. 8.
12 Quoted without bibliographical information by Elio Gioanola in his *Cesare Pavese: la poetica dell'essere* (Milan, 1977), p. 109.
13 Ibid.
14 The theme of 'there hath passed away a glory from the earth', which is central to 'Paolo e Virginia', is most in evidence in Pavese's so-called 'Poesie del disamore' (Poems of disaffection) which were never published during the poet's lifetime and which represent a temporary phase in his work, brought about by his 'spiritual' collapse following his return from Brancaleone.
15 In the context of the development of the *immagine–racconto* technique, there is an interesting passage in Pavese's thesis, where he comments on Whitman's style in the poem 'Spontaneous me': 'the fusion being brought about, as the poem takes shape, of all its descriptive elements *into a fantastic natural landscape* [my italics] – a wood, the trees, the sea – which is in no sense bounded or determined by spatial considerations, but which, for that very reason, is all the more suggestive; and this landscape, peopled by images of lovers, which move through it, not as characters in a scenario, but drawing all their internal reality, their poetry, precisely from the spiritual relationship of "suggestions" – as Whitman puts it – that they are establishing with their environment' (fols. 99–100). This is, in essence, what Pavese himself was to attempt with the *immagine–racconto* – as he explains in *Il mestiere di poeta* (see *Poesie* p. 199).
16 'L'influsso degli eventi' (The influence of events) in *La letteratura americana e altri saggi* (American literature and other essays – hereafter *La lett. am.*) (Einaudi, Turin, 1962), pp. 246–7. The article, dated 5 February 1946, was not published until after Pavese's death (i.e. in the first edition of *La Lett. am.*, 1951).
17 *Il mestiere di poeta*, in *Poesie* p. 198.
18 The title is in English.
19 Letter to Federica Pavese, 9 June 1950 in *Lettere 1945–1950* (Einaudi, Turin, 1966), p. 542. Hereafter *Lett. II*.
20 Published by Frassinelli (Turin, 1932).
21 See p. 25.
22 'Pensieri di Dina' (Dina's thoughts) in *Poesie* p. 46.
23 'Pensieri di Deola' (Deola's thoughts) in *Poesie* p. 34.
24 'Atavismo' (Atavism), 'Esterno' (Out of doors), 'Civiltà antica' (Ancient civilisation) and 'Ulisse' (Ulysses) in *Poesie* pp. 103–12.
25 'Il vino triste', 'La pace regna' (Peace reigns) and 'Creazione' (Creation) in *Poesie* pp. 108–10.

26 Ten poems (eight in Italian and two in English) written between 11 March and 11 April 1950.
27 The reader is referred in general to all the poems of Ungaretti, Montale and Quasimodo, which were written in the late nineteen-twenties and early thirties, when considering these poems of Pavese's. In particular Ungaretti's 'Quiete' (Quiet) and 'Sera' (Evening), both dating from 1929, Montale's 'Portami il girasole' (Bring me a sunflower) and 'Delta' (Delta), both dating from 1927, and Quasimodo's 'Oboe sommerso' (Sunken oboe) and 'Parola' (Word) of 1930–2 have many affinities with Pavese's poems.

3. Imprisonment, solitude and salvation in 'Il carcere'

1 *Notte di festa* (Festival night), 4th edn (Einaudi, Turin, 1961), p. 54.
2 *Il carcere* (The political prisoner), published together with *La casa in collina* under the joint title *Prima che il gallo canti*, 9th edn (Einaudi, Turin, 1962), p. 20 Hereafter *Carcere*.
3 See *Notte di festa*, pp. 25 and 175.
4 F. R. Leavis, *The great tradition* (London, 1948), p. 2.

4. 'Paesi tuoi' and the myth of America

1 *Il sangue d'Europa* (Einaudi, Turin, 1965), p. 149.
2 Ibid. pp. 155–6.
3 Ibid. p. 153.
4 Published by Bompiani, Milan, 1941.
5 See 'Narratori italiani' in *Nuova antologia*, 420 (1942), 66.
6 It should be remembered that *Il carcere* was not actually published until 1949, whilst the first collection of short stories, *Notte di festa*, did not appear until 1953.
7 'Pavese e l'America', in *Studi americani*, 4 (1958), 402.
8 The *stracittà* cultural movement grew out of Futurism, espousing its myths of progress and modernism. Massimo Bontempelli's *Novecento* was historically the first of the *stracittà* journals, taking an anti-positivistic, anti-idealistic, anti-Romantic stand in the early and mid nineteen-twenties, concerned to promote the myth of the new Fascist Italy as 'the hope of the world'. As Fascism was gradually transformed into dictatorship, and rhetoric supplanted 'action', the movement became more and more nationalistic and imperialistic, and, like Fascism itself, was characterised by extreme conformism in the thirties. *Strapaese* was in many ways diametrically opposed to *stracittà*, being strongly traditionalistic and anti-internationalistic in cultural matters, locating the 'truest' values in the Italian regions and the countryside – values which, more and more, the movement regarded as having been betrayed by the Fascist 'revolution'. For a much fuller account of the two movements, the reader is referred to G. Luti, *Cronache letterarie tra le due guerre, 1920–1940* (Bari, 1966), pp. 143–66.
9 In connection with Pavese's interest in America and the Italian 'myth' of America, the following works are extremely useful: Italo Calvino's introduction to *La lett. am.* (Turin, 1962); G. Pintor, *Il sangue d'Europa* (Turin, 1965); N. d'Agostino, 'Pavese e l'America' (see n. 7); R. H. Chase, 'Cesare Pavese and the American novel' in *Studi americani*, 3 (1957); L. Sommariva, 'Scoperta dell'America' in *Saggi di umanesimo cristiano*, VII (1952); D. Fernandez, 'Il mito degli Stati Uniti per gli intellettuali italiani nel periodo fascista' in *Lettere italiane*, XXIX (October–December 1977); D. Fernandez, *Il mito dell' America negli intellettuali italiani dal 1930 al 1950* (Caltanisetta–Rome, 1969); N. Carducci, *Gli intellettuali e l'ideologia americana nell'Italia letteraria degli anni trenta* (Lacaita, 1973).

10 Barbara Reynolds, in her *The linguistic writings of Alessandro Manzoni* (Cambridge, 1950), observes that: 'It was only when [Manzoni] began work as a novelist that he became fully aware of the limitations imposed on an Italian author by the absence of a standard form of Italian, representative of both spoken and written usage. In one of the Introductions to the earliest version of his novel (which he entitled *Gli sposi promessi* and which was never published in his lifetime), he gives an account of the methods by which he has attempted to overcome these limitations: he has made use, he states, of words derived from Lombard, French and Latin, as well as from Tuscan, and has even had recourse to inventing words, wherever analogy or extension of meaning made this a reasonable procedure' (p. 2).
11 *Paesi tuoi*, 8th edn (Einaudi, Turin, 1961), pp. 88–9. Hereafter *Paesi*.
12 Written between 5 and 29 March 1937, it was not published until after Pavese's death, in the homonymous collection of short stories of 1953. (See chapter 3, note 1.)

5. The 'search for a style' in 'La bella estate' and 'La spiaggia'

1 *La bella estate*, published together with *Il diavolo sulle colline* and *Tra donne sole* under the joint title of *La bella estate* (Einaudi, Turin, 1949); *La spiaggia* (Lettere d'oggi, Rome, 1942; new edn by Einaudi, Turin, 1956).
2 *La bella estate*, 3rd edn (Mondadori, Milan, 1961), p. 83. Hereafter *Estate*. Gian-Paolo Biasin, in his *The smile of the gods* (Ithaca, New York, 1969), observes that 'the original title of the novel – *The Curtain* – had its own precise significance in relation to what I call the *poétique du regard*: the dark, heavy curtain that divides Guido's studio in half is the theatrical back cloth, a stage curtain, for the looks that hover, meet and turn away. This truly theatrical function is emphasised even by Ginia's thoughts: "How pleasant it would be to be snugly ensconced there, spying on someone who thought he was alone in the room." The final title, *The Beautiful Summer*, seems instead to give bitter emphasis to the girl's lively, joyous hopes as she discovers herself and the world, and the terrible final disillusionment, projected into the cycle of the seasons' (p. 97–8).

What Biasin does not point out is that the curtain, which divides the 'sleeping' from the 'living' part of the room, also symbolises the emotional and experiential barrier which separates the 'light' or innocent part of Ginia's life (childhood, the beautiful summer) from the 'dark', adult world, so aptly represented by the bed, itself the symbol of the sexual mysteries which so much torment her. There is a great irony built into Ginia's wish, expressed here, in that she herself later becomes the victim of precisely the situation she imagines.
3 Biasin suggests that 'Ginia becomes a woman more through her own reflection in the mirror than through the actual act of carnal love: the self sees itself as another before it even has an awareness of itself' (*Smile of the gods*, p. 96).
4 Biasin, quite rightly, points out that 'In *The Beautiful Summer* Pavese continued and intensified his efforts to take hold of and understand reality, to strip it of its more obvious and contingent aspects in order to get at the marrow, the essence' (*Smile of the gods*, p. 99).
5 *La spiaggia*, 4th edn (Einaudi, Turin, 1961), p. 49. Hereafter *Spiaggia*.
6 The reader is referred particularly to 'Terra d'esilio' (Land of exile), 1936, in *Notte di festa*.
7 L. Bergel (trans. L. Wainstein), 'L'estetica di Cesare Pavese' in *Lo spettatore italiano*, VIII, 10 (October 1955), 407–21.
8 Ibid.

6. Symbolic reality in 'Feria d'agosto'

1 *L'Unità* (of Turin), 22 October 1953.
2 'Il nuovo romanticismo' in *Primato*, 15 August 1953. Later published in *Il sangue d'Europa*, of which see p. 102.
3 L. Bergel, in the already cited article 'L'estetica di Cesare Pavese' (see chapter 5, n. 7), suggests that '*Feria d'agosto* was produced by a sense of isolation, of having no-one but himself. Pavese must have found relief from his loneliness in reliving his past.'
4 *Feria d'agosto*, 4th edn (Mondadori, Milan, 1961). Hereafter *Feria*.
5 Quoted by Pavese in his essay 'Il mito', published in *Cultura e realtà*, 1 (May–June 1950). Now in *La lett. am.* p. 348.
6 The reasons for his failure to act were probably not 'theoretical', as this particular explanation seems to imply (or not entirely so), but rather practical and humanitarian. See chapter 8 for a fuller discussion of this question.

7. The language of myth in 'Dialoghi con Leucò'

1 *Dialoghi con Leucò*, 4th edn (Einaudi, Turin, 1961). Hereafter *Dialoghi*.
2 J. Gatt-Rutter, *Writers and politics in modern Italy* (London, 1978), p. 41.
3 See Eugenio Corsini, 'Orfeo senza Euridice: I *Dialoghi con Leucò* e il classicismo di Pavese' in *Sigma* (December 1964), 121–46.
4 See their *Introduction to a science of mythology* (London, 1949).
5 The reader is referred to the following studies of *Dialoghi*: A. Pellegrini, 'Mito e poesia nell'opera di Cesare Pavese' in *Belfagor*, 10 (September 1955); M. L. Premuda. 'I *Dialoghi con Leucò* e il realismo simbolico di Pavese' in *Annali della Scuola Normale Superiore di Pisa*, 3–4 (1957), and chapter 8 of Biasin, *Smile of the gods*.
6 See chapter 6, n. 5.
7 In connection with this particular statement, the reader is referred to my study, 'The "colloquio tra il divino e l'umano" in Pavese and Leopardi' in *Bulletin of the Society for Italian Studies*, 12 (November 1979), 19–30.
8 The reference is to Jane Ellen Harrison's *Prolegomena to the study of Greek religions* (Cambridge, 1903).
9 The reader is referred to *MV* 1 January 1946, where Pavese writes: 'discovered a new form which draws together many threads (the dialogue of Circe)'. In all probability, it was this dialogue which also suggested the general title of the collection to him, for in *Le streghe* Leukothea (Leucò) is the other interlocutor. In a letter to Bianca Garufi, dating possibly from March 1946 (*Lett. II*, p. 62), he says: 'I have found a collective title for my dialogues: *Dialoghi con Leucò*. Eh?'
10 The antipathy which Pavese often shows towards the Olympians, particularly as described here, quite possibly had some connection with his own, and the general Italian, rejection of the regimenting principle of Fascism, which had stifled Italian creativity for over twenty years. Certainly, this 'child of the mountain' could well be a caricature of Mussolini.
11 'I am your lover and so your enemy', Pavese had written in his diary on 18 November 1945.
12 'East Coker' in *Four Quartets*, ll. 186–8.
13 See p. 116
14 Pavese's references to the work in letters written to friends and critics seem to lend weight to this view. In a letter to P. Pancrazi (22 August 1947, in *Lett. II*, p. 153) he speaks of the forthcoming *Dialoghi* 'from which you will see just how corrupt I am becoming'; to F. Fortini (27 October 1947, p. 189), he says: 'In the meantime I'm sending you my big scandal, *Leucò*'; to P. Milano (25 November 1947, p. 196), he recalls that 'A few days ago I took the liberty of sending you my *Dialoghi*, a heretical book and one which is very dear to my heart'; to Sibilla

Aleramo: 'I thank you for reading *Leucò*. It's a book which is destined to please no-one, so that the few positive responses to it are all the more precious' (2 December 1947, p. 199); while three days before his death, in a letter to Nino Frank, he spoke of the work as 'a book which no-one reads and which, of course, is the only one of any value' (25 August 1950). Despite the ironical tone of many of these comments – or rather, because of it – Pavese's lack of confidence in the way in which the book would be received is clear enough.

8. 'Not fear, not the usual sort of cowardice'

1 *La casa in collina*, in *Prima che il gallo canti*, 9th edn (Einaudi, Turin, 1962), p. 254. Hereafter *Casa*.
2 'Ritorno all'uomo' in *L'Unità* (of Turin), 20 May 1945. Now in *La lett. am.* p. 218.
3 'Pieretto' in *L'Unità*, 19 May 1946. Now in *La lett. am.* p. 257.
4 'Le parole' in *L'Unità*, 8 May 1946. Now in *La lett. am.* p. 253.
5 'Paesi tuoi' in *L'Unità*, 11 July 1946. Now in *La lett. am.* p. 260.
6 'Il compagno' in *L'Unità*, 1 May 1946. Now in *La lett. am.* pp. 251–2.
7 *Il compagno* 8th edn (Einaudi, Turin, 1961), p. 10. Hereafter *Compagno*.
8 G. Venturi, *Pavese* (*Il castoro*, 25, Florence, 1970), p. 95.
9 'Dino' is an abbreviated, diminutive form of 'Corrado' i.e. Corra*dino*.
10 There is a close similarity between Pavese's insistence on 'stupore' in this novel and Camus's definition of 'l'absurde' in *Le mythe de Sisyphe* and his description of the reaction it provokes: 'L'absurdité naît d'une comparaison. Je suis donc fondé à dire que le sentiment de l'absurdité ne naît pas du simple examen d'un fait ou d'une impression mais qu'il jaillit de la comparaison entre un état de fait et une certaine réalité, entre une action et le monde qui la dépasse. L'absurde est essentiellement un divorce. Il n'est ni dans l'un ni dans l'autre des éléments comparés. Il naît de leur confrontation' (*Le mythe de Sisyphe*, Paris, 1942, p. 48). Clearly, 'l'absurde' and 'lo stupore' are not the same, though the former always carries an element of 'stupore' inherent in the discovery and the new awareness it brings. 'Stupore' certainly derives from 'confrontation' and always implies 'un divorce'.
11 There is a curious, if deliberate, irony in the fact that Corrado does eventually seek refuge in such a place, and that for a time he does find the peace-in-order that he so desperately needs.
12 Here one is reminded strongly of Eliot's almost contemporary statement 'The whole earth is our hospital' ('East Coker' l. 157) and its similar close connection with the orthodox religious organisation of life.
13 Originally, Pavese had classed the *selvaggio* as mindless rhythm, as Titanic, in fact, whilst the rational element in man's makeup had been seen as an exclusively humanising and civilising force, and this was the Olympian. However, the experience of the two orders in *Dialoghi* brought him to the realisation that the gods, the Olympians, were capable of using their rationality deviously, in ways which were anti-human, indeed inhuman. Man, in short, had within him not only a mindless *selvaggio* (instinct), but, much worse, a *selvaggio* which could press all his rationality into its service. War, which to the individual caught up in it appears mindless (as *Casa* continually demonstrates), in reality always has the 'rational' decisions of remote (Olympian) minds behind it. This is not a denial, on Pavese's part, of rationality as a power for good, simply a recognition of its possibilities for evil – a theme explored and developed in his next novel, *Il diavolo sulle colline*. The 'mindless' *selvaggio* is not a moral category, simply a question of chance, but it can be 'harnessed' by the mind working in harmony

with its rhythms, as, for example, in the case of the farming year following the lead of the seasons. It was this harmony, rather than pure rationality or total irrationality, which ever remained Pavese's ideal.

9. Structure and style in 'Il diavolo sulle colline'

1 *Il diavolo sulle colline*, in *La bella estate*, 3rd edn (Mondadori, 1961), p. 114. Hereafter *Diavolo*.
2 The significance of her name, 'rose white', should not go unnoticed – ironical as it is, particularly in this sequence.
3 Very much later in the novel, a specific connection is made between 'dance music' and the *selvaggio*: 'The music had stopped. In the silence, you could hear the crickets through the windows' (p. 178), implying perhaps that there is little difference between them, as well as illustrating Pavese's conviction that the 'Titan' always survives and re-emerges when the 'civilised' – real or illusory (as here) – disappears.
4 For example, Oreste's passion for hunting, which Poli describes as 'a drug', and which evokes in him the same disgust as 'spilled blood' evokes in Corrado, in *Casa*.
5 In this context, the reader is referred to *MV* 30 January 1950: 'The superstitious man is one who still *believes* in a myth which has already been overtaken by history – that is, in a myth for which the means of dissolution already exist.' It is a part of the thesis of this chapter that the narrator's attitude to the countryside is covered by this definition.
6 The reader is referred to the whole of the diary entry for 9 January 1950, from which this phrase is taken, for further light on the effect of this contradiction on his work.
7 This motif is found in the diary entry for 7 December 1947, here quoted in full: 'There has been so much talk, so much description, so much alarm about our life, our world and our culture, that seeing the sun and the clouds, going out into the street and finding grass, stones, dogs, moves us like grace itself, like a gift from God, like a dream. Yet a real dream, *which lasts*, which is there.' It recurs in the poem 'Mania di solitudine' (1933):

> Basta un po' di silenzio e ogni cosa si ferma
> nel suo luogo reale, cosí com'è fermo il mio corpo.
> ...Ogni pianta e ogni sasso
> vive immobile.

(All you need is a bit of silence and everything is still in its proper place, just as my body is still ... Every plant and every stone lives in stillness.)

8 This passage, incidentally, in part endorses Pieretto's view, expressed earlier p. 95), that now, in the countryside, 'the smell which dominates is that of petrol'.
9 See *Diavolo* p. 187: 'I asked him [i.e. Poli] then whether cocaine was a part of that peace of mind. His answer was that we all of us use some drug or other, from wine to sleeping-pills, from nakedness to the cruelties of the hunt: "What's nakedness got to do with it?" A lot, in fact: there are those who go out naked amongst people just for the pleasure of feeling how ugly they are and to violate a social norm.'
10 The reader is reminded of Pavese's statement in *MV* 28 December 1947, which seems to be as pertinent for the narrator as it is for Poli: 'The Greek myth teaches us that we are always at war with a part of ourselves, that part which has already been defeated, Zeus against Typhon, Apollo against Pytho. Looked at another way, what we are fighting against is always a part of ourselves, a former

self. We fight first and foremost so as *not* to be something, to free ourselves. Anyone who doesn't have aversions doesn't fight.'
11 Pavese's use of the colour white, for example, is unusual, for it rarely suggests purity; rather is it indicative of evil – the connotation it had for Melville with his 'great white whale'. In this development of a 'new language' it is difficult not to see the later Pavese as the 'post-Modernist'.
12 L. Pirandello, *L'uomo dal fiore in bocca* (Mondadori, Milan, 1951), p. 131.
13 Armanda Guiducci, *Il mito Pavese* (Florence, 1967), p. 418.

10. Being and seeming in 'Tra donne sole'

1 *Tra donne sole*, in *La bella estate*, 3rd edn (Mondadori, Milan, 1961), p. 221. Hereafter *Donne*.
2 See *In famiglia* in *Dialoghi* (p. 155) and the discussion of it in chapter 7 of this work (pp. 137–8).
3 Letter dated 18 January 1950, now in *Lett. II*, p. 460.

11. History, symbol and myth in 'La luna e i falò'

1 Translation by J. D. Sinclair, *Inferno* (Oxford and London, 1971), p. 325.
2 *La luna e i falò*, 12th edn (Einaudi, Turin, 1961), p. 12. Hereafter *Luna*.
3 Bruce Merry, 'Artifice and structure in *La luna e i falò*' in *Forum Italicum*, v, 3 (September 1971), 351–2.
4 The reader's attention is drawn to Eliot's 'The Dry Salvages' (in *Four Quartets*), where the same contrast between 'natural' and 'historical' time is a central motif:

> And under the oppression of the silent fog
> The tolling bell
> Measures time not our time, rung by the unhurried
> Ground swell, a time
> Older than the time of chronometers ... (ll. 34ff.)

5 From a very early date – certainly as early as the essay 'Tradition and the individual talent' (1920) – Eliot moved towards an ideal of 'impersonality' in his poetry: 'the poet has, not a "personality" to express, but a particular medium, which is only a medium and not a personality, in which impressions and experiences combine in peculiar and unexpected ways'. In that 'medium', according to Eliot, the poet was concerned with the expression of '*significant* emotion, emotion which has its life in the poem and not in the history of the poet' (see *The sacred wood* (London, 1974), pp. 56 and 59). Pavese, with his rejection of the 'need' for characters who were well-rounded, was carrying Eliot's view a step further in that the 'rhythm of events', the patterns of history, that is, contained and expressed precisely that '*significant* emotion' which Eliot called for. The roles and importance of characters and '*significant* emotion' were in a sense reversed.
6 This principle of the negation of the individual is embodied within Mussolini's well-known dictum of 'Everything inside the State, nothing outside the State, nothing against the State.'
7 Translation by Sinclair, *Inferno*, p. 49.
8 The dissolution of the individual within the collective was the principle underlying each of these Fascist institutions, in the belief that strength was derived from single-mindedness, which in its turn depended on order, discipline and hierarchy.

12. The celebration of a rite: last poems, 1945–1950

1 'Appunti sulla tecnica poetica di Pavese' in *Astrazione e realtà* (Mîlan, 1960). p. 315.
2 See chapter 2 above.
3 Written in Rome between 27 October and 3 December 1945. Published initially in *Le tre Venezie* (Padua), XXI, fasc. 4–6 (1947); later by G. Spagnoletti in *Antologia della poesia italiana 1909–1949* (Modena, 1950). Published after Pavese's death by Einaudi in the volume *Verrà la morte e avrà i tuoi occhi*. (See n. 4.)
4 Written for Constance Dowling, probably in Turin, between 11 March and 11 April 1950. First published together with *La terra e la morte* by Einaudi (Turin, 1951).
5 There are, of course, other phonological features, not considered here, which in this poem do contribute particularly to the rhythm, e.g. the repetition of individual sounds, groups of sounds, words and whole phrases; they also contribute to the 'binding' effect in the form-creating process.
6 The original title was in English, as was the case with five other poems in this sequence.
7 This poem and the last one in the sequence, 'Last blues, to be read some day', were written in English.
8 A reference to the dialogue *Schiuma d'onda* (*Dialoghi*), in which Aphrodite, the goddess of love, is thus named.

13. 'To bring order and design where there is chaos'

1 'L'influsso degli eventi' in *La lett. am.* p. 248.
2 Ibid.
3 The aim which Pavese had originally attributed to Sherwood Anderson. See 'L'Arte: l'ordine dov'è il caos' in *La lett. am.* p. 45.

Bibliography of Pavese's works

(Date of composition appears in parentheses after each title)

Lavorare stanca (poems, 1931–43)
   1st edn: Solaria, Florence, 1936
   New and enlarged edn (poems, 1931–40): Einaudi, Turin, 1943.
   Translation: selected poems by Pavese were translated by Margaret Crosland in *A mania for solitude: selected poems 1930–50* (Peter Owen, London, 1969)

Notte di festa (short stories, 1936–8)
   1st edn: Einaudi, Turin, 1953
   Edn used: 4th, 1961
   Translation: A. E. Murch, *Festival night* (Peter Owen, London, 1964)

Il carcere (1938–9)
   1st edn: with *La casa in collina* under the joint title of *Prima che il gallo canti* (Einaudi, Turin, 1949)
   Edn used: 9th, 1962
   Translation: W. J. Strachan, *The political prisoner* (Peter Owen, London, 1959)

Paesi tuoi (1939)
   1st edn: Einaudi, Turin, 1941
   Edn used: 8th, 1961
   Translation: A. E. Murch, *The harvesters* (Peter Owen, London, 1961)

La bella estate (1940)
   1st edn: with *Il diavolo sulle colline* and *Tra donne sole* under the joint title of *La bella estate* (Einaudi, Turin, 1949)
   Edn used: 3rd (Mondadori, Milan, 1961)
   Translation: W. J. Strachan, 'The beautiful summer', in *The political prisoner* (Peter Owen, London, 1959)

La spiaggia (1940–1)
   1st edn: Lettere d'oggi, Roma, 1942
   Edn used: 4th (Einaudi, Turin, 1961)
   Translation: W. J. Strachan, *The beach* (Peter Owen, London, 1963)

Feria d'agosto (Stories and prose, 1941–4)
   1st edn: Einaudi, Turin, 1946
   Edn used: 4th (Mondadori, Milan, 1961)
   Translation: selected stories from *Feria d'agosto* trans. by A. E. Murch, *Summer storm* (Peter Owen, London, 1966)

Racconti (short stories, 1936–44)
   1st edn: Einaudi, Turin, 1960

La terra e la morte (poems, 1945)
   1st edn: in *Le tre Venezie* (Padua, 1947)

Dialoghi con Leucò (1945–6)
   1st edn: Einaudi, Turin, 1947
   Edn used: 4th, 1961
   Translation: W. Arrowsmith and D. S. Carne-Ross, *Dialogues with Leucò* (University of Michigan Press, Ann Arbor, 1966)

Fuoco grande (1946; incomplete)
   1st edn: Einaudi, Turin, 1959
   Translation: W. J. Strachan, 'A great fire' in *The beach* (Peter Owen, London, 1963)
Il Compagno (1946)
   1st edn: Einaudi, Turin, 1947
   Edn used: 8th, 1961
   Translation: W. J. Strachan, *The comrade* (Peter Owen, London, 1959)
La casa in collina (1947–8)
   1st edn: in *Prima che il gallo canti*, 1949
   Edn used: 9th, 1962
   Translation: W. J. Strachan, *The house on the hill* (Walker, New York, 1959)
Il diavolo sulle colline (1948)
   1st edn: in *La bella estate*, 1949
   Edn used: 3rd, 1961
   Translation: D. D. Paige, *The devil in the hills* (Noonday Press, New York, 1959)
Tra donne sole (1949)
   1st edn: in *La bella estate*, 1949
   Edn used: 3rd, 1961
   Translation: D. D. Paige. *Among women only* (Peter Owen, London, 1953)
La luna e i falò (1949)
   1st edn: Einaudi, Turin, 1950
   Edn used: 12th, 1961
   Translation: Louise Sinclair, *The moon and the bonfires* (John Lehmann, London, 1952)
Verrà la morte e avrà i tuoi occhi (poems, 1950)
   1st edn: Einaudi, Turin, 1951 (together with *La terra e la morte*)
   Translation: in Crosland, *Mania for solitude*
La letteratura americana e altri saggi (essays and articles 1930–50)
   1st edn: Einaudi, Turin, 1951
   Edn used: 1962
Il mestiere di vivere (diary, 1935–50)
   1st edn: Einaudi, Turin, 1952
   Translation: A. E. Murch: *This business of living* (Peter Owen, London, 1962)
Lettere (1924–50)
   1st edn: vol. I (1924–44), vol. II (1945–50): Einaudi, Turin, 1966

Translations by Pavese

Sinclair Lewis, *Our Mr Wrenn*   *Il nostro signor Wrenn* (Bemporad, Florence, 1931)
Herman Melville, *Moby-Dick*   *Moby Dick* (Frassinelli, Turin, 1932)
Sherwood Anderson, *Dark laughter*   *Riso nero* (Frassinelli, Turin, 1932)
James Joyce, *Portrait of the artist as a young man*   *Dedalus* (Frassinelli, Turin, 1934)
J. Dos Passos, *Forty-second parallel*   *Il 42° parallelo* (Mondadori, Milan, 1935)
J. Dos Passos, *Big money*   *Un mucchio de quattrini* (Mondadori, Milan, 1937)
Gertrude Stein, *Autobiography of Alice B. Toklas*   *Autobiografia di Alice Toklas* (Einaudi, Turin, 1938)
Daniel Defoe, *Moll Flanders*   *Moll Flanders* (Einaudi, Turin, 1938)
Charles Dickens, *David Copperfield*   *David Copperfield* (Einaudi, Turin, 1939)
Gertrude Stein, *Three lives*   *Tre esistenze* (Einaudi, Turin, 1940)
Herman Melville, *Benito Cereno*   *Benito Cereno* (Einaudi, Turin, 1940)

G. M. Trevelyan, *The English revolution of 1688–89*   *La rivoluzione inglese del 1688–89* (Einaudi, Turin, 1941)
Christopher Morley, *The Trojan horse*   *Il cavallo di Troia* (Bompiani, Milan, 1941)
William Faulkner, *The hamlet*   *Il borgo* (Mondadori, Milan, 1942)
R. Henriques, *Captain Smith*   *Capitano Smith* (Einaudi, Turin, 1947)

Selected criticism of Pavese's works

d'Agostino, N., 'Pavese e l'America' in *Studi americani*, 4 (1958)
Amoruso, V., 'Cecchi, Vittorini, Pavese e la letteratura americana' in *Studi americani*, 6 (1960)
Antonicelli, F., 'Le favole di Pavese' in *Il ponte*, VI (1950)
Antonielli, S., 'I versi di Pavese' in *Belfagor*, 6 (1951)
Barberi-Squarotti, G., 'Appunti sulla tecnica poetica di Pavese' in *Questioni*, I–IV (1959) (reprinted in *Astrazione e realtà*, Milan, 1960)
  'Pavese o la fuga nella metafora' in *Sigma* (December 1964)
Barnett, L. K., 'Notes on Pavese's critical view of American literature' in *Forum Italicum*, VIII, 3 (September 1974)
Beccaria, G. L., 'Il lessico, ovvero "la questione della lingua" in Cesare Pavese' in *Sigma* (December 1964).
Bergel, L., 'L'estetica di Pavese' in *Lo spettatore italiano*, VII, 10 (1955)
Biasin, G-P., 'Il rapporto Io–altri nei romanzi "politici" di Cesare Pavese' in *Italica*, 43 (1966)
  The smile of the gods (Ithaca, New York, 1968)
  'L'inconscio di Pavese' in *Italica*, 46 (1969)
Catalano, E., *Cesare Pavese fra politica e ideologia* (Bari, 1976)
Chase, R. H., 'Cesare Pavese and the American novel' in *Studi americani*, 3 (1957)
Corsini, E., 'Orfeo senza Euridice: I *Dialoghi con Leucò* e il classicismo di Pavese' in *Sigma* (December 1964)
Dionisotti, C., '*Lavorare stanca*' in *La nuova Europa*, II, 34 (Rome, 1945)
Fernandez, D., 'Cesare Pavese' in *Le roman italien et la crise de la conscience moderne* (Paris, 1958)
  L'échec de Pavese (Paris, 1967)
Fiedler, L., 'Introducing Pavese' in *Kenyon Review*, XVI (1954)
Fontana, P., 'Il primo Pavese da *Lavorare stanca* a *La spiaggia*' in *Aevum*, 32 (1958)
Foster, D. W., 'The poetic vision of "le colline": an introduction to Pavese's *Lavorare stanca*' in *Italica*, 42 (1965)
Freccero, J., 'Mythos and logos: the moon and the bonfires' in *Italian Quarterly*, IV (1961)
Gioanola, E., *Cesare Pavese: la poetica dell'essere* (Milan, 1977)
Grassi, C., 'Osservazioni su lingua e dialetto nell'opera di Pavese' in *Sigma* (December 1964)
Guglielmi, G., 'Mito e logos in Pavese' in *Convivium*, n.s. 26 (1958)
Guglielminetti, M., 'Racconto e canto nella metrica di Pavese' in *Sigma* (December 1964)
Guiducci, A., *Il mito Pavese* (Florence, 1967)
Hahn, O., 'Pavese ou la création lucide' in *Temps Modernes*, 16 (January 1961)
Hoesle, J., *Cesare Pavese* (Berlin, 1961)
Jesi, F., 'Cesare Pavese, il mito e la scienza del mito' in *Sigma* (December 1964)
Kibler, L., 'Patterns of time in Pavese's *La luna e i falò*' in *Forum Italicum*, XII, 3 (September, 1978)

Lajolo, D., *Il vizio assurdo*, 4th edn (Milan, 1961)
Longobardi, F., 'Ancora Pavese' in *Belfagor*, 20 (November 1965)
Merry, B., 'Artifice and structure in *La luna e i falò*' in *Forum Italicum*, v, 3 (September 1971)
Mila, M., Introduction to *Cesare Pavese: Poesie* (Turin, 1961)
Mollia, F., *Cesare Pavese* (Padua, 1960)
Mondo, L., *Cesare Pavese* (Milan, 1961)
  'Fra Gozzano e Whitman: le origini di Pavese' in *Sigma* (December 1964)
Norton, P. M., 'Cesare Pavese and the American nightmare' in *Modern Language Notes*, LXXVII (January 1962)
Pampaloni, G., 'Cesare Pavese' in *Terzo programma*, 3 (1962)
Paris, R., 'Delphes sur les collines' in *Sigma* (December 1964)
Pautasso, S., 'Vent'anni di *Lavorare stanca*' in *Questioni*, IV-V (1956)
Pellegrini, A., 'Mito e poesia nell'opera di Cesare Pavese' in *Belfagor*, 10 (September 1955)
Premuda, M. L., 'I *Dialoghi con Leucò* e il realismo simbolico di Pavese' in *Annali della Scuola Normale Superiore di Pisa*, 3-4 (1957)
Renard, P., '*Dialoghi con Leucò*: la conquête du mythe comme polarisation de l'inconciliable' in *Italianistica*, 1 (January-April 1972)
Sbrocchi, L. G., *Stilistica nella narrativa pavesiana* (Florence, 1967)
Schneider, F., 'Quest, romance and myth in Pavese's *Devil in the hills*' in *Italica*, 49 (1972)
Solmi, S., 'Il diario di Pavese' in *Scrittori negli anni* (Milan, 1963)
Thompson, A. D, 'Anti-Fascism and the resistance in Pavese's last novels (1945-1950)' in *Journal of the Association of Teachers of Italian*, 27 (1979)
  '"Slow rotation suggesting permanence": history, symbol and myth in Pavese's last novel' in *Italian Studies*, XXXIV (1979)
  'The "colloquio tra il divino e l'umano" in Pavese and Leopardi' in *Bulletin of the Society for Italian Studies*, 12 (November 1979)
Venturi, G., *Pavese* (*Il castoro*, 25, Florence, 1970)

Index

'A proposito di certe poesie non ancora scritte', 78
Agostino, Nemi d', 58
Aleramo, Sibilla, 275 n. 14
Alfieri, Vittorio, 62
alienation, 4, 31, 32, 40, 51, 52, 90, 98, 99, 154, 187, 262; in *La casa in collina*, 167, 171, 172; in *Il compagno*, 162; in *Dialoghi con Leucò*, 145; in *Il diavolo sulle colline*, 187, 192; in *La luna e i falò*, 241, 242; in *Paesi tuoi*, 68, 99; in *Tra donne sole*, 217, 221
Alighieri, Dante, 4, 87, 134; *Divina Commedia* by, 227, 242; journey motif in, 223, 230, 262, 267
America amara, see Cecchi, Emilio
America, United States of: articles on literature of, 6, 58; cinema of, 56; culture of, 5, 25; materialism of, rejected, 242, 243; myth of, 55–62, 273 n. 9; neo-Realism in, 57, 58; translations of literature of, 6, 57, 58; in *La luna e i falò*, 223, 230, 241, 242, 244
'Amici', 84
Anceschi, Luciano, 249
Anderson, Sherwood, 59–60, 67, 98, 243, 262, 279, n.3 to ch. 13
anguish, see inquietudine
Annunzio, Gabriele d', 4, 30, 43, 64, 118, 147
antithesis, 262, 268; as 'symbolic representation of the divided self', 262
art and pictorial artists: in *La bella estate*, 73, 78, 81; in *La spiaggia*, 78, 83, 86; in *Tra donne sole*, 78, 208–212 *passim*

Badoglio, Marshall Pietro, 96
Bàrberi-Squarotti, Giorgio, 249, 279, n.1 to ch. 12
Baretti, Il, 3

'being' and 'seeming', theme of: in *La bella estate*, 76; in *Tra donne sole*, 204–22
'basic stratum', *see strato fondamentale, lo*
bella estate, La: homonymous novel, 52, 71–82, 268; trilogy, 11
Bergel, Leinhard, 91, 92–3, 274, n.7, 275, n.3 to ch. 6
Biasin, Gian-Paolo, 259, 274 nn. 2–4
Boccaccio, Giovanni, 118
Bottai, Giuseppe, 58

Cajumi, Arrigo, 6
Calvino, Italo, *Il sentiero dei nidi di ragno* by, 69
Camerino, Aldo, 231
campagna, see città–campagna motif
Camus, Albert, 276 n. 10
carcere, Il, 10, 36, 40–54, 58, 61–9 *passim*, 78, 79, 89, 91, 92, 99, 151, 161, 193, 264, 268; concept of antithesis in, 262–3; imprisonment and alienation in, 40, 264; will and Destiny in, 130
Carocci, Alberto, 6, 7
'Carogne', 40
casa in collina, La, 53, 149–53 *passim*, 165–77, 207, 219; historical representativeness of, 150; the intellectual and 'creation of consciousness' in, 167; nature as 'hope for the world' in, 175; organic structure of, 173–7; rejection of violence in, 153, 170; war as hazard in, 168–9, 170; war as refuge in, 165, 166
Catholicism, see myth and religion
Cecchi, Emilio, 55, 57, 58, 64, 69
characterisation in Pavese's works, 12, 69, 158–9, 240, 278 n. 6
childhood: as 'beautiful summer' or 'festa', 73–5, 87, 185; and Destiny, 108, 110, 129, 132, 172, 191, 192–3, 210, 228, 264–5; and discovery, 224;

Index

formative years and environment of, 99, 100, 108, 166, 177, 181, 185, 194, 214–15, 226, 229; and freedom, 31, 32, 34, 108, 207, 262, 272, n. 24; as 'lost paradise', 108, 184, 207; and memory, 85, 89, 91, 100, 109, 112, 185, 215; *occhio vergine* of, 16, 69, 199, 271, n. 6 to ch. 2; *lo scappato di casa*, 16; and *stupore*, 50, 169, 230; in *Feria d'agosto*, 108–10 *passim*; in Pavese's poetry, 16, 22, 28

città, see *città–campagna* motif

città–campagna motif: in Anderson's novels, 60; in *Il diavolo sulle colline*, 183–9 *passim;* in *Feria d'agosto*, 85, 110, 112; in *Lavorare stanca*, 22, 32, 98, 262; in *Paesi tuoi*, 63, 112; in *La spiaggia*, 85, 91

Cocchiara, Giuseppe, 232

Coleridge, S. T., 242

come è stato, così sarà (what has been determines what will be), 53, 118, 124, 125, 134, 155, 191, 220, 265

commitment, 14–15, 31, 116, 145–6, 162, 168, 222, 262; failure of, 87, 160, 174

compagno, Il, 115, 149–64; character of dialogue in, 156–7; *donna–mago* in, 132, 162; Turin and Rome in, 163–4; weaknesses of, 150, 155

compagno, Il (political dialogue), 155; 276 n.6

confino, 271 n. 5; Pavese's, 7, 74; in *Il carcere*, 40–54 *passim*, 177

contemplative observer: as narrator, 16, 90, 143, 272 n. 8; of self, 192

Conversazione in Sicilia, see Vittorini, Elio

Corsini, Eugenio, 116–18, 275 n. 3

Cristo si è fermato a Eboli, see Levi, Carlo

Croce, Benedetto, 4

cultura, La, 6

Cultura e realtà, 100

Defoe, Daniel, 79, 80

Deledda, Grazia, 60

Destiny, law of, 135, 142, 146, 228; and childhood, *see* childhood; ecstasy as escape from, 133–4, 144; and freedom, 129–30, 141, 142, 147–8, 234, 245, 246, 248; and the gods, 120, 147; 'hope or destiny' 142; and

inquietudine (anxiety), 128; as 'the mother within us', 131; as 'natural forces', 147; opposition to, 126, 127; politics and, 155, 247–8; as social relationships, 135–6, 245; will and, 129–34 *passim*, 142, 146, 164

dialoghi col compagno, I, 154

Dialoghi con Leucò, 34, 85, 114, 151, 153, 162, 192, 218, 222, 231, 243, 245, 249, 260, 275, n. 5 to ch. 7; character of ('search for human autonomy'), 116, 141, 142, 146; language of myth in, 115–48; preface to, 165, 178, 219; *La belva*, 137, 138–40, 260; *Gli dèi*, 117, 125–6, 210; *Il diluvio*, 142–3; *In famiglia*, 137–8, 278, n. 2 to ch. 10; *L'inconsolabile*, 133–4; *L'isola*, 120, 132–4; *La madre*, 131–2; *Il mistero*, 123–5; *Le muse*, 117, 143; *La nube*, 122, 124; *La rupe*, 135–7, 141–2; *Schiuma d'onda*, 123, 130, 131, 134, 138, 279 n. 8; *La strada*, 128–30, 135, 143; *Le streghe*, 119–20, 125–8 *passim*, 219; *Gli uomini*, 121, 125, 126

diavolo sulle colline, Il, 92, 111–12, 178–203; anthropomorphism in, 184, 186–7; countryside in, 183–4, 188–9; *donna–mago in*, 132, 179–80, 190; human and natural in harmony in, 187–9; lost harmony between the human and natural in, 185–9 *passim*, 198; magic in the commonplace in, 185, 275 n. 7; 'the new language' of, 193–203 *passim;* Oreste's 'cry' in, 92, 180; search for innocence in, 178,179, 181, 184, 191; search for self in, 192

Dickens, Charles, 79

Divina commedia, see Alighieri, Dante

Doeblin, Alfred, 79

Dos Passos, John, 79

Dostoyevsky, Fyodor, 79–80, 83, 93

Dowling, Constance, 11, 257

Einaudi, Luigi, 6

Einaudi Publishing House, 6, 10, 96

Eliot, Thomas Stearns, 136 141, 223, 224, 225, 233, 236, 238, 239–40, 241, 242, 244, 255, 275 n. 12, 276 n. 12, 278 n. 4

Fascism (in Italy), 3, 5, 6, 14, 53, 57, 96, 149, 150, 153, 157, 158, 236; and America, 55–6; anti-Fascism, 157,

158, 161, 163, 236; censorship under, 6; cultural revolt under, 70; culture of, 66, 69; emotional appeal of, 161; isolationist policy.of, 6, 58; regimentation under, 240–4 *passim*, 278 n. 6; 'resignation of responsibility' under, 180

Feria d'agosto, 69, 82–5 *passim*, 95, 96–114, 132, 249, 266, 268; child narrators in, 109; 'Il campo di granturco', 112; 'La città', 110–12; 'Le feste', 109; 'Fine d'agosto', 100; 'La giacchetta di cuoio', 109; 'Mal di mestiere', 108–9; 'Il mare', 84, 109–10; 'Nudismo', 112–14; 'Primo amore', 109; 'La vigna', 112

festa (feasts and other celebrations), 110, 175–80 *passim*, 204–10 *passim*, 236–8, 246

Flora, Francesco, 14

Formalism, 232–3

Fortini, Franco, 275 n. 14

Four Quartets: 'The Dry Salvages', 244–5, 278 n. 4; East Coker', 241, 275 n. 12; 'Little Gidding', 223, 233, 239, 240, 244; *see also* Eliot, Thomas Stearns

Frank, Nino, 275 n. 14

Frazer, Sir J. G., 78

Freud, Sigmund, 78, 118, 184

Futurism, 57

Garufi, Bianca, 275 n. 9

Gatt-Rutter, John, 275, n. 2 to ch. 7

Gerratana,Valentino, 97

Genoa, 1; in *La luna e i falò*, 225, 228, 236, 239, 244; in *La spiaggia*, 84–91 *passim*, 99

'ginestra, La', *see* Leopardi, Giacomo

Ginzburg, Leone, 5, 6, 11, 97

Giustizia e Libertà movement, 5, 7

Gobetti, Piero, 3

Gozzano, Guido: character of verse of, 17, 19; influence of, 15–19 *passim*, 26, 272 n. 14; 'Il gioco del silenzio' by, 17; 'Invernale' by, 17; 'Paolo e Virginia' by, 18–19; 'La signorina Felicità ovvero la Felicità' by, 17

Gramsci, Antonio, 3, 59, 66, 158, 161, 221

Guiducci, Armanda, 195, 196, 198, 202, 278 n. 13

Hamlet, cockcrow in, 207

Harrison, Jane Ellen, 119, 120, 275 n. 8

hazard, *see selvaggio, Il*

Hemingway, Ernest, 25, 69, 156–7

Hermetic poetry, *see poesia ermetica*

Herodotus, 140

Hesiod, 121

Homer, 51–2, 140

immagine–racconto, 19, 27, 48, 51, 265, 268, 272 n. 15

imprisonment, theme of: in *Il carcere*, 36, 40–54, 264; in *La casa in collina*, 171–2; in *Il compagno*, 162–4; in *Dialoghi con Leucò*, 142; in *Paesi tuoi*, 63; in 'Semplicità', 36; in short stories, 36, 63

incest: in *La luna e i falò*, 92; in *Paesi tuoi*, 64–5, 92

indifferenti, Gli, see Moravia, Alberto

individuating function of poetry, 249

individuation process, 102–3, 106, 185, 232

'influsso degli eventi, L', 82, 261, 272 n. 16, 279, n. 1 to ch. 13

inquietudine (anguish), 27, 97, 108, 261–70 *passim;* in *La bella estate*, 71, 72, 77; in *Il carcere*, 41, 46–7, 51, 264; in *Il compagno*, 156; in *Dialoghi con Leucò*, 123, 128, 133, 138, 140, 142; in *Il diavolo sulle colline*, 189; in *La spiaggia*, 71, 72, 90; in *La terra e la morte*, 257; in *Tra donne sole*, 206; in *Verrà la morte e avrà i tuoi occhi*, 250

'intruso, L', 40–1

Ithaca, as symbol of self, 132–4

Italian Civil War (1943–5), 10, 53, 96, 97, 150, 151, 153, 166, 170, 246, 247

journey, as 'descent into self', 192, 224, 262; as self-discovery, 109, 112, 126–7, 132–3, 134, 170, 215; Ulysses theme, *see luna e i falò, La; see also* Alighieri, Dante

Jung, Carl Gustav, 78, 112, 117, 118, 185, 193, 269, 275, n. 4 to ch. 7

Kérényi, Carl, 117, 275, n. 4 to ch. 7

Lajolo, Davide, 5, 138, 271, n. 2 to ch. 1

Langhe, the: character of, 1; in *Feria d'agosto*, 83, 100, 109–10; in *Lavorare stanca*, 98, 262; in *La luna e i falò*,

223–6, 233, 236, 239–47 *passim*, 266; in 'I mari del Sud', 20–6 *passim*, 194, 223, 226; in 'Paesaggio I', 28, in *La spiaggia*, 84, 85
Lavorare stanca, 13–39, 48, 78, 82, 83, 98, 100, 156, 253, 265; Einaudi (1943) edition of, 13, 250; Solaria (1936) edition of, 7, 13, 14, 19, 20, 22, 26–30 *passim*, 33, 58, 132, 249, 250, 261, 271, n. 4 to ch. 1, n. 2 to ch. 2; childhood in, 50, 74; *padroni di se stessi* in, 71; sex in, 29–32 *passim*, 262; *tecnica*, in post-Brancaleone poems, 34–8; work in, 29–32 *passim*, 262
Leaves of grass: 'Song of myself', 16; 'There was a child went forth', 15, 16; *see also* Whitman, Walt
Leavis, F. R., 189, 273, n. 4 to ch. 3
Leopardi, Giacomo: themes in common with Pavese, 32, 33, 36, 103, 113, 114, 118, 124, 147, 240–1, 270; and Enlightenment tradition, 128, 140; and 'l'infausta verità', 126; and the 'onslaught of reason,' 118, 230–1; on superiority of the 'active life', 85; 'La ginestra' by, 33, 114, 240–1; *Operette morali* by, 118
Levi, Carlo, 52, 70; *Cristo si è fermato a Eboli* by, 52
Lewis, Sinclair, 59–60, 243
Liberation, War of, *see* Italian Civil War
loneliness, *see* solitude
luna e i falò, La, 92, 156, 221, 223–48, 260; *campanilismo* (belonging/rootlessness) in, 241, 242; *donna–mago* in, 132, 161; mutability in, 239–40; reality in, 232, 238; 'sameness in difference' in, 236–8; search for wholeness in, 244; symbolism in, 225, 226, 229–30, 240, 242, 243; theme of return in, 224–6, 232, 244; time in, (cyclic, mythical or natural) 227, 228, 233, 234, 236, 240, 245, (historic or linear) 226, 233, 236, 245, (levels of, 232, 237, 238; Ulysses theme in, 223, 224, 230, 242, 243

Mann, Thomas, 193, 269
Manzoni, Alessandro: *I promessi sposi* by, 36, 61, 274 n. 10
Masters, Lee, 59
Melville, Herman, 25, 57, 59, 80, 278 n. 11; *Moby-Dick* by, 25, 80, 272, n. 20
Mérimée, Prosper, 81
Merry, Bruce, 232, 278, n. 3 to ch. 11
mestiere di poeta, Il, 13–14, 15, 25, 27, 272 n. 17
Mexico, 243
'Middle West e Piemonte', 59–60, 62
Mila, Massimo, ix, 6, 97
Milano, Paolo, 275 n. 14
'minute particular', the: in *La luna e i falò*, 224, 226, 228; in *Tra donne sole*, 215
'mito, Il', 100–1
Moby-Dick, *see* Melville, Herman
Mondo, Lorenzo, 16–17, 256
Montale, Eugenio, 14, 17, 272 n. 11
Monti, Augusto, 2–5, 61, 219
Moravia, Alberto, 14, 60, 157; *Gli indifferenti* by, 157
Munich and appeasement (1938), 51
music and musicians: in *La bella estate*, 75; in *Il compagno*, 156, 157; in *Dialoghi con Leucò*, 134; in *Il diavolo sulle colline*, 179–80, 277 n. 3; in *Feria d'agosto*, 110; in *Tra donne sole*, 208, 211, 212
Mussolini, Benito, 96, 154, 161
myth, 10, 18, 49, 54, 98, 100, 118, 125, 126, 148, 230, 233; of America, *see* America, United States of; 'artificial preservation' of, 103–4, 183, 230, 277 n. 5; and childhood, 109, 110, 112, 229, 230; 'clarifying one's own myths' (*ridurre a chiarezza i propri miti*), 98, 102–6, 112, 114, 136–7, 141–7 *passim*, 194–5, 230, 231, 248–50, 267, 270; and Destiny, 132, 179, 245, 248, 277 n. 10; 'of discovery', 16, 271, n. 6 to ch. 2; of Eurydice, 135, 137; Greek, 114, 117, 147; and history, 103, 105, 106, 114, 149, 188, 230–4, 261; of 'nature and rural virtues', 181, 182; of the 'once and for all event', 101, 236; origins of, 106, 145; personal, 4, 18, 21, 24, 48, 50, 74, 78, 102, 104, 107, 114, 132, 182, 229, 231; and poetry, 105–14 *passim*, 140–5, 235, 245, 250, 259; and religion, 102, 107–8, 114, 182, 202; of 'sick humanity', 174; and society, 106–7; as style, 178–203; as superstition, 103–4, 182, 230, 277 n. 5; theory of, 10, 16, 50, 94–5, 98,

101–8 passim, 114, 149, 193, 265–70 passim; word-myths, 175; of youth, 90

narrator as character: in 'L'intruso', 40–1; in *la luna e i falò*, 224; in 'I mari del Sud', 26; in *Paesi tuoi*, 78, 79; in *La spiaggia*, 27, 78–9, 90; in 'Terra d'esilio', 41; in *Tra donne sole*, 204; in other poems, 1930–5, 27
Naturalism, 15, 26, 27, 61, 67, 78–81
Neoplatonism, 144
neo-Realism, 20, 66–70 passim, 115; see also America, United States of
Nietzsche, Friedrich, 83
Notte di festa, (short stories) 272 n. 12, (homonymous short story) 63
nudity: in *La bella estate*, 72–8 passim; in *Il diavolo sulle colline*, 183, 184, 193, 196, 197, 277 n. 9; in 'Nudismo', 112–13; in Pirandello, 76

objective correlatives, see punti di riferimento
occhio vergine, see childhood
Of mice and men, see Steinbeck, John
Olympian, see Titan–Olympian conflict
'once and for all event', the, see myth
Operette morali, see Leopardi, Giacomo
'order in the midst of chaos', 171, 187–9, 209, 222, 233, 249, 255, 261–70 passim, 279, n. 3 to ch. 13
ordine nuovo, L', 3; see also Gramsci, Antonio

Paesi tuoi, 10, 52, 78–82 passim, 92, 99, 112, 131, 184, 268; language of, 67–8; and the myth of America, 55–70; see also America, United States of
'Paesi tuoi' (political dialogue), 276 n. 5
Pajetta, Gaspare, 11
Pampaloni, Geno, 48
Pancrazi, Pietro, 149, 275 n. 14
Papini, Giovanni, 4
'parole, Le' (political dialogue), 154, 276 n. 4
Pascoli, Giovanni, 47
'passage to other men' (*passaggio agli altri*), 98, 135, 137, 148, 217, 221, 257
Pavese, Cesare (1908–50): birth, 1; character, 1–12 passim, 29, 115–16; childhood of, 1–4 passim; death by suicide, 12, 231; father of, 1, 2; and Italian Communist Party, 3, 11, 82, 84, 101, 107, 115, 149–56 passim, 173, 180, 183, 212–14; and Italian Fascist Party, 6, 271, n. 3 to ch. 1; Maria, sister of, 1, 2, 10, 96; mother of, 2, 5, 96, 131, 139; pastimes of, 5; political awareness of, 3, 6, 12, 107, 113, 149; world of, 1–12
Pavese, Federica (cousin's daughter), 24, 272 n.19
'Pieretto' (political dialogue), 276 n. 3
Pintor, Giaime, 11, 56–7, 97, 273 n. 9, 275, n. 2 to ch. 6
Pirandello, Luigi, 76, 135, 194, 209, 215; *L'uomo dal fiore in bocca* by, 194, 278 n. 12; *Vestire gli ignudi* by, 76
Plato and Platonism, 124, 147
Po, river, 2, 5, 162, 164, 196, 197
poems (1945–50), 249–60; character of, 249–60 passim; as *mimesis*, 250, 251; as symbolic 'possession of experience', 250
poesia ermetica (Hermetic poetry), 14, 38, 53, 57, 249, 271 n. 3, 273 n. 27
poesia–racconto, 14, 19, 20
Poesie del disamore, 13, 37–8, 272 n. 14; 'L'amico che dorme', 37; 'Risveglio', 37–8; 'Ritorno di Deola', 37
Poesie edite e inedite, 13, 39, 271; n. 1 to ch. 2; 'Antenati', 16, 27, 29–30, 88; 'Atavismo', 272 n. 24; 'Atlantic oil', 23; 'Balletto', 29; 'Casa in costruzione', 29; 'The cats will know', 259; 'Città in campagna', 32; 'Civiltà antica', 74, 272 n. 24; 'Creazione', 272 n. 25; 'Crepuscolo di sabbiatori', 29; 'Il dio-caprone', 63, 64, 84, 214; 'Disciplina antica', 29; 'Donne perdute', 27; 'Due sigarette', 28–34 passim; 'E allora noi vili', 256; 'Estate di San Martino', 26; 'Esterno', 272 n. 24; 'Fumatori di carta', 27, 32–3; 'Gente che non capisce', 32; 'Hai un sangue un respiro', 251; 'Indisciplina', 29; 'Last blues, to be read some day', 279 n. 7; 'Lavorare stanca' (1933), 29; 'Lavorare stanca' (1934), 28, 31; 'Legna verde', 40; 'Le maestrine', 18–19; 'Mania di solitudine', 27, 277 n. 7; 'I mari del Sud', 16, 17, 20–6, 29, 34, 35, 62, 72, 85, 92, 100, 111, 194,

205, 218, 223, 225, 230, 243, 244; 'I mattini passano chiari', 251; 'Mattino', 38; 'Mito', 34–6, 38; 'La notte', 38; 'Notturno', 38, 39; 'La pace regna', 272 n. 25; 'Paesaggio I', 16, 27, 28, 29, 272 n. 8; 'Paesaggio VI', 34; 'Paesaggio VIII', 38; 'Parole del politico', 40; 'Passerò per Piazza di Spagna', 258; 'Paternità', 36; 'Pensieri di Dina', 272 n. 22; 'Pensieri di Deola', 272 n. 23; 'Piaceri notturni', 30; 'Poetica', 34; 'Poggio Reale', 40; 'Sei la terra e la morte', 258; 'Semplicità', 36; 'Sempre vieni dal mare', 250, 256; 'Lo steddazzu', 36, 37; 'Il tempo passa', 29; 'Terra rossa terra nera', 251–5; 'Terre bruciate', 40; 'To C from C', 258; 'Tolleranza', 46; 'Tradimento', 29; 'Tu non sai le colline', 256; 'Tu sei come una terra', 255; 'Ulisse', 272 n. 24; 'Verrà la morte e avrà i tuoi occhi', 251, 259; 'Il vino triste', 26, 272 n. 25; 'You, wind of March', 257, 258, 260.

politics (in Pavese's works), 33; in *La casa in collina*, 167; in *Il compagno*, 149, 158, 160, 161; in *La luna e i falò*, 236, 247–8; in *Tra donne sole*, 220

Pratolini, Vasco, 60, 70

Prima che il gallo canti, 53

promessi sposi, I, see Manzoni, Alessandro

Propp, Vladimir, 232–3

punti di riferimento (objective correlatives), 28, 86, 232

Quasimodo, Salvatore, 14

rationality: failure of, 147, 169–70; 'growth of, in history', 118, 128, 136; as 'guiding principle', 108, 113, 114, 118, 121, 122, 141, 146–7, 153, 158, 161, 162, 170, 178, 181, 233, 249, 250, 270

realism, character of Pavese's, 158–60, 193, 278 n. 11

regionalism: Fascist attitudes to, 66; in Italian literature, 60–2; regional language and national, literary language, 61–2, 66–8

repetition: 'every action repeats a divine model', 145, 238, 250; motif of return, 37, 84, 132–3, 236, 237, 269;

as 'pattern of experience', 50, 103, 105, 146, 171, 201, 228–9, 232, 236, 238, 247; and self-discovery, 144; as stylistic feature, 15, 25–6, 28, 35–6, 48, 69, 171, 175, 176, 237, 265, 266

Resistance, the, 10, 107, 157, 161, 166, 240

Reynolds, Barbara, 274 n. 10

rhythm (*ritmo*), 35, 45–6, 266; as 'animated reality', 140, 240; of 'cycle of the seasons', 175, 176, 234, 236, 238; as Destiny, 140; of events, 12, 51, 69, 140, 149, 171; of 'inner life', 72, 228–9, 246, 248; of life, 99, 237, 238; of religious life, 171, 219, 246; as *selvaggio* ('mindless rhythm of nature'), 124, 172, 179–80, 276 n. 13; see also *selvaggio, Il*

ridurre a chiarezza i propri miti, see myth, 'clarifying one's own myths'

riforma sociale, La, 6

Rilke, Rainer Maria, 133, 140

Rinascita, 152

riprese, see repetition as stylistic feature

'Ritorno all'uomo', 276 n. 2

rivoluzione liberale, La, 3

Rome (in Pavese's writings), 150, 160, 160–4 *passim*, 210

ronda, La, 56

Roosevelt, Franklin D., 56

Ruata, Adolfo, 7–8

Salò, Republic of, 10, 96, 236

Sangone, river, 5

Santo Stefano Belbo, 1–3 *passim*

scienza nuova, La, see Vico, Giambattista

selvaggio, Il, 104, 112–13, 114, 118, 119, 124, 125, 132, 137, 139, 151, 152, 153, 162, 178, 180, 204, 218, 221, 222, 230, 233, 235, 250, 259; as 'carnage of war', 151, 170; as hazard, 165, 169–70, 178, 233, 276 n. 13; as 'mindless rhythm', 276 n. 13; as primeval chaos, 188–9, 249, 270, 277 n. 3; as 'symbol of a mistaken way of life', 189, 220

Senilità, see Svevo, Italo

sentiero dei nidi di ragno, Il, see Calvino, Italo

Sereni, Vittorio, 14

Serralunga (Monferrato), 10, 96, 97

Shakespeare, William, 255

Shelley, Percy Bysshe, 128
Silone, Ignazio, 14
Solaria: edition of *Lavorare stanca*, see *Lavorare stanca;* Press, 6, 7, 34; *Solaria* review, 7
solitude (*la solitudine*): as 'dream, myth, illusion', 140; love, war and, 257, 258; as maturity ('solitude which is self-sufficiency'), 72, 74, 77, 88–91 *passim*, 143, 156, 205, 206, 221; as misfortune, 87, 89, 107–8; war and 'breaking of', 152, 165, 166; in *Il carcere*, 40–54 *passim*; in *La casa in collina*, 53, 151, 172, 173–4; in *Il diavolo sulle colline*, 192; in post-Brancaleone poems, 31–6 *passim*; in *Solaria Lavorare stanca*, 29–31 *passim*; in *Tra donne sole*, 205, 207, 218
Southern Italy (in Pavese's works), 41, 52, 98–9, 100, 262
Spanish Civil War, 157
spiaggia, La, 27, 39, 52, 58, 82–95, 99, 268, 269
Spinelli, Altiero, 7
Steinbeck, John, *Of mice and men* by, 58, 64
stile, see style
stracittà and *strapaese*, 60, 273 n. 8
strato fondamentale, lo, ('basic stratum') search for, 71, 72, 76, 83, 86, 192
Strega Prize, 11
stupore, lo, 16, 21, 50, 61, 164, 169, 170, 230, 235, 276 n. 10
Sturani, Mario, 3, 4, 30, 271, n. 1 to ch. 1
style (*stile*): concept of in Pavese, 52, 71, 219, 222, 249, 261–70 *passim*; 'fabulising aspect' of Pavese's, 235; maturity and, in *La bella estate*, and *La spiaggia*, 71–95; as myth in *Il diavolo sulle colline*, 178–203; Pintor on, 57; 'search for a', 58, 79, 82, 93, 249, 268; as search for wholeness, 262–9 *passim*; in *La casa in collina*, 173–7 *passim*; in *Dialoghi con Leucò*, 115, 147; in *La luna e i falò*, 237; in *Paesi tuoi*, 66–70 *passim*; in *La spiaggia*, 93–4
suicide: as 'defeat', 146; as escape from Destiny, 130; in *Tra donne sole*, 205, 209, 210, 218, 220
'Suicidî', 43, 161
Surrealism, 56–7

Svevo, Italo, 60; *Senilità* by, 52, 81
symbolic reality: in *Feria d'agosto*, 96–114 *passim*; in *La luna e i falò*, 238, 239, 242

'Terra d'esilio', 40, 41, 52, 99, 274 n. 6
terra e la morte, La (collection), 250, 279 nn. 3, 4
thesis, Pavese's degree, *see* Whitman, Walt
Thompson, A. D., 273 n. 7
Thoreau, Henry David, 59
Titan–Olympian conflict, 118, 121, 141, 145–6, 188, 233; in the Golden Age, 139, 142; Olympian gods, 119, 123, 231, (as 'the wreckers') 121, 122, 275 n. 10; significance of Olympian and/or Titan, 117, 119, 121, 122, 142, 175, 255, 276 n. 13; Titans as reality (*il vero*), 121, 125, 135, 137, 175, 188, 233, 255
Tra donne sole, 78, 178, 180, 204–22; art and prostitution in, 211–13; compassion in, 221; correlation between 'civilisation' and 'cruelty' in, 218, 222; dehumanisation in, 209–10, 213–14, 218; material success, the meaning of, in, 205–6, 221, 231; 'new awareness' in, 207, 208, 216–17, 219, 222; responsibility in, 216–20 *passim*; return through time in, 215–16; sexual love as a 'diversion' in, 210–11; solitude in, 205, 207, 221; symbolism in, 205, 221
Turin, 1, 2, 7, 11, 21, 96, 262; character of, 2; character of, in Pavese's works, 33, 34, 68, 150, 156, 163, 181, 204–10 *passim*, 218, 243; political life of, 3, 10, 96; university of, 4, 5

Ungaretti, Giuseppe, 14
Unità, L', 3, 97, 275, n. 1 to ch. 6; Pavese's articles in, 11, 115, 152
Untersteiner, Mario, 116, 142
uomo dal fiore in bocca, L', see Pirandello, Luigi

Venturi, Gianni, 156, 276 n. 8
Verga, Giovanni, 60, 64, 78
verismo, see Naturalism *and* Verga, Giovanni
Verrà la morte e avrà i tuoi occhi (collection), 37, 250, 257, 273 n. 26, 279 nn. 2, 3 to ch. 12

Vestire gli ignudi, see Pirandello, Luigi
'Viaggio di nozze', 43, 161
Vico, Giambattista, 78, 102, 110, 118; *La scienzia nuova* by, 102
'villa in collina, La', 87
Vittorini, Elio, 7, 56, 57, 58, 60, 70; *Conversazione in Sicilia* by, 57
voce, La, 56
voluttuoso, rejection of, 108, 158, 161, 182, 189, 219, 270

'what has been determines what will be', *see come è stato, così sarà*
Whitman, Walt, 59; influence of, 15, 17, 271, n. 6 to ch. 2; Pavese's degree thesis on ('Interpretazione della poesia di W. W.'), 5, 15, 16, 99–100, 199, 271, n. 4 to ch. 2, 272 n. 9

woman: as conflict, 256; cruelty towards, 30; as death, 251, 255, 256, 260; as Destiny, 132, 250; as destructiveness, 109, 138, 139, 158, 190–1; and the earth (motif of), 68, 186, 187, 190; exploitation of, 42–3, 63; as hoped-for salvation, 158, 192; insignificance of, 29, 162, 192; as mystery (*donna–mago*), 38, 39, 89, 132, 137, 162, 179–80, 184, 190–1, 250–1, 260; rejection of; 158, 160, 161, 192, 217; as *selvaggio*, 137, 139, 218, 255, 260, *see also selvaggio, Il*; as silence, 137, 139, 255, 260
'woman with the hoarse voice', the, 5, 7, 8, 139
Wordsworth, William, 267